OUR
FIFTY
STATES

OUR FIFTY STATES

by Mark H. Bockenhauer
and Stephen F. Cunha

Foreword by Former President Jimmy Carter

NATIONAL GEOGRAPHIC
WASHINGTON, DC

TABLE OF CONTENTS

★ FOREWORD ★ 7 ★
by Former President Jimmy Carter

Map of Our Fifty United States ★ 8
Washington, D.C. ★ 11

★ THE NORTHEAST ★ 13 ★

Ancient Wilderness Meets Modern Megalopolis ★ 14

Connecticut ★ 17
Delaware ★ 21
Maine ★ 25
Maryland ★ 29
Massachusetts ★ 33
New Hampshire ★ 37

New Jersey ★ 41
New York ★ 45
Pennsylvania ★ 49
Rhode Island ★ 53
Vermont ★ 57

★ THE SOUTHEAST ★ 61 ★

Tradition and Change Between Two Coasts ★ 62

Alabama ★ 65
Arkansas ★ 69
Florida ★ 73
Georgia ★ 77
Kentucky ★ 81
Louisiana ★ 85

Mississippi ★ 89
North Carolina ★ 93
South Carolina ★ 97
Tennessee ★ 101
Virginia ★ 105
West Virginia ★ 109

★ THE MIDWEST ★ 113 ★

Land of Plenty Under the Prairie Sky ★ 114

Illinois ★ 117
Indiana ★ 121
Iowa ★ 125
Kansas ★ 129
Michigan ★ 133
Minnesota ★ 137

Missouri ★ 141
Nebraska ★ 145
North Dakota ★ 149
Ohio ★ 153
South Dakota ★ 157
Wisconsin ★ 161

★ THE SOUTHWEST ★ 165 ★

Enchanted Places and Multicultural Faces ★ 166

Arizona ★ 169
New Mexico ★ 173

Oklahoma ★ 177
Texas ★ 181

★ THE WEST ★ 185 ★

A Restless and Enduring Frontier ★ 186

Alaska ★ 189
California ★ 193
Colorado ★ 197
Hawai'i ★ 201
Idaho ★ 205
Montana ★ 209

Nevada ★ 213
Oregon ★ 217
Utah ★ 221
Washington ★ 225
Wyoming ★ 229

U.S. Territories ★ 232

Facts & Figures and Map Key ★ 234 | Resources ★ 235 | Index ★ 236 | Credits ★ 240

FOREWORD

I AM SURE that every American can name a favorite place that brings spiritual comfort, a fresh outlook, peaceful and refreshing repose. I have found many such sanctuaries throughout our fifty states, in many different corners of this great country.

Growing up on a farm in southwest Georgia, I first fell in love with this part of America, and have many boyhood memories, such as hunting for arrowheads as I worked in the fields and fishing with a cane pole in a wooded creek near our home, eyes always open for snakes and an occasional otter. Much later, I recall lying on my back on the lawn of the Governor's Mansion in Atlanta watching a horde of Monarch butterflies as they migrated south.

There were times during my presidency when our family would climb to the roof of the White House to watch the Canada geese fly overhead, their faint, haunting calls just audible above the noise of the capital city at night. I have fond memories with my wife, Rosalynn, and our children of quiet moments at Camp David on a mountaintop in northern Maryland, cross-country skiing on pristine trails, and heading to Pennsylvania streams to cast for trout.

On the wild Alaska lands I was privileged to help protect, we witnessed timber wolves, musk-ox, polar bears, and a herd of caribou—100,000 strong—migrating across the land in stately grandeur.

But America's greatness comes not just from a collection of beloved corners like these, but from its diverse and vibrant whole. The richness of this land in a myriad of special places has shaped the character of our people and our history. We citizens love our country, and it is our duty and our pleasure to know it well—from "amber waves of grain" to "alabaster cities."

This book puts geographic knowledge about our country at your fingertips. Enjoy your special places, and then discover new ones. From this process, you will know even better the beauty that is America.

Jimmy Carter

Jimmy Carter is the 39th President of the United States, the recipient of the Nobel Peace Prize, and the Co-Chair, along with his wife, Rosalynn, of the Carter Center in Atlanta, Georgia.

The Fourth of July is a happy and patriotic event for these two girls (opposite). Each year Americans in all 50 states celebrate Independence Day with fireworks, parades, and picnics in honor of the freedoms that make the United States a very special place.

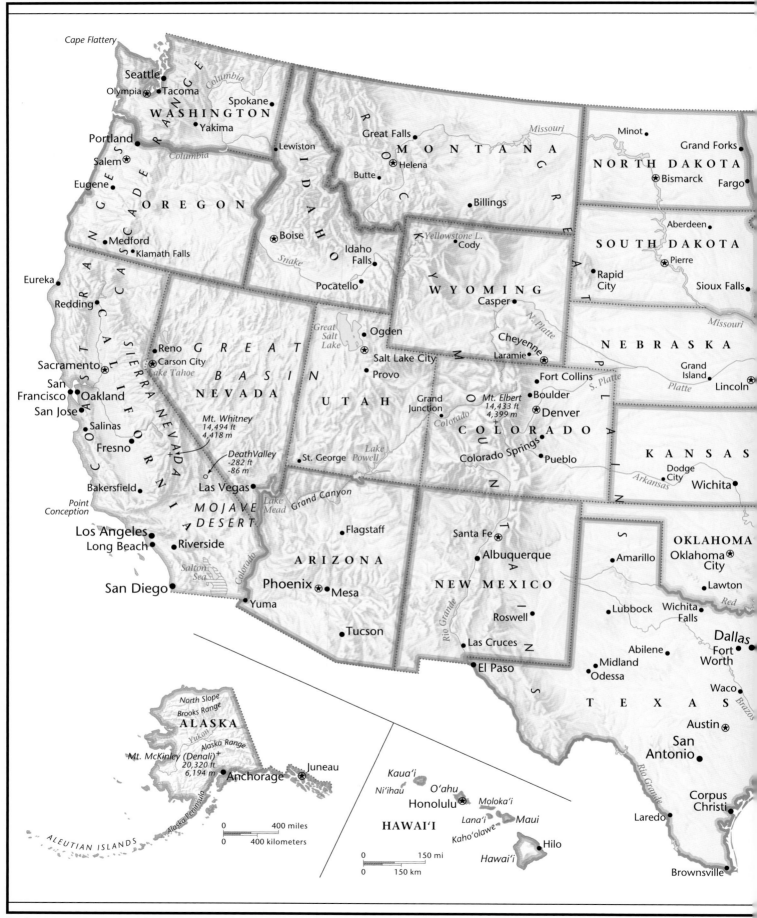

Cape Flattery

Seattle
Olympia ⊛ • Tacoma
• Spokane

W A S H I N G T O N

• Yakima

Portland
Salem ⊛

Eugene •

Medford •
• Klamath Falls

O R E G O N

Columbia

Great Falls •

M O N T A N A

Helena ⊛
Butte •

• Billings

N O R T H   D A K O T A

Minot •

Grand Forks •

Bismarck ⊛
Fargo •

Aberdeen •

S O U T H   D A K O T A

Pierre ⊛

Boise ⊛

Snake

Idaho
Falls •

Pocatello •

Rapid
City •

Sioux Falls •

Yellowstone L.
• Cody

W Y O M I N G

Casper •

N E B R A S K A

Grand
Island •

Lincoln •

Eureka •

Redding •

Sacramento ⊛
San
Francisco •
San Jose •

Salinas •

Fresno •

Bakersfield •

Point
Conception

Reno •
Carson City ⊛
Lake Tahoe

N E V A D A

**G R E A T
B A S I N**

Mt. Whitney
14,494 ft
4,418 m +

Death Valley
-282 ft
-86 m

Las Vegas •

**M O J A V E
D E S E R T**

Great
Salt
Lake

• Ogden

Salt Lake City ⊛
• Provo

U T A H

St. George •

Lake
Powell

Colorado

Lake
Mead

Grand Canyon

Cheyenne
Laramie ⊛

Fort Collins •
Boulder •
Mt. Elbert
14,433 ft
4,399 m +
⊛ Denver

C O L O R A D O

Grand
Junction •

N. Platte

S. Platte

Platte

Colorado Springs •
• Pueblo

K A N S A S

Dodge
City •
Wichita •

Arkansas

Salton
Sea

Los Angeles •
Long Beach •
• Riverside

San Diego •

• Yuma

Colorado

Flagstaff •

A R I Z O N A

Phoenix ⊛ • Mesa

Tucson •

Santa Fe •
Albuquerque •

N E W   M E X I C O

Roswell •

Rio Grande

Las Cruces •

El Paso •

Amarillo •

Oklahoma ⊛
City

Lawton •

Lubbock •

Wichita
Falls •
Red

O K L A H O M A

T E X A S

Abilene •
Midland •
Odessa •

Dallas •
Fort
Worth •

Waco •

Brazos

Austin ⊛
San
Antonio •

Corpus
Christi •

Laredo •

Brownsville •

North Slope
Brooks Range

A L A S K A

Yukon
Alaska Range

Mt. McKinley (Denali) +
20,320 ft
6,194 m
• Anchorage

Juneau ⊛

ALEUTIAN ISLANDS
Alaska Peninsula

0 ___ 400 miles
0 ___ 400 kilometers

Kaua'i
Ni'ihau
O'ahu
Honolulu ⊛
Moloka'i
Lana'i
Maui
Kaho'olawe
Hilo •
Hawai'i

H A W A I ' I

0 ___ 150 mi
0 ___ 150 km

OUR FIFTY UNITED STATES

★

International Falls
Lake of the Woods
Isle Royale
Lake Superior
Duluth
Superior
Marquette
MINNESOTA
MICHIGAN
Lake Huron
Minneapolis
St. Paul
WISCONSIN
Green Bay
Lake Michigan
Grand Rapids
Lansing
Madison
Milwaukee
Detroit
Mississippi
Cedar Rapids
Rockford
I O W A
Chicago
Gary
Fort Wayne
O H I O
Toledo
Cleveland
Erie
PENNSYLVANIA
Omaha
Des Moines
Davenport
Peoria
Columbus
Harrisburg
Pittsburgh
ILLINOIS
INDIANA
Dayton
Cincinnati
Ohio
Springfield
Indianapolis
Louisville
Frankfort
Kansas City
Jefferson City
St. Louis
Wabash
Evansville
Lexington
WEST VIRGINIA
Topeka
Charleston
KENTUCKY
VIRGINIA
Richmond
MISSOURI
Springfield
Paducah
Roanoke
Norfolk
Tulsa
Knoxville
Mt. Mitchell + 6,684 ft 2,037 m
NORTH CAROLINA
Nashville
TENNESSEE
Chattanooga
Charlotte
Fort Smith
Memphis
Greenville
ARKANSAS
Little Rock
Huntsville
Columbia
SOUTH CAROLINA
Atlanta
Birmingham
GEORGIA
Charleston
ALABAMA
Macon
MISSISSIPPI
Jackson
Columbus
Savannah
Montgomery
Shreveport
LOUISIANA
Red
Natchez
Mobile
Jacksonville
Baton Rouge
Biloxi
Mississippi River Delta
Mobile Bay
Apalachee Bay
F L O R I D A
Tallahassee
Gainesville
Beaumont
Lafayette
New Orleans
Apalachee Bay
Orlando
Cape Canaveral
Houston
Tampa
St. Petersburg
Lake Okeechobee
Fort Lauderdale
THE EVERGLADES
Miami
Florida Keys

MAINE
Bangor
Augusta
Burlington
Lake Champlain
Montpelier
VT.
N.H.
Portland
Concord
Boston
Cape Cod
Syracuse
Albany
MASS.
Rochester
NEW YORK
Providence
Buffalo
Hartford
CONN.
RHODE ISLAND
Lake Ontario
Lake Erie
Newark
Long Island
New York
Trenton
Harrisburg
NEW JERSEY
Philadelphia
Baltimore
Dover
Washington
DELAWARE
D.C.
MARYLAND
Annapolis
Chesapeake Bay
Greensboro
Raleigh
Cape Hatteras
Virginia Beach

APPALACHIAN MOUNTAINS

0   300 miles
0   300 kilometers
Albers Conic Equal-Area Projection

Alaska (U.S.)
UNITED STATES
Hawaii (U.S.)

WASHINGTON, D.C.

FOUNDED	1790
TOTAL AREA	68 sq mi; 177 sq km
LAND AREA	61 sq mi; 159 sq km
POPULATION	601,723
POPULATION DENSITY	8,848 people per sq mi
MAJOR RACIAL/ ETHNIC GROUPS	50.7% African American; 38.5% white; 3.5% Asian; 0.3% Native American. Hispanic (any race) 9.1%.
INDUSTRY	government, services, tourism

WOOD THRUSH   AMERICAN BEAUTY ROSE

Did you know?

License plates in the nation's capital bear the slogan "Taxation without Representation."

THE NATION'S CAPITAL. To the people of the United States it is a place of symbol and power like no other. It is the seat of the U.S. government where decisions are made that affect not only the country but the world. It is a magnet for tourists, who come to see its splendid monuments and museums, and home to 563,000 ordinary citizens.

In 1790 Northern and Southern leaders agreed on a capital location somewhere along the Potomac River, but it was President Washington who chose the exact spot the following year. He selected French architect Pierre L'Enfant to design a grand city on land originally donated by Maryland and Virginia. Congress used Maryland's share but gave back Virginia's land in 1846.

Washington ranks among the world's great capital cities, but life in the District is not everywhere so grand. From a high of more than 800,000 people in the 1950s, population has declined, as many have chosen to leave the high costs, congestion, and crime of District life. Hundreds of thousands of commuters work in the city but live—and spend their money—in surrounding states. City leaders are working to find ways to improve life for all its residents, but without a voting representative in Congress, change is slow and often difficult. Still, Washington, D.C.—a city honoring the Father of Our Country and a district named for Columbus—is a source of pride for all Americans.

The United States Capitol (opposite) anchors the District of Columbia and the nation. Atop its dome, the imposing Statue of Freedom stands nearly 308 feet (94 m) above ground level. The west entrance overlooks the National Mall, with its monuments and museums, and the White House, where the President lives.

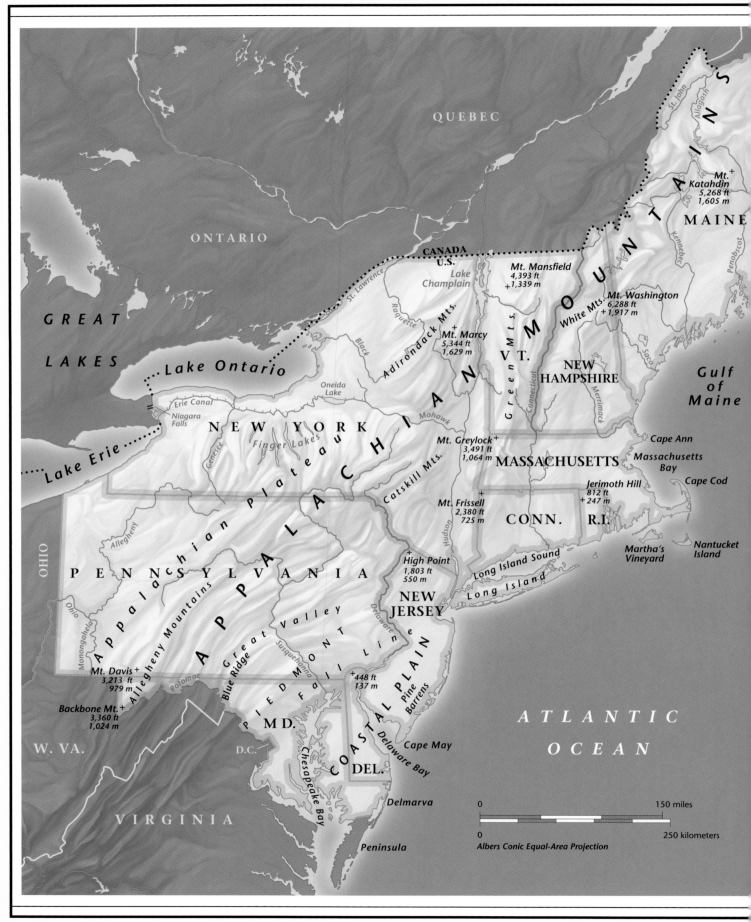

QUEBEC

ONTARIO

MAINE

Mt.
Katahdin
5,268 ft
1,605 m

CANADA
U.S.

Lake
Champlain

Mt. Mansfield
4,393 ft
+1,339 m

Mt. Washington
6,288 ft
+1,917 m

St. Lawrence

Raquette

Adirondack Mts.

Mt. Marcy
5,344 ft
1,629 m

V.T.

Green Mts.

White Mts.

NEW
HAMPSHIRE

Gulf
of
Maine

GREAT

LAKES

Lake Ontario

Black

Oneida
Lake

Mohawk

NEW YORK

Finger Lakes

Appalachian Plateau

Erie Canal

Niagara
Falls

Genesee

Lake Erie

Catskill Mts.

Mt. Greylock +
3,491 ft
1,064 m

MASSACHUSETTS

Cape Ann

Massachusetts
Bay

Cape Cod

Mt. Frissell
2,380 ft
725 m

CONN.

R.I.

Jerimoth Hill
812 ft
+247 m

Hudson

Connecticut

Merrimack

Saco

Kennebec

Penobscot

St. John

Allagash

APPALACHIAN MOUNTAINS

OHIO

PENNSYLVANIA

Allegheny

Allegheny Mountains

APPALACHIAN

Great Valley

Blue Ridge

Susquehanna

High Point
1,803 ft
550 m

Long Island Sound

Long Island

NEW
JERSEY

Martha's
Vineyard

Nantucket
Island

Ohio

Monongahela

Mt. Davis +
3,213 ft
979 m

Backbone Mt. +
3,360 ft
1,024 m

W. VA.

Potomac

D.C.

MD.

PIEDMONT

Fall Line

Delaware

+448 ft
137 m

COASTAL PLAIN

Pine
Barrens

Cape May

Delaware Bay

DEL.

ATLANTIC

OCEAN

VIRGINIA

Chesapeake Bay

Delmarva

Peninsula

0   150 miles

0   250 kilometers

Albers Conic Equal-Area Projection

The Northeast

RETREATING GLACIERS helped shape this crumpled landscape. The forested mountains, fertile valleys, navigable rivers, and excellent harbors attracted settlers. Over time, the northeast has become the country's most densely populated region. The ancient Appalachian Mountains, stretching from Maine to southwestern Maryland and beyond, form the geologic backbone. The chief ranges—the White Mountains and Green Mountains of New Hampshire and Vermont, the Catskills of New York, and the Alleghenies and Blue Ridge of Pennsylvania and Maryland—provide mineral wealth, timber resources, and recreational playgrounds. Croplands and towns fill the valleys. Rivers flowing east out of the mountains onto the flat Atlantic Coastal Plain help power the industry and commerce of some of the country's oldest and largest cities from Boston to Baltimore. Waterways flowing west link the region to the Great Lakes and the Mississippi Valley.

Ancient Wilderness Meets Modern Megalopolis

THIS COMPACT LANDSCAPE of rocky coastline, fertile valleys, and rolling mountains inspired local author Emily Dickinson to "Think New Englandy." The Northeast's rich history of self-governing began in the 1500s (and perhaps much earlier) when five Native American tribes agreed to mutual trade and peaceful treaties under the Iroquois Confederacy. The original Mohawk, Oneida, Onondaga, Cayuga, and Seneca tribes thrived by hunting, fishing, collecting berries, and trading these and other resources with nearby tribes.

In 1620 the region's first European colonists arrived and began gradually displacing the Indians. Employing "Yankee ingenuity" and a strong dose of Puritan work ethic, America's colonial economy literally sprang from the earth. Trees cut from the dense forests provided ample wood to craft into homes, barns, and ships. On this newly cleared land, settlers raised corn, wheat, and livestock. They also tapped maple trees for tasty syrup. From the mountains to the coastal plain, they harnessed water to drive mills—initially to grind flour and mill lumber and then, as the economy developed, to power textile factories. Although most people farmed, whalers, fishermen, ship builders, barrel makers, blacksmiths, and shop keepers all played important roles in this emerging economy.

For two centuries, waves of immigrants helped propel the Northeast into the center of American manufacturing and trade. By the early 1800s, cities and family farms dominated the region. An expanding network of post roads built to deliver mail, canals, and railroads linked the growing population and their markets. Ports such as Philadelphia and Baltimore became key centers of international trade.

Throughout the 19th century, the Northeast was a global industrial powerhouse. Coal, railroads, and labor powered vast iron/steel works and manufactured goods. Although during the Civil War the Border States had some Southern leanings, the Northeast was the core of the Union, and its rich resources and industrial might eventually overwhelmed the South.

During the 20th century, the economy began to change. Rapidly expanding cities such as New York, Boston, and Hartford swallowed up farms, while many factories relocated to the South and abroad, where land and labor cost less. As manufacturing declined, the Northeast was reborn into a powerful center of international business. Today, suburbs link cities into a giant interconnected metropolitan area—called a megalopolis—that stretches from Boston to Washington, D.C., and that is home to one in five Americans. Cities and transportation routes mirror those first built during colonial times. The region's cities and suburbs still welcome new waves of immigrants from home and abroad, who arrive seeking jobs in banking,

insurance, education, technology, and other service businesses.

Gigantic traffic jams, sprawling suburbs, trees damaged by acid rain, and polluted rivers are signs of a population struggling to cope with its own success. Yet, squeezed between the farms and cities are stunning remnants of the dense forests once inhabited by various native peoples. Tourism is providing new jobs as people flock to some of America's largest parks and seashores. Researchers are working to find ways to rebuild the dwindling oyster population in Chesapeake Bay. Elsewhere, the return of moose and black bear hint that some of this ancient wilderness will flourish alongside a modern megalopolis.

> "I never saw an autumnal landscape so beautifully painted....It was like the richest rug imaginable spread over an uneven surface."
>
> HENRY DAVID THOREAU

Far from bustling Northeast cities, a lone canoeist finds solitude on a lake in the Adirondack Mountains. Every autumn, shortened days and falling temperatures turn the green leaves of these hardwoods flaming shades of red, orange, and yellow.

CONNECTICUT

★ *Constitution State* ★

YANKEE QUALITY IS ASSURED. The word "Yankee" probably started out as *Jankes (Yahn kes)*, a name the Dutch used to make fun of the tradespeople they competed with in the New World. By the Revolution, people were happy to call themselves Yankees. With a long tradition of excellence and leadership in politics, seafaring, inventions, and insurance, Connecticut Yankees have plenty of reasons to be proud.

The Dutch were the first to scout the coast in 1614, but it was English colonists from Massachusetts, led by Thomas Hooker and others, who established a series of permanent settlements, including Hartford in 1635. The Pequots, the most powerful of several native groups, attacked settlements that they saw as a challenge to their regional power. In 1637, the Pequot threat was largely eliminated by soldiers who burned a native fort, killing hundreds of Indians. Competing colonies, centered at

Hartford and New Haven, joined together in the 1660s. By then, Connecticut—from an Algonquin term for "on the long tidal river"—was a colony chartered by the English king.

Critical ideas about a government "by the people" came from Connecticut. The early Hartford community's Fundamental Orders, based on a sermon by Thomas Hooker, became law in 1639, giving people the right to elect government officials. Nearly 150 years later the Connecticut Compromise was adopted at the Constitutional Convention. By providing that each state would be represented by two Senators, it ensured that states with small populations would be fairly represented in the new nation's Congress. Connecticut became the fifth state in early 1788, with Hartford as its capital.

The state has hummed with industry since colonial times, beginning with clocks, tin pots and pans, and silverware by the 1740s. Fertile

1635
Minister Thomas Hooker and a group of followers founded Hartford. He preached that government should be by consent of the people.

1790S
Just as his cotton gin revolutionized the South, Eli Whitney's concept of mass production revolutionized industry in the North.

1839–1840
The ruling that freed the slaves of the Amistad *was a landmark decision, recognizing the right of all people to rebel against injustices.*

Present day
Groton, home to the U.S. Naval Submarine Base, is where the country's newest nuclear attack sub, the Virginia-*class, is built.*

This restored whaling ship at Mystic Seaport (opposite) is part of the state's maritime history. Connecticut shipyards produced warships for the British in colonial days, whalers in the 1800s, clipper ships and steamers into the 20th century, and submarines today.

MASSACHUSETTS

+ Mt. Frissell
2,380 ft
725 m
Twin Lakes
Highest point in Connecticut

Canaan

Norfolk

Lakeville

Sharon

APPALACHIAN
NATIONAL
SCENIC TRAIL

Winsted

Torrington

MACEDONIA BROOK
STATE PARK

Litchfield

Kent

West Branch Farmington

FARMINGTON NATIONAL
WILD & SCENIC RIVER

New Hartford

Nepaug Reservoir

Harwinton

Bantam Lake

Bethlehem

Congamond Lakes

East Hartland

Barkhamsted Reservoir

Granby

E. Granby

Compensating Reservoir

Simsbury

Collinsville

Unionville

Staffordville Reservoir

Enfield

Windsor Locks

Hazardville

Broad Brook

Windsor

Bloomfield

West Hartford

North Grosvenor Dale

Quaddick Reservoir

Stafford

Ellington

Shenipsit Lake

Vernon

Manchester

Storrs

Mansfield Hollow Lake

Thompson

Putnam

Dayville

Danielson

Brooklyn

Moosup

C O N N E C T I C U T

NEW YORK

Taconic Range

Housatonic

Shepaug

Watertown

New Milford

Oakville

Lake Candlewood

Lake Lillinonah

New Fairfield

Danbury

Bethel

Lake Zoar

Housatonic

Ridgefield

WEIR FARM N.H.S.

Saugatuck Reservoir

Trumbull

Wilton

New Canaan

Westport

Fairfield

Stratford Point

Bridgeport

Stratford

Milford

STEWART B. McKINNEY N.W.R.

West Haven

Orange

Shelton

Ansonia

Seymour

Hamden

New Haven

North Haven

Naugatuck

Naugatuck

Prospect

Waterbury

Meriden

Cheshire

Quinnipiac

Wallingford

Lake Gaillard

Southington

New Britain

Newington

Plainville

Bristol

Terryville

Plainville

Hartford

East Hartford

Glastonbury

Wethersfield

DINOSAUR S.P.

Rocky Hill

Pocotopaug Lake

Marlborough

Portland

East Hampton

Colchester

Middletown

Durham

Moodus

Gardner Lake

Baltic

Yantic

Chesterfield

Haddam

Hammonasset

Deep River

Essex

Connecticut

Willimantic

Willimantic Reservoir

Shetucket

Quinebaug

Jewett City

Plainfield

Norwich

Pachaug Pond

MOHEGAN I.R.

MASHANTUCKET PEQUOT I.R.

Quaker Hill

Thames

New London

Niantic

Groton

Pawcatuck

Mystic Seaport

Mystic

Roquonock

Pawcatuck

Bridge

Westbrook

North Branford

Branford

East Haven

Guilford

Madison

East River

Clinton

Old Saybrook

RHODE ISLAND

Greenwich

Stamford

Darien

Norwalk

Willimantic

Natchaug

Coventry

Farmington

Scantic

Hockanum

Connecticut

LONG ISLAND SOUND

0   10   20 miles
0   10   20 kilometers
Albers Conic Equal-Area Projection

Building on a successful tradition of firearms manufacturing, Connecticut became a center of defense contracting in World War II. Today, submarines, jet aircraft components, helicopters, and more contribute to the nation's military. Sikorsky Aircraft Corporation, based in Stratford, has made helicopters since 1939. Here, the crew of the U.S. Air Force Sikorsky HH-60 Pave Hawk practices aerial maneuvers.

Connecticut River Valley farmlands grew plenty of corn, beans, and tobacco, and its coastal waters produced seafood. During the Revolution, cannon, cannonballs, and shot for muskets rolled from ironworks to American fighting ships and army units, starting a long tradition of military manufacturing and defense support. Connecticut inventors provided revolutionary ideas in industry. Eli Whitney came up with the idea of interchangeable parts, which made mass production possible. Samuel Colt invented the repeating pistol in 1836, and Charles Goodyear patented his method of vulcanizing, or strengthening, rubber in 1844.

Connecticut's trade and shipbuilding also flourished in the 1800s. At mid-century, whaling was a huge enterprise. Though the industry soon declined, Connecticut's ties to the sea have not. New London is home to the U.S. Coast Guard Academy, while just across the Thames River is Groton, site of the U.S. Naval Submarine Base. Sea connections helped launch another key activity. After the Revolution, some state businessmen helped a shipowner by "insuring" his vessel and cargo. They agreed to pay for lost cargo in return for a share of the profits if the voyage was successful. Thus was born the U.S. insurance business.

In the late 20th century, many New York City-based companies moved their headquarters to Connecticut. This brought many high-paying, white-collar jobs, but it did little to help old industrial cities, which began to lose jobs by the 1970s. The state government has begun efforts to revitalize cities and has enacted policies to limit sprawl and preserve the state's scenic rural areas. Connecticut fights to keep its industrial jobs and attract more technology business. These are good Connecticut Yankee ideas likely to ensure success and keep the state a leader.

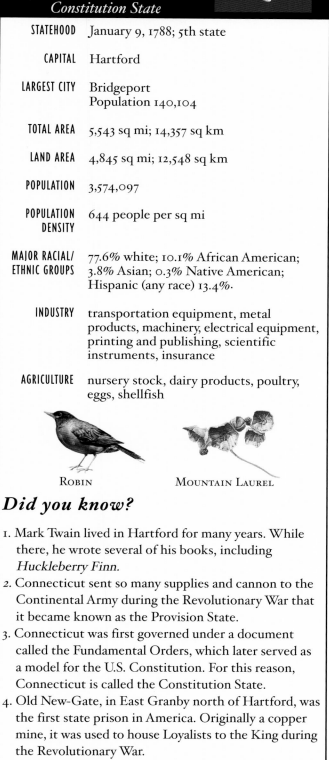

CONNECTICUT
Constitution State

STATEHOOD	January 9, 1788; 5th state
CAPITAL	Hartford
LARGEST CITY	Bridgeport Population 140,104
TOTAL AREA	5,543 sq mi; 14,357 sq km
LAND AREA	4,845 sq mi; 12,548 sq km
POPULATION	3,574,097
POPULATION DENSITY	644 people per sq mi
MAJOR RACIAL/ ETHNIC GROUPS	77.6% white; 10.1% African American; 3.8% Asian; 0.3% Native American; Hispanic (any race) 13.4%.
INDUSTRY	transportation equipment, metal products, machinery, electrical equipment, printing and publishing, scientific instruments, insurance
AGRICULTURE	nursery stock, dairy products, poultry, eggs, shellfish

ROBIN   MOUNTAIN LAUREL

Did you know?

1. Mark Twain lived in Hartford for many years. While there, he wrote several of his books, including *Huckleberry Finn.*
2. Connecticut sent so many supplies and cannon to the Continental Army during the Revolutionary War that it became known as the Provision State.
3. Connecticut was first governed under a document called the Fundamental Orders, which later served as a model for the U.S. Constitution. For this reason, Connecticut is called the Constitution State.
4. Old New-Gate, in East Granby north of Hartford, was the first state prison in America. Originally a copper mine, it was used to house Loyalists to the King during the Revolutionary War.
5. The first fully operational steel mill in the U.S. opened in Simsbury in 1728.

DELAWARE

★ *First State* ★

"A JEWEL AMONG STATES," said Thomas Jefferson about Delaware. Though the second smallest state in area, its economic importance has long been huge. Favorable laws for starting and operating businesses have attracted a variety of enterprises. More than half of the country's largest companies call themselves Delaware corporations—even if their offices in the state are just on paper. Delaware's place in the nation's history is oversize, too. When the time came to approve the U.S. Constitution, Delaware was at the head of the line. The First State signed on December 7, 1787.

Barrier island beaches stretch for 28 miles (45 km) along Delaware's southeastern Atlantic coast. Spanning its southernmost border with Maryland is the Cypress Swamp, home of one of the northernmost stands of cypress trees in the country. Northward, the state's shoreline faces the Delaware Bay. Salt marshes here provide nesting sites for birds and breeding grounds for shellfish. In the south, farms grow soybeans and corn, which help feed the quarter-billion broiler chickens produced annually. A wide variety of vegetables and fruits are grown for processing or transporting from "truck farms" to nearby cities. In the north, where the state narrows to less than 10 miles (16 km) in width, the Chesapeake and Delaware Canal links the two great bays. More than 60 percent of Delaware's population lives in this largely urban and industrial region.

When Henry Hudson sailed into Delaware Bay in 1609, Lenni-Lenape, Nanticoke, and Minqua peoples lived there. The next year, English ship captain Samuel Argall named a point of land Cape De La Warr, for the governor of Virginia. Later, the bay, river, and state all took the name Delaware. Dutch, Swedish, and English interests competed for control of the region. New Sweden, a small colony of Swedes

1638

The Swedish and Finnish pioneers who founded New Sweden were skilled woodsmen who built the first log cabins in the New World.

1802—early 1900s

This E.I. du Pont mill, which made gunpowder during the War of 1812, developed into Delaware's giant chemical industry.

1951

The Delaware Memorial Bridge opened in 1951, providing a faster and more direct route to New Jersey and New York.

Present day

Delaware has been a leader in coastal conservation since 1971 when it passed laws protecting its beaches from polluting industries.

Du Pont family wealth supports schools, roads, and public projects across Delaware. Winterthur, once a private du Pont estate, is now a world-famous garden, museum, and study center for Americana. Its latest feature is a fantasy garden for children (opposite).

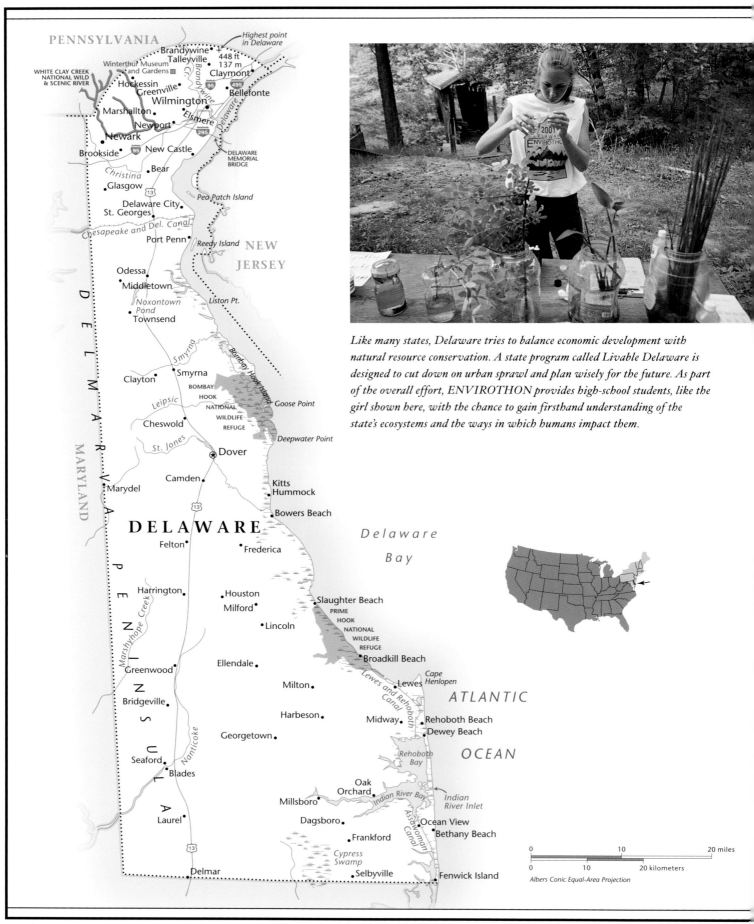

PENNSYLVANIA

WHITE CLAY CREEK
NATIONAL WILD
& SCENIC RIVER

Highest point
in Delaware
+ 448 ft
137 m

Brandywine
Talleyville
Winterthur Museum
and Gardens
Claymont

Hockessin
Greenville
Wilmington
Bellefonte

Marshallton
Elsmere

Newport

Newark
New Castle

Brookside

Bear

Christina

Glasgow

Delaware City
St. Georges

Chesapeake and Del. Canal

Port Penn

Odessa

Middletown

Noxontown
Pond
Townsend

Smyrna

Clayton
Smyrna

Leipsic

Cheswold

St. Jones

Dover

Camden

Marydel

DELAWARE

Felton
Frederica

Harrington

Houston
Milford

Lincoln

Ellendale

Greenwood

Milton

Bridgeville

Harbeson

Georgetown

Seaford
Blades

Laurel

Delmar

Marshyhope Creek

Nanticoke

Cypress
Swamp

Selbyville

DELMARVA PENINSULA

MARYLAND

NEW
JERSEY

DELAWARE
MEMORIAL
BRIDGE

Pea Patch Island

Reedy Island

Liston Pt.

Bombay Hook Island

BOMBAY
HOOK

NATIONAL

WILDLIFE

REFUGE

Goose Point

Deepwater Point

Kitts
Hummock

Bowers Beach

Delaware
Bay

Slaughter Beach

PRIME
HOOK
NATIONAL
WILDLIFE
REFUGE

Broadkill Beach

Cape
Henlopen

Lewes and Rehoboth Canal

Lewes

ATLANTIC

Midway
Rehoboth Beach
Dewey Beach

Rehoboth
Bay

OCEAN

Oak
Orchard

Millsboro

Indian River Bay

Indian River Inlet

Dagsboro

Assawoman Canal

Ocean View
Bethany Beach

Frankford

Fenwick Island

Like many states, Delaware tries to balance economic development with natural resource conservation. A state program called Livable Delaware is designed to cut down on urban sprawl and plan wisely for the future. As part of the overall effort, ENVIROTHON provides high-school students, like the girl shown here, with the chance to gain firsthand understanding of the state's ecosystems and the ways in which humans impact them.

0   10   20 miles
0   10   20 kilometers
Albers Conic Equal-Area Projection

and Finns, was founded in 1638. A Dutch force from New Amsterdam took over in 1655, and the English finally secured the area in 1674. Eight years later, it was made part of Pennsylvania. Over time, Delaware began to operate like, then finally became, an independent colony. Its population was split between Loyalists and those wanting independence, but Delaware voted to break away.

Industry came to northern Delaware in the person of a French immigrant named Éleuthère Irénée du Pont de Nemours, who opened a gunpowder factory on Brandywine Creek in 1802. Water powered Wilmington-area mills that made flour, paper, and cloth. Though some landowners in its southern counties used slaves, Delaware stayed in the Union. But pro-Southern feelings grew during the Civil War, and Delaware did not approve the U.S. Amendments securing racial equality until 1901. Integration of schools in the 1950s and housing in the 1960s was difficult here.

Delaware continued its industrial growth in the 20th century, and thousands of European workers moved in to take factory jobs. Spurred on by the demands of two world wars, oil refineries were built, as were shipyards, auto-making plants, and metal-working factories. The creek-side gunpowder mill grew into one of the world's top chemical companies. Among the many products staff at the DuPont Company invented and manufactured was the world's first human-made fiber—nylon—in 1935. Today, Delaware enjoys better economic conditions than many states and has added 11,000 jobs since 2000. But two centuries of industrial pollution have made environmental clean-up a top state priority. Also underway are attempts to save remaining natural areas from development. These efforts will take time, money, and dedication, but Delaware, the "Small Wonder," can make it happen.

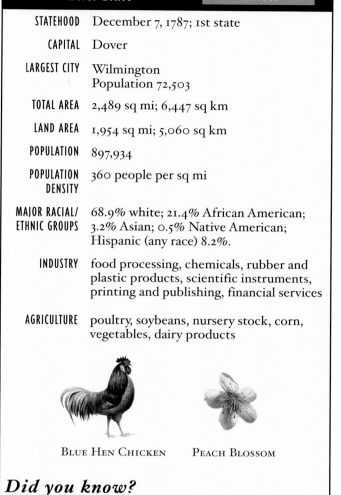

DELAWARE
First State

STATEHOOD	December 7, 1787; 1st state
CAPITAL	Dover
LARGEST CITY	Wilmington Population 72,503
TOTAL AREA	2,489 sq mi; 6,447 sq km
LAND AREA	1,954 sq mi; 5,060 sq km
POPULATION	897,934
POPULATION DENSITY	360 people per sq mi
MAJOR RACIAL/ ETHNIC GROUPS	68.9% white; 21.4% African American; 3.2% Asian; 0.5% Native American; Hispanic (any race) 8.2%.
INDUSTRY	food processing, chemicals, rubber and plastic products, scientific instruments, printing and publishing, financial services
AGRICULTURE	poultry, soybeans, nursery stock, corn, vegetables, dairy products

BLUE HEN CHICKEN   PEACH BLOSSOM

Did you know?

1. A portion of the Delaware-Pennsylvania border is the only rounded boundary in the United States.
2. Delaware's nickname, First State, refers to the fact that it was the first state to ratify the U.S. Constitution.
3. In 1880 the country held the first Miss United States pageant in Delaware. Inventor Thomas Edison was one of the judges.
4. During the Revolutionary War, a company of soldiers under Captain Jonathan Caldwell amused themselves by staging cockfights with their captain's blue hen chickens. The men distinguished themselves in several key battles and became known as the Blue Hen's Chickens. The state bird symbolizes this fighting spirit.
5. Delaware is sometimes called the Diamond State. This nickname can be traced back to Thomas Jefferson, who called Delaware a jewel among states because of its strategic position along the Atlantic coast.

MAINE

★ *Pine Tree State* ★

COASTLINE AND PINE. Maine is known especially for these, and both have helped make the state what it is today. Evergreen forests reach right down to the Atlantic shore, along the rocky 3,500-mile- (5,600-km-) long ocean edge of the Pine Tree State.

Massive Ice Age glaciers left Maine's jagged coastline with perhaps 1,100 islands, big and small. Sculpted by the moving ice and then partly submerged by rising sea level as the huge sheets of ice melted, once-onshore hilltops became offshore islands.

While Viking Leif Ericson probably visited the coast here about A.D. 1,000, the English and French definitely began scouting it in the 1500s. Maine is believed to have taken its name from English explorers who called the shore the "maine-land" to set it apart from the many islands. Several English communities were founded along the southern coast by 1623. After decades of ownership disputes, Massachusetts gained control of the territory of Maine by 1677. The French gave up all claims after the French and Indian War in 1763, but many French settlers stayed and played a key role in the economy's development. Treaties cost the Algonquin-speaking peoples most of their land.

Maine's people, like other Americans, hated what they saw as unfair British rule and taxes. Thousands of men joined the fight for freedom. After the Revolution, Maine's population grew quickly. Eventually, people wanted to separate from Massachusetts, and in 1819 they voted to do just that. In a "package deal" known as the Missouri Compromise, made between anti-slavery and pro-slavery states, Maine entered the Union "slave free" as the 23rd state in 1820. (Missouri entered as a slave state the next year.)

Logging, shipping, and shipbuilding in Maine grew from the 1600s onward. The

1498

John Cabot probably reached the Maine coast in 1498, claiming it for England. Conflicting claims with the French ended in 1763.

1809–1891

A strong voice against slavery, Hannibal Hamlin served as Lincoln's first Vice President and supported freedom for slaves.

1942–1945

During World War II, Maine shipyards built 236 Liberty Ships to haul grain, ore, munitions, and troops to our Allies in Europe.

Present day

Lobsters are at the heart of Maine's seafood industry. The state supplies more than half of the nation's total harvest.

Lighthouses have long helped sailors avoid disaster from pounding surf and strong tides along Maine's dangerous coast. The Portland Head light (opposite), built in 1791, is no longer operated by a keeper. Its light is electronically controlled.

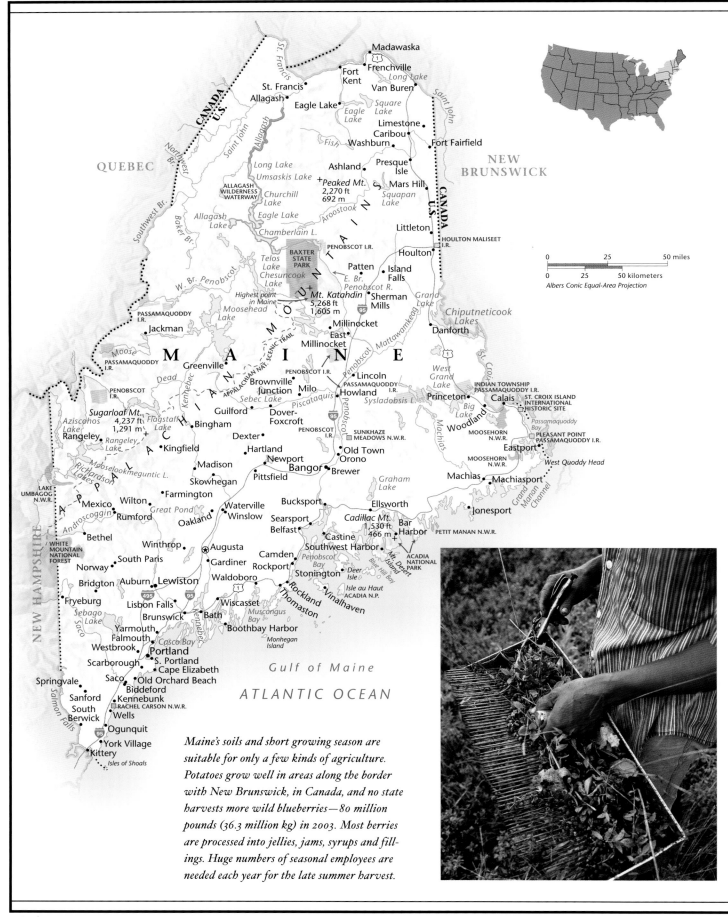

QUEBEC

CANADA
U.S.

NEW
BRUNSWICK

St. Francis

Madawaska
Frenchville
Fort Kent
Van Buren
Long Lake
St. Francis
Allagash
Eagle Lake
Square
Lake
Eagle
Lake
Limestone
Caribou
Washburn
Fort Fairfield
Ashland
Presque
Isle
Long Lake
Umsaskis Lake
+ Peaked Mt.
2,270 ft
692 m
Mars Hill
Squapan
Lake
Fish

ALLAGASH
WILDERNESS
WATERWAY

Churchill
Lake

Allagash
Lake

Eagle Lake

Chamberlain L.

Aroostook

CANADA
U.S.

Littleton

Houlton

HOULTON MALISEET
I.R.

PENOBSCOT I.R.

BAXTER
STATE
PARK

Telos
Lake
Chesuncook
Lake

Patten

Island
Falls

E. Br.
Penobscot R.

Grand
Lake

Chiputneticook
Lakes

Danforth

Highest point
in Maine

Mt. Katahdin
5,268 ft
1,605 m

Sherman
Mills

Moosehead
Lake

Millinocket

East
Millinocket

Mattawamkeag

West
Grand
Lake

Danforth

Jackman

Moose

MAINE

Greenville

Dead

Kennebec

APPALACHIAN NAT. SCENIC TRAIL

Lincoln

Howland

PENOBSCOT I.R.

PASSAMAQUODDY
I.R.

Princeton

INDIAN TOWNSHIP
PASSAMAQUODDY I.R.

Calais

ST. CROIX ISLAND
INTERNATIONAL
HISTORIC SITE

PASSAMAQUODDY
I.R.

PENOBSCOT
I.R.

Brownville
Junction
Milo

Sebec Lake

Guilford

Sugarloaf Mt.
4,237 ft
1,291 m

Flagstaff
Lake

Aziscohos
Lake

Rangeley

Rangeley
Lake

Kingfield

Bingham

Dover-
Foxcroft

Piscataquis

Penobscot

PENOBSCOT
I.R.

SUNKHAZE
MEADOWS N.W.R.

Old Town
Orono

Sysladobsis L.

Machias

West
Grand
Lake

Big
Lake

Woodland

MOOSEHORN
N.W.R.

Passamaquoddy
Bay

PLEASANT POINT
PASSAMAQUODDY I.R.

Eastport

MOOSEHORN
N.W.R.

West Quoddy Head

Dexter

Hartland

Newport

Bangor
Brewer

Graham
Lake

Mooselookmeguntic L.

Richardson
Lakes

Madison

Skowhegan

Pittsfield

LAKE
UMBAGOG N.W.R.

Mexico
Rumford

Androscoggin

Great Pond

Farmington

Wilton

Oakland

Waterville
Winslow

Bucksport

Searsport
Belfast

Ellsworth

Machias
Machiasport

Jonesport

Cadillac Mt.
1,530 ft
466 m

Bar
Harbor

PETIT MANAN N.W.R.

Bethel

Winthrop

WHITE
MOUNTAIN
NATIONAL
FOREST

South Paris

Norway

Augusta

Gardiner

Camden
Rockport

Castine

Southwest Harbor

Stonington

ACADIA
NATIONAL
PARK

Deer
Isle

Penobscot
Bay

Blue Hill Bay

Mt. Desert
Island

NEW HAMPSHIRE

Bridgton

Fryeburg

Sebago
Lake

Auburn
Lewiston

Lisbon Falls

Brunswick

Wiscasset

Bath

Waldoboro

Thomaston
Rockland

Vinalhaven

Isle au Haut
ACADIA N.P.

Muscongus
Bay

Boothbay Harbor

Monhegan
Island

Yarmouth
Falmouth

Westbrook

Portland
S. Portland
Cape Elizabeth

Casco Bay

Gulf of Maine

ATLANTIC OCEAN

Springvale

Sanford
South
Berwick

Saco
Old Orchard Beach
Biddeford
Kennebunk
RACHEL CARSON N.W.R.

Wells

Ogunquit

York Village
Kittery

Isles of Shoals

Salmon Falls

Saco

*Maine's soils and short growing season are
suitable for only a few kinds of agriculture.
Potatoes grow well in areas along the border
with New Brunswick, in Canada, and no state
harvests more wild blueberries—80 million
pounds (36.3 million kg) in 2003. Most berries
are processed into jellies, jams, syrups and fill-
ings. Huge numbers of seasonal employees are
needed each year for the late summer harvest.*

tallest, straightest white pines were perfect for the masts of sailing ships. When two centuries of cutting took most of these giants, loggers turned to woods such as oak and maple to make other products. Using river power, textile and shoe-making industries grew in the mid-1800s—though many mills moved south in the early 1900s. By then, Maine's rivers were harnessed for hydroelectric power, especially for paper and pulp mills. Shipbuilding cities like Bath and Portland, using first wood and then steel, launched thousands of vessels for military and merchant use and for fishing and lobstering, too.

Largest of the six New England states in area, Maine has the lowest population density of any state east of the Mississippi River. Most "Mainers" live near the coast in a string of communities that arc from the New Hampshire border to Bangor. The state's northern two-thirds are, in Henry David Thoreau's words, "all mossy and moosey" and much less populated. The cool, moist climate and shallow soils make much of the state's lands unsuitable for crops. Areas in the Aroostook River Valley have some of the best soils, and they make Maine a big potato producer. Food processing has grown in importance, as has tourism.

Like other New England states, Maine has lost industrial jobs, such as in paper mills. Even so, Maine remains a big producer of paper and wood products, while working to preserve its forests. As a pioneer in restoring free-flowing waterways, Maine removed the 160-year-old Edwards Dam in Augusta to allow salmon and other fish to ascend the Kennebec River. The state works hard to build "new economy" businesses, such as the making of computer components. People increasingly see that sustaining state environments will pay off with a prosperous future.

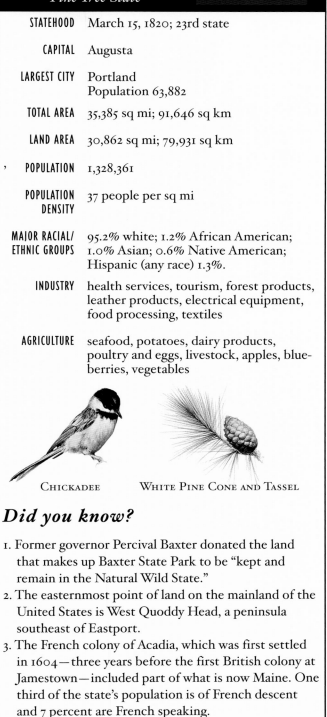

MAINE
Pine Tree State

STATEHOOD	March 15, 1820; 23rd state
CAPITAL	Augusta
LARGEST CITY	Portland Population 63,882
TOTAL AREA	35,385 sq mi; 91,646 sq km
LAND AREA	30,862 sq mi; 79,931 sq km
POPULATION	1,328,361
POPULATION DENSITY	37 people per sq mi
MAJOR RACIAL/ ETHNIC GROUPS	95.2% white; 1.2% African American; 1.0% Asian; 0.6% Native American; Hispanic (any race) 1.3%.
INDUSTRY	health services, tourism, forest products, leather products, electrical equipment, food processing, textiles
AGRICULTURE	seafood, potatoes, dairy products, poultry and eggs, livestock, apples, blueberries, vegetables

CHICKADEE WHITE PINE CONE AND TASSEL

Did you know?

1. Former governor Percival Baxter donated the land that makes up Baxter State Park to be "kept and remain in the Natural Wild State."
2. The easternmost point of land on the mainland of the United States is West Quoddy Head, a peninsula southeast of Eastport.
3. The French colony of Acadia, which was first settled in 1604—three years before the first British colony at Jamestown—included part of what is now Maine. One third of the state's population is of French descent and 7 percent are French speaking.
4. Maine covers nearly as much area as the other five New England states combined.
5. Acadia is the only national park in New England. The park's Cadillac Mountain is the highest point along the Atlantic coast of North America.

MARYLAND

★ Old Line State ★

"SAVE THE BAY!" Heard across Maryland and beyond, this slogan reminds people to care for their beautiful Chesapeake Bay. This estuary, largest in the country, is the state's greatest economic and environmental resource. Both Maryland's history and its future are tied to this vast yet vulnerable arm of the Atlantic Ocean.

Splitting Maryland almost in half, the Chesapeake separates most of the Atlantic Coastal Plain from the state's strip of Piedmont and oddly shaped Appalachian panhandle. Fed by the Susquehanna and other rivers, the bay has offered passage and protection for ships since colonial times. Here lie the state's main seaports, Baltimore and Annapolis. Watermen have long made their living from the bay's rich populations of oysters, blue crabs, and fish.

In 1608 John Smith became the first European to chart the bay. George Calvert, whose title was Lord Baltimore, received a grant from English King Charles I for the northern part of the Virginia Colony. His son settled Maryland in 1634, naming the area in honor of the king's wife, Queen Henrietta Maria. Planters in some Tidewater areas used slaves to farm tobacco. Such labor was not needed on small, mixed-crop and wheat farms to the east, north, and west. When the Revolution came, most Marylanders supported it. The Treaty of Paris, which ended the war, was ratified in 1784 in the statehouse in Annapolis. The building was used as the new nation's capitol for a nine-month period beginning the previous year. Maryland became the seventh state in 1788. Three years later it donated land for the building of a federal city in the District of Columbia.

Maryland grew quickly in the 19th century. A fine harbor and many waterfalls to power industry resulted in Baltimore's rise as a major East Coast port. Key road and canal routes

1634
Maryland's first settlement, St. Marys City, near the Potomac's confluence with the Chesapeake, was founded by Leonard Calvert.

1814
Watching Fort McHenry defend Baltimore in the War of 1812 inspired Francis Scott Key to write "The Star-Spangled Banner."

1862
The Battle of Antietam, on September 17, 1862, was the costliest day of the Civil War in terms of lives lost.

Present day
Harborplace, which opened in 1980 as a tourist, cultural, and business center, has brought new life to the port of Baltimore.

The Hooper Strait Lighthouse and an oyster-dredging skipjack (opposite) are among the symbols of Chesapeake Bay life that are preserved at the Chesapeake Bay Maritime Museum in St. Michaels. The skipjack was named the state boat in 1985.

MARYLAND
The Old Line State

STATEHOOD	April 28, 1788; 7th state
CAPITAL	Annapolis
LARGEST CITY	Baltimore Population 638,614
TOTAL AREA	12,407 sq mi; 32,133 sq km
LAND AREA	9,774 sq mi; 25,314 sq km
POPULATION	5,773,552
POPULATION DENSITY	465 people per sq mi
MAJOR RACIAL/ ETHNIC GROUPS	58.2% white; 29.4% African American; 5.5% Asian; 0.4% Native American; Hispanic (any race) 8.2%.
INDUSTRY	real estate, federal government, health services, business services, engineering services, electrical and gas services, communications, banking, insurance
AGRICULTURE	poultry and eggs, dairy products, nursery stock, soybeans, corn, seafood, cattle, vegetables

NORTHERN (BALTIMORE) ORIOLE   BLACK-EYED SUSAN

Did you know?

1. Maryland's nickname stems from praise its "troops of the line" earned from George Washington during the Revolutionary War.
2. The Maryland State House in Annapolis is the oldest state capitol still in continuous use for meetings of the state legislature.
3. The first successful passenger balloon flight in the U.S. took place in Baltimore on June 24, 1784. The only person onboard was 13-year-old Edward Warren.
4. In 1860 Baltimore had more free African Americans than any other major U.S. city. The Chesapeake Marine Railway and Dry Dock Company, founded in 1869, was operated by African Americans. Today, Prince George's County is one of the wealthiest predominantly black communities in the country.

The Chesapeake and Ohio Canal, built between 1828 and 1850, stretches for 184.5 miles (297 km) from Georgetown, in the District of Columbia, west to Cumberland, Maryland. Bedrock and tough competition from the railroads stopped the digging and ended the original vision of the canal as a link between the Atlantic and the Ohio Valley. The canal was used mostly for hauling Appalachian coal east in barges until 1924. Today, it is a national historical park, where tourists (above) can travel back in time.

linked it to the state's far-western reaches and beyond, and the Baltimore & Ohio Railroad began service in 1830. As the Civil War loomed, Maryland was divided on the issue of slavery. It stayed in the Union as a Border State, seeing many skirmishes and some major battles.

In the post-war period, Maryland became a bustling rail and ship transport center reconnecting North and South. Steelmaking, shipbuilding, and aircraft manufacturing attracted more workers during the two world wars. Nearly 90 percent of all Marylanders now live in the 35-mile- (56-km-) long corridor between D.C. and Baltimore, which has become a huge swath of suburban homes, shopping centers, and office parks. The state boasts

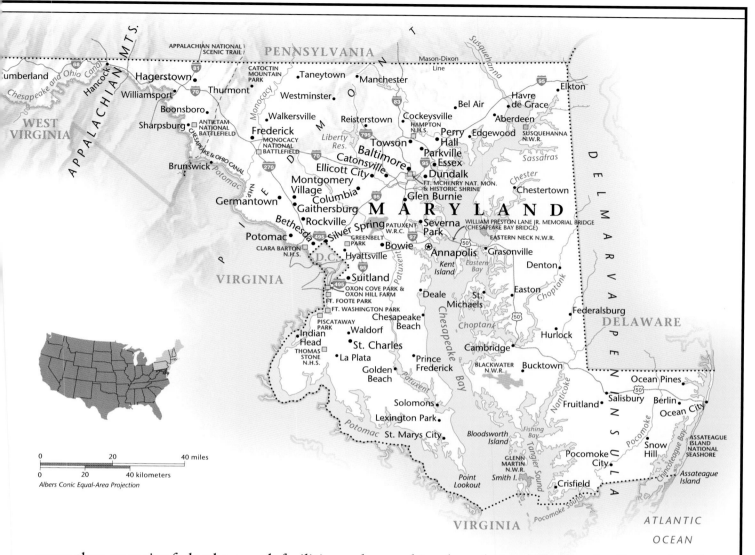

Map labels:

PENNSYLVANIA

Mason-Dixon Line

Appalachian National Scenic Trail

Cumberland
Chesapeake and Ohio Canal
Hancock
Hagerstown
Williamsport
Thurmont
Boonsboro
Sharpsburg
Antietam National Battlefield
Chesapeake & Ohio Canal N.H.P.
Brunswick
Potomac
WEST VIRGINIA
Catoctin Mountain Park
Taneytown
Manchester
Westminster
Walkersville
Reisterstown
Frederick
Monocacy National Battlefield
Monocacy
Liberty Res.
Cockeysville
Hampton N.H.S.
Bel Air
Havre de Grace
Aberdeen
Perry Hall
Edgewood
Susquehanna N.W.R.
Elkton
Susquehanna
Towson
Baltimore
Parkville
Essex
Dundalk
Ft. McHenry Nat. Mon. & Historic Shrine
Catonsville
Ellicott City
Montgomery Village
Columbia
Gaithersburg
Rockville
Germantown
Bethesda
Silver Spring
Patuxent W.R.C.
Severna Park
Glen Burnie
MARYLAND
Sassafras
Chester
Chestertown
Sassafras
William Preston Lane Jr. Memorial Bridge (Chesapeake Bay Bridge)
Eastern Neck N.W.R.
DELMARVA
Potomac
Clara Barton N.H.S.
Greenbelt Park
Bowie
Annapolis
Grasonville
Kent Island
Eastern Bay
Denton
D.C.
Hyattsville
Suitland
Oxon Cove Park & Oxon Hill Farm
Ft. Foote Park
Ft. Washington Park
St. Michaels
Deale
Easton
Choptank
Federalsburg
Piscataway Park
Indian Head
Thomas Stone N.H.S.
Waldorf
Chesapeake Beach
St. Charles
La Plata
Golden Beach
Prince Frederick
Cambridge
Hurlock
DELAWARE
Choptank
Blackwater N.W.R.
Bucktown
Chesapeake Bay
Ocean Pines
VIRGINIA
Solomons
Lexington Park
St. Marys City
Bloodsworth Island
Fishing Bay
Nanticoke
Fruitland
Salisbury
Berlin
Ocean City
Snow Hill
Pocomoke City
Assateague Island National Seashore
Glenn Martin N.W.R.
Point Lookout
Smith I.
Tangier Sound
Crisfield
Pocomoke
Chincoteague Bay
Assateague Island
VIRGINIA
Pocomoke Sound
ATLANTIC OCEAN

0   20   40 miles
0   20   40 kilometers
Albers Conic Equal-Area Projection

more than 50 major federal research facilities and has become a magnet for high-tech businesses. Traffic clogs roadways, despite the huge numbers of Maryland commuters who carpool and ride mass transit. Though more than a third of the state is still forested and agriculture—led by poultry raising—remains important, more and more land is being shifted to urban uses.

Tourists and residents alike sail, fish, swim, bird-watch, and simply soak up sun and sea breezes on Chesapeake Bay. The Bay Bridge has enabled easier travel both to Eastern Shore fishing villages and to Ocean City beaches along the state's Atlantic coast. But the mighty Chesapeake is in danger. Runoff from farm fields, backyards, and parking lots drains billions of gallons of pollutants into the estuary. Oysters, which serve as natural filters to clean the bay's waters, have declined dramatically. Between 1885 and 2003, the state's annual oyster harvest fell from 15 million bushels to 15 thousand bushels. Amazingly, the Chesapeake still supports a wide array of wildlife, plus a variety of jobs for Maryland residents. Millions of migrating birds feed here, and the state harvests more blue crabs than any other. Efforts now focus on reducing runoff, upgrading sewage treatment plants, and slowing suburban sprawl. Research to rebuild oyster populations advances. If all goes well, Maryland's people will one day be able to say, "We saved the bay!"

MASSACHUSETTS

★ *Bay State* ★

NEW LIFE, NEW IDEAS. That's what the Pilgrims wanted when they voyaged across the Atlantic in 1620. Landing first near the tip of Cape Cod, then crossing the bay to a mainland spot they named Plymouth, these settlers eventually found a better life. New ideas arose when they set down rules to govern themselves—the Mayflower Compact. Ever since, Massachusetts ideas have had enormous influence on American life—in government, education, business, and culture.

The Bay State's best-known feature is Cape Cod, curling like an arm around its large bay. This and many landscapes were shaped as gigantic glaciers pushed south. The Connecticut River Valley was scooped out, and then later filled in with fertile soils. Thin soils elsewhere limit farming. Ice sheets piled up sandy ridges, which remain today as Cape Cod and the famous islands Nantucket and Martha's Vineyard. West of the coastal plain rise rolling mountains, including the Berkshires.

The Pilgrims' new home became known as Massachusetts, after one of the groups of Algonquin-speaking peoples who lived there. Following a terrible first winter, the Pilgrims owed their lives to Native Americans who showed them how to plant corn and beans and otherwise survive. Other immigrants settled nearby in Naumkeag (Salem) and Shawmut (Boston), which became part of the Massachusetts Bay Colony. Here, political freedoms and representative government were begun, though everyone still had to be a Puritan.

Conflict had a role in colonial history here, too. Relations between settlers and native peoples began on friendly terms, but over time grew hostile. King Philip, chief of the Wampanoag people, declared war on the colonists in 1675 to protect his people and homeland.

1620
The men aboard the Mayflower *signed the Mayflower Compact, agreeing to write and obey "just and equal laws" in the new land.*

1775
The first battles of the American Revolution were fought in Lexington and Concord, where 95 Americans and 273 British died.

1800s
The state became a center of the textile, woolen, and tanning industries, which often hired women and immigrants at low pay.

1991—Present
The "Big Dig," a huge, almost-completed highway-tunnel project in Boston, will spur economic vitality and ease congestion.

The Old State House (opposite), built in 1713, was a center of political life in 18th-century Boston. The lion and unicorn are symbols of British authority, as was the council chamber of the royal governors inside.

MASSACHUSETTS
Bay State

STATEHOOD	February 6, 1788; 6th state
CAPITAL	Boston
LARGEST CITY	Boston Population 589,281
TOTAL AREA	10,555 sq mi; 27,336 sq km
LAND AREA	7,840 sq mi; 20,306 sq km
POPULATION	6,547,629
POPULATION DENSITY	620 people per sq mi
MAJOR RACIAL/ ETHNIC GROUPS	80.4% white; 6.6% African American; 5.3% Asian; 0.3% Native American; Hispanic (any race) 9.6%.
INDUSTRY	electrical equipment, machinery, metal products, scientific instruments, printing and publishing, tourism
AGRICULTURE	fruits, nuts and berries, nursery stock, dairy products

CHICKADEE

MAYFLOWER

Did you know?

1. The country's first planned industrial community was built in Lowell around a complex of textile mills beginning in 1822. By the 1840s the city had become the leading textile manufacturing center in America.
2. Lake Webster's Algonquin name is Lake Chargoggagoggmanchaugagoggchaubunagungamaug, which reportedly means "You fish on your side; I fish on my side; nobody fish in the middle."
3. The U.S.S. *Constitution* ("Old Ironsides"), the oldest, fully commissioned ship in the U.S. Navy, is permanently docked at Charlestown Navy Yard.
4. Massachusetts is the home of the country's first institute of higher learning (Harvard, 1636), its first printing press (Cambridge, 1638), its first post office (Richard Fairbanks's tavern, Boston, 1639), and its first ironworks (Lynn, 1643).

Hundreds died on both sides until, eventually, the colonists won. After decades of changes in how they governed the colonies, the English combined Plymouth and Massachusetts Bay in 1691. Later, the colonists helped the British win the French and Indian War, which ended in 1763. Shipping became a huge business, including the trading of slaves. Colonists up and down the Atlantic coast grew frustrated over control of trade and other rights by faraway England. In April 1775, British troops and colonists fought the opening battles of the Revolutionary War at Lexington and Concord. Many early battles took place in Massachusetts before action shifted south. Great leaders, such as early patriots John and Samuel Adams, made lasting impacts on the new nation. Massachusetts became the sixth state in 1788, with Boston as its capital.

Hardships caused by a law halting trade with European countries and then the War of 1812 brought huge changes for the state. Textile mills sprouted along state rivers, beginning with Lowell in 1814. Massachusetts's ties to the sea grew stronger. Shipping flourished in ports like Boston and Salem. Whalers sailed from New Bedford and Nantucket for decades until about 1900. The state contributed nearly 150,000 men and many ships to the Union effort in the Civil War. Industrial-ization increased for the rest of the century. By 1900 Massachusetts produced half the shoes made in America, as well as woolens and other clothing. The 20th century brought difficulties with labor strife and jobs leaving the state.

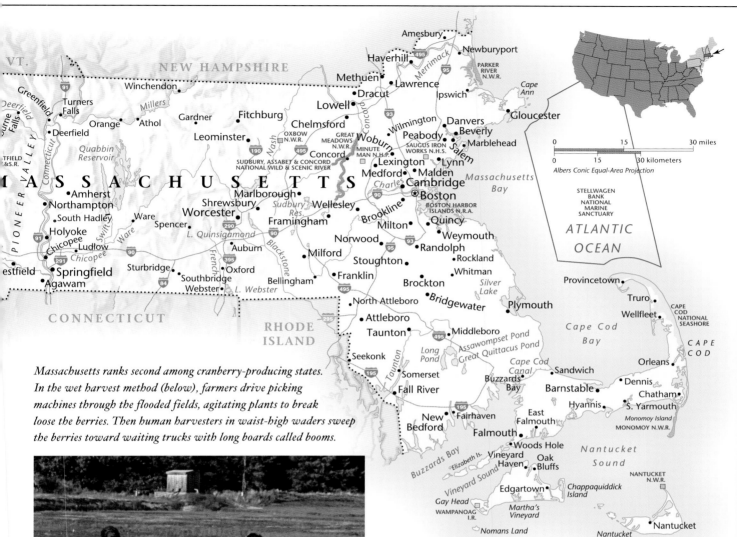

Massachusetts ranks second among cranberry-producing states. In the wet harvest method (below), farmers drive picking machines through the flooded fields, agitating plants to break loose the berries. Then human harvesters in waist-high waders sweep the berries toward waiting trucks with long boards called booms.

World War II sparked shipbuilding and other war-materials business, but by the 1960s the shift from old industries to high-tech research and products, like computers and electronics, was underway. Thousands of new jobs have recently been created.

Though there are many positives, Massachusetts's 6.4 million people face challenges, too. It's a crowded and expensive place. Boston is choked with the traffic and sprawl of modern urban life. There is a shortage of affordable housing and a wealth of traffic congestion. Whatever the problems, it seems certain Massachusetts will seek—and most likely find—new ideas to solve them.

NEW HAMPSHIRE

★ *Granite State* ★

THE GRANITE STATE. Though named for hard rock formations under the state, the nickname also reflects New Hampshire's strong feelings about liberty. First of the British colonies to become self-governing, it's no surprise that the state motto, written by Revolutionary War hero John Stark, declares "Live Free or Die."

The Appalachians form New Hampshire's backbone. Highest of the Northeast's peaks is 6,288-foot (1,917-m) Mount Washington, in the Presidential Range of the White Mountains. Famed for fearsome winter storms, a weather station atop the mountain once recorded winds of 231 mph (372 kph)! The Connecticut River flows out of the mountains to form most of the state's boundary with Vermont. More than four-fifths of the state is forested with spruce, fir, maple, oak, beech, and other trees. White-tailed deer abound, as do black bear and moose.

A short but important 18-mile (29-km) coastline stretches between Maine and Massachusetts.

To this shore came the English, founding their first settlements in 1623 along the Piscataqua River near present-day Portsmouth and Dover. Nearby communities Hampton and Exeter were soon established, and New Hampshire was made a royal colony in 1679. Long-running boundary disputes were settled with Massachusetts in the 1740s, with New York in the 1790s, and with Canada in 1842. Settlers and Abenaki peoples got along at first, but greater numbers of newcomers caused increased conflicts over hunting grounds and fishing rights. Native resistance ended by the close of the French and Indian War in 1763.

New Hampshire's patriotic colors showed early. A key event—which some consider the first strike in the fight for independence—was the taking of gunpowder from an English fort at

1777

Native son General John Stark's victory at the Battle of Bennington, in Vermont, was a turning point in the Revolution.

1850S

Mills producing lumber, paper, textiles, and woolens industrialized the state. It became a leader in child labor laws.

1944

World attention focused on the state when President Franklin Roosevelt hosted a global economic conference at Bretton Woods.

2004

Every four years, New Hampshire's tradition of holding the first presidential primary election draws national attention.

New Hampshire's spectacular fall colors attract busloads of tourists from across the country to places like Marlow (opposite). Its trademark white-steepled church and town hall are typical of rural New England towns.

QUEBEC

Third L.

First
Connecticut
Lake

Second
Lake

Lake
Francis

CANADA
U.S.

• Colebrook

Blue Mt.
3,723 ft
+ 1,135 m

*Umbagog
Lake*

LAKE
UMBAGOG
N.W.R.

North
Stratford

Upper Ammonoosuc

• Groveton

Mt. Cabot
4,160 ft, 1,268 m +

WHITE MOUNTAIN
NATIONAL FOREST

Lancaster

*Highest point in
New Hampshire*

Berlin•

APPALACHIAN
NATIONAL
SCENIC
TRAIL

• Gorham

MAINE

*Moore
Reservoir*

• Whitefield

• Littleton

Mt. Washington
6,288 ft
+ 1,917 m

Ammonoosuc

93

Franconia
• Lisbon

Bretton Woods•

WILDCAT BROOK NATIONAL
WILD & SCENIC RIVER

HAVERHILL-
BATH BRIDGE

CRAWFORD
NOTCH
S.P.

Saco

Woodsville \

Mt. Lafayette
5,249 ft, 1,600 m

North Conway•

FRANCONIA
NOTCH S.P.

WHITE MOUNTAIN
NATIONAL FOREST

VERMONT

Lincoln

North Conway•

• Haverhill

NEW

Conway•

*Conway
Lake*

• Orford

Warren•

HAMPSHIRE

Bearcamp

*Ossipee
Lake*

Ossipee

APPALACHIAN
NATIONAL
SCENIC
TRAIL

*Squam
Lake*

Center
Sandwich•

• Hanover

*Newfound
Lake*

Ashland•

Center
Ossipee•

Lebanon•

• Enfield Canaan•

*Lake
Winnipesaukee*

Meredith•

Lake Wentworth

*Mascoma
Lake*

Bristol•

Wolfeboro•

Sanbornville•

*Winnisquam
Lake*

Laconia•

*Merrymeeting
Lake*

SAINT-
GAUDENS
N.H.S.

Franklin•

Tilton•

*Crystal
L.*

Alton Bay•

• Milton

New
London•

Northfield•

Farmington•

Cocheco

*Sunapee
Lake*

*Suncook
Lakes*

Sugar

JOHN
HAY
N.W.R.

89

Canterbury•

Rochester•

Salmon Falls

Claremont•

Newport•

MT.
SUNAPEE
S.P.

Mt. Sunapee
2,743 ft
836 m

Contoocook•

Pittsfield•

Somersworth•

• Charlestown

Henniker•

Concord

*Bow
Lake*

Dover•

North
Walpole•

Hillsboro•

393

Durham•

Piscataqua

LAMPREY
NATIONAL WILD
& SCENIC RIVER

•Walpole

Antrim•

Suncook•

*Highland
Lake*

Contoocook

Raymond•

Newmarket•

Portsmouth•

Lamprey

*Great
Bay*

*Surry Mt.
Lake*

*Nubanusit
Lake*

*Massabesic
Lake*

Exeter•

Rye•

*Isles of
Shoals*

Keene•

Monadnock Mt.
3,165 ft
965 m

Peterborough•

WAPACK
N.W.R.

Manchester

293

East
Derry•

Kingston•

Hampton•

ATLANTIC

Wilton•

Londonderry•

Derry•

Plaistow•

OCEAN

Hinsdale•

Troy•

Jaffrey•

Milford•

93

Atkinson•

495

Greenville•

Salem•

Winchester•

New Ipswich•

Nashua•

Merrimack

MASSACHUSETTS

Connecticut (river labels throughout)

Merrimack

Pemigewasset

Ashuelot

Southegan

New Hampshire's rivers have provided industrial
power for more than two centuries. In recent
years, fisheries have proven increasingly valuable
to state residents and visitors alike. New
Hampshire takes pride in the wide variety of
both its fresh- and saltwater fishing. Efforts to
restore stream habitats and to restock the
endangered Atlantic salmon are underway.
Here, a fly-fisher tries his luck on the
Piscataquog River near Manchester.

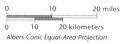

0   10   20 miles
0   10   20 kilometers

Albers Conic Equal-Area Projection

Portsmouth by a band of the colony's men in late 1774. Six months before the Declaration of Independence, New Hampshire declared its freedom from England on January 5, 1776. The state was the ninth and deciding state to approve the U.S. Constitution in mid-1788. New Hampshire was strongly against slavery. During the Civil War, it supported the Union with troops and supplies.

Industrialization started up early. The textile and woolen industries threaded their way through the Merrimack River Valley. Manchester's massive Amoskeag Mills stretched along the river and canals below its original power source, Amoskeag Falls. By 1915 this single company employed 17,000 workers—many from Canada, Ireland, Greece, and Poland—in 30 mills and turned out 50 miles (80 km) of finished cloth per hour! Change came when many mills slowed or closed due to major labor strikes and competition from lower-cost mills in Southern states. World War II helped the state rebound from the Great Depression. New businesses replaced old industries by the 1980s. Portsmouth, Nashua, and other cities benefit from their closeness to Boston, attracting high-technology companies that take advantage of an educated, skilled workforce. Some traditional state work is still strong. The Portsmouth Naval Shipyard repairs nuclear submarines; maple trees are still tapped for syrup; and forests still supply wood products and pulp to mills.

Natural resources have long been important to the state's economy. Conservation measures protecting river headwaters and large tracts of woodland have been in place since the early 1900s, and four-season tourism has begun to play a larger role in the state. Today, state residents understand that natural resources sustained can be even more valuable than those removed.

NEW HAMPSHIRE
Granite State

STATEHOOD	June 21, 1788; 9th state
CAPITAL	Concord
LARGEST CITY	Manchester Population 108,398
TOTAL AREA	9,350 sq mi; 24,216 sq km
LAND AREA	8,968 sq mi; 23,227 sq km
POPULATION	1,316,470
POPULATION DENSITY	140 people per sq mi
MAJOR RACIAL/ ETHNIC GROUPS	93.9% white; 2.2% Asian; 1.1% African American; 0.2% Native American; Hispanic (any race) 2.8%.
INDUSTRY	machinery, electronics, metal products
AGRICULTURE	nursery stock, poultry and eggs, fruits and nuts, vegetables

PURPLE FINCH   PURPLE LILAC

Did you know?

1. The famous naturally carved granite profile known as The Old Man of the Mountain, in Franconia Notch State Park, was destroyed by a rock slide in 2003. It can be seen on the U.S. Mint's quarter for the state.
2. The first strike organized by women workers in the United States occurred in December 1828. Several hundred workers walked out of the Dover Cotton Factory to protest new management policies that forbid them to talk on the job, reduced wages from 58 cents a day to 53 cents, and docked them a fourth of a day's wage if they arrived after the morning bell stopped ringing.
3. New Hampshire was named by Captain John Mason after his home county of Hampshire in England.
4. In 1964 New Hampshire became the first U.S. state to revive the use of a legal lottery in the 20th century. Since it started, the lottery has raised more than 850 million dollars to aid education.

NEW JERSEY
★ *Garden State* ★

CROSSROADS OF THE EAST. New Jersey's location has placed it squarely in the middle of Atlantic coast action for four centuries. Benjamin Franklin called it a "barrel tapped at both ends," referring both to its abundant farm production and to its position between New York City and Philadelphia.

The Dutch set up their first trading post here near present-day Jersey City in 1618 as part of New Netherland. They surrendered the land to England in 1664, and it was renamed New Jersey after the English Channel Isle of Jersey. Following decades of legal tug-of-war between leaders from New York City and Philadelphia, New Jersey became its own royal colony in 1738. It was in the thick of things during the Revolution, with more than 90 battles fought here, including important victories at Trenton, Princeton, and Monmouth. New Jersey was the third state to ratify the Constitution in late 1787, and Trenton was made its capital three years later.

By the 19th century, the state was in the middle of the industrial revolution. There was still farming, but factories produced textiles, shoes, bricks, and more. Roads were built, canals dug, and rail lines laid down. New Jersey gave soldiers, supplies, and monetary support to the Union during the Civil War. The war fueled industries and attracted thousands of European immigrants. Most factory workers crowded into Newark and other northern cities, often living in poverty. Manufacturing eventually declined—as did the health of New Jersey's urban neighborhoods. Riots broke out in Newark in 1967, calling attention to the need for change.

New Jersey's economy has turned increasingly to a wide range of service and trade businesses. The state has long been a top research center. Manufacturing has not died, though:

1524—early 1600s

The Lenni-Lenape, a peaceful farming people, greeted a succession of Europeans who came ashore in what is now New Jersey.

1778

George Washington honored Mary Ludwig Hays McCauly (Molly Pitcher) for her bravery at the Battle of Monmouth.

1879

Thomas Edison, the "Wizard of Menlo Park," is credited with more than 1,000 inventions, including the electric light bulb.

Present day

Though service industries have begun to dominate, the manufacture of drugs and chemicals continue to be key industries.

Tourists first came to Atlantic City by train in 1854. It enjoyed a century of popularity until other destinations drew visitors away. In the past two decades, the city has been revitalized. Its celebrated Boardwalk (opposite) of Monopoly fame is once again a favorite stroll.

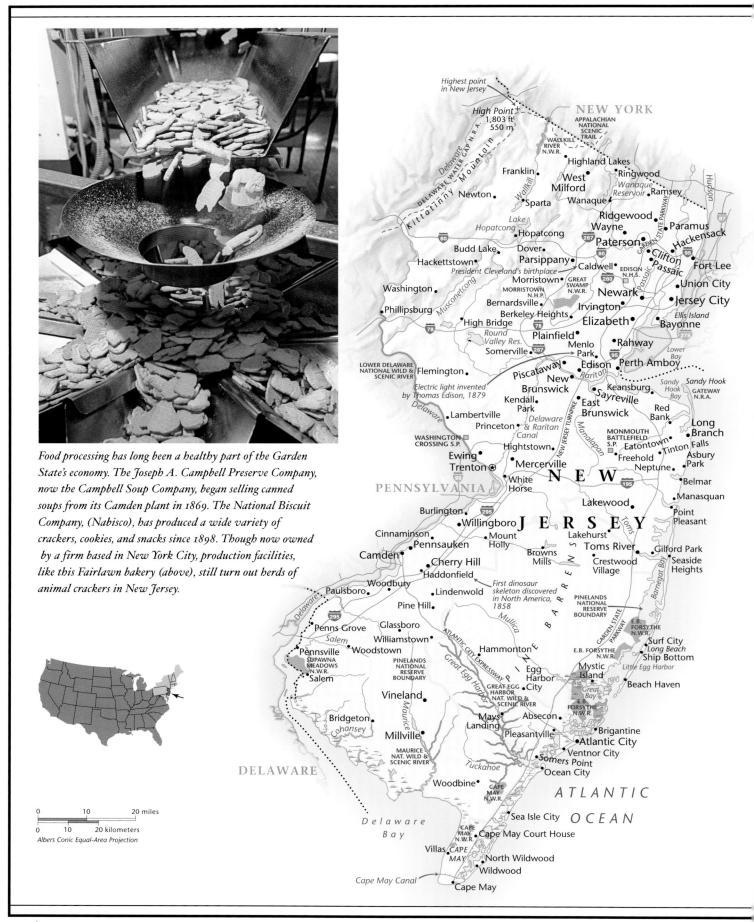

Food processing has long been a healthy part of the Garden State's economy. The Joseph A. Campbell Preserve Company, now the Campbell Soup Company, began selling canned soups from its Camden plant in 1869. The National Biscuit Company, (Nabisco), has produced a wide variety of crackers, cookies, and snacks since 1898. Though now owned by a firm based in New York City, production facilities, like this Fairlawn bakery (above), still turn out herds of animal crackers in New Jersey.

0   10   20 miles
0   10   20 kilometers
Albers Conic Equal-Area Projection

Highest point in New Jersey

High Point
1,803 ft
550 m
DELAWARE WATER GAP N.R.A.
APPALACHIAN NATIONAL SCENIC TRAIL
WALLKILL RIVER N.W.R.
NEW YORK

Kittatinny Mountain

Franklin
West Milford
Highland Lakes
Ringwood
Ramsey
Wanaque Reservoir
Newton
Sparta
Wanaque
Ridgewood
Paramus
Hackensack
Lake Hopatcong
Wayne
Paterson
Clifton
Passaic
Fort Lee
Hopatcong
Budd Lake
Dover
Parsippany
Caldwell
EDISON N.H.S.
Union City
Hackettstown
President Cleveland's birthplace
Morristown
GREAT SWAMP N.W.R.
Newark
Jersey City
Washington
MORRISTOWN N.H.P.
Bernardsville
Irvington
Ellis Island
Phillipsburg
Berkeley Heights
Elizabeth
Bayonne
High Bridge
Plainfield
Round Valley Res.
Somerville
Menlo Park
Rahway
Lower Bay
LOWER DELAWARE NATIONAL WILD & SCENIC RIVER
Flemington
Piscataway
Edison
Perth Amboy
Sandy Hook Bay
Sandy Hook
GATEWAY N.R.A.
Electric light invented by Thomas Edison, 1879
New Brunswick
Keansburg
Sayreville
Delaware
Kendall Park
East Brunswick
Red Bank
Long Branch
Lambertville
Delaware & Raritan Canal
Princeton
MONMOUTH BATTLEFIELD S.P.
Eatontown
Tinton Falls
WASHINGTON CROSSING S.P.
Hightstown
Freehold
Neptune
Asbury Park
Ewing
Mercerville
Belmar
Trenton
White Horse
NEW
Manasquan
PENNSYLVANIA
Lakewood
Point Pleasant
Burlington
JERSEY
Toms
Willingboro
Lakehurst
Cinnaminson
Mount Holly
Toms River
Gilford Park
Camden
Pennsauken
Browns Mills
Crestwood Village
Seaside Heights
Cherry Hill
PINE
Haddonfield
First dinosaur skeleton discovered in North America, 1858
BARRENS
Barnegat Bay
Woodbury
Lindenwold
PINELANDS NATIONAL RESERVE BOUNDARY
Paulsboro
Pine Hill
Mullica
E.B. FORSYTHE N.W.R.
Penns Grove
Glassboro
Surf City
Long Beach
Salem
Williamstown
Hammonton
E.B. FORSYTHE N.W.R.
Ship Bottom
Pennsville
Woodstown
ATLANTIC CITY EXPRESSWAY
Little Egg Harbor
SUPAWNA MEADOWS N.W.R.
PINELANDS NATIONAL RESERVE BOUNDARY
Egg Harbor City
Mystic Island
Beach Haven
Salem
Great Egg Harbor
GREAT EGG HARBOR NAT. WILD & SCENIC RIVER
Great Bay
Vineland
E.B. FORSYTHE N.W.R.
Bridgeton
Cohansey
Maurice
Absecon
Brigantine
Mays Landing
Millville
MAURICE NAT. WILD & SCENIC RIVER
Pleasantville
Atlantic City
Ventnor City
Somers Point
Ocean City
Tuckahoe
Woodbine
CAPE MAY N.W.R.
ATLANTIC OCEAN
Delaware Bay
Sea Isle City
DELAWARE
CAPE MAY N.W.R.
Cape May Court House
Villas
CAPE MAY
North Wildwood
Cape May Canal
Wildwood
Cape May

New Jersey still has 10,000 firms producing a vast array of products.

New Jersey boasts a wide range of landscapes. Its northern third, covered by glaciers 20,000 years ago, is hilly, rocky, and spotted with lakes and wetlands. Ancient Kittatinny Mountain stretches along its northwestern border. From Sandy Hook to Cape May, the Jersey Shore sports some of the Atlantic coast's best beaches. Most of southern New Jersey is low coastal plain that supports a people-light, wildlife-heavy region called the Pine Barrens. Called "barren" only because it wasn't good for farming, its forests, bogs, and swamps are home to more than a thousand plant and animal species. In 1978 Congress set aside 1.1 million acres (450,000 ha) as the first national reserve. This wilderness survives in the country's most densely populated state. Despite the state's overall urban and industrial character, dozens of different kinds of fruits and vegetables are grown on nearly 10,000 farms that give it the nickname Garden State. New Jersey ranks in the top five states in output of blueberries, cranberries, peaches, head lettuce, and bell peppers. Produce is either trucked fresh to regional cities or processed in factories.

All ten of New Jersey's largest cities are within 30 miles (48 km) of New York City or Philadelphia. In New Jersey, as across the U.S., people have chosen for decades to leave cities and build suburbs. The state's Smart Growth Plan and other strategies have made it a national leader in efforts to slow this sprawl and protect farmlands. By the end of 2003, a total of 120,000 acres (49,000 ha) of croplands had been preserved. By working to balance the needs of its cities, countryside, and connections to its neighbors, New Jersey seeks a lasting and vital middle ground.

NEW JERSEY
Garden State

STATEHOOD	December 18, 1787; 3rd state
CAPITAL	Trenton
LARGEST CITY	Newark Population 277,000
TOTAL AREA	8,721 sq mi; 22,588 sq km
LAND AREA	7,417 sq mi; 19,211 sq km
POPULATION	8,791,894
POPULATION DENSITY	1,008 people per sq mi
MAJOR RACIAL/ ETHNIC GROUPS	68.6% white; 13.7% African American; 8.3% Asian; 0.3% Native American; Hispanic (any race) 17.1%.
INDUSTRY	machinery, electronics, metal products, chemicals
AGRICULTURE	nursery stock, poultry and eggs, fruits and nuts, vegetables

AMERICAN GOLDFINCH   VIOLET

Did you know?

1. Beneath the Pine Barrens lie aquifers that hold 17 trillion gallons (64 trillion kl) of fresh water.
2. The first dinosaur skeleton found in North America was excavated at Haddonfield in 1858. It was named Hadrosaurus in honor of its discovery site.
3. Cape May became the nation's first seaside resort in 1761. It was named by the Dutch sea captain Cornelius Jacobsen Mey, who explored the region in the 1620s. In recognition of its well-preserved Victorian houses, it was named a National Historic Landmark City in 1976.
4. Famed inventor Thomas Edison filed for more than 400 patents from his laboratory in Menlo Park. During the seven years he worked there, his achievements included perfecting the light bulb and the telephone, inventing the phonograph (record player), and inventing the multiplex telegraph.
5. Early settlers mined the bogs of the Pine Barrens for iron to make kettles and cannonballs.

NEW YORK
★ *Empire State* ★

GATEWAY TO A NATION. New York has long been America's front door, welcoming millions of people from all over the world to new homes. Now the largest Northeast state in both area and population and long the nation's chief commercial center, New York fits the Empire State nickname traceable to George Washington.

The Appalachians and Adirondacks arc across the state's eastern half, while the Alleghenies rise in the west. Glaciers scooped out Lakes Ontario and Erie as well as the narrow Finger Lakes. Long Island is a great ridge of sand and rock left behind by retreating ice. Western lowlands and broad valleys carved by the Mohawk and Hudson Rivers offer fertile croplands.

Long before Europeans walked its lands, the powerful Iroquois Confederacy and Algonquin-speaking peoples lived here. In 1609 French explorer Samuel de Champlain explored the lake that today bears his name, and Englishman Henry Hudson explored the river now named for him. Acting on Hudson's reports, a Dutch company set up the New Netherland colony, including a settlement near present-day Albany and another on the island of Manhattan. The colony was taken over by the English in 1664 and renamed for England's Duke of York. New York was the site of many conflicts in the French and Indian War. Split loyalties among the Iroquois then and during the American Revolution cost them dearly. They had lost most of their land by the time New York became the 11th state in 1788.

New York City has been the nation's most populous city ever since the first U.S. Census in 1790. The key factor in its 19th-century growth was the digging of the Erie Canal, which by 1825 connected it—via the Hudson River—with Lake Erie and western lands beyond. Vast waves of immigrants flowed to and through New York City. Many newcomers stayed on, making the

1626

Peter Minuit, governor-general of New Amsterdam, bought Manhattan Island for goods worth about 60 Dutch guilders ($24).

1825

The opening of the Erie Canal linked the Atlantic and the Great Lakes, bringing prosperity to New York cities along its route.

1892–1954

More than 17 million people entered the U.S. through Ellis Island (now shared with New Jersey) between 1892 and 1954.

2001

The attack that killed almost 2,800 people and destroyed the World Trade Center changed forever everyday life in America.

Standing 1,250 feet (381 m) tall, the Empire State Building (opposite) has been a towering symbol of New York City since it was completed in 1931. From the tower's 86th-floor observation deck, visitors can see New York and four neighboring states!

The Niagara River is known for its magnificent waterfalls—American, Bridal Veil, and Horseshoe—along the New York-Ontario border. Known collectively as Niagara Falls, they are visited each year by roughly 12 million people. Each minute, an average of 40 million gallons (150 million liters) of water thunder 175 feet (53 m) over its ledges of limestone and shale.

city a "melting pot" of peoples and cultures. African Americans moved to the city from the South in the decades after the Civil War, and the Harlem neighborhood grew into a focal point for black cultural life. Already the nation's leading trade center, New York soon sewed up the top spot in the country's garment (clothing) industry, too. Printing and publishing boomed, and Wall Street in Manhattan became the country's financial hub. The 20th century saw New York City grow into an international stage for theater, television, film, advertising, and music recording. And the United Nations has been headquartered in the city since 1946.

New Yorkers call almost all of the state north of New York City "Upstate," and it's a different world from "The City." A quarter of state lands are devoted to agriculture, including dairy farming, fruits, and vegetables. Only Vermont taps more sugar maples for syrup. Industrial cities include Buffalo, Schenectady, Syracuse, and Utica. Rochester is known for photographic and optical equipment. Tourism is huge in the state, too, with both urban and natural areas drawing visitors year-round.

Today, the state of New York ranks third in population, with the New York City metropolitan area one of the biggest on Earth, with more than 21 million people. Both the city and state are working to rebound from the enormous impacts of the 9/11 terrorist attack. While New York's role as a commerce capital remains, its old industries face long-term decline. The state works to attract new industry and to clean up its natural environments. By 2009, the 400th anniversary of Hudson's voyage, the state plans to restore the long-polluted Hudson River. In New York City's harbor, the Statue of Liberty stands as a beacon of freedom and an invitation to people everywhere.

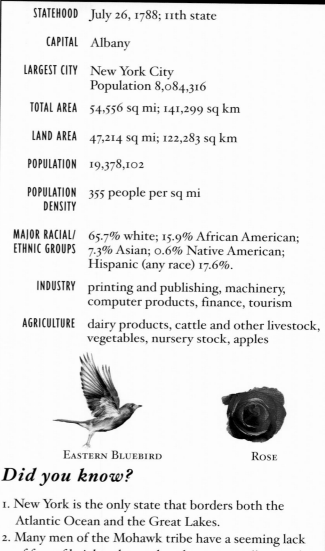

NEW YORK
Empire State

STATEHOOD	July 26, 1788; 11th state
CAPITAL	Albany
LARGEST CITY	New York City Population 8,084,316
TOTAL AREA	54,556 sq mi; 141,299 sq km
LAND AREA	47,214 sq mi; 122,283 sq km
POPULATION	19,378,102
POPULATION DENSITY	355 people per sq mi
MAJOR RACIAL/ ETHNIC GROUPS	65.7% white; 15.9% African American; 7.3% Asian; 0.6% Native American; Hispanic (any race) 17.6%.
INDUSTRY	printing and publishing, machinery, computer products, finance, tourism
AGRICULTURE	dairy products, cattle and other livestock, vegetables, nursery stock, apples

EASTERN BLUEBIRD   ROSE

Did you know?

1. New York is the only state that borders both the Atlantic Ocean and the Great Lakes.
2. Many men of the Mohawk tribe have a seeming lack of fear of heights that makes them especially suited to working as riveters on steel bridges and skyscrapers. The Empire State Building, the George Washington Bridge, and Rockefeller Center are among the many structures they have helped build.
3. Adirondack Park is the largest park in the lower 48 states . It is almost as big as Yellowstone, Yosemite, Grand Canyon, and Olympic National Parks combined.
4. The Finger Lakes, a series of glacially carved lakes in upstate New York, bear the names of various Native American tribes, including the Seneca, Cayuga, and Canandaigua. The region is second only to California in the production of grapes.

PENNSYLVANIA

★ *Keystone State* ★

THE KEYSTONE STATE. To a builder, the keystone is at the center of an arch, the stone that binds the others together. Pennsylvania was key to the nation's successful start, and a major force in holding the Union together during its toughest time.

William Penn's heavily forested colony was named for his father, Admiral William Penn. (*Sylvania* is a Latin word meaning "woodlands.") In October 1682, the younger William brought 360 settlers who believed in religious freedom and a fair government to form this 12th of the 13 English colonies. Penn treated Native Americans with respect, signing a fair treaty with Delaware chiefs. In 1701, the colony's Charter of Privilege gave its elected assembly greater power than any other in the English world. Though Penn was a Quaker, people of other religions were welcome. The colony expanded farther west, too. There, settlers met resistance from native peoples and the French. These conflicts did not end until 1763, after the French and Indian War.

Pennsylvania's lands were packed with resources above and below ground. Beech and maple uplands plus lowlands of oak and hickory made up "Penn's woods." Fertile valley soils, especially in the southeast, proved perfect for grain and dairy farming. Coal, iron, limestone, and oil supplied the minerals for industry. The many rivers and streams—and later a link to Lake Erie—offered water power and transportation.

Wealthy, populous Pennsylvania took center stage in the move to gain independence. Representatives from the 13 Colonies met in Philadelphia to adopt the Declaration of Independence, which local resident Benjamin Franklin helped draft. Pennsylvania became the second state in 1787. In the next century, the stately merchant city of Philadelphia became a brawny industrial giant—Workshop of the

1682

William Penn founded his colony in 1682 on land west of the Delaware River granted to him by King Charles II in a charter.

1863

At Gettysburg, the Union withstood "Pickett's Charge," stopping the South's advance. This was the turning point in the Civil War.

1870–1970s

Pittsburgh grew to be a steel powerhouse. By 1900, the city's mill workers turned out two-thirds of the country's steel.

1979

The near-disaster at the Three Mile Island nuclear power plant near Harrisburg stopped all U.S. development of nuclear plants.

Though a crack ended its ringing days, no symbol of freedom could ring truer than the Liberty Bell—Philadelphia's top attraction. While London-made, it became clearly American when it was rung at the first public reading of the Declaration of Independence.

"Penn's woods" are wildlife-rich. One of the largest deer populations in the country and thousands of black bears live along its forested ridges. Elk, once eliminated from the state, have made a difficult and finally successful return. But the state's best-known animal is the world's most famous groundhog. In a playful 117-year tradition, Punxsutawney Phil (left) sees his shadow on February 2, 2004. His prediction: six more weeks of winter!

0   25   50 miles
0   25   50 kilometers
Albers Conic Equal-Area Projection

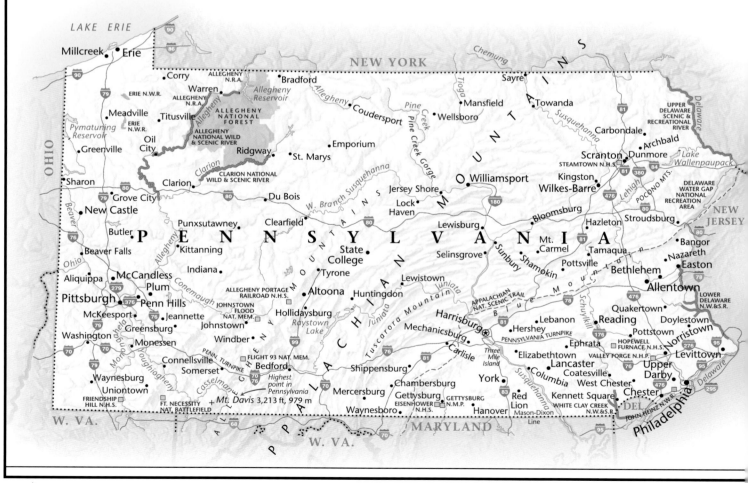

World. It launched steamships, rolled out locomotives, and milled textiles, clothing, paper, and more. Immigrants came from Ireland, Germany, and elsewhere. Located at the junction of three rivers, Pittsburgh used in-state coal and Great Lakes iron ore to make iron and later steel. Other cities boomed, too, making a thousand different products. The state contributed huge volumes of material and tens of thousands of soldiers to the Civil War.

After the war the industrial boom continued, and waves of immigrants poured in from Europe and the rural South to work in the state's mines and factories. Owners became wealthy, but life was tough and often dangerous for workers. To gain safer working conditions and better pay, labor unions were formed, leading to violent strikes in the late 1800s and early 1900s. Though industrial success continued through the two world wars, the steel industry began to decline. Less coal was needed as the steel business moved overseas, where it could be made more cheaply.

Today, Pittsburgh's mills are gone, but the city still has advanced manufacturing—plus world-class medical and life sciences research. Philadelphia is becoming a center for information technology and financial services. But Pennsylvania is still a mining and industrial force, ranking fourth in coal production and fifth in steel output. It's an agricultural state, too, with 50,000 farms producing dairy products, fresh vegetables, and eggs. Tourists increasingly find the state's rural landscapes, plentiful wild spaces, and key historic sites unbeatable destinations. Though Pennsylvania is a different fit now from when Penn and Franklin walked its cobblestones, the Keystone State still has a key place in the workings of the nation.

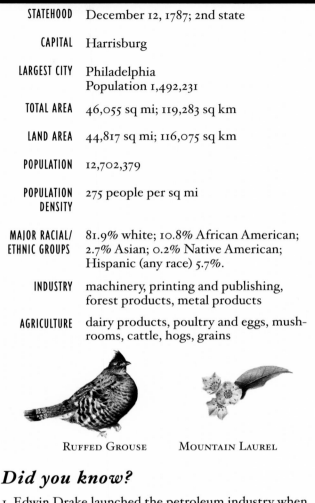

PENNSYLVANIA
Keystone State

STATEHOOD	December 12, 1787; 2nd state
CAPITAL	Harrisburg
LARGEST CITY	Philadelphia Population 1,492,231
TOTAL AREA	46,055 sq mi; 119,283 sq km
LAND AREA	44,817 sq mi; 116,075 sq km
POPULATION	12,702,379
POPULATION DENSITY	275 people per sq mi
MAJOR RACIAL/ ETHNIC GROUPS	81.9% white; 10.8% African American; 2.7% Asian; 0.2% Native American; Hispanic (any race) 5.7%.
INDUSTRY	machinery, printing and publishing, forest products, metal products
AGRICULTURE	dairy products, poultry and eggs, mushrooms, cattle, hogs, grains

RUFFED GROUSE   MOUNTAIN LAUREL

Did you know?

1. Edwin Drake launched the petroleum industry when he drilled the first oil well in 1859 at Titusville.
2. During the American Revolution, the Liberty Bell was moved from Philadelphia to Allentown. It was returned after the British evacuated Philadelphia.
3. Hershey is known as the Chocolate Capital of the World. Among its most popular candies are Hershey's Kisses. Between its factory in Hershey and the one in Oakdale, California, the company can turn out 80 million of these candies each day.
4. The first federal building whose construction was specifically authorized by the Constitution was the U.S. Mint. Philadelphia was selected for the site because, when construction began in 1792, it was the nation's capital. It is believed that some of the silver used in making the first silver coins was donated by President George Washington, who lived a few blocks from the mint at the time.

RHODE ISLAND

★ *Ocean State* ★

SMALL SPACE, SPECIAL PLACE. Rhode Island is the smallest state in area—tinier than some *counties* in other states—but it's founded on freedoms still revered across the nation. There's much that makes Rhode Island special.

The Dutch explored the coastline in 1614— possibly giving it the name *Roodt Eylandt* (Red Island)—but it was Roger Williams who began white settlement there in 1636. Forced to leave Massachusetts because he disagreed with its Puritan leaders, Williams wanted to create a place of religious freedom. He obtained land along a large bay from the Narragansett people, naming his community Providence. Other like-minded people later established Newport, Portsmouth, and Warwick. The settlements joined together for protection. Over time, relations with the Indians worsened. King Philip's War ended native resistance to white settlement in 1676.

Rhode Island steered an independent course as a colony, avoiding outside affairs. But the people soon realized that such connections were needed and began trading their harvests and catches for goods from other colonies and countries. In the 1700s, Newport emerged as the leading port in the very profitable "triangle trade," in which ships carrying lumber to the West Indies returned with molasses for making rum. Rum was then sent to Africa in exchange for slaves. In the 1780s a state law banned the slave trade and provided for the gradual emancipation of children of slaves.

In the first years of the United States, Rhode Island's independent attitude kept it from signing the Constitution. It pressed for greater freedom of worship and other rights, for slavery to be abolished, for changes in trade rules and in taxes, and for a method of representation in Congress that was not based on

1636

Roger Williams founded Rhode Island and Providence Plantations and also wrote America's first document separating church and state.

1793

Samuel Slater's use of water to power a cotton mill started the industrial revolution in the U.S. and New England's textile empire.

1890s

The Breakers was one of several "cottages" built in Newport by wealthy business barons from New York in the 1890s.

Present day

Providence's worn-out harbor area has been revitalized by an award-winning urban renewal project called WaterPlace Park.

Historical home of the America's Cup yacht races, Newport still hosts sailing crews from across the globe. Here, the crew of the Spirit of Rhode Island *enjoys a sun-splashed day on the water.*

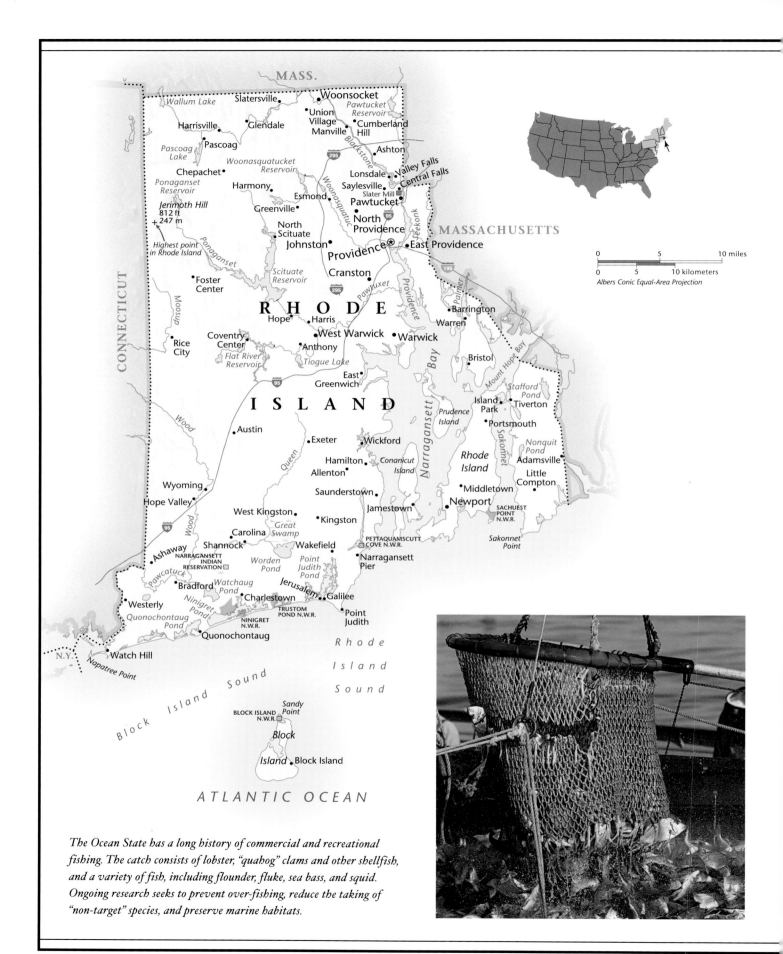

MASS.

Wallum Lake · Slatersville · Woonsocket

Pawtucket Reservoir

Harrisville · · Glendale · Union Village · Cumberland Hill

· Pascoag · Manville · Ashton

Pascoag Lake

Woonasquatucket Reservoir

Chepachet · Lonsdale · Valley Falls · Central Falls

Harmony · Esmond · Saylesville · Pawtucket

Ponaganset Reservoir

Greenville · Slater Mill □

Jerimoth Hill 812 ft + 247 m

North Scituate · North Providence · MASSACHUSETTS

Highest point in Rhode Island

Johnston · Providence ⊛ · East Providence

R H O D E

Scituate Reservoir

· Cranston

· Foster Center

Ponaganset

I - 295

Hope · Harris · Barrington

Moosup

Pawtuxet

· Warren

Providence

Palmer

I S L A N D

Rice City

Coventry Center · West Warwick · Warwick

· Anthony · Bristol

Flat River Reservoir

Tiogue Lake

Mount Hope Bay

Stafford Pond · Tiverton

Wood

· Austin

East Greenwich · Island Park

· Exeter · Wickford · Portsmouth

Hamilton · *Conanicut Island* · *Prudence Island*

· Allenton · *Rhode Island* · *Nonquit Pond*

Queen · Adamsville

· Wyoming · Saunderstown · Little Compton

Hope Valley · Middletown

· West Kingston · Jamestown · Newport

· Kingston · SACHUEST POINT N.W.R.

Great Swamp

· Carolina · Wakefield

· Shannock · PETTAQUAMSCUTT COVE N.W.R.

Ashaway · *Sakonnet Point*

NARRAGANSETT INDIAN RESERVATION □ · Narragansett Pier

Pawcatuck · *Worden Pond* · *Point Judith Pond*

· Bradford · *Watchaug Pond* · Jerusalem

Westerly · Charlestown · · Galilee

Ninigret Pond

Quonochontaug Pond · TRUSTOM POND N.W.R. · Point Judith

NINIGRET N.W.R.

· Quonochontaug

Rhode

N.Y. · Watch Hill

Napatree Point · *Island*

Sound

Block Island Sound

Sandy Point

BLOCK ISLAND N.W.R. □

Block Island · Block Island

ATLANTIC OCEAN

CONNECTICUT

0   5   10 miles
0   5   10 kilometers
Albers Conic Equal-Area Projection

The Ocean State has a long history of commercial and recreational fishing. The catch consists of lobster, "quahog" clams and other shellfish, and a variety of fish, including flounder, fluke, sea bass, and squid. Ongoing research seeks to prevent over-fishing, reduce the taking of "non-target" species, and preserve marine habitats.

population alone. With the addition of the Bill of Rights and the provision that each state would have two Senators in Congress plus a number of Representatives based on state population, Rhode Island finally signed the Constitution in 1790 and became the 13th state.

Rhode Island had what was needed to be a leader in the new U.S. economy: wealth from trade, power from its rivers, and cheap labor. Dozens of textile mill towns prospered, attracting immigrants first from Ireland, England, and Scotland and later from Italy and Portugal. Providence, linked by sea and rail, became Rhode Island's biggest commercial center. Newport developed as a vacation spot for the wealthy. In spite of its cotton-trade ties to the South, the state's anti-slavery stand made it a Union supporter in the Civil War.

Textiles began a gradual decline that continued into the 20th century. Labor strikes caused by a gap between wealthy business owners and poor workers developed in the 1920s. Tough times continued during the Depression. World War II helped the state's economy, but it suffered later when military bases were closed in the 1970s.

In recent years, Rhode Island has seen economic improvement. It has a thriving jewelry and silverware industry and manufactures electronics, scientific instruments, machines, and some textiles. Like other old industrial states, Rhode Island is switching to a more service-based economy. Biotechnology is growing, and the state is working to preserve the environment of Narragansett Bay, source of much of its wealth. The Ocean State also looks to expand tourism, drawing visitors with its rich history and a variety of water sports. No place in this small state is more than a half-hour drive from the ocean or bay—something special that no big state can match.

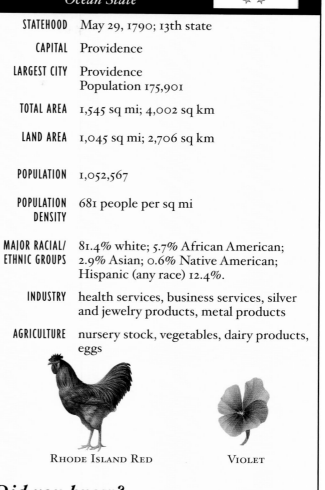

RHODE ISLAND
Ocean State

STATEHOOD	May 29, 1790; 13th state
CAPITAL	Providence
LARGEST CITY	Providence Population 175,901
TOTAL AREA	1,545 sq mi; 4,002 sq km
LAND AREA	1,045 sq mi; 2,706 sq km
POPULATION	1,052,567
POPULATION DENSITY	681 people per sq mi
MAJOR RACIAL/ ETHNIC GROUPS	81.4% white; 5.7% African American; 2.9% Asian; 0.6% Native American; Hispanic (any race) 12.4%.
INDUSTRY	health services, business services, silver and jewelry products, metal products
AGRICULTURE	nursery stock, vegetables, dairy products, eggs

RHODE ISLAND RED   VIOLET

Did you know?

1. The Rhode Island Red was one of the first chicken breeds developed to increase the quality and quantity of egg and meat production.
2. In colonial times, Newport was an important port in the Triangle Trade, which centered on slaves, sugar products—especially molasses—and rum. The Sugar Act of 1764 threatened Rhode Island's economy and caused the colony to be among the first to push for an end to British rule.
3. The Quonset hut takes its name from Quonset Point, the Naval Air Station on Narragansett Bay where this type of structure was first built.
4. The rights guaranteed to all Americans in the First Amendment to the Constitution, including freedom of religion, speech, and assembly, were among the rights promised much earlier to settlers in Rhode Island by Roger Williams, the colony's founder.

VERMONT
★ *Green Mountain State* ★

GREEN MOUNTAIN MAJESTY. When the French explorer Samuel de Champlain viewed a ridge of a long, forest-cloaked dividing range, he called it *vert mont*—"green mountain." Ever since, these granite and green slopes of the northern Appalachians have defined the region. Still four-fifths wooded and split north to south by rugged lines of peaks, Vermont proudly wears its nickname: Green Mountain State.

The only New England state without direct access to the Atlantic, Vermont has a freshwater sea instead: Lake Champlain. Shared with New York and Quebec, the glacially-carved, 120-mile- (193-km-) long lake is the sixth-largest in the country. Vermont has plentiful water elsewhere, too. Among its many rivers, the Connecticut forms the state's long eastern boundary. Vermont's northern location and high ridges bring heavy snows during cold winters. Cool, short summers and poor, rocky soils limit most agriculture to lake and river lowlands.

The French traded in the area and built their first settlement in 1666, but it did not last. In 1724 the English founded Fort Dummer near present-day Brattleboro. The two empires fought over Vermont, with the French retreating to Canada at the close of the French and Indian War in 1763. Shaped like a rocky wedge between New York and New Hampshire, Vermont once divided those colonies. Each wanted the territory, and they actually fought over Vermont. Among the battlers was fiercely proud Ethan Allen, who at first led efforts to join these lands to New Hampshire. But once the Revolutionary War began, he and his Green Mountain Boys switched to fight the British. Allen's daring capture of Fort Ticonderoga sparked early war efforts by patriots all across New England and beyond.

1609

Samuel de Champlain, with the aid of Huron people, was the first European to explore the region, claiming it for France.

1775

Ethan Allen and his Green Mountain Boys won fame by capturing Fort Ticonderoga, on Lake Champlain, from the British.

1811–1850s

Merino sheep imported from Spain gave rise to woolen mills and made the breed the state's chief livestock animal until the 1850s.

Present day

Tourism is now a top state business. This snowboarder competed in the 2001 Winter X Games, which attracted huge crowds.

It's fair time in Tunbridge, a classic New England small town (opposite). In Vermont such communities are known for their tradition of "town meetings"—gatherings where every citizen can have a say in local issues, such as education and taxes.

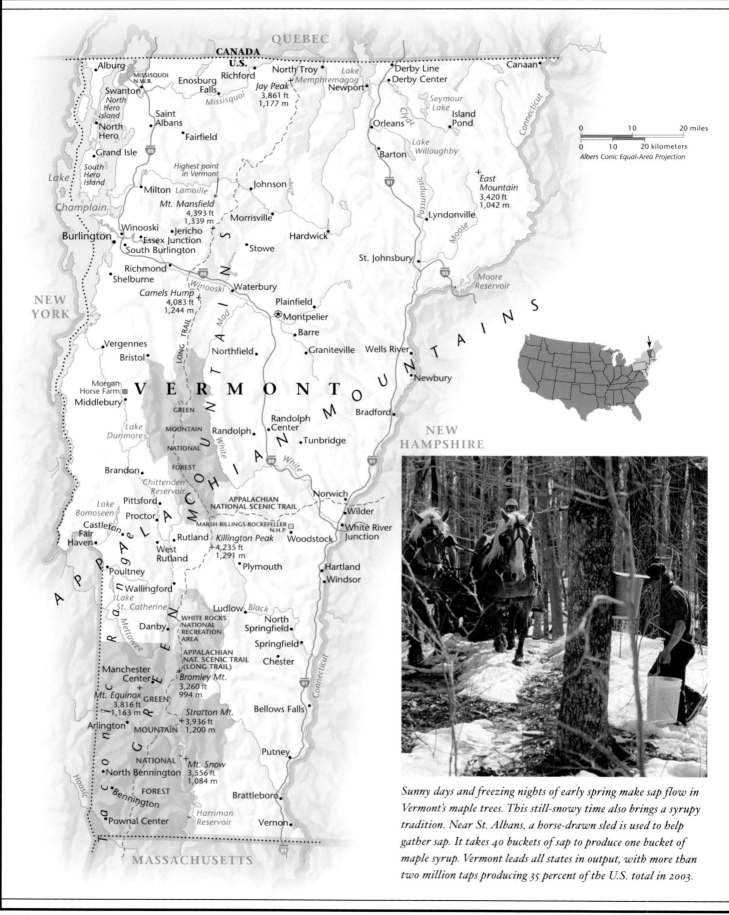

QUEBEC

CANADA
U.S.

Alburg
MISSISQUOI N.W.R.
Swanton
North Hero Island
North Hero
Grand Isle
South Hero Island

Lake Champlain

NEW YORK

Enosburg Falls
Richford
North Troy
Jay Peak
3,861 ft
1,177 m

Missisquoi

Saint Albans
Fairfield

Milton
Lamoille
Highest point in Vermont

Mt. Mansfield
4,393 ft
1,339 m

Johnson
Morrisville
Stowe
Hardwick

Winooski
Jericho
Essex Junction
South Burlington

Burlington

Richmond
Shelburne

Winooski
Waterbury

Camels Hump
4,083 ft
1,244 m

Mad

Plainfield
✪ Montpelier
Barre

Vergennes
Bristol

Northfield
Graniteville

Morgan Horse Farm
Middlebury

V E R M O N T

GREEN

MOUNTAIN

NATIONAL

FOREST

Lake Dunmore

Randolph
White

Randolph Center
Tunbridge

Brandon
Chittenden Reservoir

Pittsford
Proctor

Lake Bomoseen

Castleton
Fair Haven

Rutland
West Rutland

Killington Peak
4,235 ft
1,291 m

MARSH-BILLINGS-ROCKEFELLER N.H.P.
Woodstock

Plymouth

APPALACHIAN NATIONAL SCENIC TRAIL

Norwich
Wilder
White River Junction

Poultney

Wallingford
Lake St. Catherine

Danby

WHITE ROCKS NATIONAL RECREATION AREA

APPALACHIAN NAT. SCENIC TRAIL (LONG TRAIL)

Ludlow
Black
North Springfield
Springfield
Chester

Mettowee

Manchester Center

Mt. Equinox
3,816 ft
1,163 m

GREEN

Bromley Mt.
3,260 ft
994 m

Stratton Mt.
3,936 ft
1,200 m

MOUNTAIN

Arlington

Bellows Falls

NATIONAL

Mt. Snow
3,556 ft
1,084 m

North Bennington

FOREST

Bennington

Putney

Hoosic

Pownal Center

Harriman Reservoir

Brattleboro

Vernon

MASSACHUSETTS

North Troy
Derby Line
Derby Center
Canaan

Lake Memphremagog
Newport

Seymour Lake

Orleans
Clyde
Island Pond

Barton
Lake Willoughby

+East Mountain
3,420 ft
1,042 m

Passumpsic
Lyndonville

Moose

St. Johnsbury

Moore Reservoir

Wells River
Newbury

Bradford

NEW HAMPSHIRE

Connecticut

Hartland
Windsor

Connecticut

A P P A L A C H I A N   M O U N T A I N S

T A C O N I C   R A N G E

L O N G   T R A I L

0   10   20 miles
0   10   20 kilometers
Albers Conic Equal-Area Projection

Sunny days and freezing nights of early spring make sap flow in
Vermont's maple trees. This still-snowy time also brings a syrupy
tradition. Near St. Albans, a horse-drawn sled is used to help
gather sap. It takes 40 buckets of sap to produce one bucket of
maple syrup. Vermont leads all states in output, with more than
two million taps producing 35 percent of the U.S. total in 2003.

Vermonters' independent attitudes caused them to declare freedom not just from British rule in 1777, but from all their neighbors, too. After some talk of joining with Canada, Vermont joined the U.S. as the 14th state in 1791. Montpelier became its capital in 1805. Stability brought more immigrants to Vermont, and sheep farming and woolen mills proved successful for the first half of the 19th century. Railroads arrived in 1849 to help tranport Vermont resources.

Vermont's geology plays a key role in its economy. The world's largest granite quarry (east of Barre) and the largest underground marble quarry (near Danby) produce building stone. Above ground, Vermont's green treasures include hardwoods for furniture and softwoods for pulp and paper. Milk and cheese are produced from dairy herds grazed on mountain pastures. For years, tourists have enjoyed the state's country roads, hiking trails, water activities, and winter sports. In recent decades, computer and other high-tech companies have found Burlington and other Vermont cities fine spots to locate operations.

Vermonters have traditionally blazed their own path in politics, and ideas born here often led the country. Vermont's 1777 constitution banned slavery and gave the vote to all men even if they did not own land—two ideas that were way ahead of their time. By 1970 Vermont was a national leader in environmental legislation. Today the state struggles to balance environmental protection and economic growth. Recent problems include an increase in part-time residents who bring money to the state but reduce its rural nature, the loss of dairy farms, and pollution. Success in preserving Vermont's natural resources will safeguard opportunities for future generations of Green Mountain boys and girls.

VERMONT
Green Mountain State

STATEHOOD	March 4, 1791; 14th state
CAPITAL	Montpelier
LARGEST CITY	Burlington Population 39,466
TOTAL AREA	9,614 sq mi; 24,901 sq km
LAND AREA	9,250 sq mi; 23,956 sq km
POPULATION	625,741
POPULATION DENSITY	65 people per sq mi
MAJOR RACIAL/ ETHNIC GROUPS	95.3% white; 1.3% Asian; 1.0% African American; 0.4% Native American; Hispanic (any race) 1.5%.
INDUSTRY	health services, tourism, finance, real estate, computer components, electrical parts, printing and publishing, machine tools
AGRICULTURE	dairy products, maple products, apples

HERMIT THRUSH

RED CLOVER

Did you know?

1. Almost three-quarters of Vermont's electricity is generated by the nuclear power plant at Vernon, south of Brattleboro, along the Connecticut River.
2. From 1777 until it became a state in 1791, Vermont had its own postal and monetary systems.
3. Morgan horses, an American breed known for its stamina, vigor, and all-purpose usefulness, have been raised on farms throughout Vermont since just after the Revolution. The First Vermont Cavalry rode Morgans in the Civil War, and Confederate General Stonewall Jackson's horse "Little Sorrel" was a Morgan.
4. The Long Trail is a 265-mile- (426-km-) long hiking trail that runs along the ridges of the Green Mountains for the entire length of the state.
5. Vermont has never been heavily populated. Today, only Wyoming has fewer residents.

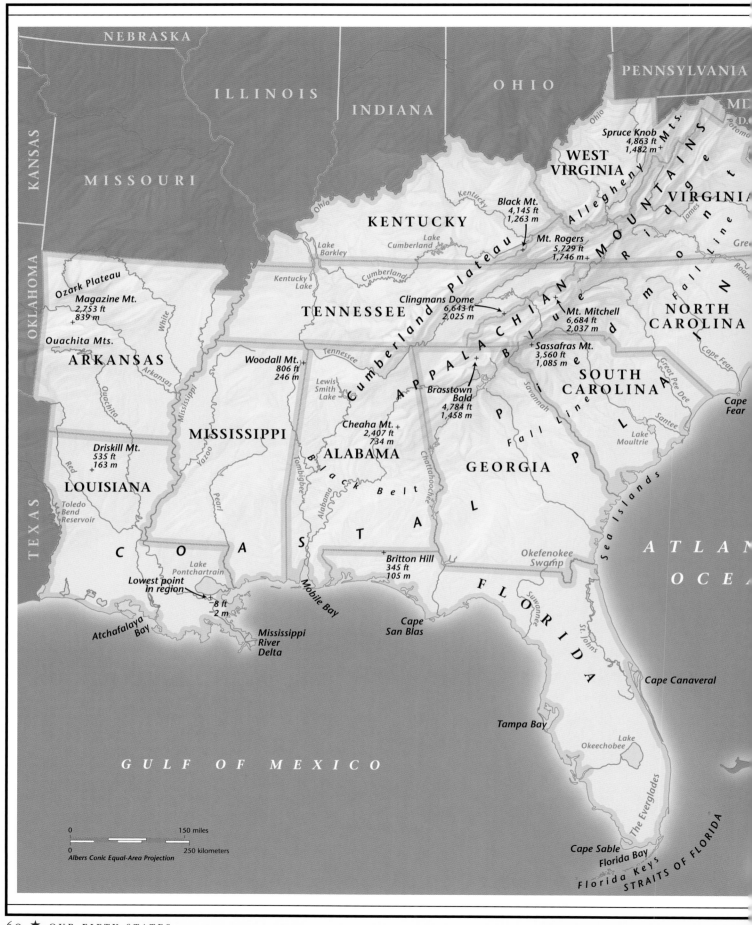

NEBRASKA

ILLINOIS

INDIANA

OHIO

PENNSYLVANIA

KANSAS

MISSOURI

MD.

WEST
VIRGINIA

Spruce Knob
4,863 ft
1,482 m +

Allegheny Mts.

VIRGINIA

Ohio

Kentucky

Black Mt.
4,145 ft
1,263 m
+

Mt. Rogers
5,729 ft
1,746 m +

James

Piedmont

KENTUCKY

Lake
Barkley

Lake
Cumberland

Cumberland

Kentucky
Lake

MOUNTAINS

Roan

OKLAHOMA

Ozark Plateau

Magazine Mt.
2,753 ft
+ 839 m

TENNESSEE

Clingmans Dome
6,643 ft
2,025 m

+ *Mt. Mitchell*
6,684 ft
2,037 m

Blue

Ridge

Fall Line

NORTH
CAROLINA

Ouachita Mts.

White

Sassafras Mt.
3,560 ft
1,085 m

APPALACHIAN

Great Pee Dee

Cape Fear

ARKANSAS

Arkansas

Tennessee

Woodall Mt. +
806 ft
246 m

Lewis
Smith
Lake

Brasstown
Bald
4,784 ft
1,458 m

SOUTH
CAROLINA

Santee

Cape
Fear

Ouachita

MISSISSIPPI

Cheaha Mt. +
2,407 ft
734 m

+

Savannah

Lake
Moultrie

Driskill Mt.
535 ft
+ 163 m

Yazoo

ALABAMA

Black

Belt

GEORGIA

Fall Line

P

I

LOUISIANA

Red

Pearl

Alabama

Tombigbee

Chattahoochee

L

Sea Islands

ATLAN

OCEA

Toledo
Bend
Reservoir

C

O

A

S

T

A

L

Okefenokee
Swamp

FLORIDA

TEXAS

Lake
Pontchartrain

Britton Hill
345 ft
105 m

Suwannee

Lowest point
in region
+ –8 ft
–2 m

Mobile Bay

Cape
San Blas

St. Johns

Atchafalaya
Bay

Mississippi
River
Delta

Cape Canaveral

Tampa Bay

Lake
Okeechobee

GULF OF MEXICO

The Everglades

STRAITS OF FLORIDA

0   150 miles

Cape Sable
Florida Bay

Florida Keys

0   250 kilometers

Albers Conic Equal-Area Projection

The Southeast

ROUNDED MOUNTAINS, big rivers, and fertile plains characterize the Southeast. Southern ranges of the Appalachians—the Allegheny, Blue Ridge, and Cumberland Plateau—form a divide through the region. Streams flowing west of this divide join and enlarge the mighty Mississippi. Those draining east cross the Piedmont to a coastal plain that wraps around the southern tip of the Appalachians to Louisiana's Gulf Coast—a watery world of meandering rivers, deltas, swamps, and barrier islands.

West of the Mississippi the Ouachita Mountains and Ozark Plateau overlook Arkansas. The Florida peninsula is built on a limestone foundation punctuated by numerous lakes, sinkholes, islands, and America's most famous swamp—the Everglades. Throughout the Southeast needle-leaf, broadleaf, and mixed forests thrive in a mostly mild climate where rainfall occurs in every month.

N.J.

DEL.

Delmarva
Peninsula

Chesapeake Bay

Dismal
Swamp

Albemarle
Sound

Outer Banks

Pamlico
Sound

Cape
Hatteras

Outer

Cape Lookout

TIC

N

Tradition and Change Between Two Coasts

ABUNDANT natural resources have always shaped how people live in this well-watered land. Native Cherokee, Shawnee, Choctaw, and Seminole tribes thrived by hunting in the forest, fishing, and gathering fruits, nuts, and berries that appear to grow everywhere. Many tribes also planted the "three sisters"—corn, squash, and beans.

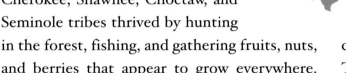

Europeans arrived from three directions. Spain's Ponce de León reached Florida in 1513. By 1565 the Spanish had founded the first permanent colony in America at St. Augustine, Florida—55 years before the Pilgrims landed in Massachusetts. In 1673 two Frenchmen, missionary Jacques Marquette and explorer Louis Joliet, paddled down the Mississippi River to the mouth of the Arkansas River. Within a decade France claimed the entire area drained by the Mississippi River. The English colonized Virginia in the early 1600s and slowly extended settlements south to Georgia by the 1730s. Although the Europeans were few in number, their guns and "Old World" diseases such as smallpox devastated Indian populations.

The colonists quickly took advantage of the natural resources. They planted tobacco on the fertile coastal lands, mined rich deposits of coal and iron ore in the Appalachians, and turned marshlands into rice fields. The rivers plus Atlantic and Gulf waters were chock-full of fish, while the broadleaf and pine forests yielded plenty of game and timber. Along the fall line, where Appalachian streams tumble from the Piedmont onto the Atlantic Coastal Plain, water-powered factories helped cities such as Richmond and Raleigh prosper.

Spanish and French control of the Southeast dwindled in the late 1700s. After frontiersman Daniel Boone blazed the Wilderness Road across the Appalachians in 1775, American farmers migrated into the Kentucky, Ohio, and Tennessee River Valleys. Elsewhere the rise of tobacco and cotton created a plantation economy dependent upon slave labor. East of the Appalachians fine seaports promoted trade with the Northeast and Europe, while areas west of the mountains turned to the Ohio and Mississippi Rivers. To open lands for settlers in the 1830s, the government forced thousands of Native Americans westward along what became known as the Trail of Tears.

By 1850 a diverse mix of people of European heritage firmly controlled this thriving region. However, by 1861 tensions over slavery between northern and southern states erupted in Civil War. All the states in this region except Kentucky and West Virginia seceded from the Union to form the Confederacy. The Union victory after four years of war left most of the region in ruins for the next half century.

By the 1930s two events changed the Southeast. The first was a 1920s plague of boll weevils that devastated cotton crops and forced farmers to diversify. The second was the Tennessee Valley Authority, which built dams to control flooding and provide power. The abundant electricity coupled with nonunion labor and air-conditioning attracted northern-based companies and people—a process that still continues.

"...Louisiana bayous,... sun, cotton fields, lonesome roads, train whistles in the night,...."

LANGSTON HUGHES, *"Music at Year's End,"* The Chicago Defender, *January 9, 1943*

Today, crops like Georgia peaches, Louisiana rice, and Florida oranges are known worldwide. The region also produces varied products such as Arkansas chickens, Kentucky racehorses, North Carolina timber, and oil along the Gulf Coast. Sandy coastal beaches attract visitors. Cities such as Atlanta, New Orleans, Miami, and Raleigh-Durham are leaders in business, research, and tourism.

All this development has brought water shortages, pollution, and crowded commutes, but it is also a sure sign that the Southeast is thriving again.

A shady lane of stately oak trees stretches to the white columns and porches of this restored Louisiana plantation home (above). Built in 1839, the mansion provides a glimpse into the lifestyle of wealthy Southerners before the Civil War brought lasting change.

ALABAMA
★ *Heart of Dixie* ★

"OH, I WISH I was in the land of cotton, old times there are not forgotten!" So begins the famous song, "Dixie," a favorite of Confederate troops as they battled to maintain their way of life. Today, Alabama's nickname is Heart of Dixie, which fits as well in today's South as when the state anchored the Confederate States of America.

The Spanish explored the region in the 1500s, but it was the French who established the first permanent European settlement along Mobile Bay in 1702. They named the region for Indians who called themselves "Alibamu." The British won control of the land after the French and Indian War, but lost it to the U.S. after the Revolution. Andrew Jackson's defeat of Creek warriors in the War of 1812 and the rising demand for cotton spurred immigration from Tennessee and Georgia. The Territory of Alabama was formed in 1817 and became a state

two years later. Native Americans were forced to relocate to Oklahoma during the 1830s.

Alabamans settled a state of mostly low, rolling plains. The rugged southern reaches of the Cumberland Plateau and the Appalachian Mountains stretch into the northeast. Except for the Tennessee River, which arcs through Alabama's northern districts, most rivers flow from northeast to southwest, emptying into Mobile Bay. Spanning the middle is the Black Belt, a band of rich, dark soil that made cotton Alabama's chief crop. Wealthy landowners, using slaves for labor, established big plantations in fertile bottomlands. They led the state to secession from the Union in 1861.

The Confederacy's government was formed in Montgomery, which acted as its capital for a time. Selma was a center of ammunition manufacture, and Mobile was a critical port. The Civil War cost 15,000 Alabama soldiers their

1813–1814
Defeated after the massacre of settlers at Fort Mims, the Creek people were forced to give up their lands to the U.S. government.

1880
Alabama's iron and steel industry was launched with the opening of Birmingham's first blast furnace, Alice No. 1.

1955
When Rosa Parks refused to give up her bus seat to a white man in Montgomery, her arrest was a key event in the civil rights movement.

Present day
U.S. Space Camp, in Huntsville, is one of several NASA programs that provide jobs and revenue for the state.

Cave-dwelling peoples lived for nearly 8,000 years in the rugged region around DeSoto Falls (opposite) in northeastern Alabama. Named for Spanish gold seeker Hernando de Soto, who trekked through in 1540, it is part of Little River Canyon National Preserve.

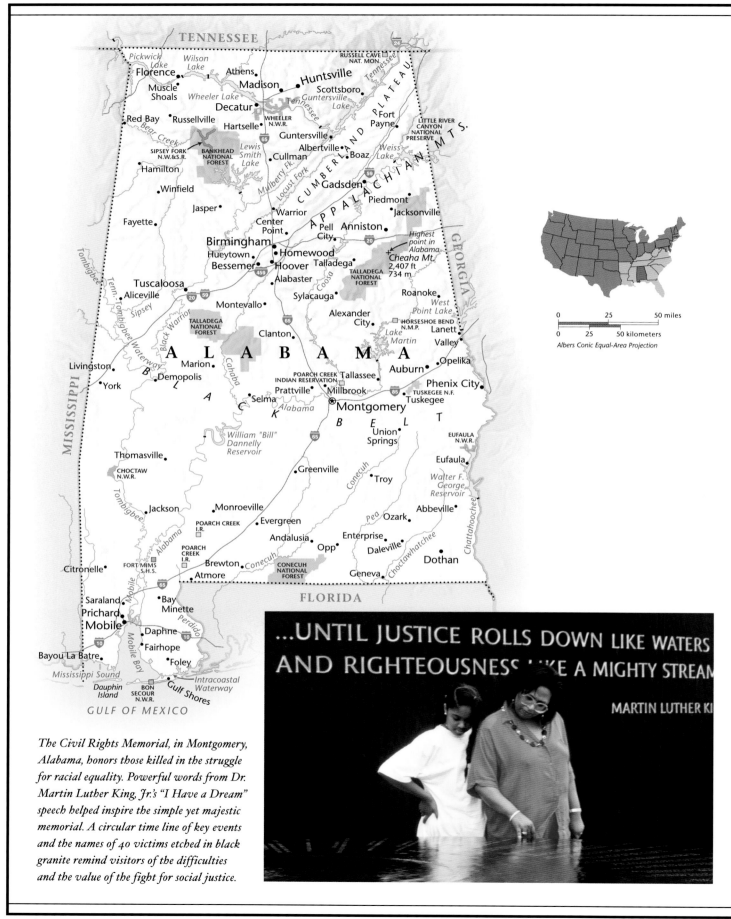

TENNESSEE

Pickwick Lake
Wilson Lake
Florence
Athens
Muscle Shoals
Madison
Huntsville
Scottsboro
RUSSELL CAVE NAT. MON.
Red Bay
Russellville
Decatur
Wheeler Lake
Guntersville Lake
Fort Payne
LITTLE RIVER CANYON NATIONAL PRESERVE
Hartselle
WHEELER N.W.R.
Guntersville
Bear Creek
SIPSEY FORK N.W.&S.R.
BANKHEAD NATIONAL FOREST
Lewis Smith Lake
Cullman
Albertville
Boaz
Weiss Lake
Hamilton
Mulberry Fk.
Locust Fork
Gadsden
Piedmont
Winfield
Jasper
Warrior
Center Point
Jacksonville
Fayette
Birmingham
Pell City
Anniston
Highest point in Alabama
Hueytown
Homewood
Talladega
Cheaha Mt. 2,407 ft 734 m
Bessemer
Hoover
Alabaster
TALLADEGA NATIONAL FOREST
Tuscaloosa
Aliceville
Sylacauga
Roanoke
West Point Lake
Montevallo
Alexander City
HORSESHOE BEND N.M.P.
Lanett
TALLADEGA NATIONAL FOREST
Clanton
Lake Martin
Valley
Livingston
Marion
Auburn
Opelika
York
Demopolis
POARCH CREEK INDIAN RESERVATION
Tallassee
Phenix City
Selma
Prattville
Millbrook
TUSKEGEE N.F.
Tuskegee
Montgomery
William "Bill" Dannelly Reservoir
Union Springs
EUFAULA N.W.R.
Thomasville
Greenville
Eufaula
CHOCTAW N.W.R.
Troy
Walter F. George Reservoir
Jackson
Monroeville
Ozark
Abbeville
POARCH CREEK I.R.
Evergreen
Andalusia
Enterprise
Daleville
Citronelle
POARCH CREEK I.R.
Opp
Dothan
FORT MIMS S.H.S.
Brewton
Geneva
Saraland
Atmore
CONECUH NATIONAL FOREST
Prichard
Bay Minette
Mobile
Daphne
Bayou La Batre
Fairhope
Foley
Mississippi Sound
Dauphin Island
BON SECOUR N.W.R.
Intracoastal Waterway
Gulf Shores

GULF OF MEXICO

MISSISSIPPI

A L A B A M A

BLACK BELT

GEORGIA

FLORIDA

Tombigbee
Tenn-Tombigbee Waterway
Sipsey
Black Warrior
Cahaba
Coosa
Alabama
Conecuh
Pea
Choctawhatchee
Chattahoochee
Perdido
Mobile Bay

0   25   50 miles
0   25   50 kilometers
Albers Conic Equal-Area Projection

The Civil Rights Memorial, in Montgomery, Alabama, honors those killed in the struggle for racial equality. Powerful words from Dr. Martin Luther King, Jr.'s "I Have a Dream" speech helped inspire the simple yet majestic memorial. A circular time line of key events and the names of 40 victims etched in black granite remind visitors of the difficulties and the value of the fight for social justice.

...UNTIL JUSTICE ROLLS DOWN LIKE WATERS AND RIGHTEOUSNESS LIKE A MIGHTY STREAM

MARTIN LUTHER KI

lives. Post-war Reconstruction brought corrupt governments and the persistence of racial inequalities and injustices. It also saw the rise of Birmingham as the "Pittsburgh of the South" as railroads carried Alabama coal, iron ore, and limestone to the city's steel mills. But it took a tiny insect to spark a transformation in the economy.

In the 1920s the boll weevil destroyed the cotton harvest. Together with declining soil fertility caused by planting cotton year after year, the weevil infestation forced farmers to finally break away from a single crop. Cotton is still important, but so are peanuts, sweet potatoes, pecans, chickens, and pond-raised catfish. Vast stands of oak and pine support a giant forest-products industry. Beginning in 1933, the Tennessee Valley Authority's dam at Muscle Shoals provided plentiful and cheap electricity. The completion of the Tennessee-Tombigbee Waterway in 1985 dramatically increased barge traffic by linking the Tennessee River and Mobile Bay. Huntsville has attracted space-related and high-tech businesses since NASA's Marshall Space Flight Center opened in 1960.

Alabama's 4.5 million people have not forgotten their state's past. More than one-fourth of the population is African American, and those who are old enough remember terrible days of violence and racial injustice. But in the 1950s and 1960s gains in voting and other civil rights were achieved across the country.

The economy continues to diversify. An auto assembly plant built in the 1990s has doubled production. Efforts are underway to bolster military bases, increase Mobile's cruise ship and container-port facilities, and expand the state's space industry. While learning from its "old times" Alabama is marching forward to new and better ones.

ALABAMA
Heart of Dixie

STATEHOOD	December 14, 1819; 22nd state
CAPITAL	Montgomery
LARGEST CITY	Birmingham Population 239,416
TOTAL AREA	52,419 sq mi; 135,765 sq km
LAND AREA	50,744 sq mi; 131,426 sq km
POPULATION	4,779,736
POPULATION DENSITY	91 people per sq mi
MAJOR RACIAL/ ETHNIC GROUPS	68.5% white; 26.2% African American; 1.1% Asian; 0.6% Native American; Hispanic (any race) 3.9%.
INDUSTRY	retail and wholesale trade, services, government, finance, insurance, real estate, transportation, construction, communication
AGRICULTURE	fruits and vegetables, dairy products, cattle, forest products, commercial fishing

NORTHERN FLICKER   CAMELLIA

Did you know?

1. In 1955 Alabama became the first state to have a state-owned television station.
2. Dismals Canyon, a few miles south of Russellville, has natural bridges, waterfalls, and one of the few stands of virgin forest east of the Mississippi River. Aaron Burr used the area as a hideout for several months after killing Alexander Hamilton in a duel in 1804.
3. The Tennessee-Tombigbee Waterway, the world's biggest earth-moving project to date, is five times longer than the Panama Canal.
4. George Washington Carver, a freed slave who helped revolutionize the economy of the South through his experiments with peanuts, soybeans, alternatives for cotton, and sweet potatoes, was the director of agricultural research at the Tuskegee Institute.

ARKANSAS
★ *Natural State* ★

DIVERSE LANDSCAPES and outdoor activities aplenty earn Arkansas its nickname, the Natural State. On its north and west rise the rugged Ouachita Mountains and the Ozark Plateau. Between them flows the Arkansas River, south and east across the state to the Gulf Coastal Plain. There it joins the Mississippi River, with its many oxbow lakes along Arkansas's eastern border.

Spaniard Hernando de Soto ventured into the region in 1541, and French explorers scouted its resources in the 1670s. The French learned of a native group named for the south wind. The Algonquin called them the *Oo-ka-na-sa,* and French missionary Father Marquette wrote "Arkansas" (pronounced ARK-an-saw). While the French, Spanish, and British each controlled the land for periods of time, Arkansas became part of the U.S. with the Louisiana Purchase in 1803. The Arkansas Territory was formed in 1819, and settlement increased with the forced departure of most Choctaw and Cherokee peoples. Slaveholding Southern planters arrived to grow cotton in the Mississippi bottomlands. The wide valley of the Arkansas River provided fine farmlands, too. Poorer settlers from the southern Appalachians began moving into the Ozarks and Ouachitas, bringing their traditions of music and crafts.

As for the territory's largest city and future state capital, French traders crossed the Arkansas River at a spot where a "petite roche" offered a good landmark. Little Rock was on the map—founded in 1821. Improved river transport was key to early territorial expansion. A steamboat first chugged 300 miles (480 km) up the snag-filled Arkansas River in 1822.

Arkansas entered the Union as the 25th state in 1836. Difficult times followed after the state joined the Confederacy in 1861. The Union

1686

Fur trader Henri de Tonty, the Father of Arkansas, founded the first permanent European settlement on the Arkansas River.

1862

After their victory at Pea Ridge, the largest Civil War battle west of the Mississippi, the Union Army went on to capture Little Rock.

1957

Amid violent protests, this girl and eight other African Americans began attending formerly all-white Little Rock Central High School.

Present day

Arkansas-based Wal-Mart, the world's largest retailer, attracts many suppliers and other businesses to the state.

Natural wonders as diverse as hot springs, a diamond mine open to the public, and miles of scenic trails await visitors to Arkansas. Hikers (opposite) stand atop Hawksbill Crag, or Whitaker Point as the locals call it, overlooking the Buffalo National River.

MISSOURI

Bella Vista
Bentonville
Rogers
Siloam Springs
Springdale
Fayetteville

PEA RIDGE N.M.P.
Eureka Springs
Berryville
Beaver Lake
Harrison
Bull Shoals Lake
Mountain Home
Norfork Lake

Cherokee Village
MAMMOTH SPRING S.P.
Corning
Horseshoe Bend
Pocahontas
Walnut Ridge
Paragould

White

OZARK N.F.

OZARK PLATEAU

Buffalo

BUFFALO N.W.&S.R.
BUFFALO NATIONAL RIVER

OZARK NATIONAL FOREST
NORTH SYLAMORE CREEK N.W.&S.R.

Jonesboro
Manila
BIG LAKE N.W.R.
Blytheville

OKLAHOMA

OZARK NATIONAL FOREST
Boston Mountains

RICHLAND CREEK NATIONAL WILD & SCENIC RIVER

OZARK N.F.

Mountain View
Batesville
Tuckerman
Newport
Trumann

Osceola
Marked Tree

TENNESSEE

OZARK N.F.

Mulberry

HURRICANE CR. N.W.&S.R.
Fairfield Bay
Clinton
MULBERRY NATIONAL WILD & SCENIC RIVER

Van Buren
Ozark
Clarksville
BIG PINEY CREEK NATIONAL WILD & SCENIC RIVER
Greers Ferry Lake
Heber Springs

Arkansas

Fort Smith
Lake Dardanelle
Paris
Dardanelle
Russellville

CACHE RIVER N.W.R.
Wynne
WAPANOCCA N.W.R.
Earle
West Memphis

Highest point in Arkansas
Magazine Mt. 2,753 ft 839 m
OZARK N.F.
Morrilton
Greenbrier
Searcy
Bald Knob
Little Red

Crowleys Ridge

L'Anguille

Cache

White

Greenwood
Booneville

HOLLA BEND N.W.R.
Conway
Beebe
CACHE RIVER N.W.R.

Waldron

Maumelle
Cabot
Jacksonville
CACHE RIVER N.W.R.
Brinkley
Marianna
ST. FRANCIS NATIONAL FOREST

OUACHITA NATIONAL FOREST

Little Rock
North Little Rock
Bryant
Forrest City

St. Francis

ARKANSAS

Ouachita Mountains

Mena
Lake Ouachita
HOT SPRINGS N.P.
Benton
England
Stuttgart
West Helena
Helena

LITTLE MISSOURI N.W.&S.R.
Hot Springs
De Gray Lake
Malvern
Sheridan
White

COSSATOT N.W.&S.R.
Lake Greeson
Pine Bluff
De Witt
WHITE RIVER N.W.R.

MISSISSIPPI

De Queen
Nashville
Murfreesboro
CRATER OF DIAMONDS S.P.
Arkadelphia
Saline
Arkansas
Bayou Bartholomew
ARKANSAS POST NAT. MEM.

COSSATOT N.W.R.
Gurdon
Little Missouri
Fordyce
Dumas

Little
Millwood Lake
Prescott
White Oak Lake
Monticello
McGehee

Ashdown
Red
Hope
Camden
Warren
Dermott

Ouachita

TEXAS
Texarkana
Stamps
Smackover
Lake Village

Magnolia
El Dorado
FELSENTHAL N.W.R.
Hamburg
Eudora

Lake Erling
Lake Jack Lee
Crossett
OVERFLOW N.W.R.

Red

LOUISIANA

0   25   50 miles
0 25 50 kilometers
Albers Conic Equal-Area Projection

Arkansas raises enough poultry to strut about, including these chickens in a Tyson Foods facility near Fayetteville in the northwestern corner of the state. In 2003 the state ranked second in the nation in the production of broiler chickens. More than one in five people in Arkansas work in agriculture, food processing, or related jobs.

Army occupied the northern part of the state by early 1863. After the war, the state was not re-admitted to the Union until African Americans were given the right to vote in 1868. While advances came for Arkansas in the decades that followed, many of its people—both white and black—remained poor. Some left for northern industrial cities in the early 20th century, while others migrated west during the Great Depression.

The past few decades have brought better days to Arkansas. State population is now about 2.7 million, with nearly one in six residents of African-American heritage. Agriculture is thriving. Soggy Mississippi River lowlands provide fine rice-growing conditions. Rice fields are flooded to farm fish, too, with nutrients from the fish providing great fertilizer for the next rice crop. The state is second in catfish production, third in turkeys, fourth in cotton, and a leader in raising and processing chickens for sale. Arkansas is the top U.S. producer of bauxite and bromine, and oil and natural gas are also extracted.

Arkansas's economic success is tied to sustainable use of its varied natural resources. Visitors flock to the scenic wooded trails and whitewater routes of the Ozarks and Ouachitas, where forests are managed for recreation, wildlife habitat, and a variety of wood products. Recently, though, a combination of drought, insects, and disease has killed large numbers of red oak trees across these highlands. Wise water management is also critical to the state's economy, since both surface and underground sources provide for drinking, industry, and irrigation. Continued growth—both urban and rural—depends upon adequate and clean water supplies. People of the Natural State know they need to care for the natural environment that nurtures them.

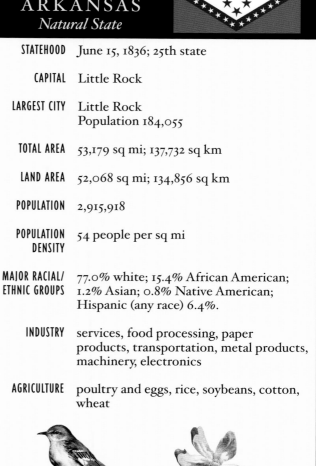

ARKANSAS
Natural State

STATEHOOD	June 15, 1836; 25th state
CAPITAL	Little Rock
LARGEST CITY	Little Rock Population 184,055
TOTAL AREA	53,179 sq mi; 137,732 sq km
LAND AREA	52,068 sq mi; 134,856 sq km
POPULATION	2,915,918
POPULATION DENSITY	54 people per sq mi
MAJOR RACIAL/ ETHNIC GROUPS	77.0% white; 15.4% African American; 1.2% Asian; 0.8% Native American; Hispanic (any race) 6.4%.
INDUSTRY	services, food processing, paper products, transportation, metal products, machinery, electronics
AGRICULTURE	poultry and eggs, rice, soybeans, cotton, wheat

MOCKINGBIRD   APPLE BLOSSOM

Did you know?

1. Crater of Diamonds State Park is the only diamond-producing area in the world that allows the public to keep what they find, and near Murfreesboro is the only diamond mine in North America that is open to the public.
2. The average temperature of the waters in the 47 springs that flow out of Hot Springs Mountain is 143°F (62°C).
3. Arkansas has been the country's leading producer of rice since 1973. It produces about 45 percent of the total U.S. crop.
4. In 1932, Arkansas elected the first woman to the U.S. Senate. Her name was Hattie Caraway.
5. Nine million gallons (34,000,000 L) of water flow from Mammoth Spring each hour. The spring forms a scenic 10-acre (4-ha) lake in Mammoth Spring State Park. It is the world's largest single spring.

FLORIDA

★ *Sunshine State* ★

COAST TO COAST—to coast! Florida boasts three distinct shores. A long strand of hard-packed sand stretches along 400 miles (640 km) of Atlantic beachfront. Across the giant peninsula are softer, seashell-rich beaches, lining the Gulf of Mexico. To the northwest people play on Panhandle beaches with the color and feel of white sugar. Once a limestone seafloor, the low-relief platform that makes up the state was uncovered as sea level dropped. Florida is the lowest and flattest state.

The Spanish founded St. Augustine in 1565, making it the continent's oldest permanent European settlement. Spain lost the territory to Britain in 1763 but regained it 20 years later. Farmland attracted American settlers in the early 1800s, and a treaty with Spain allowed the U.S. to obtain the territory in 1821. Native Seminoles fought to keep their lands, but most were forced west. When Florida became the 27th

state in 1845, Tallahassee was made its capital city.

Florida joined the Confederacy and seceded from the Union just 16 years after statehood. It was readmitted in 1868. Florida's modernization followed the railroads built along its Atlantic and Gulf coasts in the 1890s. Land sales boomed, orange groves were planted, and tourists began to visit from the chilly north. Beachfront hotels and resorts sprang up along the train routes. The Spanish-American War of 1898 and two world wars boosted Florida's growth, with an ever-greater need for military bases and agricultural products. The state soon became a retirement haven for senior citizens, as well as a refuge for immigrants after the Cuban Revolution in 1959. Miami grew to become the nation's major gateway to the Caribbean and much of Latin America.

Since 1950, Florida's population has blossomed from about 3 million people to more

1513

Juan Ponce de León, seeker of the fabled Fountain of Youth, claimed Florida for Spain, naming it Pascua Florida (*Flowery Easter*).

1835

Although the Seminole Wars cost these native people most of their lands, some found refuge and new homes in the Everglades.

1896—1912

By building the Florida East Coast Railway to Miami and then Key West, Henry M. Flagler opened the state to development.

Present day

Cape Canaveral, site of NASA's Kennedy Space Center, is a hub for space-age technology as well as a major tourist attraction.

Looking almost like the long Florida peninsula where it lives, an American alligator (opposite) waits in the duckweed-filled water of the Everglades where it is a key part of the ecosystem. Clean waters and adequate habitat are needed to ensure the reptile's survival.

FLORIDA
Sunshine State

STATEHOOD	March 3, 1845; 27th state
CAPITAL	Tallahassee
LARGEST CITY	Jacksonville Population 762,461
TOTAL AREA	65,755 sq mi; 170,304 sq km
LAND AREA	53,927 sq mi; 139,670 sq km
POPULATION	18,801,310
POPULATION DENSITY	285 people per sq mi
MAJOR RACIAL/ETHNIC GROUPS	75.0% white; 16.0% African American; 2.4% Asian; 0.4% Native American; Hispanic (any race) 22.5%.
INDUSTRY	tourism, health services, business services, communications, banking, electronic equipment, insurance
AGRICULTURE	citrus fruits, vegetables, field crops, nursery stock, cattle, dairy products

MOCKINGBIRD

ORANGE BLOSSOM

Did you know?

1. Hurricane Andrew, which struck the Homestead area of South Florida in August 1992, was the most expensive natural disaster to date in U.S. history.
2. Clearwater has the highest rate of per capita lightning strikes of any U.S. city.
3. Citrus fruits originated in Southeast Asia. Ponce de León planted the first citrus in Florida in the early 1500s.
4. Counting bays and barrier islands along its Atlantic and Gulf coasts, Florida has 8,500 miles (14,000 km) of shoreline. Alaska is the only state with more.
5. The Overseas Highway, which spans 113 miles (182 km) between Key Largo and Key West, has more than 42 bridges and links more than a hundred islands. The longest is the Seven Mile Bridge.
6. Britton Hill, Florida's highest point, is only 345 feet (105 m) above sea level.

than 17 million. This almost six-fold increase has made Florida the nation's fourth-largest state in population. One in six Floridians is Hispanic, many of them Cuban. A slightly smaller number are African American. Vacationers arrive year-round, but especially in the winter and spring seasons. Spectacular theme parks in Orlando entertain millions annually. Tourists *ooh* and *ah,* watching space launches from NASA's Kennedy Space Center. The Everglades, a unique ecosystem of marsh and swamp fed by waterways linked to Lake Okeechobee, is another major attraction. Alligators and crocodiles live here, as do hundreds of bird species and the endangered Florida panther.

Fertile soils and a warm, wet subtropical climate in the Sunshine State provide farming riches, too. Florida tops the nation in sugarcane and citrus fruit and ranks second in output of tomatoes, strawberries, and greenhouse and nursery products. There are huge harvests of dozens of other fruits and vegetables as well as thousands of beef-cattle operations, especially in the Panhandle. Military bases plus related defense and research companies play a large role in the state's economy and have helped Florida lead the country in job growth in the past two years.

Though Florida continues to prosper, both natural and human-caused difficulties confront the state. Years-long droughts have been damaging in recent years, as have monster storms such as Hurricane Andrew. For decades, abundant water resources have been directed away from the Everglades and other natural needs to those of expanding farms and cities. Efforts are underway to restore this life-giving flow of water. Florida's fast population growth strains all resources. The challenge will be to grow without sacrificing the state's natural treasures.

ALABAMA

Highest point in Florida

POARCH CREEK I.R.

Britton Hill
345 ft
105 m

Crestview

Marianna

GEORGIA

Lake Seminole

OKEFENOKEE N.W.R.

Pensacola

Niceville

Fort Walton Beach

Panama City

Fort Pickens

GULF ISLANDS NATIONAL SEASHORE

Choctawhatchee

Apalachicola

APALACHICOLA NATIONAL FOREST

Ochlockonee

⊛ Tallahassee

ST. MARKS N.W.R.

Perry

Live Oak

OSCEOLA NATIONAL FOREST

St. Marys

Fernandina Beach

TIMUCUAN ECOLOGICAL AND HISTORIC PRESERVE

FORT CAROLINE NAT. MEM.

Jacksonville

Jacksonville Beach

CASTILLO DE SAN MARCOS NAT. MON.

ATLANTIC OCEAN

Lake City

F L O R I D A

Intracoastal Waterway

ST. VINCENT N.W.R.

Gainesville

Palatka

St. Augustine

FORT MATANZAS NAT. MON.

Palm Coast

LOWER SUWANNEE N.W.R.

CEDAR KEYS N.W.R.

Lake George

OCALA N.F.

LAKE WOODRUFF N.W.R.

Daytona Beach

Ocala

De Land

New Smyrna Beach

CANAVERAL NATIONAL SEASHORE

CRYSTAL RIVER N.W.R.

Deltona

St. Johns

Titusville

Homosassa Springs

Leesburg

Sanford

MERRITT ISLAND N.W.R.

CHASSAHOWITZKA N.W.R.

Spring Hill

Walt Disney World & EPCOT Center

Orlando

John F. Kennedy Space Center

Cape Canaveral

Bayonet Point

Kissimmee

Merritt Island

GULF

OF

MEXICO

Tarpon Springs

Lakeland

Haines City

Melbourne

Clearwater

TAMPA I.R.

Winter Haven

Palm Bay

PELICAN ISLAND N.W.R.

St. Petersburg

Tampa

Tampa Bay

Vero Beach

PINELLAS N.W.R.

Sebring

Indian

Fort Pierce

EGMONT KEY N.W.R.

DE SOTO NAT. MEM.

Bradenton

Peace

Arcadia

FORT PIERCE I.R.

Port St. Lucie

Sarasota

BRIGHTON SEMINOLE I.R.

Lake Okeechobee

St. Lucie Canal

LOXAHATCHEE N.W. & S.R.

HOBE SOUND N.W.R.

Venice

Port Charlotte

Jupiter

Punta Gorda

Caloosahatchee

Miami Canal

Belle Glade

West Palm Beach

Charlotte Harbor

Fort Myers

ARTHUR R. MARSHALL LOXAHATCHEE N.W.R.

Delray Beach

Cape Coral

J. N. "DING" DARLING N.W.R.

IMMOKALEE I.R.

Boca Raton

Immokalee

BIG CYPRESS SEMINOLE I.R.

Coral Springs

COCONUT CREEK I.R.

Naples

MICCOSUKEE I.R.

SEMINOLE I.R.

Fort Lauderdale

Big Cypress Swamp

BIG CYPRESS NAT. PRESERVE

Hollywood

HOLLYWOOD I.R.

Hialeah

Miami Beach

Kendall

Miami

The Everglades

Biscayne Bay

EVERGLADES NATIONAL PARK

BISCAYNE N.P.

Homestead

Cape Sable

FLORIDA KEYS NATIONAL MARINE SANCTUARY

GREAT WHITE HERON N.W.R.

NAT KEY DEER REFUGE

Florida Bay

Key Largo

KEY WEST N.W.R.

FLORIDA KEYS

Marathon

STRAITS OF FLORIDA

DRY TORTUGAS NATIONAL PARK

Key West

0   50   100 miles

0   50   100 kilometers

Albers Conic Equal-Area Projection

The king of the nation's theme parks, Disney's Magic Kingdom attracts more than ten million visitors annually. When it opened in 1971 as the first portion of Walt Disney World, the park transformed Orlando from an agricultural area to a fantasy getaway destination. Florida entertains more than 50 million visitors each year, providing more than 800,000 jobs directly involved in tourism.

GEORGIA

★ *Empire State of the South* ★

"EMPIRE STATE OF THE SOUTH." A regal-sounding nickname for a U.S. state may seem odd, but it fits Georgia. From majestic, forested highlands to a grand seaport on a palm-fringed coast, Georgia is as landscape-rich as any state. Last established of the 13 British colonies, it's even named for royalty: King George II.

Scouted by one empire and settled by another, the territory was of interest to the Spanish as early as the 1500s, but under English control from 1733. While begun as a place for poor English to start life anew after serving time in debtors' prisons, Georgia soon was like other southern colonies, exporting products such as rice, cotton, lumber, and deerskins to England—with slave labor. After the American Revolution, it ratified the Constitution in 1788, the fourth state to do so. At the time, Augusta was the capital city. Georgia's slave-based plantation economy boomed after the invention of the cotton gin in 1793. Gold discovered in its northern region in 1828 further speeded settlement and signaled the end of Creek and Cherokee success in resisting the newcomers. These Native Americans were among those forced to walk the Trail of Tears in the 1830s.

Georgia tilts southeastward, from Appalachian heights to a coastline dotted with wildlife refuges that are a birder's paradise. Spanning the Florida border, the Okefenokee National Wildlife Refuge harbors alligators, river otters, and bears in 700 square miles (1,820 sq km) of untamed swamps, bogs, and marshes. Between its low coastal plain and northern wooded heights lies a broad area of rolling forested hills and farmlands—the Piedmont.

It was on the Piedmont, at the foot of the Blue Ridge Mountains, that a settlement named Terminus was founded in 1837 at the endpoint of the promising new rail line. Within a decade

1733

James Oglethorpe founded Savannah as part of a slave-free colony but soon discovered that slave labor brought greater profits.

1793

Eli Whitney helped make cotton king by inventing a gin that could separate cotton seeds from fiber faster than could be done by hand.

1864

After burning Atlanta, Union General Sherman began his march to the sea, destroying property and railroads as he went.

1996

Hosting the Summer Olympics not only brought billions in revenue to Atlanta but also created jobs and world-class facilities.

Atlanta (opposite) has been called the Economic Capital of the Southeast. The metro area population increased by nearly 40 percent in the 1990s—from 2.9 million to 4.1 million. But growth has its costs: too much pollution and too great a demand on limited resources.

GEORGIA
Empire State of the South

STATEHOOD	January 2, 1788; 4th state
CAPITAL	Atlanta
LARGEST CITY	Atlanta Population 424,868
TOTAL AREA	59,425 sq mi; 153,909 sq km
LAND AREA	57,906 sq mi; 149,976 sq km
POPULATION	9,687,653
POPULATION DENSITY	163 people per sq mi
MAJOR RACIAL/ ETHNIC GROUPS	59.7% white; 30.5% African American; 3.2% Asian; 0.3% Native American; Hispanic (any race) 8.8%.
INDUSTRY	textiles and clothing, transportation equipment, food processing, paper products, chemicals, electrical equipment, tourism
AGRICULTURE	poultry and eggs, cotton, peanuts, vegetables, sweet corn, melons, cattle

BROWN THRASHER   CHEROKEE ROSE

Did you know?

1. The carvings of Confederate leaders Robert E. Lee, Stonewall Jackson, and Jefferson Davis on Stone Mountain near Atlanta make up the world's largest high relief sculpture.
2. Delta Airlines started as a company that dusted crops for boll weevils and developed into one of the country's leading commercial airlines.
3. Martin Luther King, Jr., charismatic African-American civil rights leader and recipient of the Nobel Peace Prize, was born in Atlanta in 1929.
4. The U.S. first gold rush happened in 1828 near Dahlonega, which means "yellow money" in Cherokee.
5. Coca-Cola was invented in 1886 in Atlanta by Dr. John Pemberton and was first sold at the soda fountain in a local pharmacy. First-year sales averaged nine drinks a day for a year-end earning of $50.

Peanuts have been grown in Georgia since colonial times. In 2003 the state grew almost 45 percent of the nation's harvest. Related to beans and alfalfa, peanuts grow on the roots of the plant. Peanuts are eaten roasted, shelled, salted, or as peanut butter or oil. They are even used in livestock feed.

the prospering city took a name invented from the Georgia and Atlantic Railroad: Atlanta. The city and the state supplied food and other resources for the Confederate war effort. Atlanta and Georgia became Civil War targets by 1864. Union forces devastated the state in the fall of that year. Destroying everything in its path, Sherman's Army burned most of Atlanta and left a 50-mile- (80-km) wide swath of ruin to the sea.

Georgia suffered through decades of post-Civil War poverty. Sharecropping, soil erosion, and the boll weevil invasion of the early 20th century hurt farming. Savannah declined in importance, but Atlanta was quickly rebuilt after the war and developed into the transportation, trade, and financial hub of the South.

Though still a leader among states in cotton production, Georgia's agriculture has diversified. It is first in producing broiler chickens and a leader in egg output. Georgia is widely known for peanuts, pecans, peaches, and sweet Vidalia onions. Vast pine forests help make it a leader in forest products, and it is number one in paper production. From northeastern quarries, Georgia produces the Greene County granite used to form the plaza of the new National World War II Memorial on the Mall in Washington, D.C.

Georgia has 8.7 million residents. Almost three in ten Georgians have African-American heritage. In 1967, racial violence erupted in Atlanta, which became a center of the civil rights movement. Georgia native Jimmy Carter, who was governor before becoming President in 1976, pushed strongly for equal opportunity. Rapid population gains have caused resource strains on education, healthcare, and highways. Georgians will likely solve these problems and continue to weave prosperity into the future of their southern empire.

KENTUCKY

★ *Bluegrass State* ★

BLUEGRASS STATE. Whether one hears the state's nickname, or hears the refrain from the state song "My Old Kentucky Home," pleasant rural images come to mind. Though Kentucky contains plenty of southern hospitality, it's also a mining and manufacturing state like industrial states to the north.

In the language of local Native American people, *kentake* meant "prairie," for the open, grassy spaces among its hardwood forests. Kentucky has more than a thousand miles (1,600 km) of navigable waterways, including the Tennessee, Cumberland, Green, Kentucky, and Licking Rivers, which all flow into the Ohio. This broad and deep river, which forms the state's northern border, joins the Mississippi at Kentucky's southwestern tip. High ridges and deep, narrow valleys of the Appalachians and adjoining Cumberland Plateau make up most of eastern Kentucky. Rivers rushing from the

heights have carved twisting gorges called gaps through the mountains.

Through these passages pioneers reached central and western Kentucky. When a treaty with the Cherokee opened the region to easterners in 1775, the legendary but real-life Daniel Boone was quick to travel through the Cumberland Gap. The famed pioneer brought his family and others to build Boonesborough. When the American Revolution ended, streams of settlers flowed into what was then a huge, western "county" of Virginia. Kentucky became the 15th state in 1792, with the town of Frankfort as its capital.

After the last Native American claims to Kentucky lands were resolved in 1818, the state developed a booming tobacco-based economy. A pro-slavery/anti-slavery split developed, dividing Kentucky between plantation owners and small-scale farmers and crafts people.

1775
Daniel Boone opened up the Northwest Territory by leading settlers through the Cumberland Gap from Virginia to Kentucky.

1852
A Kentucky slave auction inspired Harriet Beecher Stowe to write her powerful anti-slavery novel Uncle Tom's Cabin.

1930s
The attempt by labor unions to secure better wages and working conditions for coal miners led to violent strikes in Harlan County.

Present day
More than 2.5 million Louisville Sluggers, the official bat of major league baseball, are produced in Kentucky each year.

Kentucky's Thoroughbred horses (opposite), a breed originally from England, are famous for their racing ability. Lexington is the bustling Bluegrass hub of the state's horse-raising operations, where the first racecourse was set up in 1789.

KENTUCKY
Bluegrass State

STATEHOOD	June 1, 1792; 15th state
CAPITAL	Frankfort
LARGEST CITY	Louisville Metro Population 693,604
TOTAL AREA	40,409 sq mi; 104,659 sq km
LAND AREA	39,728 sq mi; 102,896 sq km
POPULATION	4,339,367
POPULATION DENSITY	107 people per sq mi
MAJOR RACIAL/ ETHNIC GROUPS	87.8% white; 7.8% African American; 1.1% Asian; 0.2% Native American; Hispanic (any race) 3.1%.
INDUSTRY	manufacturing, services, government, finance, insurance, real estate, retail trade, transportation, wholesale trade, construction, mining
AGRICULTURE	tobacco, horses, cattle, corn, dairy products

CARDINAL   GOLDENROD

Did you know?

1. Mammoth Cave, with its 360 miles (580 km) of mapped passageways, is the longest cave system in the world. Visitors have come to explore it since 1816.
2. Kentucky bluegrass gets its name not from the color of the grass (which is green) but from the bluish buds the grass produces in the spring and that make meadows look blue.
3. Pike County has produced more than 1.33 billion tons of coal, more than any other county in the country.
4. Abraham Lincoln, President of the United States, and Jefferson Davis, President of the Confederacy, were both born in log houses in Kentucky. Lincoln's birthplace was Sinking Spring Farm, southeast of Elizabethtown (1809); Davis's was in Fairview (1808).

Officially neutral at the outbreak of the Civil War, Kentucky eventually sided with the Union even though about one-third of its soldiers fought for the Confederacy.

First worked in the 1750s, eastern Kentucky's enormous deposits of soft bituminous coal have been mined in great quantities for 150 years. This natural resource provided wealth, fueled labor movements, and caused disastrous environmental problems. Deep-shaft mines and dangerous hand labor were the rule for decades. Eventually, machines did much of the work. Later, shallower western Kentucky coal reserves were strip-mined by huge power shovels and bulldozers. Since the 1970s, federal laws have required that stripped lands be restored to their original condition, but many older mines leave scars on the land.

Kentucky's central Bluegrass region provided green alternatives to the coal economy. A long, warm growing season and calcium-rich soils here yield excellent tobacco and winning horses. At its heart is Lexington. Louisville, home to the famous Kentucky Derby horse race, is a major Ohio River port and highway and air-transport center.

Long a victim of a boom-and-bust mining economy, eastern Kentucky is still the state's poorest region, but it is culturally rich. Its Scotch-Irish heritage is preserved in its distinctive crafts and music. Its forests of oak, walnut, and hickory help make Kentucky a leader among hardwood producing states. Tourism is increasing in this region of pioneer history, state parks, and federal recreation lands.

In a state that combines traits from North and South, Kentuckians retain old customs and activities as they blaze new trails. Long a mostly rural state, most Kentuckians now live in cities. Still a major coal producer, the state explores clean-burning coal technology. Manufacturing remains a force, too, with the fourth-largest production of motor vehicles in the United States. Kentucky seeks to better its standard of living by improving education, by making technology part of everyday life, and by developing strong ties to the national and global economy. People here want to share their ideas and culture with the world as they build their "new" Kentucky homes.

A long tradition of folk music is alive and well in Kentucky. bluegrass music has roots in the tunes of Scotch-Irish immigrants to the Appalachians, as well as in the music of African-American slaves. The name came from Kentuckian Bill Monroe, who called his 1939 band the Blue Grass Boys, after his home state.

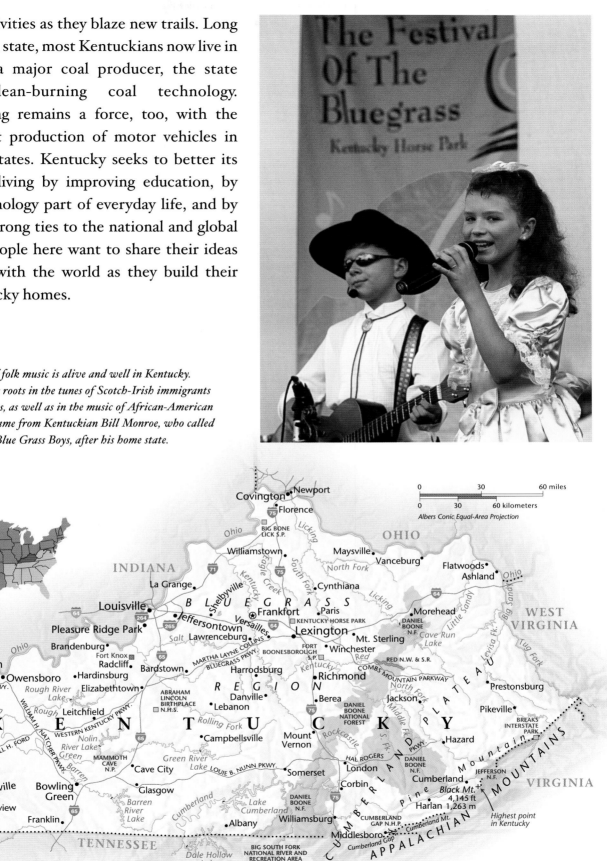

LOUISIANA

★ *Pelican State* ★

THE BAYOU STATE or the Pelican State. Take your pick, both nicknames are about water. Looking like a boot on the Gulf of Mexico shore, Louisiana stands between Texas and Mississippi, with Arkansas to its north. Fresh, salty, or a mix of both called brackish, water is the source of the state's successes—and some of its troubles.

Water was the highway when French explorer La Salle sailed down the Mississippi River in 1682, claiming—and naming—the entire valley for his king, Louis XIV. "Louisiana" was a vast realm then, but the territory eventually was reduced to form the state of today, surrounding the lower reaches of the great river.

With the Louisiana Purchase in 1803, New Orleans, founded almost a century before on a strip of land along a sweeping bend of the Mississippi, was positioned to become the commercial focus for the sprawling river basin.

Steamboats reached Louisiana at about the time it became the 18th state in 1812. The state capital traveled upriver to Baton Rouge in 1849. By that time, New Orleans had become not just a bustling port for cotton and other plantation products, but also the biggest slave-trading market in the South. The state joined the Confederacy, but by 1862 it was in Union hands.

Louisiana's post-Civil War decades brought hard times—corrupt leadership, a declining cotton economy, and continued racial inequalities. Poor African-American farmers struggled to survive in an unfair system. Oil and gas, discovered there in 1901, helped change the state's fortunes. Today, rigs in all sections of the state and in Gulf waters make Louisiana the fourth-largest oil producer in the nation. Refineries and petrochemical plants line the riverbanks from New Orleans to Baton Rouge, turning natural resources into hundreds of products.

1803

The raising of the American flag in New Orleans celebrated the Louisiana Purchase, which doubled the size of the United States.

1862

Confederate sharpshooters failed to keep the Union from capturing New Orleans and gaining control of the mouth of the Mississippi.

1928–1932

Huey Long, a strong advocate of education, the poor, and state's rights, was the most influential politician in Louisiana history.

Present day

Massive oil-and-natural-gas rigs in the Gulf of Mexico help make the state one of the top five U.S. producers of these energy resources.

Fancy floats and feasts mean it's Mardi Gras in New Orleans (opposite). Each year the celebration attracts millions of visitors to this French-founded city. Its picturesque French Quarter, unique foods, and home-grown jazz music make it a popular attraction year-round.

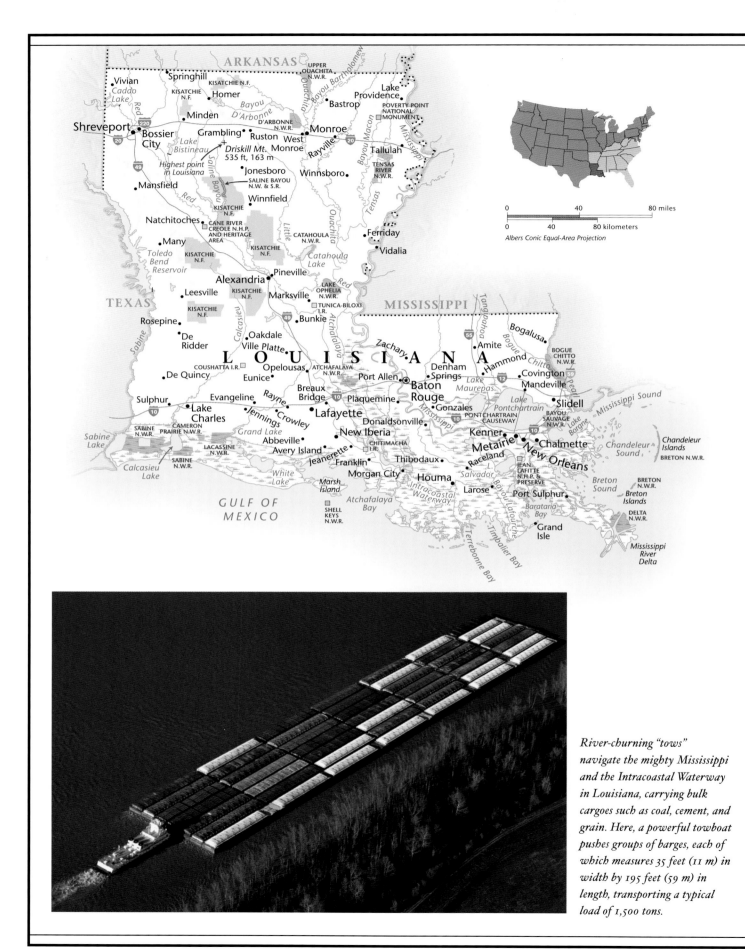

LOUISIANA

ARKANSAS

Vivian

Caddo Lake

Springhill

KISATCHIE N.F.

Homer

KISATCHIE N.F.

Bayou D'Arbonne

Minden

Shreveport

Bossier City

D'ARBONNE N.W.R.

Grambling

Ruston

West Monroe

Monroe

Rayville

Tallulah

Driskill Mt.
535 ft, 163 m
Highest point
in Louisiana

Jonesboro

SALINE BAYOU
N.W. & S.R.

Winnsboro

TENSAS RIVER N.W.R.

Mansfield

Saline Bayou

Winnfield

Red

KISATCHIE
N.F.

Natchitoches

CANE RIVER
CREOLE N.H.P.
AND HERITAGE
AREA

KISATCHIE
N.F.

Little

CATAHOULA
N.W.R.

Ferriday

Vidalia

Many

*Toledo
Bend
Reservoir*

KISATCHIE
N.F.

*Catahoula
Lake*

Ouachita

TEXAS

Rosepine

Leesville

Alexandria

Pineville

KISATCHIE N.F.

Marksville

LAKE
OPHELIA
N.W.R.

Red

MISSISSIPPI

TUNICA-BILOXI
I.R.

De
Ridder

Oakdale

Bunkie

Ville Platte

ATCHAFALAYA
N.W.R.

Zachary

Amite

Bogalusa

BOGUE
CHITTO
N.W.R.

Bogue Chitto

Sabine

COUSHATTA I.R.

Opelousas

Denham
Springs

Hammond

De Quincy

Eunice

Breaux
Bridge

Port Allen

Baton
Rouge

*Lake
Maurepas*

Covington

Mandeville

Sulphur

Evangeline

Rayne

Plaquemine

Gonzales

Slidell

Lake
Charles

Jennings

Crowley

Lafayette

Donaldsonville

*Lake
Pontchartrain*

BAYOU
SAUVAGE
N.W.R.

*Lake
Borgne*

Mississippi Sound

SABINE
N.W.R.

CAMERON
PRAIRIE N.W.R.

Abbeville

Avery Island

CHITIMACHA
I.R.

New Iberia

Kenner

Metairie

Chalmette

*Chandeleur
Sound*

*Chandeleur
Islands*

*Sabine
Lake*

LACASSINE
N.W.R.

Jeanerette

Franklin

Thibodaux

New Orleans

Bayou Lafourche

BRETON N.W.R.

*Calcasieu
Lake*

SABINE
N.W.R.

*White
Lake*

Grand Lake

Morgan City

Houma

Raceland

JEAN
LAFITTE
N.H.P. &
PRESERVE

*L.
Salvador*

BRETON
N.W.R.

*Breton
Sound*

BRETON
Islands

*Marsh
Island*

Larose

Port Sulphur

*Baratria
Bay*

DELTA
N.W.R.

**GULF OF
MEXICO**

SHELL
KEYS
N.W.R.

*Atchafalaya
Bay*

*Intracoastal
Waterway*

Terrebonne Bay

Timbalier Bay

Grand
Isle

*Mississippi
River
Delta*

0   40   80 miles
0   40   80 kilometers
Albers Conic Equal-Area Projection

River-churning "tows" navigate the mighty Mississippi and the Intracoastal Waterway in Louisiana, carrying bulk cargoes such as coal, cement, and grain. Here, a powerful towboat pushes groups of barges, each of which measures 35 feet (11 m) in width by 195 feet (59 m) in length, transporting a typical load of 1,500 tons.

Louisiana owes its very existence to upstream erosion. Borne by the Mississippi and other rivers, sediment has built up the river's lower reaches and shifting delta for millions of years. Well-watered Louisiana lies low, averaging just 100 feet (30 m) above sea level. From hills near Shreveport, the land descends to marshes, swamps, and slow-moving streams called bayous along its Gulf Coast. Here live Cajuns, whose ancestors—the Acadians—were forced from French Canada by the British in the 1700s. Many Cajuns still speak French, and their spicy foods and toe-tapping music combine to make rural Louisiana culture unlike that of any other state.

Louisiana lands the nation's second-biggest commercial fish catch—including shrimp and oysters. The state ranks second among states in sweet potatoes and sugarcane and third in rice production. Fields are flooded to raise catfish and crayfish—a state specialty. Still one of the world's busiest ports for river and ocean-going traffic, New Orleans is also a famous tourist destination.

While the lives and livelihoods of Louisiana's 4.5 million people are rooted in water, threats from water keep them on guard. The enormous and shifting Mississippi has always proven hard to handle, but a disastrous flood in 1927 caused the federal government to try. An extensive system of dams and river embankments called levees are designed to control floods and improve navigation. The state has wetlands rich in wildlife, including alligators, muskrats, and waterfowl. Both urban and rural activities threaten this water-land paradise, as do pollutants from half the country that wash down the Mississippi. Louisiana residents know that water keeps state hopes afloat, so they must work to keep "water woes" from interfering with future success.

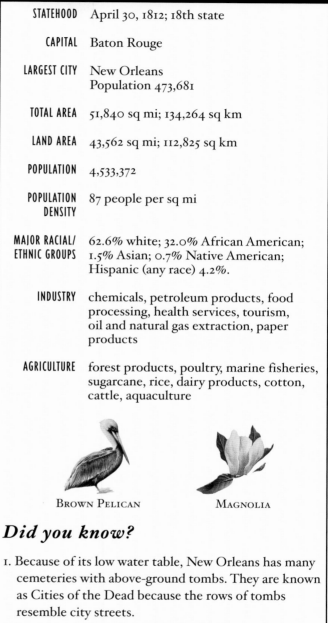

LOUISIANA
Pelican State

STATEHOOD	April 30, 1812; 18th state
CAPITAL	Baton Rouge
LARGEST CITY	New Orleans Population 473,681
TOTAL AREA	51,840 sq mi; 134,264 sq km
LAND AREA	43,562 sq mi; 112,825 sq km
POPULATION	4,533,372
POPULATION DENSITY	87 people per sq mi
MAJOR RACIAL/ ETHNIC GROUPS	62.6% white; 32.0% African American; 1.5% Asian; 0.7% Native American; Hispanic (any race) 4.2%.
INDUSTRY	chemicals, petroleum products, food processing, health services, tourism, oil and natural gas extraction, paper products
AGRICULTURE	forest products, poultry, marine fisheries, sugarcane, rice, dairy products, cotton, cattle, aquaculture

BROWN PELICAN   MAGNOLIA

Did you know?

1. Because of its low water table, New Orleans has many cemeteries with above-ground tombs. They are known as Cities of the Dead because the rows of tombs resemble city streets.
2. Louisiana is the only state in the Union that has parishes instead of counties and that refers to the Napoleonic Code in its laws.
3. The 24-mile- (39-km-) long Lake Pontchartrain Causeway is the longest bridge completely over water in the world.
4. Louisiana's Creole society is made up of descendants of people of Spanish or French heritage mixed with that of African slaves who gained their freedom before the Civil War.

MISSISSIPPI

★ *Magnolia State* ★

STOP CHANGING CHANNELS! Apparently no one told the loopy Mississippi River that. It has meandered along for ages to form the scalloped western boundary of its namesake state. When the river curls far enough back on itself, it can cut across the narrow neck of land to form what's called an oxbow lake. Dozens of these crescent-shaped water bodies lie along the lower reaches of the Mississippi. Like its great river, the state itself has seen some big changes.

Hernando de Soto scouted the Mississippi for Spain in 1540. The territory was later claimed by the French, who founded their first settlement in 1699 on the Gulf Coast near present-day Ocean Springs. Great Britain controlled the region after the French and Indian War until it passed to the U.S. in 1783. But Spain did not give up its coastal claims. Spanish West Florida, including Mississippi's present shoreline, was officially transferred to the United States in 1819.

Three major native groups were living here when Europeans arrived. The Natchez are remembered for "tracing" a trail—later used by settlers and traders—from their lowland home to hunting grounds in present-day Tennessee. The Chickasaw lived in the north and were great warriors who later helped the British battle the French. The Choctaw were the dominant group—skilled farmers who lived in the central region. Nearly all eventually were forced off their lands by the incoming Americans, and many trekked the Trail of Tears to Oklahoma in the 1830s—or died along the way. The Mississippi Territory was created in 1798, and included for a time present-day Alabama. Mississippi entered the Union as the 20th state in 1817. A small town on the Pearl River, renamed in honor of Andrew Jackson, became the state capital in 1821.

Mississippi was soon ruled by "King Cotton." For more than a century—until the

1806

Using seeds imported from Mexico, planters developed a new variety of cotton that helped make Mississippi a major cotton producer.

1863

The capture of Vicksburg after a 47-day siege gave the Union control of the Mississippi River and hastened the end of the Civil War.

1963

Medgar Evers was killed for trying to end segregation of African Americans. In 1969 his brother was elected mayor of Fayette.

Present day

The annual shrimp harvest is an important part of Mississippi's seafood industry, along with oysters and red snappers.

The American Queen (opposite), built in 1995, celebrates the 19th-century days of Mississippi River paddle-wheeling. Regular steamboat service for passengers and freight operated between New Orleans and Natchez by 1814.

MISSISSIPPI
Magnolia State

STATEHOOD	December 10, 1817; 20th state
CAPITAL	Jackson
LARGEST CITY	Jackson Population 180,881
TOTAL AREA	48,430 sq mi; 125,434 sq km
LAND AREA	46,907 sq mi; 121,489 sq km
POPULATION	2,967,297
POPULATION DENSITY	61 people per sq mi
MAJOR RACIAL/ ETHNIC GROUPS	59.1% white; 37.0% African American; 0.9% Asian; 0.5% Native American; Hispanic (any race) 2.7%.
INDUSTRY	petroleum products, health services, electronic equipment, transportation, banking, forest products, communications
AGRICULTURE	poultry and eggs, cotton, catfish, soybeans, cattle, rice, dairy products

MOCKINGBIRD

MAGNOLIA

Did you know?

1. Mississippi is the country's leading supplier of farm-raised catfish. This industry supports other segments of the economy, such as corn, soybeans, and cotton-seed, all of which are used as fish food.
2. The famous crash of the Cannonball Express, which killed folk-song hero John Luther "Casey" Jones, occurred in Vaughan on April 30, 1900.
3. In 1902 while on a hunting expedition in Mississippi, President Theodore (Teddy) Roosevelt refused to shoot a captured bear. This act resulted in the creation of the world-famous teddy bear.
4. Natchez, settled by the French in 1716, is the oldest permanent European settlement in Mississippi.
5. NASA space shuttle engines are tested at the John C. Stennis Space Center, near Bay St. Louis.

Great Depression of the 1930s—the state's economy and society were dominated by the growing, processing, and selling of the white, fluffy fiber. For much of this time, wealthy white plantation owners lived like royalty while African Americans were enslaved. Poor white, non-slaveholding farmers lived free but like peasants. Mississippi joined the Confederacy and paid dearly for it. Some 770 Civil War battles and skirmishes were fought here, Jackson was burned three times, and at least 25,000 Mississippi soldiers died.

Though slavery was officially abolished after the war, the economic and the social realities did not change much. Both white and black share-croppers were supplied with land to farm, seeds to plant, and tools to use in exchange for a heavy share of the harvest going to the wealthy landowner. Most African-American civil rights were withheld until the protests, violence, and legislation of the 1950s and 1960s finally achieved integration and began to build equal rights.

Mississippi has worked over the past half century both to broaden its farm economy and to balance it with other activities. Long, hot summers, annual rainfall averaging more than 50 inches (127 cm), and rich soils allow diverse agriculture. While cotton farmed in the Delta region, between the Yazoo and Mississippi Rivers, still makes the state a national leader, these flatlands also support huge harvests of rice, soybeans, sorghum, and other crops. Mississippi is the country's largest supplier of pond-raised catfish and a major chicken producer, too.

The state's southern yellow pine forests yield lumber and other forest products. The Gulf Coast, where residents catch and process seafood, pump and refine oil and gas, and build ships, attracts increasing numbers of tourists.

Mississippi is also home to a number of key military facilities.

Not all of Mississippi's problems are solved, and the state still works to correct the impacts of a painful past. The state's per capita income remains among the lowest in the nation. Rural poverty rates are particularly high, especially in places dominated by large groups of the state's more than one million African Americans. But the state strives to improve the lives of all its citizens by pressing for improved education and the creation of more and higher-paying jobs.

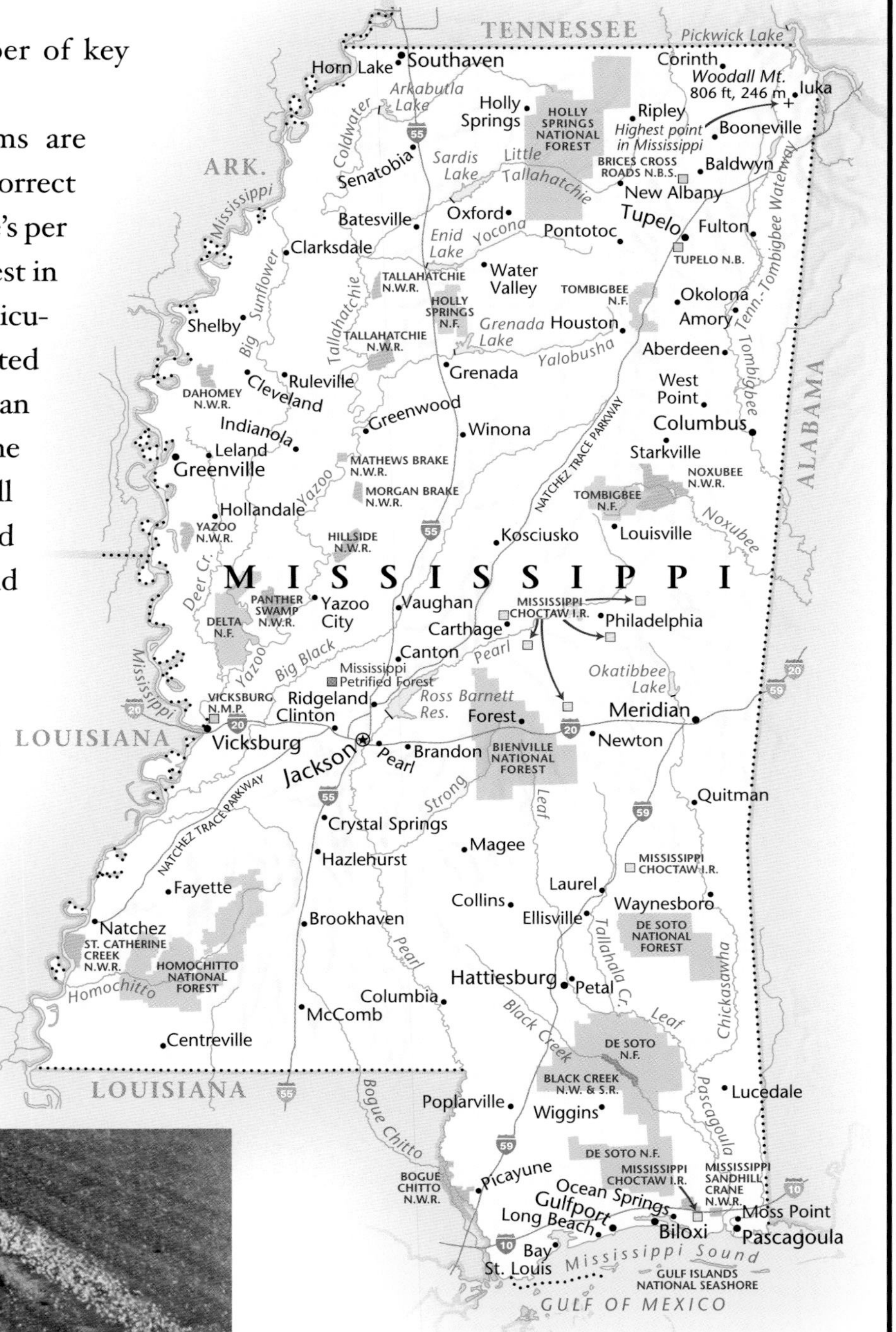

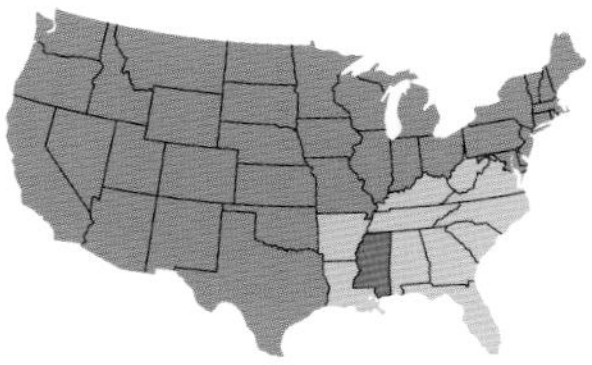

Although Mississippi has much greater agricultural diversity today than in the 19th century, the state still ranks among the top three cotton-producing states. The backbreaking method of picking cotton by hand has given way to mechanized cotton harvesters like the one shown here. Field hands traditionally were paid in pennies-per-pound picked; machines that do the job today can cost more than $300,000 each.

NORTH CAROLINA

★ *Tar Heel State* ★

FROM THE MOUNTAINS to the sea, across a broad, hilly piedmont to its wave-dashed Atlantic coastline, North Carolina holds rich and varied landscapes. Mount Mitchell—the highest point east of the Mississippi River—tops out at 6,684 feet (2,037 m) above sea level in the state's Black Mountains.

A French expedition sailed along the coast in 1524. Sixty-one years later Sir Walter Ralegh sent a colonizing expedition from England, but the settlers returned after a year. In 1587 more than a hundred people settled on and later vanished from Roanoke Island. In 1629 King Charles I split off a portion of the Virginia Colony and named it after himself (*Carolus* is Latin for Charles). In the 1650s most Indians were forced out when conflicts erupted between settlers and Creeks, Cherokees, and Algonquins. In 1729, the royal colonies of North and South Carolina were formed. The economy centered on naval stores, such as pitch, tar, and turpentine. Soon, tobacco and cotton were grown in the English-settled eastern lowlands, while Scots, Irish, and Germans moved to lands farther west. Opposition to English taxes made North Carolina eager to join the Revolution, and a victory near Wilmington helped win the region for the Americans.

Capes Hatteras, Lookout, and Fear poke seaward from the arc of barrier islands that protect species-rich sounds and bays along the coast. Battered by high winds, Outer Banks waters are hazardous: more than 600 ships have sunk here. Big rivers run swiftly southeast from the uplands, changing to wider, slower waterways the closer they get to the ocean.

North Carolina joined the Union as the 12th state in 1789 and maintained a mostly agricultural economy, which included the use of slaves on cotton and tobacco plantations. Though its citizens were split on the issue of slavery, the state

1591

The word "Croatoan" was the only evidence found of colonists who disappeared from England's first settlement on Roanoke Island.

Early 1900s

Textile mills became the state's chief employer, as farmers left their fields to work in mills, where children often provided cheap labor.

1960

A sit-in at an all-white lunch counter in Greensboro was one of many protests that led to laws banning segregation in public places.

Present day

Fort Bragg and Camp Lejeune are among the military bases that give the armed forces a large presence in North Carolina.

Flashing a powerful warning light across the treacherous Diamond Shoals, Cape Hatteras Lighthouse (opposite) is the tallest and most famous brick lighthouse in the country. Its beacon can be seen for nearly 22 miles (35 km).

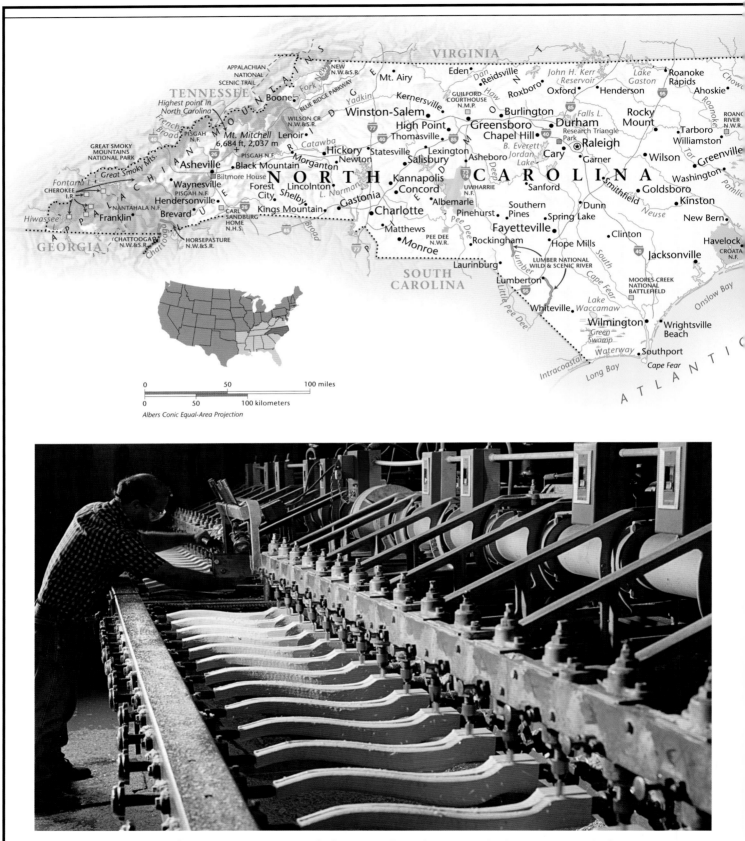

North Carolina has extensive forest resources. Large areas of softwood pine forests feed paper and pulp mills. Rich stands of hardwood trees and skilled craftspeople have combined to build a solid reputation for North Carolina furniture makers. Here, a woodworker makes chair legs on a production line. Hickory, High Point, and Thomasville are among the places famous for wooden furniture.

joined the Confederacy in 1861. North Carolina struggled after the war with rural poverty and racial inequalities that persisted well into the 20th century. In 1971 Charlotte was the site of the first major school-busing program to eliminate school segregation.

The tobacco business boomed after the invention of the cigarette-making machine in the 1880s. Textile mills found power in numerous rivers. By the 1920s, oak and maple forests supplied a huge furniture-making industry, which still leads the nation. Rich fisheries and numerous mineral resources were developed, too. Military spending began during World War II and is still strong.

Now, high-tech industries prosper in the famous Research Triangle between Chapel Hill, Durham, and the state capital, Raleigh. Charlotte has grown into one of the top banking cities in the country. Tourists flock to the seashores of the Outer Banks, while Great Smoky Mountains National Park and the Appalachian Trail draw vacationers to the wild western highlands. The state's agriculture is quite diverse. It ranks first in total tobacco harvest and in turkey production, is second only to Iowa in hog raising, and is a major producer of many other farm products.

Both highs and lows seem likely in North Carolina's future. Some businesses, like technology and finance, should continue to shine. But state manufacturing doesn't look so bright. More than 25,000 textile jobs were lost to foreign competition in 2003. State leaders are working to solve these and other problems. They hope that with its rich resources and landscapes from beachfront to rocky top, the state's future will be looking up.

NORTH CAROLINA
Tar Heel State

STATEHOOD	November 21, 1789; 12th state
CAPITAL	Raleigh
LARGEST CITY	Charlotte Population 580,597
TOTAL AREA	53,819 sq mi; 139,389 sq km
LAND AREA	48,711 sq mi; 126,161 sq km
POPULATION	9,535,483
POPULATION DENSITY	177 people per sq mi
MAJOR RACIAL/ ETHNIC GROUPS	68.5% white; 21.5% African American; 2.2% Asian; 1.3% Native American; Hispanic (any race) 8.4%.
INDUSTRY	real estate, health services, chemicals, tobacco products, finance, textiles
AGRICULTURE	poultry, hogs, tobacco, nursery stock, cotton, soybeans

CARDINAL   FLOWERING DOGWOOD

Did you know?

1. In 1903 the Wright brothers made the first successful human-powered flight at Kill Devil Hill near Kitty Hawk on the Outer Banks.
2. The state's nickname honors North Carolina's soldiers who refused to turn and run during the Civil War, as if their heels were glued to the ground with tar. Confederate General Robert E. Lee recognized their bravery, calling them "Tar Heel boys."
3. North Carolina has the nation's largest state-maintained highway system, with more than 77,000 miles (124,000 km) of roadway.
4. Edward Teach, also known as the notorious pirate Blackbeard, used Ocracoke Island, part of the Outer Banks, as a hideout. The Okracoke inlet where he was killed is known as Teach's Hole.
5. More than 1,250,000 bricks were used to build the Cape Hatteras Lighthouse.

SOUTH CAROLINA

★ *Palmetto State* ★

SHAPED LIKE A WEDGE or a spreading fan, triangular South Carolina points to the Blue Ridge and waves at the Atlantic. On its ocean edge, warm sea breezes rustle coastal grasses and stately palmetto trees. From the time a Revolutionary War fort built from these tough trees withstood a British attack, South Carolina has been known as the Palmetto State. While smaller than its neighbors, South Carolina has played a major role in the nation's history.

South Carolinians usually divide their state into two broad regions. A small slice of Appalachian highlands and a larger piece of rolling piedmont form the northwestern third of the state called the Up Country. Here, swift streams and rivers roll from the highlands.

The southeastern two-thirds of the state are the Low Country, a South Carolina name for the broad Atlantic Coastal Plain. Here, rivers slow and flow across fine lowland soil and swampy lands. Mild winters and long, hot summers dominate, always with a threat of big storms. Hurricane Hugo tore through Charleston with winds of 135 miles per hour (217 kph) in 1989.

After Spanish and French attempts to colonize the coast failed, the English succeeded at Charles Towne—later renamed Charleston—in 1670. Located a few miles inland on a point between the Ashley and Cooper Rivers, the port prospered as slave-based plantation agriculture took root. Early farming here produced cotton, indigo, and tobacco, but rice soon became the biggest export crop. North and South Carolina were made separate royal colonies in 1729. The ragged shoreline of bays and islands harbored pirates, who raided Carolina shipping and settlements. South Carolina became the eighth state in 1788, and the capital was moved from Charleston to more centrally located Columbia in 1790.

1680

Slaves, shown here unloading rice barges, taught their English masters how to grow rice, which flourished as a plantation crop.

1861

The Civil War began with a Confederate attack on the Union's Fort Sumter, which guarded Charleston harbor.

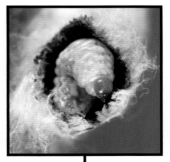

1920s

The damage done to cotton by the boll weevil forced South Carolina and other southern states to plant other crops.

1989

Hurricane Hugo, which piled up boats like toys, eroded beaches, and leveled dunes, had a devastating effect on the tourist industry.

Charleston's historic downtown district (opposite) is considered to be a living museum of early Southern life. Though damaged by Hurricane Hugo in 1989, the city's grand 18th- and 19th-century homes retain their charm and grace.

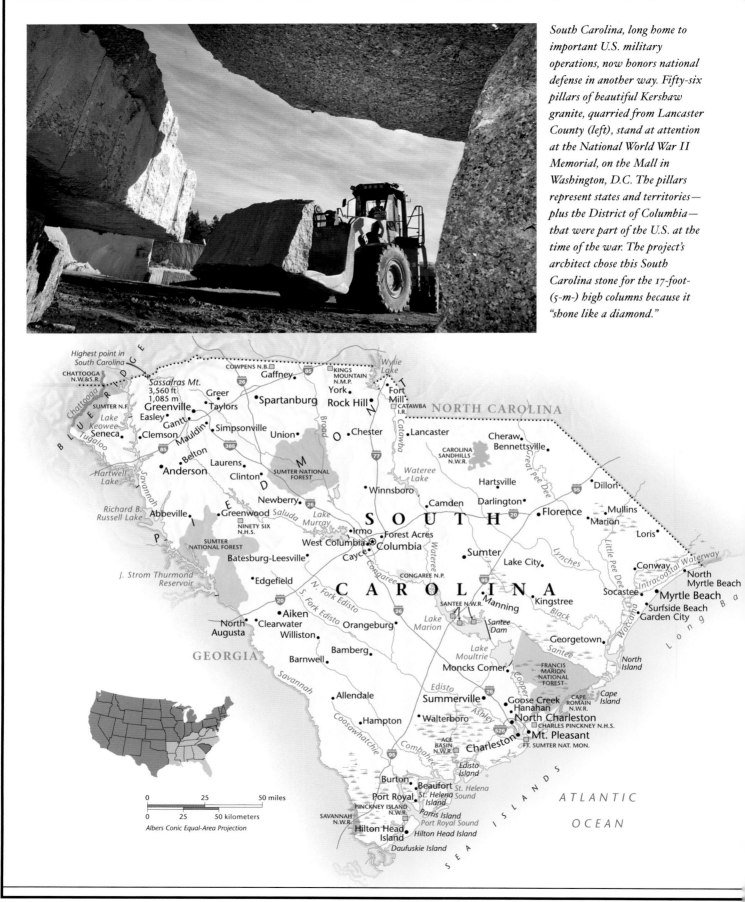

South Carolina, long home to important U.S. military operations, now honors national defense in another way. Fifty-six pillars of beautiful Kershaw granite, quarried from Lancaster County (left), stand at attention at the National World War II Memorial, on the Mall in Washington, D.C. The pillars represent states and territories— plus the District of Columbia— that were part of the U.S. at the time of the war. The project's architect chose this South Carolina stone for the 17-foot- (5-m-) high columns because it "shone like a diamond."

Highest point in South Carolina
CHATTOOGA N.W.&S.R.
COWPENS N.B.
KINGS MOUNTAIN N.M.P.
Wylie Lake
Sassafras Mt. 3,560 ft 1,085 m
Gaffney
York
Fort Mill
CATAWBA I.R.
NORTH CAROLINA
SUMTER N.F.
Greer
Taylors
Spartanburg
Rock Hill
Greenville
Easley
Gantt
Simpsonville
Chester
Lancaster
Cheraw
Bennettsville
Seneca
Clemson
Mauldin
Union
CAROLINA SANDHILLS N.W.R.
Lake Keowee
Belton
Laurens
SUMTER NATIONAL FOREST
Wateree Lake
Hartsville
Dillon
Anderson
Clinton
Winnsboro
Camden
Darlington
Mullins
Newberry
Marion
Loris
Abbeville
Greenwood
Saluda
Lake Murray
Florence
NINETY SIX N.H.S.
Irmo
Forest Acres
West Columbia
Columbia
SOUTH
SUMTER NATIONAL FOREST
Batesburg-Leesville
Cayce
Sumter
Lake City
Conway
North Myrtle Beach
Edgefield
CAROLINA
CONGAREE N.P.
Manning
Kingstree
Socastee
Myrtle Beach
Aiken
North Augusta
Clearwater
Williston
Orangeburg
SANTEE N.W.R.
Lake Marion
Santee Dam
Surfside Beach
Garden City
J. Strom Thurmond Reservoir
Bamberg
Georgetown
GEORGIA
Barnwell
Lake Moultrie
FRANCIS MARION NATIONAL FOREST
North Island
Allendale
Summerville
Moncks Corner
CAPE ROMAIN N.W.R.
Cape Island
Hampton
Walterboro
Goose Creek
Hanahan
North Charleston
CHARLES PINCKNEY N.H.S.
ACE BASIN N.W.R.
Mt. Pleasant
Charleston
FT. SUMTER NAT. MON.
Edisto Island
Burton
Beaufort
St. Helena Sound
Port Royal
St. Helena Island
PINCKNEY ISLAND N.W.R.
Parris Island
Port Royal Sound
SEA ISLANDS
ATLANTIC OCEAN
SAVANNAH N.W.R.
Hilton Head Island
Hilton Head Island
Daufuskie Island

0   25   50 miles
0   25   50 kilometers
Albers Conic Equal-Area Projection

Invention of the cotton gin in 1793 greatly increased production of the fiber crop. Low Country plantation owners, fearing loss of their wealth if slavery were abolished, led the fateful drive to withdraw from the Union in late 1860. By then, 60 percent of the state's population was African American, almost all slaves. The Civil War's first shot was fired on U.S. Fort Sumter in Charleston harbor on April 12, 1861.

South Carolina's economy suffered through hard times for decades after the war. Small-scale farmers toiled in poverty, and some migrated to Northern cities for work. Soil erosion damaged state farmlands, and cotton output was ruined by the boll weevil in the 1920s. Tobacco then increased in importance and is still a leading state crop. Soybeans now dominate in acreage planted, and the state produces more peaches than Georgia in some years.

First railroads then freeways stitched South Carolina into the nation's industrial fabric along the textile belt between Greenville and Spartanburg. Longleaf and loblolly pine forests support a thriving pulp and paper industry. High-tech businesses, nuclear plants, and military bases also contribute to the economy.

Travelers make South Carolina a top stop. Seaside resorts like Myrtle Beach on the "Grand Strand of Sand" and Hilton Head in the Sea Islands attract millions of visitors annually. Charleston's historic mansions display the lives of South Carolina's early "rich and famous," while the Old Slave Mart Museum shows the awful conditions of the slave trade. Today, South Carolina works to provide better education, jobs, and quality of life for all its citizens. With its abundant resources and diverse economy, the Palmetto State can look forward to a strong future.

SOUTH CAROLINA
Palmetto State

STATEHOOD	May 23, 1788; 8th state
CAPITAL	Columbia
LARGEST CITY	Columbia Population 117,394
TOTAL AREA	32,020 sq mi; 82,932 sq km
LAND AREA	30,110 sq mi; 77,983 sq km
POPULATION	4,625,364
POPULATION DENSITY	144 people per sq mi
MAJOR RACIAL/ ETHNIC GROUPS	66.2% white; 27.9% African American; 1.3% Asian; 0.4% Native American; Hispanic (any race) 5.1%.
INDUSTRY	service industries, tourism, chemicals, textiles, machinery, forest products
AGRICULTURE	chickens, tobacco, nursery stock, beef cattle, dairy products, cotton

CAROLINA WREN   YELLOW JESSAMINE

Did you know?

1. Sandhills along the western edge of the coastal plain are the remains of beaches from an ancient sea that once covered the area.
2. Sullivans Island, off the coast of Charleston, is known as the Ellis Island of Slavery. It was here that more than 200,000 enslaved people from West Africa first set foot on American soil.
3. From the 1920s to the 1940s, South Carolina called itself the Iodine State to draw attention to the large quantities of this mineral found in its plants.
4. Francis Marion earned the nickname Swamp Fox for his legendary ability to stage raids against the British and then disappear into the swamps of southern South Carolina during the Revolutionary War.
5. The first French settlement in South Carolina was Parris Island, founded in 1562.

TENNESSEE

★ *Volunteer State* ★

IF YOU THINK Tennessee, think "three." Three stars on Tennessee's flag represent the three physical regions of the state: East, Middle, and West. They may also symbolize that it was the third state to join the Union after the original 13.

East Tennessee is row after row of ridges, topped by the Great Smoky Mountains. Named for the combination of mist and plant vapors that hover in the steep-walled valleys, the Smokies are home to an amazing diversity of plants and animals. This region also includes the deeply eroded Cumberland Plateau. These eastern highlands give way to the gently rolling lands of Middle Tennessee. A large oval basin, the region boasts rich agricultural lands perfect for livestock grazing and crop raising—especially tobacco and corn. West Tennessee is in the flatter and lower expanses of the wide Mississippi River Valley. Its fertile lands are known for growing cotton.

The state's principal river is the Tennessee. Beginning near Knoxville, the river flows southwest past Chattanooga into northern Alabama. But then it loops back into the state, flowing north into Kentucky where it joins the Ohio River. Earthquakes sloshed water from the Mississippi into a low-lying area to form Reelfoot Lake—Tennessee's only large natural lake.

Cherokee people living along rivers of East Tennessee called one of their towns Tanasie, and the region took this name. The French scouted and traded on the rivers by the late 1600s. When Britain gained control after the French and Indian War, Virginians began to migrate to green Tennessee valleys. In 1780 Fort Nashborough was founded on the Cumberland River. This settlement later became Nashville, the state capital. An estimated 70,000 people lived in the territory when Tennessee was added to the Union in 1796. A series of treaties forced the Chickasaw from

1812

Andrew Jackson became known as a fierce Indian fighter in the War of 1812 and worked for the removal of all Native Americans.

1863

During the Civil War, Union forces captured Chattanooga, which gave them control of an important rail center.

1934

Norris Dam was the first built under the Tennessee Valley Authority, which controlled flooding and provided electricity to rural areas.

Present day

The General Motors Saturn plant at Spring Hill is part of a growing manufacturing region in central Tennessee.

Crested by Clingmans Dome (opposite), Great Smoky Mountains National Park stretches along the border between Tennessee and North Carolina. The park is world-famous for the diversity of its plant and animal species.

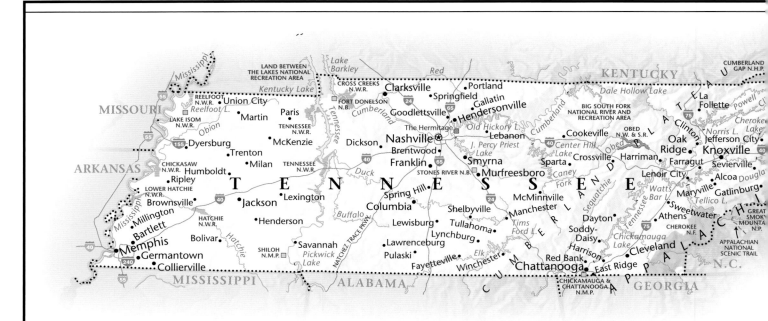

their lands in western Tennessee by 1818. After Tennessee native Andrew Jackson became President, he imposed treaties that removed remaining natives from the state in the 1830s.

Immigrants from the eastern states, Ireland, and Scotland set up small farms in the valleys of East Tennessee, while Southern cotton planters moved into western areas near the Mississippi. The Civil War found the state deeply divided. Though Tennessee became the last state to join the Confederacy, thousands of residents fought for the Union. Two bloody days of conflict at Shiloh in April 1862 took the lives of nearly 24,000 men.

Tennessee was first to be readmitted to the Union after the war, but tensions remained between whites and African Americans. The Ku Klux Klan was founded in Pulaski, Tennessee, in 1866. This racist group used threats and violence to keep freed slaves from enjoying the same rights as whites. While the state attempted to rebuild its agricultural economy after the war, there were long decades of poverty for many Tennessee small farmers, both black and white. Disease ravaged its cities, too, as cholera epidemics hit Nashville, and yellow fever killed thousands in Memphis in 1878.

In the depths of the Great Depression, the federal government launched the state into the industrial era. The Tennessee Valley Authority—or TVA—built dozens of dams along the Tennessee River and its tributaries for flood control, navigation, and electric power. The state used this new hydropower to produce aluminum, steel, weapons, chemicals, and textiles. During World War II, the U.S. government built a secret research facility at Oak Ridge where scientists worked to develop the atomic bomb.

Overall, Tennessee's future looks promising. Great Smoky Mountains National Park tops its tourism successes, attracting at least nine million visitors annually. But pollution from automobiles and distant power plants is threatening the park's health. Middle Tennessee has become a manufacturing hub, including auto assembly plants whose success is dependent on the strength of the nation's economy. And there's music—country in Nashville and blues in Memphis. Like a hard-working musical group, Tennessee's regions seek three-part harmony and prosperity for all.

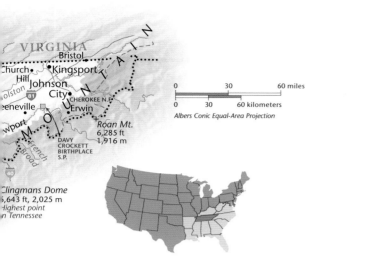

VIRGINIA
Bristol
Church
Hill
Kingsport
Johnson
City
olston
eneville
Erwin
CHEROKEE N.F.
81
wport
Roan Mt.
6,285 ft
1,916 m
DAVY
CROCKETT
BIRTHPLACE
S.P.
40

0   30   60 miles
0   30   60 kilometers
Albers Conic Equal-Area Projection

Clingmans Dome
6,643 ft, 2,025 m
Highest point
in Tennessee

TENNESSEE
Volunteer State

STATEHOOD	June 1, 1796; 16th state
CAPITAL	Nashville
LARGEST CITY	Memphis Population 648,882
TOTAL AREA	42,143 sq mi; 109,151 sq km
LAND AREA	41,217 sq mi; 106,752 sq km
POPULATION	6,346,105
POPULATION DENSITY	150 people per sq mi
MAJOR RACIAL/ ETHNIC GROUPS	77.6% white; 16.7% African American; 1.4% Asian; 0.3% Native American; Hispanic (any race) 4.6%.
INDUSTRY	service industries, chemicals, transportation equipment, processed foods, machinery
AGRICULTURE	cattle, cotton, dairy products, hogs, poultry, nursery stock

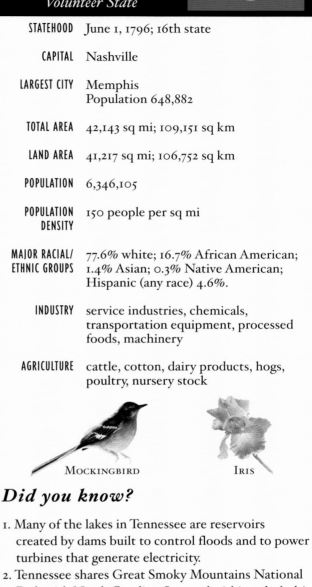

MOCKINGBIRD   IRIS

Did you know?

1. Many of the lakes in Tennessee are reservoirs created by dams built to control floods and to power turbines that generate electricity.
2. Tennessee shares Great Smoky Mountains National Park with North Carolina. Located within a day's drive of more than half the people in the United States, it is the most visited national park in the country.
3. Graceland, Elvis Presley's mansion in Memphis, is the most visited house in the United States after the White House.
4. Tennessee earned its nickname for its enthusiastic response to President Madison's call for volunteers during the War of 1812. The state sent 1,500 men to fight at New Orleans.
5. The National Civil Rights Museum is in Memphis's Lorraine Motel, site of the assassination of Martin Luther King, Jr. in 1968.

Nashville's Grand Ole Opry, first broadcast in 1925 as the "Barn Dance," is the world's longest-running live radio show. Hundreds of thousands of people attend performances of country music shows each year at the Opry, earning Tennessee's capital city the nickname Music City, USA. Nashville is also the site of the Country Music Hall of Fame and Museum.

VIRGINIA

★ *Old Dominion* ★

A STATE OF BEGINNINGS—and endings. That's Virginia. Jamestown's founding in 1607 marked the first successful English settlement in America. The American Revolution ended at Yorktown in 1781. Eighty-four years later the Civil War ended at Appomattox Courthouse. Of the first five presidents, four were Virginians.

From ocean-side Virginia Beach, it's more than a 440-mile (708-km) hike to reach the Cumberland Gap at the state's southwestern tip. The low, sandy plain that extends out from the Chesapeake Bay is known as the Tidewater region, because its inlets and rivers feel the pull of ocean tides. Next inland is the Piedmont, which reaches west to the base of the scenic Blue Ridge mountains. Beyond lie the rich farmlands of the Shenandoah Valley and the rugged Appalachian terrain. A small section of Virginia forms the southern tip of the Delmarva Peninsula, east of the Chesapeake Bay.

In the early 17th century, much of the continent not controlled by the Spanish or French was claimed by England and called Virginia (after Elizabeth I, who was known as the Virgin Queen). In 1607, an expedition sponsored by a merchant group named the Virginia Company established Jamestown along the James River. An attack led by Powhatan in 1622 killed not only a third of the colony's people but also the company, which lost its charter, or legal contract, for the land. Native American resistance was soon put down, and the territory was made a royal colony in 1624—the first in English history.

A plantation society eventually thrived in the Tidewater region, with fields of tobacco tended by thousands of African slaves. Small-scale farmers could not compete, and many moved west and south to pioneer new areas. By the 1760s, Virginians were bitter about increasing

1607

Pocahontas, by saving the life of John Smith, helped ensure the survival of Jamestown, first permanent English colony in America.

1781

The surrender of the British to George Washington at Yorktown ended the Revolutionary War and won independence for America.

1862

The first battle between ironclad ships was fought between the North's Monitor *and the South's* Virginia *at Hampton Roads.*

Present day

Supercomputers at Virginia Tech are a symbol of the state's growing reputation as the Silicon Valley of the East Coast.

At Colonial Williamsburg (opposite), a craftsman uses the same techniques Virginia bookmakers would have used in the 1700s to bind a book. The city has been restored to give visitors a glimpse of everyday life in Virginia's colonial capital city.

VIRGINIA
Old Dominion

STATEHOOD	June 25, 1788; 10th state
CAPITAL	Richmond
LARGEST CITY	Virginia Beach Population 433,934
TOTAL AREA	42,774 sq mi; 110,785 sq km
LAND AREA	39,594 sq mi; 102,548 sq km
POPULATION	8,001,024
POPULATION DENSITY	187 people per sq mi
MAJOR RACIAL/ ETHNIC GROUPS	68.6% white; 19.4% African American; 5.5% Asian; 0.4% Native American; Hispanic (any race) 7.9%.
INDUSTRY	food processing, communication and electronic equipment, transportation equipment, printing, shipbuilding, textiles
AGRICULTURE	tobacco, poultry, dairy products, beef cattle, soybeans, hogs

CARDINAL   FLOWERING DOGWOOD

Did you know?

1. King James had high hopes that Jamestown would be suitable for the production of silk. But the imported silkworms and mulberry seedlings did not thrive. Tobacco not silk saved the colony from financial ruin.
2. Arlington County was a portion of the land surveyed in 1791 to be part of the District of Columbia, but the land was returned to Virginia by the U.S. Congress.
3. Wild ponies have lived on Assateague Island for centuries. The ponies that live on the Virginia end of the island are owned by the Chincoteague Volunteer Fire Department. Each year in a roundup, young ponies swim to Chincoteague where they are auctioned off as a fund-raising event.
4. In 1989 Virginia voters elected the country's first African-American governor, Douglas Wilder.

British control and taxes. Many leaders in the movement for independence, including George Washington and Thomas Jefferson, were Virginians. The British were defeated in 1781. Virginia became the 10th state in 1788, with Richmond as its capital.

The debate over the continued use of slavery divided the country. Richmond was made capital of the Confederacy in 1861, and Virginia was a major battleground in the Civil War. At first, most conflicts fought on state soil were won by the South, but the tide turned by mid-1863. Richmond fell on April 3, 1865, and the South surrendered one week later.

The war left much of the state in ruins, and the end of slavery finished Virginia's plantation system. Virginia agriculture began to diversify. Tobacco was still the chief crop, but dairy farming expanded as did fruit and vegetable growing. The state industrialized, primarily in textiles, food processing, and ship-building. The deep-water harbor of the Hampton Roads area has long been a center of shipyards and naval bases. Virginia is also a major site for military training.

Today, Virginia's population is one of the most diverse in the nation. Proximity to Washington, D.C., and increased federal spending have boosted the state's economy and help keep employment up. Northern Virginia attracts defense and other high-tech research activities. Traffic and other growth-related issues abound, with new housing even springing up near historic battlefields. Although the state is known as the Old Dominion, Virginia is really in a constant state of new beginnings.

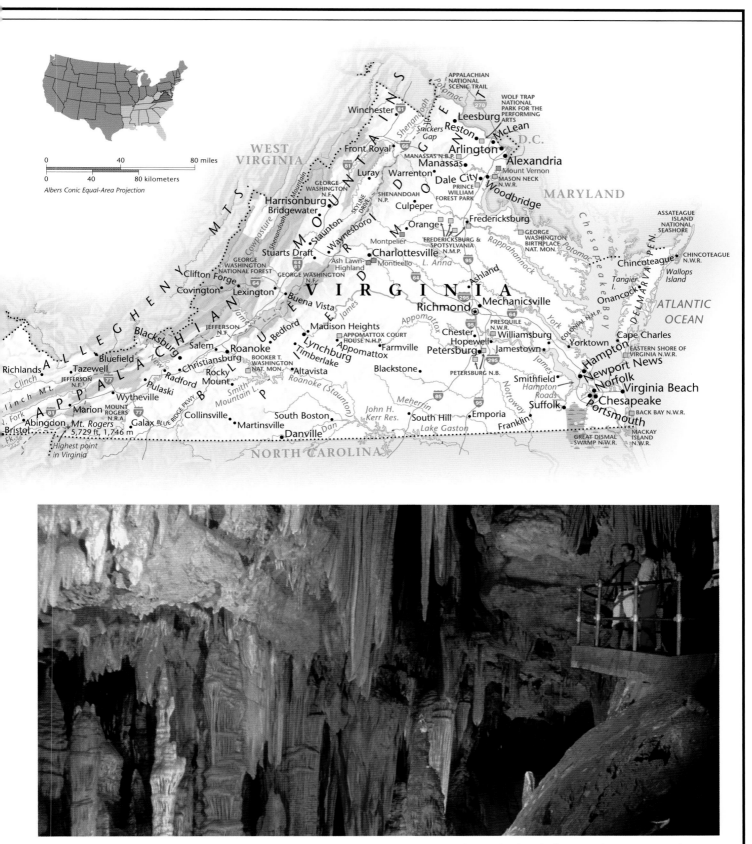

Virginia boasts more than 3,000 caves, mostly in or near the Shenandoah Valley. Acidic groundwater dissolves the limestone, leaving great underground chambers. In Luray Caverns (above), narrow passages open to "rooms" from 30 to 140 feet (9–43 m) high. Luray's stalactites (growing downward) and stalagmites (growing upward) add one cubic inch (16 cm³) to their length every 120 years as water deposits minerals on them.

WEST VIRGINIA

★ Mountain State ★

THE MOUNTAIN STATE is a rough-and-tumble landscape of steep ridges and deep valleys that is sometimes called the Colorado of the East. Enclosed within crooked boundaries that mostly follow winding rivers and uneven mountain tops, West Virginia's rugged isolation has helped shape the state's history and its people.

The thickly forested Appalachians acted as a barrier, keeping people from the east away. Many early German and Scotch-Irish settlers came from Pennsylvania, following long north-south valleys. In 1727 New Mecklenburg (now Shepherdstown) became the first permanent community. Native Americans defended their hunting grounds against the newcomers, but gave up claims to the region after a 1774 defeat.

Having little in common with wealthy, slave-holding Virginia planters who held political power over the region, people looked west to the Kanawha and Ohio Rivers for trade. Most held no slaves and did not want slavery in their region. They voted against secession from the Union in 1861. Outvoted, they decided to secede from Virginia instead. Two years later, West Virginia became the 35th state. Charleston was made its permanent capital in 1885.

The Mountain State's economy has had its highs and lows. Vast forests aboveground and abundant minerals below offered opportunities. Hardwood forests cover more than two-thirds of the state, and it has long produced lumber for the nation. Salt has been mined from the Charleston area since the early 1800s. Natural gas deposits made the state a leader in gas and oil production in the early 20th century.

But it was "Old King Coal" that really heated up state industrial growth. First discovered in the 1740s, vast deposits of soft bituminous coal lie beneath half the state. Coal provided fuel for salt and chemical works, iron and steel mills,

1859

Fiery abolitionist John Brown failed in his attempt to start a slave revolt by raiding the federal arsenal at Harpers Ferry.

1870

Stories about John Henry's skills as a steel-driving man working on the Big Bend Tunnel made him an American folk hero.

Early 1900s

As coal came to dominate the economy, labor union efforts to win better working conditions for men and boys led to mine wars.

Present day

Outdoor recreation seekers, such as these on the Gauley River, help make tourism one of West Virginia's chief businesses.

Adventurers of all kinds "dive" into West Virginia's beautiful deep valleys. Here a BASE (Building, Antenna, Span, Earth) jumper skydives off the 876-foot- (267-m-) high New River Gorge Bridge, an activity that is legal only on Bridge Day each October.

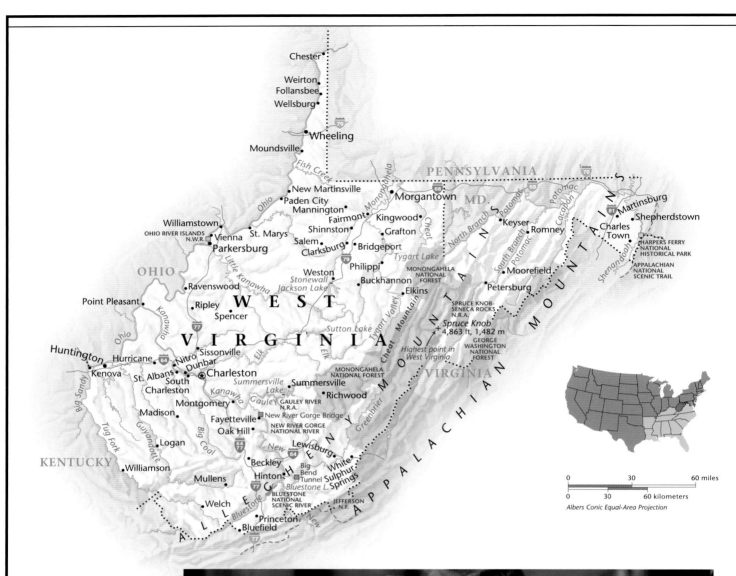

Glassmaking has long been a source of income and pride for West Virginia. Fine deposits of silica-rich sandstone provide the raw material, and natural gas furnishes the heat. Here, a glassmaker carefully shapes a fine vase in a glass works east of Huntington.

and glassworks. Steamboats paddled the state's rivers, and then trains, powered by coal, chugged through its mountains. They also transported the fuel—plus lumber and other resources—to homes and businesses across the nation. Immigrants, including whites from the North, blacks from the South, and Southern Europeans, found work in state mines and factories. Both world wars were boom times for West Virginia's economy. The chemical industry expanded and coal production peaked in 1947 with 176 million tons.

But coal mining brought darker times to the state. Years of breathing coal dust brought black lung disease to thousands of miners, and many more died in accidents. Pay was low, with workers too often mistreated and cheated by mining companies. Workers' attempts to get better wages and working conditions by unionizing often ended in violence. The Great Depression brought hard times but also U.S. laws allowing labor unions. By the 1950s, boom times for the nation's steel industry were over, and the market for coal was reduced. Later environmental laws favored cleaner-burning coal from western states. In 1983 unemployment reached a terrible 21 percent. Though West Virginia today trails only Wyoming as a coal producer, the fuel's importance as a job source is declining, and the state has much damage to repair from more than 150 years of mining.

In recent years West Virginia has turned to different resources—especially to its natural beauty—in attempts to strengthen its economy. The state's mostly rural residents work increasingly in service industries. Tourists love to hike the state's mountain trails, raft its rushing rivers, and sample its country crafts and culture. Like state residents, they seek to stay connected to the outside world but find serenity in West Virginia.

WEST VIRGINIA
Mountain State

STATEHOOD	June 20, 1863; 35th state
CAPITAL	Charleston
LARGEST CITY	Charleston Population 51,702
TOTAL AREA	24,230 sq mi; 62,755 sq km
LAND AREA	24,078 sq mi; 62,361 sq km
POPULATION	1,852,994
POPULATION DENSITY	76 people per sq mi
MAJOR RACIAL/ ETHNIC GROUPS	93.9% white; 3.4% African American; 0.7% Asian; 0.2% Native American; Hispanic (any race) 1.2%.
INDUSTRY	tourism, coal mining, chemicals, metal manufacturing, forest products, stone, clay, oil, and glass products
AGRICULTURE	poultry and eggs, cattle, dairy products, apples

CARDINAL   RHODODENDRON

Did you know?

1. Moundsville, in the northern panhandle, is one of the nation's oldest and largest Indian burial grounds.
2. The first rural free mail delivery in the United States started in Charles Town on October 1, 1896.
3. West Virginia's mean elevation of 1,500 feet (460 m) makes it the state with the highest average elevation east of the Mississippi.
4. Outdoor advertising began in Wheeling as early as the 1890s when the makers of Mail Pouch tobacco painted bridges and barns with words encouraging people to chew their product.
5. One of the most legendary family feuds in the United States involved the Hatfields, who lived on the West Virginia side of the Tug Fork River, and the McCoys, who lived on the Kentucky side. It lasted from 1863–1891.
6. West Virginia is the only state with two panhandles.

SASKATCHEWAN

MANITOBA

ONTARIO

MONT.

CANADA
U.S.

Lake of the
Woods

Rainy

Isle
Royale

Lake Superior

G
R
E
A
T

Souris

Lake
Sakakawea

Upper
Red Lake

Eagle Mt.
2,301 ft
701 m

Mt. Arvon
1,979 ft
603 m

Keweenaw
Peninsula

NORTH
DAKOTA

Badlands

Lower
Red Lake

Lake
Winnibigoshish

Upper Peninsula

WYO.

White Butte
+3,506 ft
1,069 m

Leech Lake

MINNESOTA

MICHIGAN

Strs. of Mackinac

Lake Hur.

Moreau

G
R
E

Lake
Oahe

Mille
Lacs
Lake

Mississippi

Timms Hill
1,951 ft
595 m
+

WISCONSIN

Menominee

Cheyenne

SOUTH
DAKOTA

White

Black
Hills
+
Harney Peak
7,242 ft
2,207 m

Lake
Sharpe

James

Missouri

Lake Francis
Case

A
T

Minnesota

Wisconsin

Lake
Winnebago

Lake Michigan

Lower
Peninsula

Muskegon

Saginaw B.

Niobrara

North Platte

Sand Hills

Big Sioux

Little Sioux

Hawkeye Point
1,670 ft
509 m
+

Cedar

I O W A

Iowa

Charles Mound
1,235 ft
376 m
+

Rock

Fox

Grand

Lake
St. Cla.

Panorama
Point
5,423 ft
1,653 m
+

South Platte

Platte

NEBRASKA

P
L
A
I
N
S

Missouri

Des Moines

Illinois

ILLINOIS

Wabash

INDIANA

Maumee

Wabash

1,550 ft
472 m +

Great Miami

Scio

Republican

Kansas

Smoky Hills

Smoky Hill

Mt. Sunflower
4,039 ft
1,231 m
+

KANSAS

Arkansas

Flint Hills

Neosho

Grand

MISSOURI

Missouri

Lake
of the
Ozarks

Taum
Sauk Mt.
1,772 ft
540 m
+

Black

Mississippi

White
1,257 ft
383 m +

Ohio

KENTUCKY

Cimarron

Red Hills

Harry S.
Truman
Reservoir

Ozark Plateau

Table
Rock Lake

Ohio

TENNESSEE

TEXAS

OKLAHOMA

ARKANSAS

0   150 miles

0   250 kilometers

Albers Conic Equal-Area Projection

MISSISSIPPI

ALABAMA

The Midwest

THE AMERICAN HEARTLAND stretches across the central United States from Ohio and the Great Lakes almost to the foothills of the Rocky Mountains. Several times in the last Ice Age giant glaciers flowed south from Canada across this gentle land, scooping out thousands of lakes in Minnesota, Wisconsin, and Michigan. Of these, the Great Lakes form the world's largest body of fresh water. Farther south, the ice sheets melted into countless streams that carried crushed rock and fine silt that account for the rolling hills and fertile prairie soils found throughout the lower Midwest.

There are giant rivers, too. The Ohio, Missouri, and a dozen other large rivers join the Mississippi to become the longest and most important river system in North America. Farther west in the Dakotas, sediments from rivers and ancient oceans have eroded into bizarre landforms called badlands. Nearby the Black Hills rise above the Great Plains.

Land of Plenty Under the Prairie Sky

A VAST LANDSCAPE of great forests and endless prairies, this mid-continental heartland adds geographic space and a rural spirit to the United States. Here the bold mark of nature appears in sudden tornadoes, great floods, and thunderstorms that drop hailstones the size of baseballs. Winters can be long and very cold, especially in the far north along the border with Canada. Yet each one ultimately dissolves into humid spring warmth that nurtures new crops, wildflowers, and migrating birds.

For centuries eastern woodland Indians farmed and fished while semi-nomadic prairie tribes hunted bison, elk, coyote, and other mammals on their grassy "American Serengeti." In the early 1600s French fur traders and missionaries arrived in the Great Lakes region and immediately became involved in long-standing Indian wars over territory and resources. In the 1760s France lost eastern portions of their Louisiana Territory to Britain after the French and Indian War and gave control of lands west of the Mississippi to Spain. These western lands were returned to France in 1800. America won the Northwest Territory—the area north of the Ohio River and west to the Mississippi—after the Revolution and then purchased French Louisiana in 1803.

American settlers came mostly from the Northeast. They clung to the densely forested rivers and shores of the Great Lakes and eastern prairie. Later, railroads bridged the Mississippi and steamed westward. The Homestead Act of 1862 made free tracts of land available to people looking for new places to live. Tall grasses grew in the fertile eastern prairie where rainfall was plentiful, but the thickly matted roots made the soil difficult to plow until the 1850s when John Deere's steel-bladed plow came into widespread use. Farther west the climate was drier, and the grasses were shorter. Farmers used windmills to pull water from underground reservoirs called aquifers. What had been described as the Great American Desert became vast fields of wheat. The Germans, Norwegians, Swedes, and others who came in great numbers cultivated an immense patchwork of fields that largely replaced the Native American way of life.

By 1900 the region had evolved into America's "breadbasket." Corn and soybeans thrive in a well-watered belt from Ohio to Iowa. Dairy farming flourishes in the cool, moist climate of Wisconsin and Minnesota. To the drier west, wheat rules in Kansas, Nebraska, and the Dakotas. Minneapolis grew as a grain-milling center. Cattle, hogs, and poultry are raised on large farms and feedlots across much of this region. By the end of the 19th century Chicago, St. Louis, Kansas City, and Omaha had become meat packing centers. Today, food processing is done in many rural towns. Rich deposits of iron ore and coal turned the Great Lakes region into a manufacturing empire. Steel mills and factories in Chicago, Gary, Detroit, and Cleveland employed a new wave of immigrants from Europe as well as African Americans migrating from the South. The watery highways that attracted Indians and settlers remain the principal routes for transporting grains and ores, while railroads and trucks carry manufactured goods to the rest of the country and beyond.

> "There was nothing but land...the material out of which countries are made."
>
> WILLA CATHER, *The Homesteader's World*

The population and economy of the Midwest is on the move once again. Corporate agribusiness is swallowing up traditional family farms. Computer and biotechnology firms are slowly replacing steel mills and automobile assembly plants, and expanding suburbs are causing farms to disappear. Commerce still centers on Chicago, one of the busiest air, rail, and shipping crossroads on the continent. New immigrants from Asia and Latin America arrive daily in search of jobs and a good life under the prairie sky.

Slaughtered almost to extinction, the bison (above) is still a symbol of the great rolling grasslands that covered much of the Midwest, where pigs, poultry, cattle, and dairy cows now reign. Most of the prairie has been planted in corn, soybeans, and wheat.

ILLINOIS

★ *Land of Lincoln* ★

PANCAKE FLAT—that's what most of Illinois is except for some northwest uplands and a strip of southwest hills. Until less than two centuries ago it was covered by tall, waving prairie grasses. Thousands of years ago, invading ice sheets ended their southward campaign in Illinois, grinding down landforms on their advance and leaving rich, dark soils during their retreat. Hundreds of south-flowing rivers drain to the Wabash, Ohio, and Mississippi—rivers that form most of the state's boundaries.

When French explorers Marquette and Joliet canoed down the Mississippi in 1673, they met people who called themselves the "Illini"—an Algonquin word for "men" or "warriors." The European newcomers founded Cahokia along the big river as the first Illinois settlement in 1699. British military forces and traders followed, and for a time they lived in harmony with the French and various Native American groups. Peace turned to conflict with the French and Indian War. In 1763 the victorious British took over the Illinois region.

The U.S. gained control two decades later, following independence. Illinois formed part of the Northwest Territory of 1787, and settlers swarmed to the region. Illinois became the 21st state in 1818, with its capital first in Kaskaskia and then Vandalia—both in the south. Abraham Lincoln, then an Illinois legislator, worked hard to get the capital moved in 1839 to Springfield, a more central location. Today, that city celebrates the 16th President's many accomplishments, and Illinois is often called the Land of Lincoln.

Where nature once raised grasses, settlers planted wheat. At first, the gummy soils proved tough to plow with wooden or iron blades. But that was before 1838, when a blacksmith named John Deere perfected his steel plow. The prairie

1673

French explorers Father Jacques Marquette and Louis Joliet were likely the first Europeans to enter the Illinois area.

1858

Views on slavery expressed by Abraham Lincoln in his debates with Stephen A. Douglas led to his election as President in 1860.

1908–1919

Rioting caused by racial tensions between blacks and whites in Chicago and other cities forced some people to move to safer places.

1955

The Fermi National Accelerator Laboratory near Batavia is one of the world's leading centers for the study of the atom.

Buildings of the "Loop," Chicago's main business district (opposite), are evidence of the decades when Chicago and New York City competed in raising ever-higher skyscrapers. The Sears Tower thrusts 1,454 feet (443 m) upward—the tallest building in the U.S.

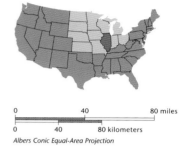

80 miles
80 kilometers
Albers Conic Equal-Area Projection

Illinois produces enormous crops of corn and soybeans on some of the most fertile farmland on the planet. Here a crew applies herbicide to soybeans, knowing they must be careful to select a chemical that will kill the weeds without damaging the crop or the soil. Some farmers have gone organic, which means they don't use chemicals on their fields.

had finally met its match. Farm machinery is still a top Illinois export, and the state usually ranks second in both corn and soybean production.

Beginning in the 1860s, Illinois grew into an industrial as well as an agricultural giant—with Chicago leading the way. Its fiery steel mills boomed, with iron ore shipped in from the Lake Superior region and coal hauled in by rail from downstate deposits. Immigrants from all across Europe plus African Americans from southern states came to work in huge and often dangerous slaughterhouses, foundries, and other factories. Protests and strikes erupted between management and workers, and unions were eventually organized to improve working conditions.

Chicago is one of the world's great cities. With almost three million people and a greater metro area population triple that, it's bigger than any other city between New York City and Los Angeles. With a great location at the southern end of Lake Michigan, Chicago has long been the top transportation center in the country—by water, rail, truck, and air. Though Chicagoland factories still churn out everything from steel and machinery to candy and gum, the industrial "city of the broad shoulders" increasingly processes ideas and information, too.

As they look forward, Illinois leaders tackle tough issues. The state has recently lost more than 160,000 manufacturing jobs, so keeping high-wage employment is a challenge. While four of five Illinois residents live in its cities, four of five state acres are farmed. But urban areas are sprawling out and taking over some of the world's best cropland. Some worry that Illinois should use that land to grow food. These and other struggles will test the minds of Illinois people as they face the future across their Prairie State.

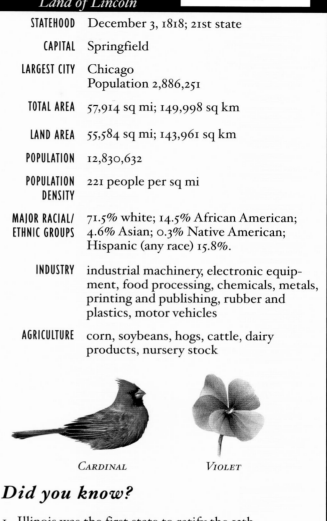

ILLINOIS
Land of Lincoln

STATEHOOD	December 3, 1818; 21st state
CAPITAL	Springfield
LARGEST CITY	Chicago Population 2,886,251
TOTAL AREA	57,914 sq mi; 149,998 sq km
LAND AREA	55,584 sq mi; 143,961 sq km
POPULATION	12,830,632
POPULATION DENSITY	221 people per sq mi
MAJOR RACIAL/ ETHNIC GROUPS	71.5% white; 14.5% African American; 4.6% Asian; 0.3% Native American; Hispanic (any race) 15.8%.
INDUSTRY	industrial machinery, electronic equipment, food processing, chemicals, metals, printing and publishing, rubber and plastics, motor vehicles
AGRICULTURE	corn, soybeans, hogs, cattle, dairy products, nursery stock

CARDINAL   VIOLET

Did you know?

1. Illinois was the first state to ratify the 13th Amendment to the U.S. Constitution, which made slavery illegal.
2. Between 1910 and 1930 Chicago's African-American population grew to nearly a quarter million, as the Great Migration brought black workers from the agricultural South to industrial cities in the North. The city also became a mecca for blues musicians, such as B.B. King, Memphis Minnie, and Muddy Waters.
3. On St. Patrick's Day the Chicago River is dyed green.
4. Chicago's nickname "Windy City" came from Charles Dana, editor of the New York *Sun,* who grew tired of hearing Chicagoans boast about the Columbian Exposition—the Chicago World's Fair of 1893.
5. The first controlled atomic chain reaction took place on a squash court at the University of Chicago in 1942 under the direction of physicist Enrico Fermi.

INDIANA
★ *Hoosier State* ★

"HOOSIER?" If someone knocked on the door of an early Indiana cabin, the pioneer inside might have called out "Who's here?" So goes one idea about how the state's nickname originated. Another is that a hardworking group of Indiana canal laborers were called Hoosier's Men, after their foreman. No one is certain, but Indiana's friendly, reliable people have been known by the name since the 1830s.

Indiana wears the results of ancient continental ice sheets across five-sixths of its land. Kettle lakes and huge piles of glacial gravel lie sprinkled across northern sections. A mixture of clay, sand, rocks, and other sediments called glacial till provides central Indiana's gentle landscape with fertile prairie soils. The state's southern reaches escaped these giant icy bulldozers and are more ruggedly landscaped with tree-covered hills and lowlands. Most of the state slopes gently to the southwest—draining to the Wabash River and from there to the Ohio River, which forms the southern border.

Early mound-building peoples left traces of their presence, but Algonquin peoples lived here when the French arrived in the 1670s. To protect their water route between the Great Lakes and the Mississippi River, the French constructed forts along Indiana rivers, including Vincennes on the lower Wabash. The earliest European settlement in the region, this became British property with the end of the French and Indian War in 1763. But in 1779, during the American Revolution, rebels from Kentucky seized Vincennes. Settlers poured in via this southern connection in the years that followed, leading to conflicts with Native Americans. The Battle of Tippecanoe in 1811 signaled the end of Native American control of the region. Most were forced to leave the land that the U.S. Congress named for them. The Indiana

1779

George Rogers Clark's capture of Vincennes from the British helped Americans gain control of the Northwest Territory.

1850s

The Underground Railroad, a network of escape routes that helped slaves find freedom, was very active in Indiana.

Early 1900s

Enormous mills built by U.S. Steel in Gary attracted migrant workers and laid the foundation for Indiana's steel industry.

Present day

The Indianapolis 500 auto race, held each Memorial Day weekend, attracts huge crowds and celebrates Indiana's auto heritage.

This covered bridge (opposite) is one of about 90 that are still preserved in Indiana. Built in the 19th century, these bridges were often the largest roofed area in a community, which made them good sites for weddings and political rallies.

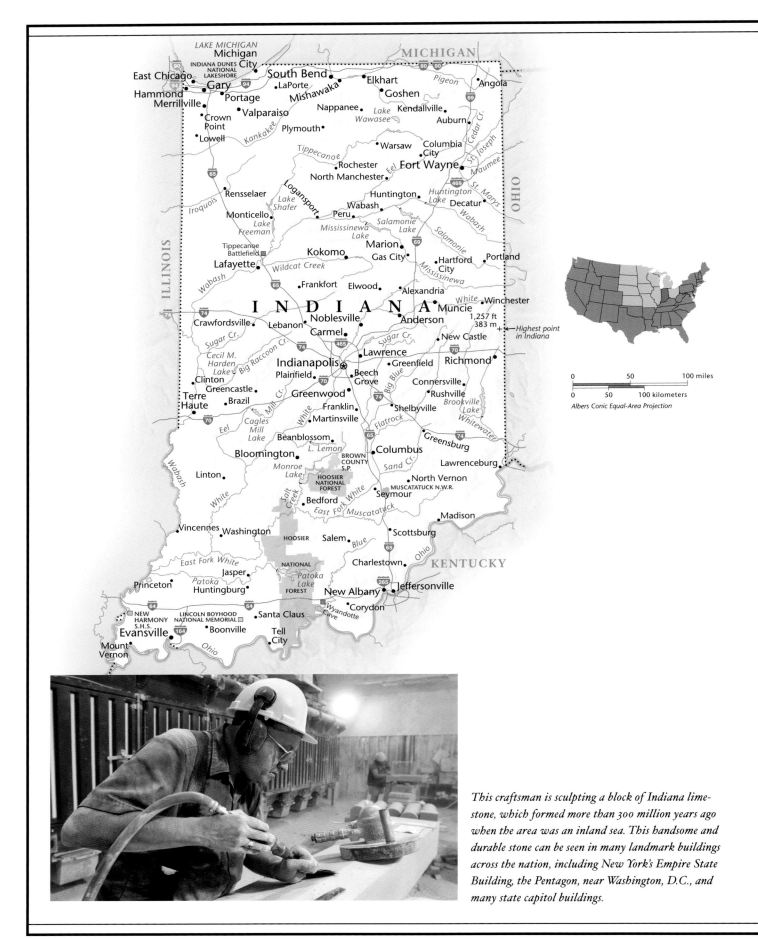

LAKE MICHIGAN

MICHIGAN

Michigan City

INDIANA DUNES NATIONAL LAKESHORE

East Chicago
Hammond
Gary
Portage
Merrillville
Valparaiso
Crown Point
Lowell

South Bend
LaPorte
Mishawaka
Elkhart
Goshen
Angola

Nappanee
Kendallville
Auburn

Lake Wawasee

Plymouth

Warsaw
Columbia City
Fort Wayne

Rochester
North Manchester

Huntington
Huntington Lake
Decatur

Rensselaer

Logansport
Lake Shafer
Wabash
Peru

Monticello
Lake Freeman

Kokomo
Mississinewa Lake
Salamonie Lake
Marion
Gas City
Hartford City
Portland

Tippecanoe Battlefield

Lafayette

Wildcat Creek

Frankfort
Elwood
Alexandria
Winchester

I N D I A N A
White
Muncie
1,257 ft
383 m
Highest point in Indiana

Crawfordsville
Lebanon
Noblesville
Carmel
Anderson
New Castle

Sugar Cr.

Cecil M. Harden Lake

Indianapolis
Lawrence
Greenfield
Richmond

Clinton
Plainfield
Beech Grove

Greencastle
Connersville

Terre Haute
Brazil
Greenwood
Rushville
Brookville Lake

Cagles Mill Lake
Franklin
Shelbyville

Martinsville
Flatrock

Beanblossom
Greensburg

L. Lemon
Columbus

Bloomington
BROWN COUNTY S.P.
Lawrenceburg

Monroe Lake
HOOSIER NATIONAL FOREST
North Vernon
MUSCATATUCK N.W.R.

Linton
Seymour

Bedford
East Fork White
Muscatatuck
Madison

Vincennes
Washington
Salem
Scottsburg

HOOSIER
Blue

East Fork White
NATIONAL
Charlestown
KENTUCKY

Jasper
Patoka Lake
Princeton
FOREST
New Albany
Jeffersonville

Huntingburg
Corydon

NEW HARMONY S.H.S.
LINCOLN BOYHOOD NATIONAL MEMORIAL
Santa Claus
Wyandotte Cave

Evansville
Boonville
Tell City

Mount Vernon
Ohio

ILLINOIS

OHIO

0   50   100 miles
0   50   100 kilometers
Albers Conic Equal-Area Projection

This craftsman is sculpting a block of Indiana limestone, which formed more than 300 million years ago when the area was an inland sea. This handsome and durable stone can be seen in many landmark buildings across the nation, including New York's Empire State Building, the Pentagon, near Washington, D.C., and many state capitol buildings.

Territory was separated from the larger Northwest Territory at the turn of the 19th century, and statehood was welcomed in 1816.

Abundant rains and warm summers made the state a farming leader. Indiana industry sprouted with the arrival of the railroads at mid-century. Manufactured goods were joined by a giant steel-making effort at the beginning of the 20th century. Labor movements got an early start in Indiana. By 1920, the state had almost three million people. Indiana's economy "bottomed out" during the Great Depression but boomed both during and after World War II, producing automobile parts, electrical goods, and communications equipment.

Indiana's central location gave rise to the nickname Crossroads of America. Indianapolis became an early hub of farm product shipping and processing. An early auto-making center that lost its lead to Detroit, the city celebrates each Memorial Day weekend with the famous Indianapolis 500 race. From bike racing to basketball, other sports also draw attention to the Hoosier State. College and university athletes from across the country are honored in the new NCAA Hall of Champions in Indianapolis.

Indiana's economy, like others in the region, is shifting from an emphasis on heavy industry to a more technology-oriented job market. As factories close, workers who were accustomed to high union wages often have to settle for lower paying jobs. But there are bright spots. The opening of automobile assembly plants has brought thousands of new jobs over the past two decades. Indiana continues to be a top-ranking agricultural state, and jobs in service industries, such as tourism and pharmaceuticals, are increasing. Overall the future looks promising for the Hoosier State's 6.2 million residents.

INDIANA
Hoosier State

STATEHOOD	December 11, 1816; 19th state
CAPITAL	Indianapolis
LARGEST CITY	Indianapolis Population 783,612
TOTAL AREA	36,418 sq mi; 94,321 sq km
LAND AREA	35,867 sq mi; 92,895 sq km
POPULATION	6,483,802
POPULATION DENSITY	178 people per sq mi
MAJOR RACIAL/ ETHNIC GROUPS	84.3% white; 9.1% African American; 1.6% Asian; 0.3% Native American; Hispanic (any race) 6.0%.
INDUSTRY	transportation equipment, steel, pharmaceutical and chemical products, machinery, petroleum, and coal
AGRICULTURE	corn, soybeans, hogs, poultry and eggs, cattle, dairy products

CARDINAL

PEONY

Did you know?

1. Indiana has more miles of interstate highway for each square mile of territory than any other state, and more major interstate highways intersect in Indiana than anywhere else in the country.
2. Between 1900 and 1920, more than 200 different kinds of cars, including Duesenburgs, Auburns, Stutzes, and Maxwells, were manufactured in Indiana.
3. John Chapman, better known as Johnny Appleseed, is buried in Archer Park in Fort Wayne. Every year Fort Wayne hosts the Johnny Appleseed Festival to commemorate the man who planted apple orchards from Pennsylvania to Illinois.
4. In 1880 Wabash became the first city in the country to be lighted by electric lights.
5. Johnny Gruelle, who got his start as a newspaper cartoonist in Indianapolis, created the Raggedy Ann doll.

IOWA

★ *Hawkeye State* ★

IOWA IS RICH from the ground up. Its soils are legendary—some layered hundreds of feet deep. More than nine of every ten acres of the state are used for agriculture. Long, warm summer days, plenty of rainfall, and winters that preserve plant nutrients combine to make Iowa croplands the envy of other farm states. The state produces more corn, soybeans, hogs, and eggs than any other. Iowa's treasure lies not in silver or gold but in abundant and fertile soil.

Iowa is held in the arms of two great rivers, the Mississippi to the east and Missouri to the west. Thousands of years ago massive sheets of ice from the north formed most of Iowa's gently-rolling landscape. Iowa's other streams flow in southerly paths to meet up with one of the two river giants. In some years, spring snowmelt or summer downpours cause flooding and damage along some or all of Iowa's rivers.

In the summer of 1673, French explorers Marquette and Joliet canoed down the Mississippi, meeting natives on its western shore who called themselves "the people." That word, translated and changed by French and later English speakers, is "Iowa." The region was not settled by large numbers of whites until the 1830s. Its prairie soils, which supported grasses as high as riders on horseback, were difficult to plow until the invention of the steel plow. The federal government fought the Sauk and Fox peoples for Iowa lands in the Black Hawk War in 1832. Within 20 years, most of the Native American groups were forced out to the west.

At first part of the Michigan and then the Wisconsin Territory, Iowa became the 29th state in late 1846. The state's population grew as immigrants from northern Europe arrived. Steamboats moved settlers in and goods out. The completion of a bridge over the Mississippi River at Davenport paved the way for the railroad.

1832

The defeat of the Sauk Indians at the Battle of Bad Axe along the Mississippi River helped open Iowa to white settlers.

1867

The arrival of the railroad at Council Bluffs opened a new and faster way to get goods to market. It also brought more settlers.

1930s

During the Depression, farmers seeking more money for their products tried to decrease supply by blocking roads to market.

1993

The Great Flood of 1993 was one of the worst in Iowa's history, causing more than two billion dollars in property damage.

Today, Iowa's farmers produce more than any previous generation. This bounty is due in part to the use of multipurpose agricultural machines (opposite), satellite weather data, and careful soil testing. Seed companies contribute by offering high-yield crop types.

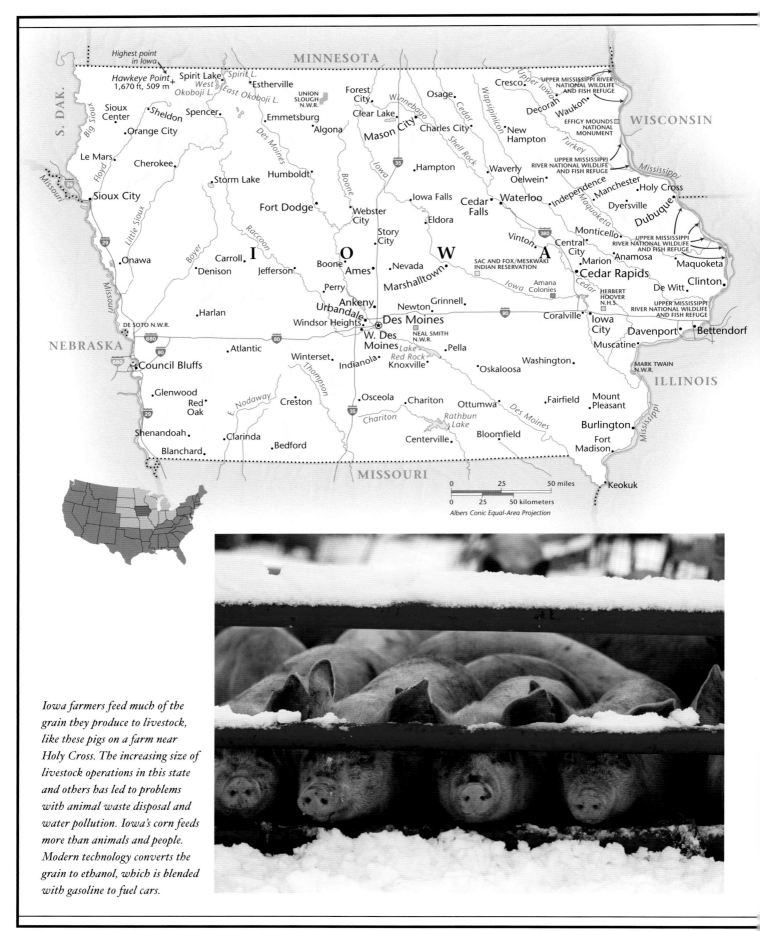

MINNESOTA

Highest point in Iowa
Hawkeye Point
1,670 ft, 509 m

Spirit Lake · Spirit L. · Estherville
West Okoboji L. · East Okoboji L.

S. DAK.

Sioux Center · Sheldon · Spencer · Emmetsburg · Algona · Forest City · Clear Lake · Mason City · Osage · Cresco · Decorah · Waukon

UNION SLOUGH N.W.R. · Winnebago · Charles City · New Hampton · Waverly · Oelwein

Orange City · Le Mars · Cherokee · Storm Lake · Humboldt · Fort Dodge · Webster City · Iowa Falls · Eldora · Cedar Falls · Waterloo · Independence · Manchester · Holy Cross · Dyersville · Dubuque

UPPER MISSISSIPPI RIVER NATIONAL WILDLIFE AND FISH REFUGE

EFFIGY MOUNDS NATIONAL MONUMENT

WISCONSIN

Sioux City · Onawa · Carroll · Denison · Jefferson · Boone · Ames · Nevada · Marshalltown · Vinton · Central City · Marion · Anamosa · Maquoketa · Monticello · Cedar Rapids · Clinton

I O W A

Story City

SAC AND FOX/MESKWAKI INDIAN RESERVATION

Amana Colonies

De Witt

Harlan · Perry · Ankeny · Urbandale · Windsor Heights · Des Moines · Newton · Grinnell · Coralville · Iowa City · Davenport · Bettendorf

DE SOTO N.W.R.

HERBERT HOOVER N.H.S.

NEBRASKA

W. Des Moines · NEAL SMITH N.W.R. · Muscatine

Atlantic · Winterset · Indianola · Pella · Washington

Lake Red Rock · Knoxville · Oskaloosa

Council Bluffs

ILLINOIS

Glenwood · Red Oak · Creston · Osceola · Chariton · Ottumwa · Fairfield · Mount Pleasant

MARK TWAIN N.W.R.

Shenandoah · Clarinda · Bedford · Centerville · Bloomfield · Burlington · Fort Madison

Blanchard

Rathbun Lake

MISSOURI

Keokuk

0   25   50 miles
0 25 50 kilometers
Albers Conic Equal-Area Projection

Iowa farmers feed much of the grain they produce to livestock, like these pigs on a farm near Holy Cross. The increasing size of livestock operations in this state and others has led to problems with animal waste disposal and water pollution. Iowa's corn feeds more than animals and people. Modern technology converts the grain to ethanol, which is blended with gasoline to fuel cars.

When men boarded trains to fight in the Civil War, women kept the farms going.

The completion of a railroad across the state after the war helped bring growth and prosperity. But good times were mixed with hard times in the late 1800s. Organizations like the Grange were formed to help insure farmers fair prices for their crops. With the development of cars and trucks in the early 20th century, Iowans built better roads to bring their crops to market, and in the 1930s rural electric cooperatives made power available to every house and farm. The Great Depression hit Iowa farmers hard, but World War II helped restore prosperity by boosting demand for farm products. Tough times returned in the 1980s, forcing thousands of farmers to go out of business. The state population fell by nearly 140,000 between 1980 and 1990.

Efforts to diversify the economy helped the population rebound to a slow-growing 2.9 million. But Iowa is still tied to its soil. Recent years have seen bigger farms but fewer farmers, who use huge machinery and satellite technology to precisely plant, weed, and harvest their sprawling fields. On average, one Iowa farm grows enough food to feed 280 people. Agriculture has long fed the state's chief industry—food processing—which includes cereal milling, meat packing, and even popcorn bagging. The manufacture of farm machinery, the sale of ethanol for fuel, and the use of wind farms to generate electricity are all sources of income for Iowa's farmers. Its cities are known for insurance, banking, and printing and publishing.

To ensure the future health of its agriculture and its citizens, Iowa plans to improve water quality by curbing farm run-off and to fight erosion by continuing conservation efforts to keep its rich soil right where it belongs.

IOWA
Hawkeye State

STATEHOOD	December 28, 1846; 29th state
CAPITAL	Des Moines
LARGEST CITY	Des Moines Population 198,076
TOTAL AREA	56,272 sq mi; 145,743 sq km
LAND AREA	55,869 sq mi; 144,701 sq km
POPULATION	3,046,355
POPULATION DENSITY	54 people per sq mi
MAJOR RACIAL/ ETHNIC GROUPS	91.3% white; 2.9% African American; 1.7% Asian; 0.4% Native American; Hispanic (any race) 5.0%.
INDUSTRY	real estate, health services, industrial machinery, food processing, construction
AGRICULTURE	hogs, corn, soybeans, oats, cattle, dairy products

AMERICAN GOLDFINCH   WILD ROSE

Did you know?

1. Iowa ranks as the nation's second largest agricultural producer after California.
2. In the 1800s Iowa's topsoil was as much as five feet (1.5 m) deep. Today, decades of farming have reduced it to an average depth of two feet (.6 m).
3. Iowa's nickname comes from Chief Black Hawk, a Sauk Indian chief who started what became known as the Black Hawk War in 1832.
4. The Amana Colonies, established in 1855 by people of German heritage who belonged to a religious group called the Community of True Inspiration, strived to achieve an ideal society that promoted equality, humility, and a simple way of life. In 1932 the community formed a corporation that became famous for making refrigerators, freezers, and air conditioners.
5. JollyTime, the first brand-name popcorn, originated in the Sioux City home of Cloid H. Smith in 1914.

KANSAS
★ Sunflower State ★

"HOME ON THE RANGE." Every American has heard—and sung—the song in school, but it was a Kansas doctor, Brewster Higley, who wrote the famous lyrics. His song describes an ideal 19th-century farming life of happy homesteads where "the skies are not clouded all day." Most Kansans would probably still agree with him about their prairie state.

The landscape of Kansas is mostly low, rolling hills, with wooded river valleys in its eastern half. Its surface slopes gently upward from Missouri to Colorado. In the east, the rocky Flint Hills preserve a 50-mile- (80-km-) long swath of prairie. The iron-colored Red Hills in the southwest and the fossil-rich Smoky Hills in the state's north-central section reveal that much of Kansas was the bottom of a vast shallow sea millions of years ago. Fossil hunters once competed for the best examples of prehistoric specimens for museums and collectors.

The state takes its name from the Kansa—"people of the south wind"—but winds are not always kind to Kansas. Storms produce hail that can ruin crops and property. Tornadoes twist their way across the Sunflower State, and blizzards howl in winter. Precipitation levels are higher in the east. The rain and snow, combined with fine soil conditions, were perfect for growing eye-high bluestem grass that covered the region before settlers arrived. Rainfall declines to the west, where shorter grasses dominate.

In 1541, the Spanish explorer Francisco Vásquez Coronado searched here in vain for a city of gold. Wichita, Cheyenne, Osage, and Kiowa peoples—among others—called the region home. U.S. control came in 1803 with the Louisiana Purchase, and the Santa Fe Trail brought settlers and traders in the 1820s. But most considered the land here unfit to settle, so eastern Kansas was set up to be used as land for

1856

The violence caused when Border Ruffians from Missouri tried to get Kansas to vote for slavery led to the nickname Bleeding Kansas.

1870s

Railroad expansion and a movement to drive Native Americans out of Kansas led to the slaughter of millions of bison.

1890s–1911

Carry A. Nation, who smashed saloons with her hatchet, was part of the reform movement that was given voice by the Populist Party.

Present day

The aviation industry, which developed after World War II, now contributes more to the state's economy than wheat does.

No other state grows wheat like Kansas (opposite). While drought and storms cause output to vary from year to year, the state produced 480 million bushels in 2003 to make it the nation's number one producer of this grain.

KANSAS
Sunflower State

STATEHOOD	January 29, 1861; 34th state
CAPITAL	Topeka
LARGEST CITY	Wichita Population 355,126
TOTAL AREA	82,277 sq mi; 213,096 sq km
LAND AREA	81,815 sq mi; 211,900 sq km
POPULATION	2,853,118
POPULATION DENSITY	34 people per sq mi
MAJOR RACIAL/ ETHNIC GROUPS	83.8% white; 5.9% African American; 4.8% Asian; 1.0% Native American; Hispanic (any race) 10.5%.
INDUSTRY	aircraft manufacturing, transportation equipment, construction, food processing, printing and publishing, health care
AGRICULTURE	cattle, wheat, sorghum, soybeans, hogs, corn

WESTERN MEADOWLARK

SUNFLOWER

Did you know?

1. So many fossils were found in Kansas in the late 1800s that competing paleontologists launched the "Kansas Fossil Wars," resorting to bribes and trickery to get the best specimens.
2. Dry air and a constant temperature of 68.5°F (20.3°C) in the underground chambers of an old salt mine near Hutchinson make them ideal for storing valuables, including thousands of original Hollywood movies.
3. Barton County is named for Clara Barton, famed Civil War nurse and founder of the American Red Cross.
4. Pizza Hut, the world's largest pizza company, opened its first restaurant in Wichita in 1958.
5. Samuel Perry Dinsmoor used 113 tons of concrete to create the Garden of Eden, in Lucas, Kansas. Visitors can still see Dinsmoor, who died in 1932. He lies in a concrete tomb with a glass top.

Rail towns like Dodge City and Abilene were once destinations for cattle drives from Texas. Kansas is still cattle country, producing 6.6 million cattle and calves in 2004—enough for every Kansan to herd two or three. But crowded feedlots, not open range, are where many cattle spend their time these days. The chance, however unlikely, of mad cow disease finding a route to its feedlots keeps Kansas on its guard.

the relocation of Native Americans in the 1830s. But within two decades, Congress decided that the land was needed for white settlement after all.

The Kansas-Nebraska Act of 1854 brought waves of immigrant settlers and allowed them to vote whether or not they wanted slavery. Newcomers began pushing Native Americans out, and groups for and against slavery battled each other. Pro-slavery "Border Ruffians" attacked Lawrence and other cities in 1856, and famous anti-slavery fighter John Brown led a raid in return. Kansas finally joined the Union as a free state in 1861, just before the Civil War.

Kansas boomed after the war. Within a few decades, enormous herds of bison that once roamed free were wiped out, and beef cattle took their place. Cowboys drove longhorns north from Texas to the railroad at Dodge City and

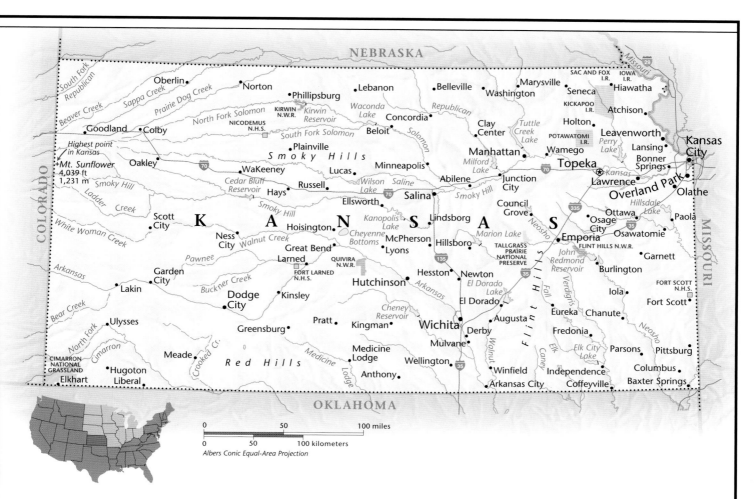

Abilene. While cattle were bought, gunfights were fought. Storybook lawmen like Bat Masterson, Wild Bill Hickok, and Wyatt Earp really did battle outlaws here in the Wild West. Another famous Kansas battler, Carry Nation, helped lead the temperance movement to control alcohol in the late 19th and early 20th centuries.

Two world wars sparked food demand, and Kansas reaped farming benefits. Then drought hit with the terrible Dust Bowl of the 1930s. Thousands left the state, but Kansas fought back with groundwater irrigation in the west and better conservation methods overall. Soon known as the breadbasket of America, Kansas still produces more wheat than any other state. Kansas is also a leader in sorghum, a grain used for livestock feed.

The state's industrial economy soared in the 20th century with airplane manufacturing based in Wichita. Meat-packing facilities have long prepared state beef for market. Huge military bases add thousands of jobs to the economy. Oil and natural gas wells dot the Kansas plains, and it is one of the few sources of helium, a gas used to float blimps and balloons.

Today, the majority of the 2.7 million Kansans live in its eastern cities. Hispanics make up the largest minority, followed by African Americans and Asians. The country recently marked the anniversary of the famous Brown v. Board of Education of Topeka court case that helped integrate the nation's schools. Looking to the future, the state seeks to expand an emerging medical sciences business, while keeping its industry, military bases, and agriculture intact. Yes, most Kansans would seldom say a "discouraging word" about their "Home on the Range."

MICHIGAN

★ *Great Lake State* ★

GREAT LAKE STATE is the perfect nickname for Michigan, with its two huge peninsulas surrounded by the country's four largest lakes: Superior, Huron, Michigan, and Erie. The state's real name is from the Chippewa word *"micigama,"* meaning "great lake."

Michigan's Upper Peninsula extends east from Wisconsin, and its Lower Peninsula juts north from Ohio and Indiana. The "Big Mac" bridge links the two at the five-mile- (8-km-) wide Straits of Mackinac. The lakes provided easy transport routes for the French in the 17th century, when they met and traded furs with Ojibwa, Ottawa, and Potawatomi peoples. Father Marquette established the first European settlement at Sault Sainte Marie in 1668.

The British defeated the French here during the French and Indian War then abandoned the region to the United States by 1796. The Michigan Territory was formed in 1805, and

New Englanders moved in, farming and building towns. By 1837, Michigan had gained the resource-rich Upper Peninsula and statehood.

For decades, Upper Peninsula mines led the U.S. in iron and copper output. Michigan also produced salt, gypsum, and oil. Loggers cut white pines on both peninsulas. Railroads and steamships hauled cargo to market, a task made easier by the completion of locks on the Soo Canals that linked Lakes Superior and Huron.

By the late 1800s, the iron and steel industry had grown strong here, ignited by several "horseless carriage" pioneers, including Henry Ford. He built an assembly line in 1913 and began mass producing cars. Assembly-line jobs gave rise to labor unions and attracted immigrants—huge numbers of African Americans from southern states plus Germans, Hungarians, Poles, Irish, Ukrainians, and Italians. During World War II, auto factories were converted to military uses, and

1763–1766

Chief Pontiac's efforts to drive the British from the region ended in defeat for the Ottawa, who were forced to sign a peace treaty.

1855

The completion of the Soo Canal provided a means of shipping iron ore mined on the Upper Peninsula to steel centers on the Great Lakes.

1913

The introduction of the auto assembly line at the Highland Park Ford Plant revolutionized mass production in industry.

Present day

Battle Creek, headquarters of cereal giants Post and Kelloggs, has long been a center for nutrition research.

Though Detroit's wheels have slowed in recent decades with changes in the auto industry (opposite), it is still known as the Motor City. Michigan produced more than one out of every five of the nation's motor vehicles in 2003.

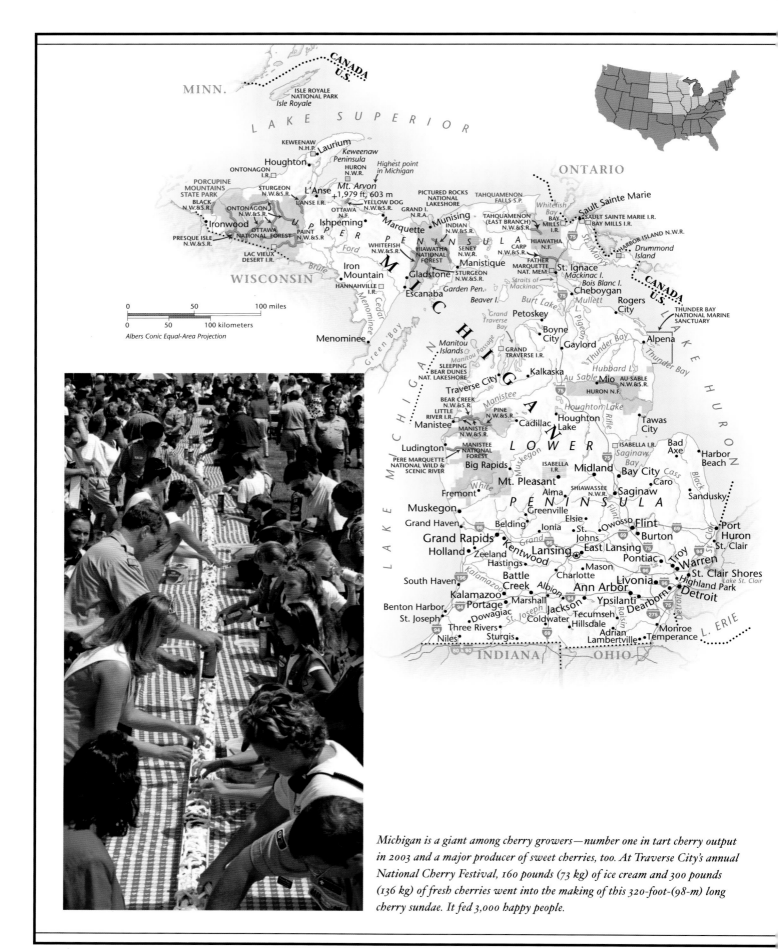

CANADA
U.S.

MINN.

ISLE ROYALE
NATIONAL PARK
Isle Royale

L A K E   S U P E R I O R

ONTARIO

KEWEENAW
N.H.P.
Laurium
Houghton
*Keweenaw
Peninsula*

ONTONAGON
I.R.
HURON
N.W.R.
*Highest point
in Michigan*

PORCUPINE
MOUNTAINS
STATE PARK
BLACK
N.W.&S.R.
STURGEON
N.W.&S.R.
L'Anse
L'ANSE I.R.
Mt. Arvon
+1,979 ft, 603 m
YELLOW DOG
N.W.&S.R.
OTTAWA
N.F.
PICTURED ROCKS
NATIONAL
LAKESHORE
GRAND I.
N.R.A.
TAHQUAMENON
FALLS S.P.

Sault Sainte Marie

*Whitefish
Bay*
BAY
MILLS
I.R.
SAULT SAINTE MARIE I.R.
BAY MILLS I.R.

Ironwood
ONTONAGON
N.W.&S.R.
OTTAWA
NATIONAL   FOREST
PRESQUE ISLE
N.W.&S.R.
PAINT
N.W.&S.R.
Ishpeming
Marquette
Munising
INDIAN
N.W.R.
TAHQUAMENON
(EAST BRANCH)
N.W.&S.R.
CARP
N.W.&S.R.
FATHER
MARQUETTE
NAT. MEM.
HIAWATHA
N.F.
HARBOR ISLAND N.W.R.
*Drummond
Island*

LAC VIEUX
DESERT I.R.
U P P E R   P E N I N S U L A
WHITEFISH
N.W.&S.R.
HIAWATHA
NATIONAL
FOREST
SENEY
N.W.R.
Manistique
St. Ignace
Mackinac I.
Bois Blanc I.

CANADA
U.S.

Ford
Brule
Iron
Mountain
STURGEON
N.W.&S.R.
Gladstone
Escanaba
HANNAHVILLE
I.R.
Garden Pen.
Beaver I.
*Straits of
Mackinac*
Cheboygan
Rogers
City
THUNDER BAY
NATIONAL MARINE
SANCTUARY

WISCONSIN

Cedar
Menominee
Menominee

M I C H I G A N

Green Bay

Burt Lake
*Mullett
L.*
Petoskey
Boyne
City
Gaylord
L. pigeon
Thunder Bay
Alpena
Thunder Bay

50   100 miles
0   50   100 kilometers
Albers Conic Equal-Area Projection

*Grand
Traverse
Bay*
*Manitou
Islands*
*Manitou
Passage*
GRAND
TRAVERSE I.R.
SLEEPING
BEAR DUNES
NAT. LAKESHORE
Traverse City
Kalkaska
Au Sable
Mio
AU SABLE
N.W.&S.R.
Hubbard L.

L A K E   H U R O N

Manistee
BEAR CREEK
N.W.&S.R.
LITTLE
RIVER I.R.
PINE
N.W.&S.R.
Cadillac
L O W E R
Houghton
Lake
HURON N.F.
Houghton Lake
Rifle
Tawas
City

Manistee
MANISTEE
N.W.&S.R.
MANISTEE
NATIONAL
FOREST
Muskegon
ISABELLA I.R.
*Saginaw
Bay*
Bad
Axe
Harbor
Beach

Ludington
PERE MARQUETTE
NATIONAL WILD &
SCENIC RIVER
Big Rapids
ISABELLA
I.R.
Midland
Bay City
Cass
Caro
Black
Sandusky

Fremont
Mt. Pleasant
SHIAWASSEE
N.W.R.
Alma
Saginaw
P E N I N S U L A

White
Greenville
Elsie
Owosso
Flint
Burton
Port
Huron

Muskegon
Belding
Ionia
St.
Johns
Flint
East Lansing
St. Clair

Grand Haven
Grand
Grand Rapids
Kentwood
Lansing
Pontiac
Troy
Warren

Holland
Zeeland
Hastings
Charlotte
Mason
Livonia
St. Clair Shores
Highland Park
Lake St. Clair

South Haven
Kalamazoo
Battle
Creek
Albion
Ann Arbor
Dearborn
Detroit

Kalamazoo
Marshall
Jackson
Ypsilanti
Detroit

Benton Harbor
Portage
St. Joseph
Dowagiac
Coldwater
Tecumseh
Hillsdale
Adrian
Monroe
Temperance
L. ERIE

St. Joseph
Three Rivers
Niles
Sturgis
Lambertville

INDIANA
OHIO

*Michigan is a giant among cherry growers—number one in tart cherry output
in 2003 and a major producer of sweet cherries, too. At Traverse City's annual
National Cherry Festival, 160 pounds (73 kg) of ice cream and 300 pounds
(136 kg) of fresh cherries went into the making of this 320-foot-(98-m) long
cherry sundae. It fed 3,000 happy people.*

the state earned the name Arsenal of Democracy.

The state's auto-making methods spread abroad, and by the 1970s, foreign competition had slowed Detroit's momentum. The city declined along with its top industry. It has lost jobs and fully half its population in the past few decades. Racial tensions, which had flared violently during the 1940s, erupted again into riots in 1967. The city has worked hard since to address racial concerns and to restart its economy.

Low rolling hills spread across the Lower Peninsula's southern half, while a higher plateau of birches, aspens, and oaks covers the northern half. Towering along Lake Michigan's shore are rows of sand dunes, which are a popular tourist attraction. The climate here is also perfect for fruit, and Michigan ranks as the top producer of cherries and blueberries. Pine forests dominate the wild "U.P." Black bear and white-tailed deer abound, while moose and wolves still live on Isle Royale in Lake Superior. Winter brings snow-sports enthusiasts to ski resorts, and summer vacationers enjoy water activities on the state's more than 10,000 lakes.

Today, nearly 90 percent of the state's 10.1 million people live south of a line stretching from Muskegon to Bay City. This ethnically diverse state includes the largest group of Arab peoples in the country. Detroit ("Motown") is a national hub of African-American entertainment and culture.

Michigan still ranks as the U.S. leader in automobile and parts production but is also known for a variety of other products, ranging from chemicals to breakfast food. Michigan is working hard to diversify its economy, focusing on service and high-technology businesses. This will be a long, difficult process, but Michigan people are fortunate to be able to count on the resources of their two big peninsulas and four Great Lakes.

MICHIGAN
Great Lake State

STATEHOOD	January 26, 1837; 26th state
CAPITAL	Lansing
LARGEST CITY	Detroit Population 925,051
TOTAL AREA	96,716 sq mi; 250,494 sq km
LAND AREA	56,804 sq mi; 147,121 sq km
POPULATION	9,883,640
POPULATION DENSITY	102 people per sq mi
MAJOR RACIAL/ ETHNIC GROUPS	78.9% white; 14.2% African American; 2.4% Asian; 0.6% Native American; Hispanic (any race) 4.4%.
INDUSTRY	motor vehicles and parts, machinery, metal products, office furniture, tourism, chemicals
AGRICULTURE	dairy products, cattle, vegetables, hogs, corn, nursery stock, soybeans, hay, fruit

ROBIN

APPLE BLOSSOM

Did you know?

1. Michigan's unique location on the Great Lakes gives it a range of climates for growing a variety of farm products. It is second only to California in crop diversity.
2. The largest registered Holstein herd of dairy cows lives in a town called Elsie.
3. The first tunnel that allowed motor vehicles to travel between two countries connects Detroit and Windsor, Ontario, in Canada.
4. Although Michigan is sometimes known as the Wolverine State because of the many wolverine pelts traded by early trappers, none of these animals are left in the state.
5. Isle Royale was designated an International Biosphere Reserve in 1980. The wolf/moose predator-prey study conducted there is the longest running such study in the world.

MINNESOTA

★ *Gopher State* ★

AWASH IN WATER—falling, flowing, still, and marshy—that's Minnesota. The state borders the greatest of the Great Lakes—Superior—and is the source of the country's mightiest river—the Mississippi. State license plates read "Land of 10,000 Lakes." Minnesotans might mention that there are actually twice that many or more. "Minnesota" comes from a Dakota term meaning "cloudy water," describing the light-colored clay suspended in the Minnesota River.

While thick woods and lakes cover Minnesota's gravelly northern third, its central and southwest areas are nearly treeless plains with soils perfect for farming. Its many rivers flow in three directions. The Mississippi drains south to the Gulf of Mexico. Northern rivers flow east to Lake Superior or north into Canada.

When French fur traders scouted Minnesota lands and waters in the late 17th century, they met eastern Dakota peoples. Within decades, rival Ojibwas armed with French guns pushed the Dakota southwest into the prairies. The territory came under American control by 1818. The U.S. Army established Fort Snelling as a key frontier outpost in the 1820s. Most of the Minnesota Territory was opened for settlement by 1851, and the 32nd state joined the Union in 1858. Fierce conflict soon arose between the settlers and the Dakota, and the Indians were largely driven north to Canada and west to the Dakota Territory. For the next half-century, Minnesota's tall timber, fertile soils, and mineral resources attracted waves of newcomers, especially from Norway, Sweden, and Germany.

Over several decades, Minnesota's vast pine forests were largely clear-cut for lumber. Eventually, many cut-over areas were reforested and are today national, state, and private forests. The use of smaller trees for pulpwood and paper has helped to keep timber an important

1680

Father Louis Hennepin, while held captive by the Dakota, was the first white person to see the site that is now Minneapolis.

1862

Outrage over the Dakota attack on New Ulm caused the Indians to be forced out of Minnesota, opening the land to white settlers.

1880s—1950s

Workers like these mined hematite iron ore from rich deposits in the Mesabi Range. Today, lower grade taconite iron ore is mined.

Present day

Each year 42 million people visit Bloomington's Mall of America, largest enclosed retail/ family entertainment complex in the U.S.

Minnesotans and visitors alike treasure great scenery, peace, and terrific fishing on the state's amazing number and variety of lakes. A lone boater (opposite) motors across a misty Lake Winnibigoshish—called Lake Win-nee by locals—near Grand Rapids.

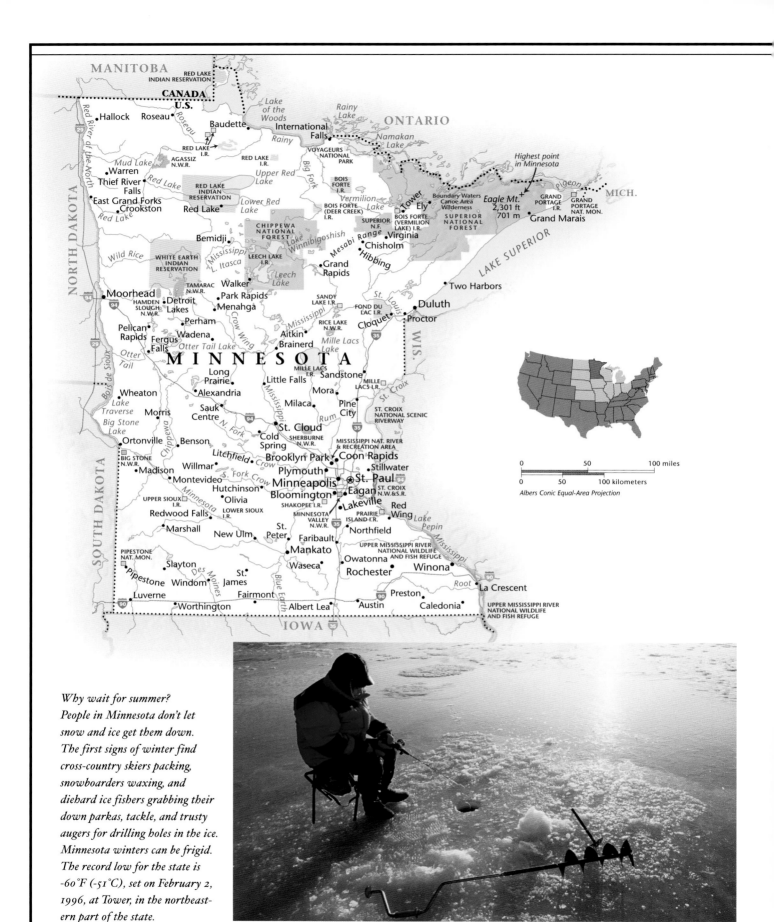

MINNESOTA

MANITOBA

RED LAKE INDIAN RESERVATION

CANADA
U.S.

Hallock • Roseau •

Baudette •

Lake of the Woods

International Falls

Rainy Lake

ONTARIO

Namakan Lake

VOYAGEURS NATIONAL PARK

Rainy

Red River of the North

Highest point in Minnesota

Pigeon

MICH.

RED LAKE I.R.

AGASSIZ N.W.R.

RED LAKE I.R.

Upper Red Lake

BOIS FORTE I.R.

Vermilion Lake

Tower • Ely •

Boundary Waters Canoe Area Wilderness

Eagle Mt. 2,301 ft 701 m

GRAND PORTAGE I.R.

GRAND PORTAGE NAT. MON.

Warren •
Thief River Falls •

Red Lake

RED LAKE INDIAN RESERVATION

Lower Red Lake

BOIS FORTE (DEER CREEK) I.R.

BOIS FORTE (VERMILION LAKE) I.R.

SUPERIOR N.F.

SUPERIOR NATIONAL FOREST

Grand Marais •

East Grand Forks •
Crookston •

Red Lake •

Mud Lake

Red Lake

NORTH DAKOTA

Bemidji •

CHIPPEWA NATIONAL FOREST

Lake Winnibigoshish

Mesabi Range

Virginia •
Chisholm •
Hibbing •

LAKE SUPERIOR

Wild Rice

WHITE EARTH INDIAN RESERVATION

L. Itasca

Mississippi

LEECH LAKE I.R.

Grand Rapids •

Two Harbors •

Moorhead •

Detroit Lakes •

TAMARAC N.W.R.

Walker •

Leech Lake

Park Rapids •
Menahga •

SANDY LAKE I.R.

FOND DU LAC I.R.

Duluth •

HAMDEN SLOUGH N.W.R.

Perham •

Crow Wing

Mississippi

St. Louis

Cloquet •
Proctor •

Pelican Rapids •

Wadena •

Aitkin •

RICE LAKE N.W.R.

WIS.

Fergus Falls •

Otter Tail Lake

Brainerd •

Mille Lacs Lake

Otter Tail

MINNESOTA

MILLE LACS I.R.

Sandstone •

Long Prairie •

Little Falls •

MILLE LACS I.R.

St. Croix

Wheaton •

Alexandria •

Mora •

Pine City •

ST. CROIX NATIONAL SCENIC RIVERWAY

Lake Traverse

Sauk Centre •

Milaca •

Bois de Sioux

Big Stone Lake

Morris •

Rum

Ortonville •

Benson •

Litchfield •

St. Cloud •

SHERBURNE N.W.R.

MISSISSIPPI NAT. RIVER & RECREATION AREA

BIG STONE N.W.R.

Cold Spring •

Brooklyn Park •

Coon Rapids •

Stillwater •

Madison •

Willmar •

Plymouth •

Minneapolis •

⊛ St. Paul

SOUTH DAKOTA

Montevideo •

Hutchinson •

Bloomington •

Eagan •

ST. CROIX N.W.&S.R.

UPPER SIOUX I.R.

Olivia •

LOWER SIOUX I.R.

SHAKOPEE I.R.

Lakeville •

PRAIRIE ISLAND I.R.

Red Wing •

Lake Pepin

Redwood Falls •

MINNESOTA VALLEY N.W.R.

Northfield •

Mississippi

Marshall •

New Ulm •

St. Peter •

Faribault •

PIPESTONE NAT. MON.

Slayton •

Des Moines

St. James •

Mankato •

Waseca •

Owatonna •

UPPER MISSISSIPPI RIVER NATIONAL WILDLIFE AND FISH REFUGE

Winona •

Pipestone •

Windom •

Rochester •

Root

La Crescent •

Luverne •

Worthington •

Fairmont •

Albert Lea •

Austin •

Preston •

Caledonia •

UPPER MISSISSIPPI RIVER NATIONAL WILDLIFE AND FISH REFUGE

Blue Earth

IOWA

0   50   100 miles
0   50   100 kilometers
Albers Conic Equal-Area Projection

*Why wait for summer?
People in Minnesota don't let
snow and ice get them down.
The first signs of winter find
cross-country skiers packing,
snowboarders waxing, and
diehard ice fishers grabbing their
down parkas, tackle, and trusty
augers for drilling holes in the ice.
Minnesota winters can be frigid.
The record low for the state is
-60°F (-51°C), set on February 2,
1996, at Tower, in the northeastern part of the state.*

Minnesota business. While wheat had grown to be the top crop by 1870, other grains and dairy farming gained importance later on. It is still a bountiful farm state, where farmers grow oats, corn, and soybeans, raise pigs and cows, and produce milk and cheese.

In 1865, rich deposits of iron ore were found in northeastern Minnesota's Mesabi Range. Mining boomed, with more than a hundred open pits by 1900. Transported to Duluth then shipped to blast furnaces along Lakes Erie and Michigan, Minnesota iron ore became U.S. steel. The state has led the nation in iron ore production ever since.

Minneapolis grew up around the Falls of St. Anthony, where the Mississippi's power was used to grind acres of wheat and cut miles of timber. Just ten miles downstream, St. Paul became Minnesota's capital. Water highways and railroad empires helped make the "Twin Cities" a premier trading and market center, serving areas all the way to the Pacific. Innovative manufacturing of plastics and other products followed. Nearly three-quarters of the people now live in cities big and small, producing processed foods, machinery, paper, printed materials, and chemical products.

Minnesota today is an exciting mix of "cold and new." Rather than letting chilly winters keep them indoors, Minnesotans celebrate the frigid season with snowy sports such as ice fishing, hockey, and snowmobiling. Summers bring great north woods swimming, fishing, and canoeing.

The state's 5.1 million residents are protecting their water resources while they plunge into new industries. A pioneer in computers and other high-tech manufacturing, Minnesota intends to lead the coming biotechnology industry. In these and other ways, Minnesota's future seems—like its sky-blue waters—limitless!

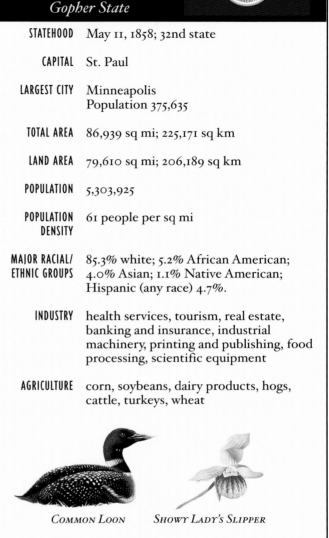

MINNESOTA
Gopher State

STATEHOOD	May 11, 1858; 32nd state
CAPITAL	St. Paul
LARGEST CITY	Minneapolis Population 375,635
TOTAL AREA	86,939 sq mi; 225,171 sq km
LAND AREA	79,610 sq mi; 206,189 sq km
POPULATION	5,303,925
POPULATION DENSITY	61 people per sq mi
MAJOR RACIAL/ ETHNIC GROUPS	85.3% white; 5.2% African American; 4.0% Asian; 1.1% Native American; Hispanic (any race) 4.7%.
INDUSTRY	health services, tourism, real estate, banking and insurance, industrial machinery, printing and publishing, food processing, scientific equipment
AGRICULTURE	corn, soybeans, dairy products, hogs, cattle, turkeys, wheat

COMMON LOON   SHOWY LADY'S SLIPPER

Did you know?

1. The first cellophane tape was developed by Minnesota Mining and Manufacturing (3M) Company in 1930.
2. The nickname Gopher State comes from an 1859 cartoon in which men who wanted to build a railroad through the state were pictured as gophers wearing top hats and pulling a train.
3. The opening of the St. Lawrence Seaway in 1959 connected the Port of Duluth and the Atlantic Ocean.
4. The world's first successful open-heart operation was performed at the University of Minnesota in 1952, and Rochester is home to the world-famous Mayo Clinic.
5. Modern in-line skates were invented by two Minnesota students. Looking for a way to practice hockey in the summer, they replaced their skate blades with wheels.

MISSOURI

★ *Show Me State* ★

"GATEWAY TO THE WEST." With its mid-continent location and the country's two longest rivers embracing the state, it was natural that Missouri would be described this way. The broad and swift Missouri River sweeps across the state from the west to join the mighty Mississippi on its eastern edge—linking its two biggest cities.

Missouri's name comes from a native group whose name meant "wooden canoe people," or the "town of large canoes." When French settlers arrived in 1700, they found Osage and Illini peoples—and valuable deposits of lead. Trappers and traders peacefully paddled the region's rivers, at least until the U.S. bought the vast Louisiana Territory from France in 1803. Lewis and Clark set out the next year up the muddy Missouri to open the American West.

Missouri was made a territory in 1812. Broken treaties with Native Americans caused violence until a pact was signed with most native groups in 1815. Settlement was stoked by the arrival of the first bellowing riverboats, which reached Missouri in 1819. The fur-trading center of St. Louis soon grew to be a major transport hub. The Missouri Compromise of 1820 allowed Missouri to join the Union as a slave state in 1821. Tent cities sprang up around the state as pioneers headed west from Independence—the jumping-off point for the Santa Fe and Oregon Trails. Pony Express riders high-tailed it west with their mailbags from St. Joseph for fast-and-furious ten-day rides to California.

But tensions grew between residents who were for slavery and those who were against it. While Missouri officially sided with the Union during the Civil War, thousands of its soldiers fought for the Confederacy. Post-war Missouri healed slowly but was prospering in both agriculture and industry by the end of the century. It celebrated its success in 1904 with two events:

1735

French settlers established Missouri's first permanent white settlement along the Mississippi at Ste. Genevieve.

1860–1861

The Pony Express delivered mail between Missouri and California in just ten days, using a central route later adopted by the railroad.

1904

The St. Louis World's Fair marked the centennial of the Louisiana Purchase and showcased electricity and early automobiles.

Present day

Branson has become a major country music center, helping to make tourism a multi-billion-dollar industry for Missouri.

Twin symbols of Missouri's central role in the nation's westward growth can be seen together today on the St. Louis waterfront (opposite): the massive Gateway Arch and a steamboat's paddle wheel churning the waters of the Mississippi River.

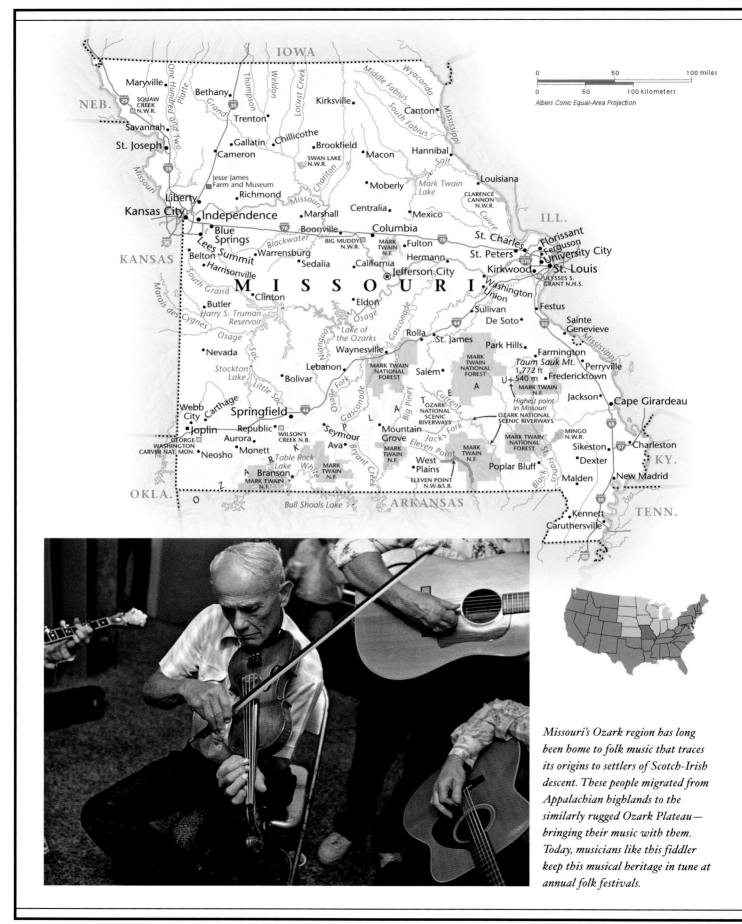

Missouri's Ozark region has long
been home to folk music that traces
its origins to settlers of Scotch-Irish
descent. These people migrated from
Appalachian highlands to the
similarly rugged Ozark Plateau —
bringing their music with them.
Today, musicians like this fiddler
keep this musical heritage in tune at
annual folk festivals.

the Olympics and World's Fair, both in St. Louis.

The rugged Ozark Plateau, coated with oak, hickory, and pine forests shared with Arkansas and Oklahoma, covers much of Missouri's south. North of the Missouri River lie hills, valleys, and glacially-formed fertile croplands of corn and soybeans, much like in neighboring Iowa and Illinois. Cotton and rice carpet the Mississippi River bottomlands as in the nearby southern states.

Missouri's economy is amazingly diverse. More than 100,000 farms, a greater number than in any other state but Texas, make Missouri a major producer of soybeans, corn, cattle, and hogs. More than three centuries after lead was first mined, Missouri still leads the nation in lead production, and barge traffic makes St. Louis one of the busiest inland ports in the nation.

Long a center of metal and chemical manufacturing, St. Louis has lost many jobs and residents in the past few decades. Giant stockyards in Kansas City closed in the 1990s, but the urban area—linked to its Kansas twin—is still a major farm supplier and a center of auto making. Springfield, in the southwest, is a fast-growing trade and manufacturing city. Nearby, the scenic Ozarks boast numerous reservoirs lined with vacation cabins and boat docks. Besides trail trekkers and river rafters, country music lovers flock to this region. Branson's dozens of theaters host famous country-western singers for national crowds.

As Missouri strengthens its traditional economic bases, it also strives to be included in a "Bio-Belt" of life-science research by encouraging the growth of high-tech industries. The spectacular Gateway Arch is more than a symbol of the state's historic role in the nation's settlement. It is also the symbol of an open doorway to Missouri's future success.

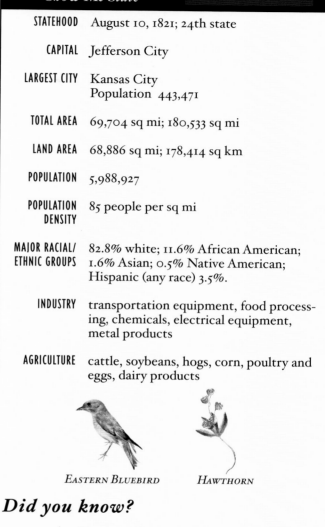

MISSOURI
Show Me State

STATEHOOD	August 10, 1821; 24th state
CAPITAL	Jefferson City
LARGEST CITY	Kansas City Population 443,471
TOTAL AREA	69,704 sq mi; 180,533 sq mi
LAND AREA	68,886 sq mi; 178,414 sq km
POPULATION	5,988,927
POPULATION DENSITY	85 people per sq mi
MAJOR RACIAL/ ETHNIC GROUPS	82.8% white; 11.6% African American; 1.6% Asian; 0.5% Native American; Hispanic (any race) 3.5%.
INDUSTRY	transportation equipment, food processing, chemicals, electrical equipment, metal products
AGRICULTURE	cattle, soybeans, hogs, corn, poultry and eggs, dairy products

EASTERN BLUEBIRD   HAWTHORN

Did you know?

1. Kansas City has a second level of roads, offices, and storage areas built into natural caves below the streets of the city.
2. Samuel Clemens (Mark Twain) used his hometown of Hannibal as the model for settings in his novels *Tom Sawyer* and *Huckleberry Finn*.
3. In late 1811 and early 1812, three of the strongest earthquakes in U.S. history rocked Missouri near New Madrid. The quakes, which scientists believe measured 8 on the Richter scale, caused the Mississippi River to flow backward temporarily.
4. According to one account, the state's nickname comes from a speech by Missouri's U.S. Congressman Willard Duncan Vandiver in 1899. He said, "...frothy eloquence neither convinces nor satisfies me. I am from Missouri. You have got to show me."

NEBRASKA

★ *Cornhusker State* ★

"THE GREAT AMERICAN DESERT." So wrote Major Stephen Long after he mapped the Nebraska plains for the U.S. government in 1820. Seeing the rolling and mostly tree-free prairies during a bad drought, his expedition found it "almost wholly unfit for cultivation." Nebraskans might chuckle today if they could show the explorer a map showing 95 percent of their state covered with farms and ranches.

Based upon Long's report, the area that included Nebraska was set up as Indian Territory—but not for long. In the 1840s, Omaha, with its fine location along the Missouri and near the Platte River, was the starting point for the long journey west for many Oregon and Mormon Trail trekkers. A natural east-west travel corridor, the broad and shallow Platte gave Nebraska its name, from an Oto Indian term meaning "flat water." Thousands of wagon trains rumbled west along-side the Platte. Some people also put down roots in the area, especially in the tall-grass eastern prairies.

Both precipitation and population decline as one travels west in Nebraska. Corn and soybeans thrive in the usually well-watered eastern sections along the Missouri River border, where corn-fed pigs and poultry are raised, too. "Dry farming" is practiced in the west, where one crop year is followed by a year or two with no planting. Water from reservoirs on the Platte and other streams provides irrigation for agriculture. Catching rainfall like a sponge, the grass-covered Sand Hills help refresh the Ogallala Aquifer, a source of groundwater tapped by thousands of wells.

Two acts of the U.S. Congress had great impacts on Nebraska in the mid-19th century. The Kansas-Nebraska Act in 1854 made the two neighbor territories part of the U.S. The

Pre 1854

Native Americans gave up their lands in eastern Nebraska to the U.S. by 1854, but tribes in the west did not surrender theirs until 1877.

1862

The Homestead Act brought a rush of settlers, many building homes of sod because so few trees grew on the Nebraska prairie.

1890

Farmers seeking relief from low prices and overuse of credit, supported Populist Party candidate William Jennings Bryan.

Present day

The Strategic Command, based near Omaha, gathers national defense information and plays a key role in the state's economy.

Hundreds of thousands of westbound Oregon, California, and Mormon Trail riders welcomed the sight of Chimney Rock (opposite), near Nebraska's western border. The limestone landmark rises above the prairie 325 feet (99 m) from base to tip.

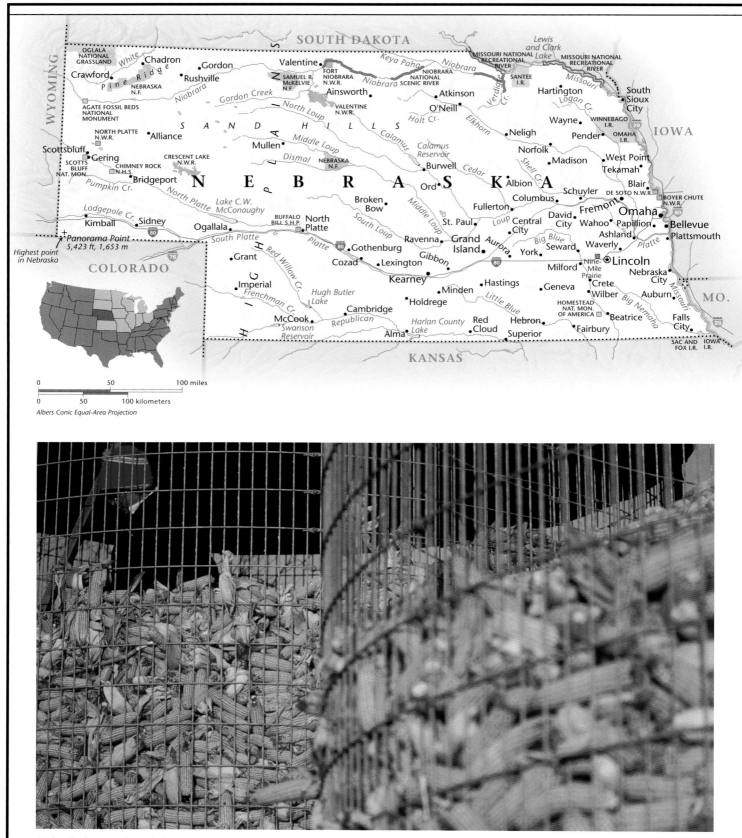

Nebraska harvested 1.13 billion bushels of corn in 2003, ranking third behind Iowa and Illinois in corn harvest. Much of the corn is fed to livestock—especially cattle—which are then processed in state meat-packing plants. Corn is also a source of ethanol, an ingredient in a variety of products, including gasohol. Twenty-two percent of the people in the Cornhusker State are employed in agriculture or related jobs.

Homestead Act of 1862 allowed white settlers to claim—and keep—a "section" of 160 acres (65 ha) of land, if they worked for five years to develop it. As immigrants swarmed to Nebraska to obtain their land, the Sioux and Cheyenne of Nebraska lost more and more of theirs. Nebraska became the 37th state in 1867. The tiny town of Lancaster was renamed Lincoln—after the 16th President—and was made the state capital.

In 1869, the Union Pacific Railroad steamed its way across the new state, bringing more immigrants both through and to Nebraska. Families fought the loneliness of a hard life on their scattered homesteads by sometimes meeting with neighbors. In most areas, wood was scarce, so many farm families built homes using prairie sod. Cut into blocks held together by strong root systems, this "Nebraska marble" proved to be a durable building material. A Nebraska newspaperman started Arbor Day in 1872—planting trees to help hold soil in place. Nebraska was known as the Tree Planter's State until 1945. It has the only national forest that was planted by people.

Nebraska's population has not grown much since 1900. The state's farmers have ridden an economic "roller coaster" of good followed by bad times over the past century. As elsewhere in the country, the size of farms has increased while the number of farmers has decreased. Some rural counties struggle to keep their people from leaving. Overall, irrigation has expanded, causing concern that overuse of groundwater may leave little for the future. Other activities are helping the state to prosper—meat packing, insurance, banking, telecommunications, health care, and the U.S. military. Nebraska's slow-growing population will continue to have its roots in the prairies and its eyes on the future.

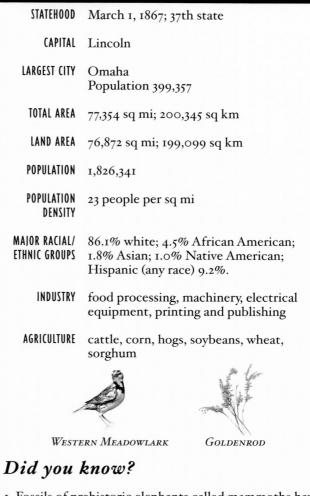

NEBRASKA
Cornhusker State

STATEHOOD	March 1, 1867; 37th state
CAPITAL	Lincoln
LARGEST CITY	Omaha Population 399,357
TOTAL AREA	77,354 sq mi; 200,345 sq km
LAND AREA	76,872 sq mi; 199,099 sq km
POPULATION	1,826,341
POPULATION DENSITY	23 people per sq mi
MAJOR RACIAL/ ETHNIC GROUPS	86.1% white; 4.5% African American; 1.8% Asian; 1.0% Native American; Hispanic (any race) 9.2%.
INDUSTRY	food processing, machinery, electrical equipment, printing and publishing
AGRICULTURE	cattle, corn, hogs, soybeans, wheat, sorghum

WESTERN MEADOWLARK   GOLDENROD

Did you know?

1. Fossils of prehistoric elephants called mammoths have been found in almost every county in Nebraska. The largest is on display at the University of Nebraska State Museum in Lincoln.
2. In 1900 a local sports writer started calling members of the University of Nebraska athletic teams "Cornhuskers." In 1945 the state legislature adopted it as the official state nickname.
3. Nebraska has more miles of river within its boundaries than any other state.
4. The largest expanse of original native prairie in the United States is in the Sand Hills region. It is an important stopover for migrating sandhill cranes.
5. The system of center pivot irrigation, which opens more land to crop production, originated in Nebraska. It is estimated that by 2010 this method of irrigation will water 70 percent of the state's cropland.

NORTH DAKOTA

★ *Flickertail State* ★

"LOOK AT THE FLICKERTAILS!" North Dakota's energetic little ground squirrels emerge from their burrows to watch the prairies as they flick their tails in expectation. The lives and livelihoods of people in the Flickertail State are also rooted in these rolling lands.

Huge Ice Age glaciers scoured the eastern two-thirds of the land, changing and blocking river courses. Several streams combined to form today's mighty Missouri, which cuts its channel across the state from west to south. West of the river, lands not smoothed by ice sheets have been eroded into rugged hills and "badlands." North and east of the Missouri Valley, thousands of pan-shaped lakes and ponds left by glaciers dot the state's Drift Prairie. These kettle holes make temporary homes for migrating waterfowl. The terrain slopes gradually downward to the state's eastern border, which is marked by the Red River of the North. This flat valley, once the bottom of a vast glacial lake, contains some of the world's best farmland—and is often subject to flooding.

Although French explorers moved through in the 1730s, it was the Corps of Discovery led by Lewis and Clark that put the area on the map. Staying with Mandan people along the Missouri River in what is now central North Dakota, they met a Shoshone woman named Sakakawea during the winter of 1804–05. As a guide and interpreter, she was indispensible to the expedition. Lake Sakakawea, formed by a dam on the Missouri River, is named in her honor.

Permanent settlement was slow, even after the Dakota Territory was formed in 1861—in part because of later conflicts with Native Americans. It took the coming of the railroad in the 1870s for farmers and ranchers to arrive in greater numbers. North Dakota entered the Union as the 39th state in 1889.

1804

Lewis and Clark met Sakakawea, who guided them across plains and mountains to the Pacific Ocean, at Fort Mandan.

1874–1890

Wheat farms as large as 65,000 acres (26,000 ha) earned such huge profits that they became known as "bonanza farms."

1951

Oil discovered near Tioga became the state's most valuable mineral. The area currently supplies much of North Dakota's propane gas.

Present day

Garrison Dam provides electricity, flood control, irrigation, and, by creating Lake Sakakawea, supports a rising recreation industry.

Rich soils, long days of summer sunshine, and plentiful rainfall grow head-high sunflowers in the Red River Valley (opposite). Used for cooking oil, birdseed, and snacks, more than half the U.S. sunflower harvest comes from North Dakota farmland.

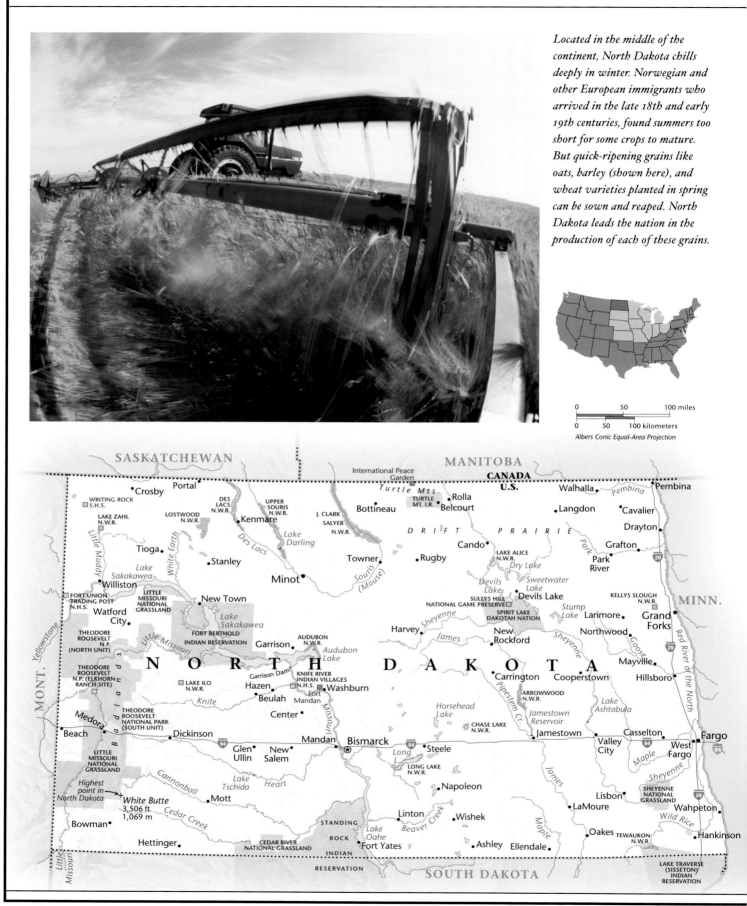

Located in the middle of the continent, North Dakota chills deeply in winter. Norwegian and other European immigrants who arrived in the late 18th and early 19th centuries, found summers too short for some crops to mature. But quick-ripening grains like oats, barley (shown here), and wheat varieties planted in spring can be sown and reaped. North Dakota leads the nation in the production of each of these grains.

0   50   100 miles
0   50   100 kilometers
Albers Conic Equal-Area Projection

SASKATCHEWAN   MANITOBA

International Peace Garden
Turtle Mts.   CANADA
                   U.S.

Crosby   Portal
WRITING ROCK S.H.S.
LAKE ZAHL N.W.R.   DES LACS N.W.R.   Rolla
                                        TURTLE MT. I.R.
LOSTWOOD N.W.R.   UPPER SOURIS N.W.R.   Bottineau   Belcourt   Walhalla   Pembina
                                                                          Langdon   Cavalier
Kenmare   J. CLARK SALYER N.W.R.   Drayton
Tioga   Lake Darling
                                                    Cando   LAKE ALICE N.W.R.   Grafton
White Earth   Towner   Rugby   Dry Lake   Park River
Lake Sakakawea   Stanley
Little Muddy   Minot   Souris (Mouse)   Devils Lake   Sweetwater Lake
Williston   SULLYS HILL NATIONAL GAME PRESERVE Devils Lake   KELLYS SLOUGH N.W.R. MINN.
FORT UNION TRADING POST N.H.S. LITTLE MISSOURI NATIONAL GRASSLAND New Town   SPIRIT LAKE DAKOTAH NATION Stump Lake Larimore Grand Forks
Watford City   Harvey   Sheyenne   New Rockford   Northwood
THEODORE ROOSEVELT N.P. (NORTH UNIT)   Little Missouri   FORT BERTHOLD INDIAN RESERVATION Garrison AUDUBON N.W.R. James Sheyenne Mayville
                                            Audubon Lake

N O R T H   D A K O T A
THEODORE ROOSEVELT N.P. (ELKHORN RANCH SITE)   Carrington Cooperstown   Hillsboro
LAKE ILO N.W.R.   Garrison Dam   KNIFE RIVER INDIAN VILLAGES N.H.S. Washburn ARROWWOOD N.W.R.
Medora   Hazen   Fort Mandan   Knife   Horsehead Lake   Lake Ashtabula
                Beulah   CHASE LAKE N.W.R. Jamestown Reservoir
THEODORE ROOSEVELT NATIONAL PARK (SOUTH UNIT) Center   Jamestown   Casselton   Fargo
Beach   Dickinson   Missouri   Mandan Bismarck   Valley City   West Fargo
LITTLE MISSOURI NATIONAL GRASSLAND   Glen Ullin New Salem   Steele   Long L.   Maple
Highest point in North Dakota   Cannonball   Lake Tschida   Heart LONG LAKE N.W.R.   Sheyenne
White Butte 3,506 ft 1,069 m   Mott   Napoleon   SHEYENNE NATIONAL GRASSLAND
Cedar Creek   Lisbon   Wahpeton
Bowman   Linton   Beaver Creek   Wishek   LaMoure   Wild Rice
Hettinger   CEDAR RIVER NATIONAL GRASSLAND STANDING ROCK   Lake Oahe Ashley Ellendale Oakes TEWAUKON N.W.R. Hankinson
Little Missouri   INDIAN RESERVATION   Fort Yates   LAKE TRAVERSE (SISSETON) INDIAN RESERVATION
                                            SOUTH DAKOTA

Pembina
Red River of the North
Goose
Maple
James
Pipestem Cr.

Farming became and is still the major economic activity in the state even though it has not always been easy. North Dakota farmers have endured drought, dust storms, invasions of grasshoppers, terrible economic times, and of course, the cold. Blizzards can reduce visibility from miles to feet in minutes. But North Dakota's summer days are long, warm—even hot. Many hours of sunshine at the state's high latitude allow the short growing season to produce fine crops.

Wheat is the top crop here, and North Dakota farms produce lots of it. A typical year's harvest is about 300 million bushels, which is more than enough to provide a bushel for every person in the country. The state leads the country in producing sunflowers, oats, barley, canola, flax seed, and dry beans.

North Dakotans look both below and above their rolling prairies for future vitality—and energy. Since the 1970s, oil and natural gas reserves have been tapped in the western half of the state. Closer to the surface lie huge deposits of a kind of coal called lignite, which is burned in nearby power plants to produce electricity. Above ground, strong winds turn towering wind turbines that generate electricity. This rich variety of energy resources makes North Dakota an exporter of energy to neighboring states and holds continued promise for its economic future.

There is concern over the recent decline in the state's population. Only two states have fewer people than the 633,837 who call North Dakota home. Building on North Dakota's fine education system, state officials work to keep young people from leaving the state to find jobs in other places. Keeping home-grown talent in the state will help ensure a future full of energy and hope.

NORTH DAKOTA
Flickertail State

STATEHOOD	November 2, 1889; 39th state
CAPITAL	Bismarck
LARGEST CITY	Fargo Population 91,204
TOTAL AREA	70,700 sq mi; 183,112 sq km
LAND AREA	68,976 sq mi; 178,647 sq km
POPULATION	672,591
POPULATION DENSITY	9 people per sq mi
MAJOR RACIAL/ ETHNIC GROUPS	90.0% white; 5.4% Native American; 1.2% African American; 1.0% Asian; Hispanic (any race) 2.0%.
INDUSTRY	services, government, finance, construction, transportation, oil and gas
AGRICULTURE	wheat, cattle, sunflowers, barley, soybeans

WESTERN MEADOWLARK   *WILD PRAIRIE ROSE*

Did you know?

1. Theodore Roosevelt National Park is the only such park named for a U.S. President.
2. Sunflowers grow as tall as 13 feet (4 m) in North Dakota.
3. Each year a demolition derby using farm combines is held at the State Fair in Minot.
4. A bronze statue of Sakakawea and her baby son Jean Baptiste stands at the entrance to the North Dakota Heritage Center on the grounds of the state capitol in Bismarck.
5. More waterfowl hatch in the many prairie kettle holes and sloughs of North Dakota than in any other state.
6. The International Peace Garden straddles the boundary between North Dakota and Manitoba, in Canada.
7. Devils Lake, the largest natural body of water in North Dakota, is known among fishermen as the Perch Capital of the World.

OHIO
★ Buckeye State ★

THREE BIG *C*s—and so much more! Shaped a bit like a deep bowl on the map, Ohio brims with natural resources, rich farmlands, lots of people, and three big *C* cities: Cleveland lies in the north on the shore of Lake Erie, Columbus anchors the middle, and in the southwest stands Cincinnati—alongside the great river that gives Ohio its name.

Long before the Iroquois named the big west-flowing river, the Adena, Hopewell, and Mississippian cultures built huge burial mounds on southern Ohio hilltops. While the French and British struggled to control the Ohio Country in the mid-1700s, the first permanent white settlement was established at Marietta—on the banks of the Ohio—in 1788. The first of many successful Ohio River ports, it was soon surpassed in importance by down-river Cincinnati. The battle of Fallen Timbers, a total victory for the U.S. Army in 1794, forced the Indians of the Northwest Territory to sign a treaty that opened much of the Ohio Valley to settlers. In 1796, New Englanders arrived on Lake Erie's shores and founded Cleveland. Ohio became the 17th state in 1803, with its capital first at Chillicothe and then Zanesville. In 1816, Ohio established Columbus as its seat of government.

Ohio prospered with its key waterways linking regions east and west. Its Lake Erie rim bustled with business, especially after the Erie Canal was finished in 1825. This provided a route for East Coast water traffic to reach the frontier. Flatboats and then steamboats navigated the Ohio River. The state grew quickly. The growing of corn, wheat, oats, and potatoes—plus the raising of cattle and hogs—made it an agricultural powerhouse by 1850. Industry soon followed, led by meat packing. By that time, rails connected most major state cities.

1794
General "Mad" Anthony Wayne's defeat of Native Americans at the Battle of Fallen Timbers helped open the Ohio Valley to settlers.

1915
Akron's first rubber products were made in the 1870s, and by 1915 it had become known as the Rubber Capital of the World.

1969
When the Cuyahoga River caught fire in 1969, it became a symbol of a polluted America and led to environmental legislation.

Present day
The Rock and Roll Hall of Fame, a centerpiece of Cleveland's cleaned-up waterfront, attracts thousands of visitors each year.

Ohio's Serpent Mound (opposite) is among the best preserved of the prehistoric effigy mounds—earthworks created in the shape of animals—that appear in several areas of the Midwest. It is 450 yards (411 m) long, with an average elevation of about 4 feet (1.2 m).

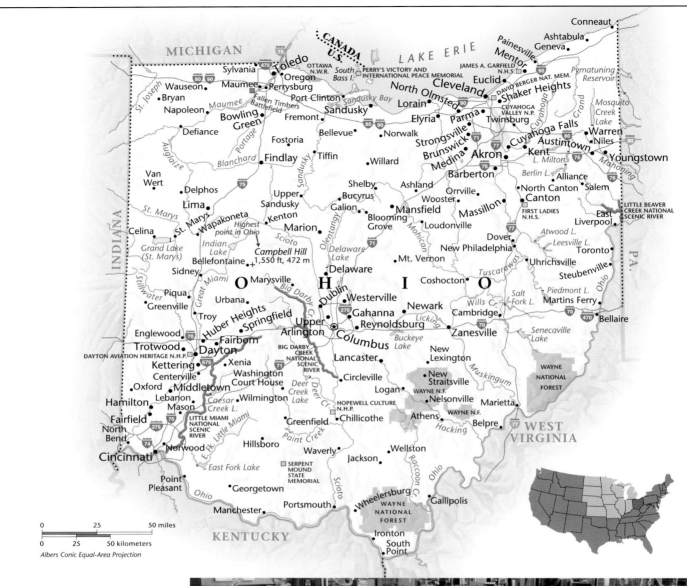

MICHIGAN

CANADA
U.S.

LAKE ERIE

Conneaut
Ashtabula
Geneva
Painesville
Mentor

Sylvania
Toledo
OTTAWA
N.W.R.
South
Bass I.
PERRY'S VICTORY AND
INTERNATIONAL PEACE MEMORIAL
JAMES A. GARFIELD
N.H.S.
Pymatuning
Reservoir

Wauseon
Maumee
Oregon
Perrysburg
Port Clinton
Cleveland
Euclid
DAVID BERGER NAT. MEM.
Shaker Heights

Bryan
Napoleon
Bowling
Green
Fallen Timbers
Battlefield
Sandusky
Sandusky Bay
North Olmsted
Lorain
Parma
CUYAHOGA
VALLEY N.P.
Mosquito
Creek
Lake

Defiance
Fremont
Bellevue
Norwalk
Elyria
Strongsville
Brunswick
Twinsburg
Cuyahoga Falls
Warren
Grand

Van
Wert
Findlay
Tiffin
Willard
Medina
Akron
Austintown
Niles

Delphos
Lima
Upper
Sandusky
Shelby
Bucyrus
Ashland
Orrville
Wooster
Barberton
Berlin L.
North Canton
Alliance
Salem
Youngstown
Mahoning
L. Milton

Celina
St. Marys
Wapakoneta
Highest
point in Ohio
Kenton
Galion
Blooming
Grove
Mansfield
Massillon
Canton
FIRST LADIES
N.H.S.
East
Liverpool
LITTLE BEAVER
CREEK NATIONAL
SCENIC RIVER

Grand Lake
(St. Marys)
Indian
Lake
Marion
Loudonville
Atwood L.
Dover
New Philadelphia
Uhrichsville
Toronto
Steubenville

Sidney
Bellefontaine
Campbell Hill
1,550 ft, 472 m
Delaware
Lake
Mt. Vernon
Coshocton
Leesville L.
Salt
Fork L.
Piedmont L.
Martins Ferry

Piqua
Greenville
Urbana
Marysville
Dublin
Delaware
Westerville
Newark
Cambridge
Bellaire

Troy
Huber Heights
Springfield
Upper
Arlington
Gahanna
Reynoldsburg
Zanesville
Senecaville
Lake

Englewood
Fairborn
Columbus
BIG DARBY
CREEK
NATIONAL
SCENIC
RIVER
Buckeye
Lake

Trotwood
Dayton
DAYTON AVIATION HERITAGE N.H.P.
Kettering
Xenia
Washington
Court House
Lancaster
New
Lexington
WAYNE
NATIONAL
FOREST

Centerville
Oxford
Middletown
Lebanon
Wilmington
Deer
Creek
Lake
Circleville
Logan
New
Straitsville
WAYNE N.F.
Nelsonville
Marietta

Hamilton
Mason
LITTLE MIAMI
NATIONAL
SCENIC
RIVER
Caesar
Creek L.
HOPEWELL CULTURE
N.H.P.
WAYNE N.F.

Fairfield
North
Bend
Norwood
Greenfield
Chillicothe
Athens
Belpre
WEST
VIRGINIA

Cincinnati
Hillsboro
Waverly
Jackson
Wellston
Ohio

Point
Pleasant
Georgetown
SERPENT
MOUND
STATE
MEMORIAL
WAYNE
NATIONAL
FOREST
Gallipolis

Manchester
Portsmouth
Wheelersburg

East Fork Lake

KENTUCKY

Ironton
South
Point

OHIO

INDIANA

PA.

0   25   50 miles
0   25   50 kilometers
Albers Conic Equal-Area Projection

Ohio has long been a manufacturing giant. The list of Buckeye State products is impressive: food, soap, iron and steel, aluminum, rubber, plastics, glass, appliances, chemicals, and more. Greater than one-fourth of the state's manufacturing is related to the production of motor vehicles. Recent annual production of cars and light trucks stands at more than 1.8 million.

The so-called Underground Railroad—a loose network of people who helped escaped slaves move north to freedom—maintained many "stations," or safehouses, in Ohio. After the Civil War, the iron and steel industry fired the state's economy. Rich deposits of coal and oil from outside and inside the state fueled this growth.

European immigrants arrived in huge numbers through the second half of the 19th century, finding work in Ohio's thriving factories. Organized labor groups were formed to promote workers' rights.

Ohio suffered huge job losses during the Great Depression, but its economy rebounded during and after World War II. Ohio became a major manufacturer of rubber and plastics. Lake Erie ports handled bulk mineral cargoes as well as finished products. The Ohio River carried huge volumes of oil and steel in multi-barge tows. By the 1960s pollution problems darkened Ohio's skies and discolored its waterways, especially Lake Erie. Decades of clean-up efforts have paid off, and the state's environment has rebounded well.

Today, the Buckeye State is prospering. With just under 11.5 million people, Ohio is the seventh most populous state and still a leading farm state. Ohio agriculture supports more than a thousand food-processing operations, making everything from jellies to sausages. Huge, efficient auto assembly and parts plants have been built recently, making the state second only to Michigan in car manufacturing. The state seeks to attract information technology and other emerging industries, while striving to make its cities and towns more livable for residents. Boding well for Ohio's future is the state's continued emphasis on education. It has more than 130 colleges and universities, graduating about 50,000 students each year.

OHIO
Buckeye State

STATEHOOD	March 1, 1803; 17th state
CAPITAL	Columbus
LARGEST CITY	Columbus Population 725,228
TOTAL AREA	44,825 sq mi; 116,096 sq km
LAND AREA	40,948 sq mi; 106,056 sq km
POPULATION	11,536,504
POPULATION DENSITY	257 people per sq mi
MAJOR RACIAL/ ETHNIC GROUPS	82.7% white; 12.2% African American; 1.7% Asian; 0.2% Native American; Hispanic (any race) 3.1%.
INDUSTRY	transportation equipment, metal products, machinery, food processing, electrical equipment
AGRICULTURE	soybeans, dairy products, corn, hogs, cattle, poultry and eggs

CARDINAL   SCARLET CARNATION

Did you know?

1. Fires set by anti-union workers in 1884 in coal mines around New Straitsville, southeast of Columbus, are still burning. Smoke from the underground fires has been seen coming up through the ground in Wayne National Forest, which surrounds the town.
2. Ohio has the largest Amish-Mennonite community in the world. The Amish and Mennonite Heritage Center is located in Berlin, near New Philadelphia.
3. Twinsburg, located just south of Cleveland, has been hosting the Twins Days Festival every August since 1976. Each year about 3,000 sets of twins from around the world gather here.
4. Marietta, Ohio's first permanent European settlement, was named for the French Queen Marie Antoinette.
5. The Cincinnati Reds were the first professional baseball team.

SOUTH DAKOTA

★ *Mount Rushmore State* ★

WHAT'S IN A WORD? "Dakota" means "allies" or "friends" to people of the Sioux nations. When French explorers moved through the area in the 1740s, they met people of the Sioux federation who treated them well, and in 1804 Lewis and Clark were allowed to pass through Indian territory as they moved up the Missouri River. But fur traders and settlers who followed in the decades after had clashes with these Native Americans.

In 1868 the Dakota Territory included both North and South Dakota. Within a few years, immigrants, especially from Central Europe and Scandinavia, began arriving by rail. Most made their homesteads in the fertile eastern half of the state. They found rich prairie-grass soils and enough precipitation there to grow wheat and other crops. To the west of the Missouri the newcomers encountered drier conditions, better suited for grazing cattle and

sheep. The Dakota Territory was split in half when both North and South Dakota were admitted to the Union on the same day in 1889. Pierre (pronounced "peer") was made the capital of the southern state.

South Dakota has only one large area of forest, the Black Hills. Named for the dark color of their stately ponderosa pines, the Black Hills are the highest peaks east of the Rocky Mountains. More important, they are sacred to the Lakota people, who see them as "the heart of everything that is." An 1868 treaty had promised to let the Lakota keep their rich hunting grounds forever, but all this changed when the U.S. Army, led by George Armstrong Custer, reported gold in the Black Hills. Although the Lakota, led by Sitting Bull and Crazy Horse, wiped out Custer's troops in neighboring Montana in 1876, they could not win against the bitter campaign launched by the Army. The last

1830s

The arrival of steamboats on the upper Missouri River stimulated the fur trade and helped open the region to development.

1874–2002

The discovery of gold in the Black Hills led to the opening of the Homestake Mine, richest and longest-producing mine in the U.S.

1930s

Dust storms called black blizzards and plagues of grasshoppers accompanied a 10-year drought, worst in the state's history.

Present day

The completion of a monument to Lakota chief Crazy Horse is part of a new drive to attract visitors and build the tourist industry.

The Badlands (opposite), strange shapes etched into layers of volcanic ash and soft sediments, frustrated early white settlers. Today, they enchant visitors to Badlands National Park, where wind, rain, snow, and ice erode an average of one inch (2.5 cm) per year.

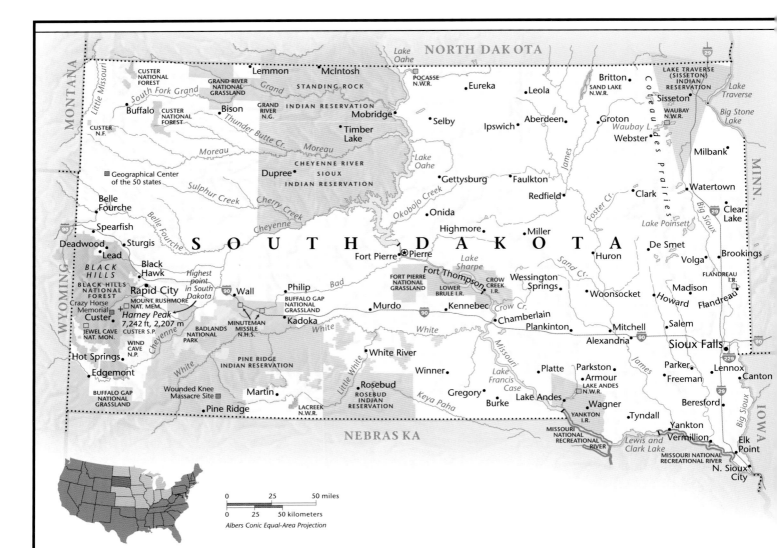

NORTH DAKOTA

MONTANA

CUSTER NATIONAL FOREST
GRAND RIVER NATIONAL GRASSLAND
GRAND RIVER N.G.
CUSTER NATIONAL FOREST
CUSTER N.F.

Little Missouri
South Fork Grand
Grand
Lake Oahe
Lemmon
McIntosh
POCASSE N.W.R.
Eureka
Leola
Britton
SAND LAKE N.W.R.
LAKE TRAVERSE (SISSETON) INDIAN RESERVATION
Sisseton
Lake Traverse

Buffalo
Bison
STANDING ROCK INDIAN RESERVATION
Mobridge
Selby
Ipswich
Aberdeen
Groton
Webster
Waubay L.
WAUBAY N.W.R.
Big Stone Lake
Milbank

Thunder Butte Cr.
Timber Lake
Moreau

Moreau
CHEYENNE RIVER
Dupree
SIOUX INDIAN RESERVATION
Gettysburg
Faulkton
Redfield
James
Clark
Watertown
Coteau des Prairies
Lake Poinsett
Clear Lake

MINN.

Geographical Center of the 50 states
Sulphur Creek
Cherry Creek
Cheyenne
Lake Oahe
Okobojo Creek
Onida
Highmore
Miller
De Smet
Volga
Brookings
Foster Cr.

Belle Fourche
Spearfish
Deadwood
Sturgis
Lead
Black Hawk
BLACK HILLS
BLACK HILLS NATIONAL FOREST
Rapid City
MOUNT RUSHMORE NAT. MEM.
Crazy Horse Memorial
Custer
JEWEL CAVE NAT. MON.
CUSTER S.P.
Harney Peak 7,242 ft, 2,207 m
WIND CAVE N.P.
Hot Springs
Edgemont

Belle Fourche
Highest point in South Dakota
Cheyenne
Wall
Philip
BUFFALO GAP NATIONAL GRASSLAND
MINUTEMAN MISSILE N.H.S.
BADLANDS NATIONAL PARK
Murdo
Kadoka
White

Fort Pierre
Pierre
Bad
FORT PIERRE NATIONAL GRASSLAND
Fort Thompson
LOWER BRULE I.R.
CROW CREEK I.R.
Wessington Springs
Huron
Sand Cr.
Howard
Madison
Flandreau
FLANDREAU I.R.

Lake Sharpe
Kennebec
Crow Cr.
Chamberlain
Plankinton
Woonsocket
Mitchell
Alexandria
Salem
Sioux Falls

WYOMING

White
WIND CAVE N.P.
White
PINE RIDGE INDIAN RESERVATION
Little White
White River
Winner
Lake Francis Case
Platte
Parkston
Armour
LAKE ANDES N.W.R.
Parker
Freeman
Lennox
Canton

BUFFALO GAP NATIONAL GRASSLAND
Wounded Knee Massacre Site
Martin
LACREEK N.W.R.
ROSEBUD INDIAN RESERVATION
Rosebud
Keya Paha
Gregory
Burke
Lake Andes
Wagner
YANKTON I.R.
Tyndall
Beresford

Pine Ridge

NEBRASKA

Missouri
Lewis and Clark Lake
MISSOURI NATIONAL RECREATIONAL RIVER
Yankton
Vermillion
MISSOURI NATIONAL RECREATIONAL RIVER
Elk Point
N. Sioux City

IOWA
Big Sioux

S O U T H   D A K O T A

0   25   50 miles
0   25   50 kilometers
Albers Conic Equal-Area Projection

Four Presidents who played key roles in the first 150 years of the nation—(left to right) George Washington, Thomas Jefferson, Theodore Roosevelt, and Abraham Lincoln—are commemorated in the Mount Rushmore National Memorial. The sculpture represents the vision of Gutzon Borglum, who began work on his Shrine of Democracy in 1927. Gazing from a granite mountainside in the Black Hills, these 60-foot- (18-m-) high figures inspire people from around the world.

major battle in the Indian Wars took place along Wounded Knee Creek on the Pine Ridge Reservation. There, U.S. troops massacred 300 Native American men, women, and children.

Today, one in twelve of South Dakota's people is American Indian. Most live on the nine reservations scattered across the state. Many battle poverty on these poor lands. Some fight through the courts for lands that were once theirs. In the Black Hills, the Lakota are honoring Chief Crazy Horse with a gigantic memorial that is being carved out of solid granite.

Another monumental structure in the Black Hills—Mount Rushmore—attracts nearly three million people each year, making the region a major source of income for the state. Vacationers find a bit of the past in herds of bison and in the "Wild West" town of Deadwood, where Wild Bill Hickok and Calamity Jane lived.

Farming and ranching still form key parts of the state's economy. South Dakota is a top producer of millet, soybeans, sunflowers, rye, sheep, and cattle. Special facilities convert corn to a motor fuel called ethanol. Meat packing and other food processing also add value to state farm products. In recent years, the manufacture of computers and the processing of credit card information have brought jobs to many workers, especially in the Sioux Falls area. A pioneering effort is also underway to turn the remains of an old industry into a brand-new one. The Homestake Mine, which closed in 2002, will work again for South Dakota. The State government has plans to turn the 8,000-foot- (2,400-m-) deep gold mine into a world-class, high-tech underground research laboratory. As they look ahead, the people of South Dakota know that the past is with them as they scout the future.

SOUTH DAKOTA
Mount Rushmore State

STATEHOOD	November 2, 1889; 40th state
CAPITAL	Pierre
LARGEST CITY	Sioux Falls Population 130,491
TOTAL AREA	77,117 sq mi; 199,731 sq km
LAND AREA	75,885 sq mi; 196,540 sq km
POPULATION	814,180
POPULATION DENSITY	10 people per sq mi
MAJOR RACIAL/ ETHNIC GROUPS	85.9% white; 8.8% Native American; 1.3% African American; 0.9% Asian; Hispanic (any race) 2.7%.
INDUSTRY	finance, services, manufacturing, government, retail trade, transportation and utilities, wholesale trade, construction, mining
AGRICULTURE	cattle, corn, soybeans, wheat, hogs, hay, dairy products

RING-NECKED PHEASANT

PASQUEFLOWER

Did you know?

1. The world's largest, most complete, and best preserved specimen of *Tyrannosaurus rex* discovered to date was unearthed on the Cheyenne River Indian Reservation in 1990. It was named Sue after the fossil hunter who found it.
2. Petrified Wood Park in Lemmon is the largest park of its kind in the world. Fossils and petrified wood are arranged in unusual shapes, including a castle and pyramids.
3. South Dakota is the home of the Dakota, Lakota, and Nakota tribes, which together make up the Sioux Nation.
4. In 1959, with the addition of Alaska and Hawaii to the Union, the geographic center of the United States moved from Lebanon, Kansas, to a point near Belle Fourche, South Dakota.

WISCONSIN

★ Badger State ★

BADGER STATE, a name that refers to lead miners who lived like burrowing animals in caves during the 1820s, is one state nickname. Another—America's Dairyland—comes from the state's cheese-making and milk-producing traditions. Wisconsinites would say that while both of these names refer to particular resources, neither captures the state's wide-ranging landscapes and activities.

Jean Nicolet, a Frenchman searching for a Northwest Passage to Asia, stepped ashore from "La Baye" (Green Bay) to meet not Chinese but Winnebago natives in 1634. Marquette and Joliet found Ojibwa and Menominee peoples as they paddled and portaged their way across the territory in 1673 to reach the Mississippi River. The explorers found waterways everywhere— lakes, streams, and wetlands of all sizes in this region the Ojibwa called "gathering of the waters," or the French called "Ouisconsin."

Gigantic fingers of continental glaciers formed much of Wisconsin's present landscape, gouging out Lake Superior and Lake Michigan. As they retreated, the glaciers left rocks in looping mounds called moraines across northern uplands and eastern lowlands. Expansive central wetlands that produce the nation's top cranberry crop were once a glacial lake bed. Ridges blocked the glaciers' paths into southwestern Wisconsin, leaving tall bluffs and steep-sided valleys untouched.

The British took control of all French lands east of the Mississippi in 1763. Green Bay became Wisconsin's first permanent European settlement the next year. The region passed to American control after the Revolutionary War, becoming part of the sprawling Northwest Territory. Native American resistance ended with the Black Hawk War in 1832, and the Wisconsin Territory was formed in 1836.

1634

Frenchman Jean Nicolet, who was seeking a water route to China, was one of the first Europeans to set foot on Wisconsin soil.

1820s

The mining of lead for use in paint and in shot for guns rose sharply, causing miners to pour into southwestern Wisconsin.

1890–1925

Wisconsin's Progressive Movement, led by "Fighting Bob" La Follette, initiated key political, social, and economic reforms.

Present day

Hundred-year-old Harley David-son Motor Company is a symbol of the state's tradition as a center of small engine manufacturing.

Two dairy farms share a bluff top in southwestern Wisconsin (opposite), a region that continental ice sheets largely missed. To prevent erosion, these steep-sided valleys that the French called "coulees" must be planted in rows parallel to the contour.

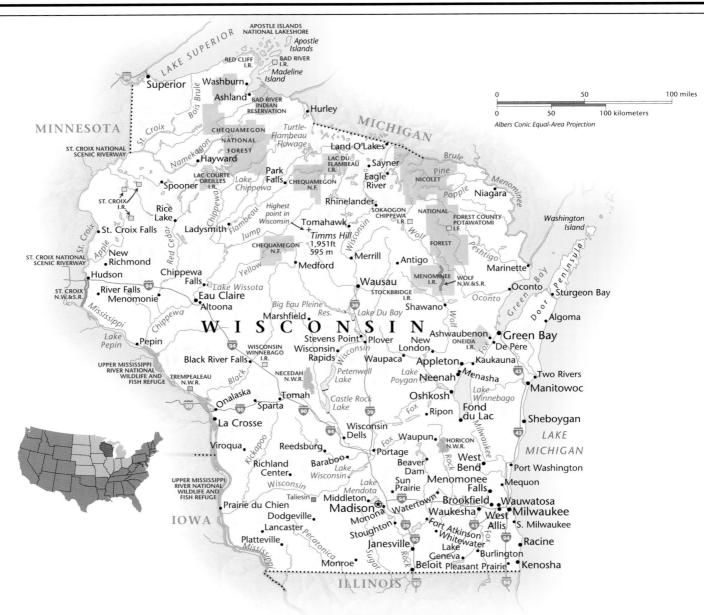

MINNESOTA

LAKE SUPERIOR

APOSTLE ISLANDS
NATIONAL LAKESHORE

Apostle
Islands

RED CLIFF
I.R.

BAD RIVER
I.R.

Madeline
Island

Superior

Washburn

Ashland

BAD RIVER
INDIAN
RESERVATION

Hurley

MICHIGAN

Bois Brule

St. Croix

Namekagon

CHEQUAMEGON

NATIONAL

FOREST

Turtle-
Flambeau
Flowage

Land O'Lakes

Brule

ST. CROIX NATIONAL
SCENIC RIVERWAY

Hayward

Park
Falls

LAC DU
FLAMBEAU
I.R.

Sayner

Pine

NICOLET

Menominee

LAC COURTE
OREILLES I.R.

Lake
Chippewa

CHEQUAMEGON
N.F.

Eagle
River

Popple

Niagara

Spooner

Rhinelander

ST. CROIX
I.R.

Rice
Lake

Chippewa

Flambeau

Highest
point in
Wisconsin

Tomahawk

SOKAOGON
CHIPPEWA
I.R.

NATIONAL

FOREST COUNTY
POTAWATOMI
I.F.

Washington
Island

St. Croix Falls

Ladysmith

Jump

Timms Hill
1,951ft
595 m

Wisconsin

FOREST

Peshtigo

New
Richmond

CHEQUAMEGON
N.F.

Yellow

Medford

Merrill

Antigo

Marinette

ST. CROIX NATIONAL
SCENIC RIVERWAY

Hudson

Chippewa
Falls

Wausau

MENOMINEE
I.R.

WOLF
N.W.&S.R.

Oconto

Sturgeon Bay

ST. CROIX
N.W.&S.R.

River Falls
Menomonie

Red Cedar

Lake Wissota

STOCKBRIDGE
I.R.

Shawano

Oconto

Green Bay

Algoma

Eau Claire

Big Eau Pleine
Res.

Lake Du Bay

Door Peninsula

Mississippi

Altoona

Marshfield

WISCONSIN

Wolf

Ashwaubenon

Green Bay
De Pere

Lake
Pepin

Pepin

Black River Falls

WISCONSIN
WINNEBAGO
I.R.

Stevens Point

Wisconsin
Rapids

Plover

Wisconsin

New
London

Waupaca

ONEIDA
I.R.

Kaukauna

Two Rivers

UPPER MISSISSIPPI
RIVER NATIONAL
WILDLIFE AND
FISH REFUGE

TREMPEALEAU
N.W.R.

NECEDAH
N.W.R.

Petenwell
Lake

Appleton

Neenah

Menasha

Lake
Poygan

Manitowoc

Black

Onalaska

Tomah

Castle Rock
Lake

Oshkosh

Fond
du Lac

Lake
Winnebago

Sheboygan

Sparta

Fox

Ripon

La Crosse

Kickapoo

Reedsburg

Fox

Waupun

HORICON
N.W.R.

Milwaukee

LAKE

MICHIGAN

Viroqua

Portage

Beaver
Dam

West
Bend

Port Washington

Richland
Center

Baraboo

Lake
Wisconsin

Sun
Prairie

Menomonee
Falls

Mequon

Wisconsin

Lake
Mendota

Middleton

Watertown

Brookfield

Wauwatosa

UPPER MISSISSIPPI
RIVER NATIONAL
WILDLIFE AND
FISH REFUGE

Prairie du Chien

Taliesin

Madison

Monona

Waukesha

West
Allis

Milwaukee

S. Milwaukee

IOWA

Dodgeville

Fort Atkinson

Racine

Lancaster

Stoughton

Whitewater

Fox

Burlington

Kenosha

Platteville

Pecatonica

Janesville

Lake
Geneva

Sugar

Rock

Monroe

Beloit

Pleasant Prairie

ILLINOIS

Mississippi

0   50   100 miles
0   50   100 kilometers
Albers Conic Equal-Area Projection

Swiss, German, and other European settlers brought their skills in raising dairy cows for milk, butter, and especially cheese to Wisconsin. Soon large milking barns appeared across the state. In Monroe, a master cheesemaker (left) racks 18-lb (8-kg) wheels of Grand Cru Gruyere cheese for drying—one of hundreds of types made in the Dairy State. In 2003 Wisconsin produced 26 percent of the country's total cheese output.

Wisconsin joined the Union in 1848 as the 30th state, with Madison as its capital. German immigrants arrived in great numbers and settled in Milwaukee. The city became a center of German culture, with its meat packing and beer brewing.

Rural settlers found soils across southern Wisconsin fertile enough to grow wheat and other crops. Loggers cut down immense stands of white pines across the northern half of the state. Wisconsin owes its trademark dairy farming to Swiss settlers. For most of the 20th century, Wisconsin was the country's largest producer of dairy products.

The 20th century also saw industrial Wisconsin reach high gear. Cities large and small built factories, turning out everything from bathroom fixtures to cooking pots. "Machine Shop of the World," Milwaukee rumbled with the manufacture of railroad cars, heavy machinery, and then small engines. Large numbers of Polish and African-American laborers arrived to fill factory jobs there. Wisconsin grew to be one of the world's top paper-making centers as sawmills and pulp mills harnessed hydropower. Wisconsin's water resources also made it a haven for hunters, fishers, and sport enthusiasts.

Today, Wisconsin is facing the decline of manufacturing and family-owned farms as well as an urgent need to protect natural resources. The state works to keep existing factories successful and sponsors research to expand biotechnology and other new businesses. It has also launched a major program to clean up industrial pollutants in the Fox River. Farmers are looking to new markets as they grow both profitable and earth-friendly organic crops. Long a leader in social and environmental action, the state is working hard to protect the future of its 5.5 million people.

WISCONSIN
Badger State

WISCONSIN
1848

STATEHOOD	May 29, 1848; 30th state
CAPITAL	Madison
LARGEST CITY	Milwaukee Population 590,895
TOTAL AREA	65,498 sq mi; 169,639 sq km
LAND AREA	54,310 sq mi; 140,663 sq km
POPULATION	5,686,986
POPULATION DENSITY	86 people per sq mi
MAJOR RACIAL/ ETHNIC GROUPS	86.2% white; 6.3% African American; 2.3% Asian; 1.0% Native American; Hispanic (any race) 5.9%.
INDUSTRY	industrial machinery, paper products, food processing, metal products, electronic equipment, transportation
AGRICULTURE	dairy products, cattle, corn, poultry and eggs, soybeans

ROBIN   WOOD VIOLET

Did you know?

1. The first hydroelectric plant in the country was built on the Fox River in Appleton in 1882.
2. The first snowmachine patent was issued to Carl Eliason of Sayner, Wisconsin. Today the state has more than 25,000 miles (40,000 km) of groomed snowmobile trails.
3. In 1856 a German immigrant named Margarethe Schurz opened the first kindergarten in the United States in Watertown. Her concept of teaching young children through play quickly spread across the U.S.
4. Door County, which includes Door Peninsula, has more than 250 miles (400 km) of shoreline, more than any other county in the United States.
5. Laura Ingalls Wilder was born in Pepin in 1867. Her famous "Little House" books are based on her childhood life in the forests and prairies of the Midwest.
6. Baraboo is the birthplace of the Ringling Bros. Circus.

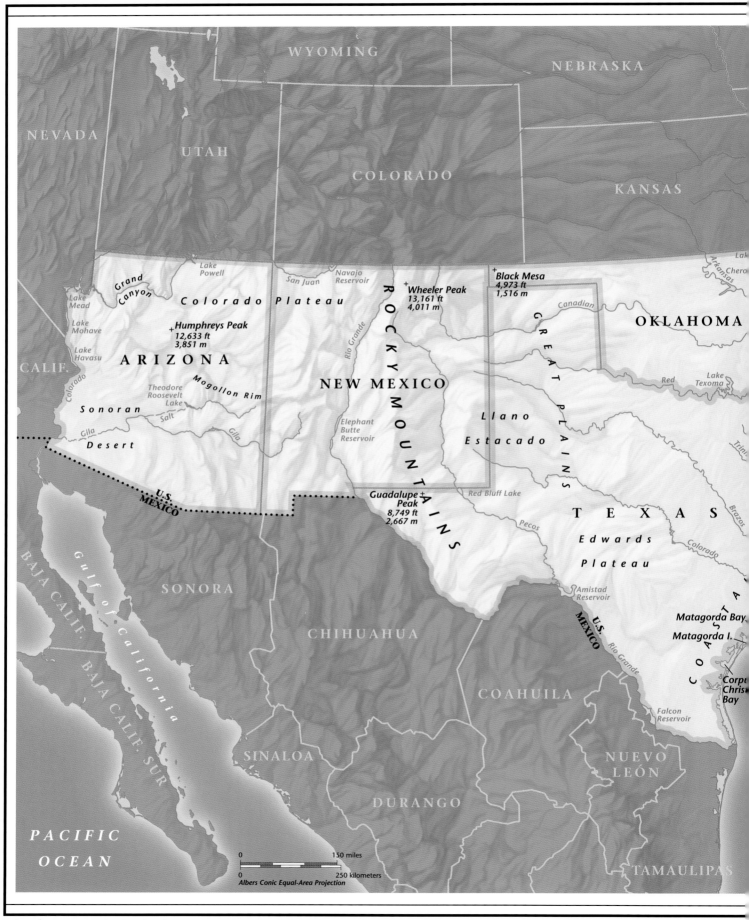

WYOMING

NEBRASKA

NEVADA

UTAH

COLORADO

KANSAS

Lake Powell

San Juan

Navajo Reservoir

Grand Canyon

Colorado Plateau

+ Wheeler Peak
13,161 ft
4,011 m

+ Black Mesa
4,973 ft
1,516 m

Canadian

OKLAHOMA

Lake Mead

+ Humphreys Peak
12,633 ft
3,851 m

Rio Grande

Lake Mohave

R
O
C
K
Y

G
R
E
A
T

Lake Havasu

ARIZONA

NEW MEXICO

CALIF.

Colorado

Theodore Roosevelt Lake

Mogollon Rim

Sonoran

Salt

Gila

Elephant Butte Reservoir

L l a n o

Red

Lake Texoma

Gila

Desert

U.S.
MEXICO

E s t a c a d o

M
O
U
N
T
A
I
N
S

P
L
A
I
N
S

Guadalupe +
Peak
8,749 ft
2,667 m

Red Bluff Lake

T E X A S

Pecos

Edwards

Colorado

Plateau

Brazos

BAJA CALIF.

Gulf of California

SONORA

Amistad Reservoir

C
O
A
S
T
A

Matagorda Bay

Matagorda I.

U.S.
MEXICO

Rio Grande

CHIHUAHUA

COAHUILA

NUEVO
LEÓN

Corpus Christi Bay

BAJA CALIF. SUR

Falcon Reservoir

SINALOA

PACIFIC
OCEAN

DURANGO

0   150 miles

0   250 kilometers

Albers Conic Equal-Area Projection

TAMAULIPAS

The Southwest

DIVERSE LANDSCAPES and sunny weather characterize the American Southwest. Deep canyons dominate the Colorado Plateau west of the Rockies, where the Colorado River winds through Arizona's Grand Canyon. Dams and reservoirs now tame this once mighty waterway, which provides water and power to cities and farms. South of the plateau the Sonoran Desert stretches into Mexico. The silt-laden Rio Grande flows out of the Rocky Mountains, carrying snowmelt to thirsty lands along the Texas-Mexico border. The windswept Great Plains stretch east of the Rockies across mostly level Texas and Oklahoma. Rivers move southeast through this short-grass prairie to the coastal plain, then empty into the Gulf of Mexico. Like the land, the climate changes with location. Precipitation is scarce except in the eastern part of the region. Southwestern winters can be cold and snowy, but summers are hot and sunny.

Enchanted Places and Multicultural Faces

LONG BEFORE COLUMBUS reached the New World resourceful Indians farmed the landscapes of the Southwest. Near rivers and springs, ancestral Puebloans, Zuni, and Hopi peoples planted fields of corn, beans, and squash. To these staples they added piñon nuts, venison, rabbit, and chili peppers. The ancestral Puebloans first built their villages with sun-baked adobe bricks high atop mesas. Later, they wedged their homes and granaries within the vertical walls of sheltered canyons. East of the Rocky Mountains, the Comanche and Apache adapted to life on the southern Great Plains by hunting buffalo and gathering plants.

In 1540 the Spanish conquistador Francisco Vásquez de Coronado rode north from Mexico to claim this "Kingdom of New Mexico." By 1610, just ten years before *Mayflower* pilgrims settled Massachusetts, Spain's cluster of buildings near Santa Fe became America's first capital city. During the next century European guns and diseases overwhelmed the Indians.

In 1821, the Santa Fe Trail broadened American trade and settlement. The next year Stephen F. Austin led the first band of American farmers into the hill country of central Texas. Farms and cattle ranches began to blanket the countryside. Although by 1824 Mexico had gained control of the Southwest from Spain, *Los Americanos* were now firmly established in this dry region. Soon they were driving herds of Texas longhorns north along the Shawnee and Chisholm Trails to railroad yards in the Midwest. In 1835 rebellious Americans in Texas revolted against Mexican rule. Ten years later Texas joined the Union. In 1848 after war with Mexico, Arizona and New Mexico became part of the United States.

Under American control, the region's economy began to change. The cattle drives ended in the 1870s as barbed wire and railroads stretched into Texas. Land-hungry settlers in Oklahoma encouraged the U.S. government to either purchase or take land promised to the Indians. Elsewhere a series of broken treaties forced Native Americans from their remaining homelands. Oil discoveries in the early 1900s attracted new settlers to Texas and Oklahoma.

Around this same time, water and electricity provided by dams built on the Rio Grande and the Colorado River, as well as dozens of smaller water projects, led to the growth of modern cities and huge farming operations. Today, the Southwest is a major exporter of grain, fruit, cotton, and vegetables, much of it harvested by workers from nearby Mexico. Sheep, goats, as well as cattle ranching and feeding operations remain important to the region.

In recent decades new industries have emerged. The cities of Dallas, Oklahoma City, Phoenix, and Albuquerque are important centers of technology and business. New Mexico is a key player in solar energy and weapons research, while Texas hosts the command post for U.S. astronauts. Since 1914 the Houston Ship Channel has linked the city's oil refineries with the Gulf Coast and the rest of the world. Abundant sunshine and a slower lifestyle attract newcomers. While growth fuels the economy, it depletes groundwater in huge aquifers that lie beneath much of the region.

The Southwest is a fast-growing region with a dynamic modern economy that retains much of its Native American, Hispanic, and Wild West heritage. Indian traditions of fine pottery, weavings, and architecture are abundantly evident throughout New Mexico and Arizona. Each year millions of tourists explore its canyons, mountains, and deserts. These landscapes, combined with the region's unique settlement history, contribute to its reputation as an enchanted and multicultural place.

> "Wildness so godful, cosmic, primeval, bestows a new sense of Earth's beauty and size."
>
> —JOHN MUIR, *STEEP TRAILS*

The famous Mitten Buttes create a magical desert landscape against a Southwestern sky. The red sandstone formations, which rise 900 feet (275 m) above the floor of Monument Valley, are part of a Navajo tribal park on the Utah-Arizona border.

ARIZONA
★ *Grand Canyon State* ★

"LITTLE SPRING"—that's the meaning of the Native American term for Arizona. Knowing this, you'd expect water to be a big deal here, and you'd be right. Very little rain falls on much of the state, and most rivers and streams flow for only part of the year. Conserving water is key to Arizona's future success.

Millions of years of tug-of-war between uplift in Earth's crust and erosion by rivers has created the spectacular scenery of the Colorado Plateau in the north. The mile- (1.6-km-) deep Grand Canyon is the plateau's crown jewel, but Monument Valley and the Painted Desert are among its other treasures. Forests of ponderosa pine grow on the Mogollon Rim, a long line of steep cliffs that provide a 2,000-foot (600-m) step-down to the Basin and Range region. Major dams have been built to harness rivers here. To the south and west, ranges are lower and basins are broader—and bone dry. The

Sonoran Desert stretches across more than 25,000 square miles (65,000 sq km) of the state into Mexico. Some areas of the desert average 5 to 6 inches (13–15 cm) of rain per year. Summer sun bakes the saguaro and other cacti, with daily summer temperatures averaging above 100°F (38°C).

Native peoples have succeeded in this challenging land for more than 2,500 years. The ancestral Puebloans inhabited cliff dwellings in Canyon de Chelly, and the Hohokam built dams and dug ditches to bring water from the Gila and Salt Rivers to fields of corn, beans, and squash. The Hopi were living in Oraibi when the Navajo and Apache peoples arrived more than 500 years ago. First Spain then Mexico ruled the region, and settlers fought the Indians for control of the land. Arizona became a U.S. territory after the Mexican-American War in 1848.

Silver and copper attracted settlers from the

1692–1821
Spanish missions like San Xavier del Bac, rebuilt in 1783, were founded to teach Arizona's Native Americans Christianity.

1886
Arizona's Indian Wars ended when a lack of food forced Apache chief Geronimo (3rd from left) to surrender to the U.S. Army.

1911
The Theodore Roosevelt Dam, first of several in the Salt River Project, brings water and electricity to fast-growing Phoenix.

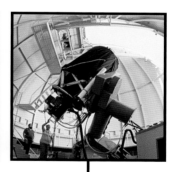

Present day
The Kitt Peak National Observatory's 20-some telescopes earn Tucson the title Astronomy Capital of the World.

The Colorado River has been carving the Grand Canyon (opposite) for millions of years, creating what President Theodore Roosevelt called "the most impressive piece of scenery I have ever looked at." Each year it attracts five million tourists.

Map Labels

COLO.
UTAH
NEVADA
CALIFORNIA
NEW MEXICO
BAJA CALIF.
BAJA CALIF.
SONORA
U.S.
MEXICO

Lake Powell
Four Corners
Monument Valley
Glen Canyon Dam
Page
GLEN CANYON N.R.A.
KAIBAB I.R.
VERMILION CLIFFS NAT. MON.
Kayenta
NAVAJO NAT. MON. (BETATAKIN RUIN)
NAVAJO NAT. MON. (KEET SEEL RUIN)
NAVAJO NAT. MON. (INSCRIPTION HOUSE RUIN)
Black Mesa
CANYON DE CHELLY NAT. MON.
Chinle
Colorado City
PIPE SPRING NAT. MON.
KAIBAB NATIONAL FOREST
Kaibab Plateau
Marble Canyon
NAVAJO NATION RESERVATION
Tuba City
HOPI
HOPI I.R.
Old Oraibi
INDIAN RESERVATION
Polacca
Fort Defiance
Window Rock
HUBBELL TRADING POST N.H.S.
Virgin
Kanab Cr.
Paria
Painted Desert
Little Colorado
GRAND CANYON-PARASHANT NAT. MON.
LAKE MEAD N.R.A.
GRAND CANYON NATIONAL PARK
Grand Canyon
Lake Mead
Hoover Dam
GRAND CANYON N.P.
HAVASUPAI I.R.
Grand Canyon
KAIBAB N.F.
Coconino Plateau
LAKE MEAD NATIONAL RECREATION AREA
Red Lake
HUALAPAI INDIAN RESERVATION
Highest point in Arizona
Humphreys Peak 12,633 ft 3,851 m
WUPATKI NAT. MON.
SUNSET CRATER VOLCANO NAT. MON.
Puerco
Lake Mohave
Dolan Springs
Seligman
Williams
Flagstaff
WALNUT CANYON NAT. MON.
Winslow
PETRIFIED FOREST N.P.
Black Mountains
Kingman
KAIBAB N.F.
COCONINO N.F.
Meteor Crater
Holbrook
ZUNI I.R.
Bullhead City
FT. MOJAVE I.R.
Big Sandy
PRESCOTT NATIONAL FOREST
Verde
Sedona
PRESCOTT N.F.
TUZIGOOT NAT. MON.
Cottonwood
CAMP VERDE I.R.
Clear Creek
Chevelon Cr.
Snowflake
Chino Valley
MONTEZUMA CASTLE NAT. MON.
St. Johns
Lake Havasu
Prescott Valley
YAVAPAI I.R.
Camp Verde
APACHE-SITGREAVES NATIONAL FOREST
Little Colorado
Lake Havasu City
BILL WILLIAMS RIVER N.W.R.
Prescott
VERDE N.W.&S.R.
Mogollon Rim
Show Low
Pinetop-Lakeside
Eagar
Bill Williams
Parker
AGUA FRIA NAT. MON.
Payson
WHITE MOUNTAIN APACHE RESERVATION
Whiteriver
COLORADO RIVER INDIAN RESERVATION
Wickenburg
Agua Fria
TONTO NATIONAL FOREST
Theodore Roosevelt Lake
Salt
White
APACHE-SITGREAVES NATIONAL FOREST
San Francisco
Quartzsite
Verde
FT. McDOWELL I.R.
Sun City
SALT RIVER I.R.
Black
Clifton
CIBOLA N.W.R.
KOFA NATIONAL WILDLIFE REFUGE
Glendale
Scottsdale
TONTO NAT. MON.
Globe
SAN CARLOS APACHE RESERVATION
Phoenix
Mesa
San Carlos
IMPERIAL N.W.R.
SONORAN
Tempe
Chandler
Safford
Gila
GILA RIVER I.R.
CASA GRANDE RUINS NAT. MON.
San Carlos Reservoir
CORONADO N.F.
MARICOPA (AK-CHIN) I.R.
Florence
GILA BEND I.R.
Coolidge
Gila
Yuma
Wellton
Gila Bend
Casa Grande
Eloy
San Manuel
CORONADO N.F.
DESERT
SONORAN DESERT NAT. MON.
Catalina
Santa Cruz
San Pedro
Gila
COCOPAH I.R.
IRONWOOD FOREST NAT. MON.
Oro Valley
CORONADO N.F.
San Luis
Ajo
TOHONO O'ODHAM INDIAN RESERVATION
SAGUARO N.P.
CORONADO N.F.
Willcox
CABEZA PRIETA NATIONAL WILDLIFE REFUGE
PASCUA YAQUI I.R.
Tucson
SAGUARO N.P.
FORT BOWIE N.H.S.
ORGAN PIPE CACTUS NAT. MON.
Kitt Peak National Observatory
SAN XAVIER I.R.
Green Valley
Benson
CHIRICAHUA NAT. MON.
CORONADO N.F.
Sells
BUENOS AIRES N.W.R.
CORONADO N.F.
Tombstone
CORONADO N.F.
TUMACACORI N.H.P.
CORONADO N.F.
Sierra Vista
Bisbee
SAN BERNARDINO N.W.R.
Nogales
Douglas
CORONADO NAT. MEM.

ARIZONA

0   50   100 miles
0   50   100 kilometers
Albers Conic Equal-Area Projection

The Navajo became sheep and goat herders early in the 19th century. Herding provided the Navajo with a steady supply of food and also with wool for the production of trade goods. Their population prospered and grew, doubling by the mid-1800s. In the past century overgrazing and erosion have resulted in loss of grazing land and reduction in the size of their herds.

East, as did cheap land for sheep and cattle ranching. But settlement didn't really begin to grow until after the fighting with the Apache ended in 1886. By the time statehood was granted in 1912, huge irrigation projects were underway. Farming of cotton and citrus fruits boomed. Year-round water meant opportunities for industries, too.

Arizona is now home to 5.6 million people, with most of this growth occurring after World War II. Before the war the population was mainly rural, but now most people live in and around Phoenix and Tucson. The state's climate and scenic beauties have attracted residents, tourists, and businesses alike. People come just to breathe its clean, dry air. The introduction of air-conditioning brought even more people. Cloud-free skies and wide-open spaces attracted the military, especially for air bases and desert warfare research. Related industries, such as aircraft and weapons manufacture, followed. Recently, electronics and other high-tech businesses have thrived.

All this growth brings challenges. For decades, Arizona's "Five Cs"—copper, cattle, cotton, citrus, and climate—were the basis for the state's prosperity. Arizona still produces more copper than all other states combined, but its importance has declined. The three agricultural Cs are still farmed but face problems with markets and water supply. Water "wars" between farmers, Native Americans, and city dwellers are ongoing. In addition, the Central Arizona Project, a massive effort to bring Colorado River water to the growing cities of Phoenix and Tucson, puts Arizona at odds with neighboring California and Nevada. If questions of water use are addressed, the state will continue to prosper, and its fifth C—climate—will always encourage people to "follow the sun" to Arizona.

ARIZONA
Grand Canyon State

STATEHOOD	February 14, 1912; 48th state
CAPITAL	Phoenix
LARGEST CITY	Phoenix Population 1,371,960
TOTAL AREA	113,998 sq mi; 295,254 sq km
LAND AREA	113,635 sq mi; 294,312 sq km
POPULATION	6,392,017
POPULATION DENSITY	56 people per sq mi
MAJOR RACIAL/ ETHNIC GROUPS	73.0% white; 4.6% Native American; 4.1% African American; 2.8% Asian. Hispanic (any race) 29.6%.
INDUSTRY	real estate, manufactured goods, retail, state and local government, transportation and public utilities, wholesale trade, health services, tourism, electronics
AGRICULTURE	vegetables, cattle, dairy products, cotton, fruit, nursery stock, nuts

CACTUS WREN   SAGUARO

Did you know?

1. Of the 21 Indian reservations in Arizona, the largest belongs to the Navajo Nation. Native Americans and the federal government own 70 percent of the state.
2. The planet Pluto was discovered from the Lowell Observatory in Flagstaff in 1930.
3. Arizona's largest lizard, the Gila monster, is the only poisonous lizard in the United States.
4. Lake Powell, the nation's second largest reservoir, is named for John Wesley Powell, the one-armed Civil War veteran who was the first white person to successfully navigate and map the Grand Canyon.
5. London Bridge, which once spanned England's River Thames, was purchased for Lake Havasu City in the 1960s. The bridge was shipped across the Atlantic and reconstructed in the Arizona desert.

NEW MEXICO

★ *Land of Enchantment* ★

THE YEAR WAS 1610. Ten years before the *Mayflower* landed on Cape Cod, Santa Fe became the capital of New Mexico, a province of New Spain. Nearly four centuries later, the handsome Palace of the Governors still stands in what is now the state capital. Spanish, Mexican, and Native American influences blend across rugged and scenic New Mexico.

The state's landscape was shaped by forces much older—the uplift of ancient seafloors, massive volcanic eruptions, and millions of years of erosion. The northwest corner contains the Colorado Plateau's deeply-cut valleys and mesas. Ship Rock, the hardened neck of an eroded volcano, stands there as a lonely reminder of a fiery past. Rolling lands of the Great Plains cover the eastern third of the state, while the rugged spine of the Rockies reaches into central New Mexico. The Rio Grande flows through its middle from

Colorado south to Texas and Mexico, and deserts cover much of the southern portion.

Immigrants have long ventured to New Mexico. The first may have been Ice-Age hunters 12,000 years ago. Evidence of their presence has been found near the town of Clovis, and tips from their spears are known worldwide as Clovis points. When the Spanish first explored here in the 1500s, they found Zuni, Hopi, and Tewa peoples living in clusters of apartment-like structures. They named these stone and adobe (mud-brick) buildings pueblos after the Spanish word for towns. Some of these centuries-old dwellings are still occupied. The newcomers settled across the region, building missions, setting up ranches, and trading with the native people.

After Mexico gained independence from Spain in 1821, it began trading with the United States. As the Santa Fe Trail brought more and

1610

Santa Fe, the oldest capital city in the nation, has been the seat of government in New Mexico since Spanish territorial days.

1863–1868

Thousands of Navajo were rounded up by the U.S. Army and forced to march to a reservation called Bosque Redondo.

1945

The first test of a U.S.-made atomic bomb was at Trinity Site in the desert near Alamogordo on July 16, 1945.

Present day

Forest fires are a yearly spring-summer threat. In 2003 a task force was created to help prevent damage to high-risk communities.

Almost one in ten residents of New Mexico is Native American. The state hosts powwows—celebrations of Native American dancing and singing—that attract participants from all across the United States.

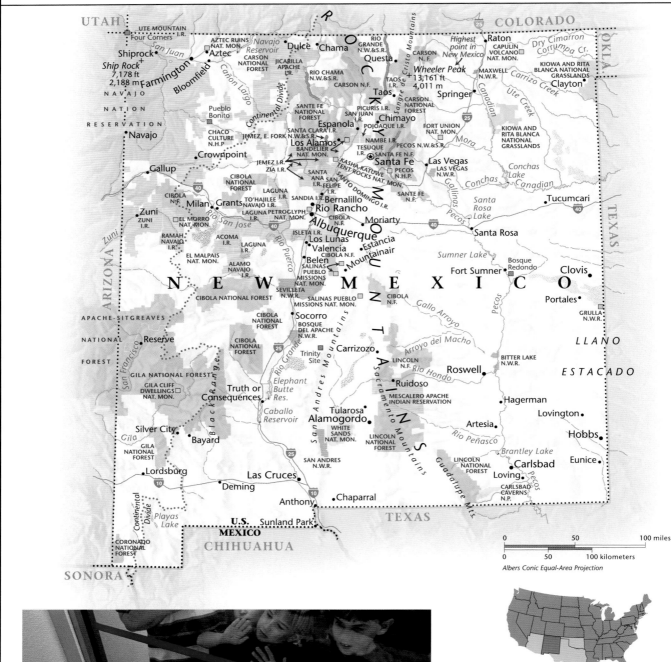

UTAH | COLORADO
Four Corners
UTE MOUNTAIN I.R.
Shiprock
Aztec
AZTEC RUINS NAT. MON.
Navajo Reservoir
Dulce
Chama
RIO GRANDE N.W.&S.R.
Raton
CAPULIN VOLCANO NAT. MON.
Dry Cimarron Cr.
CARSON N.F.
Questa
Highest point in New Mexico
Ship Rock 7,178 ft 2,188 m
Farmington
Bloomfield
Cañon Largo
CARSON NATIONAL FOREST
JICARILLA APACHE I.R.
RIO CHAMA N.W.&S.R.
CARSON N.F.
Wheeler Peak 13,161 ft 4,011 m
Springer
MAXWELL N.W.R.
KIOWA AND RITA BLANCA NATIONAL GRASSLANDS
Carrizo Creek
Clayton
NAVAJO NATION
Continental Divide
Sangre de Cristo Mountains
TAOS I.R.
Taos
CARSON NATIONAL FOREST
FORT UNION NAT. MON.
Canadian
Ute Creek
KIOWA AND RITA BLANCA NATIONAL GRASSLANDS
RESERVATION
Navajo
Pueblo Bonito
SANTA FE NATIONAL FOREST
PICURIS I.R.
Chimayo
Espanola
POJOAQUE I.R.
Mora
PECOS N.W.&S.R.
CHACO CULTURE N.H.P.
JEMEZ, E. FORK N.W.&S.R.
SANTA CLARA I.R.
Los Alamos
BANDELIER NAT. MON.
NAMBE I.R.
TESUQUE I.R.
SANTA FE N.F.
Crownpoint
JEMEZ I.R.
ZIA I.R.
KASHA-KATUWE TENT ROCKS NAT. MON.
Santa Fe
Las Vegas
LAS VEGAS N.W.R.
Conchas Lake
Gallup
CIBOLA NATIONAL FOREST
SANTA ANA I.R.
SAN FELIPE I.R.
SANTO DOMINGO I.R.
PECOS N.H.P.
SANTA FE N.F.
Conchas
Canadian
CIBOLA N.F.
LAGUNA
TO'HAJIILEE NAVAJO I.R.
SANDIA I.R.
LAGUNA PETROGLYPH NAT. MON.
Bernalillo
Rio Rancho
Santa Rosa Lake
Tucumcari
Milan
Grants
Zuni
ZUNI I.R.
EL MORRO NAT. MON.
ACOMA I.R.
Rio San Jose
CIBOLA N.F.
LAGUNA I.R.
ISLETA I.R.
Albuquerque
Moriarty
RAMAH NAVAJO I.R.
EL MALPAIS NAT. MON.
ALAMO NAVAJO I.R.
Rio Puerco
Los Lunas
Valencia
Estancia
Santa Rosa
CIBOLA N.F.
Mountainair
Belen
SALINAS PUEBLO MISSIONS NAT. MON.
Sumner Lake
Bosque Redondo
Clovis
N E W   M E X I C O
CIBOLA NATIONAL FOREST
SEVILLETA N.W.R.
SALINAS PUEBLO MISSIONS NAT. MON.
CIBOLA N.F.
Fort Sumner
Portales
GRULLA N.W.R.
CIBOLA NATIONAL FOREST
Socorro
BOSQUE DEL APACHE N.W.R.
Gallo Arroyo
Pecos
L L A N O
APACHE-SITGREAVES
CIBOLA NATIONAL FOREST
Sacramento Mountains
Arroyo del Macho
E S T A C A D O
NATIONAL
Reserve
CIBOLA NATIONAL FOREST
San Andres Mountains
Carrizozo
BITTER LAKE N.W.R.
FOREST
San Francisco
Trinity Site
LINCOLN N.F.
Rio Hondo
Roswell
GILA NATIONAL FOREST
Elephant Butte Res.
Ruidoso
Hagerman
GILA CLIFF DWELLINGS NAT. MON.
Truth or Consequences
Caballo Reservoir
MESCALERO APACHE INDIAN RESERVATION
Artesia
Lovington
Silver City
Gila
Tularosa
WHITE SANDS NAT. MON.
Alamogordo
LINCOLN NATIONAL FOREST
Rio Peñasco
Hobbs
GILA NATIONAL FOREST
Bayard
SAN ANDRES N.W.R.
Brantley Lake
LINCOLN NATIONAL FOREST
Carlsbad
Eunice
Lordsburg
Loving
Pecos
Deming
Las Cruces
Guadalupe Mts.
CARLSBAD CAVERNS N.P.
Continental Divide
Anthony
Chaparral
CORONADO NATIONAL FOREST
Playas Lake
U.S.
Sunland Park
MEXICO
TEXAS
CHIHUAHUA
SONORA

0   50   100 miles
0   50   100 kilometers
Albers Conic Equal-Area Projection

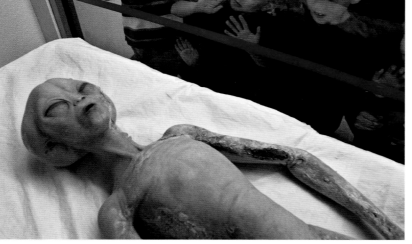

New Mexico's colorful landscapes have long attracted artists and lovers of the outdoors. Many believe they also may be inviting to beings from beyond Earth. Each summer the International UFO Museum and Research Center in Roswell hosts the Roswell UFO Festival. It commemorates the so-called Roswell Incident, in which an unidentified flying object, or UFO, reportedly crashed near the town in 1947. The alien shown here is a prop from a movie about the event.

more Americans, conflicts arose that sparked the Mexican-American War. New Mexico became a U.S. territory in 1850, soon after the war ended. More migrants arrived from the East, first by wagon train and then rail. They mined silver and gold, raised cattle and sheep, and irrigated crops in river valleys. Statehood came late, with New Mexico becoming the 47th state in 1912.

New kinds of immigrants arrived in the 20th century. Artists were lured by the state's colorful landscapes and dramatic skies. Historic Taos Pueblo and Sante Fe became world-famous art centers. Another group arrived—quietly—in 1943. Government scientists came to isolated Los Alamos to build a top-secret weapon. Their success was marked by the explosion of the first atomic bomb in the New Mexico desert in July 1945.

Today, New Mexico is still home to many specialists in military, nuclear, and space program research. Much high-tech work is concentrated around Albuquerque. Mines produce uranium, potash, and lead. Oil and natural gas wells dot the eastern plains, and mountain forests grow ponderosa pines for lumber. Cattle ranches can be upwards of a hundred square miles in area. A farming specialty is chili peppers, with New Mexico producing more than any other state. Tourists in increasing numbers visit historic sites, enjoy desert vistas, and hike wild landscapes.

New Mexico takes pride in its ethnic diversity. More than 42 percent of its population claims Hispanic heritage, the highest level in the nation, and there are more than a dozen American Indian groups. But poverty is a problem—especially among native peoples—and an overall population increase has created water-use issues that New Mexico's people must solve if their state is to remain the Land of Enchantment.

NEW MEXICO
Land of Enchantment

STATEHOOD	January 6, 1912; 47th state
CAPITAL	Santa Fe
LARGEST CITY	Albuquerque Population 463,874
TOTAL AREA	121,590 sq mi; 314,915 sq km
LAND AREA	121,356 sq mi; 314,309 sq km
POPULATION	2,059,179
POPULATION DENSITY	16 people per sq mi
MAJOR RACIAL/ ETHNIC GROUPS	68.4% white; 9.4% Native American; 2.1% African American; 1.4% Asian. Hispanic (any race) 46.3%.
INDUSTRY	electronic equipment, state and local government, real estate, business services, federal government, oil and gas extraction, health services
AGRICULTURE	cattle, dairy products, hay, chilies, onions

ROADRUNNER   YUCCA

Did you know?

1. In 1950 the town of Hot Springs volunteered to change its name to Truth or Consequences. It is the only city in the country named for a game show.
2. The roadrunner, New Mexico's state bird, can reach ground speeds of 15 miles an hour (24 kph).
3. The Big Room, the largest underground chamber in Carlsbad Caverns National Park, is big enough to hold six football fields.
4. The largest gypsum dune field in the world is in White Sands National Monument.
5. In terms of percent of its total population, New Mexico has more Native Americans and Hispanic people than any other state in the lower 48.

OKLAHOMA
★ *Sooner State* ★

THEY JUST COULDN'T WAIT to get there. Eager 1880s homesteaders who couldn't stand the wait for Oklahoma Territory to open were called "Sooners." Later, as many as 50,000 immigrants made wild "land runs," claiming lands to settle. The most famous land run, on April 22, 1889, saw a patch of prairie turn into a city of 10,000 newcomers in just a few hours. The place? Oklahoma City.

More than half a century earlier, a much different and sadder migration had begun to create the Oklahoma of today. Federal troops pushed Cherokee, Choctaw, Chickasaw, Creek, and Seminole people from their homes in the Southeast to lands west of the Mississippi River. Fifteen thousand Cherokee people endured the most tragic of these journeys during the winter of 1838–39. As many as 4,000 died along this Trail of Tears. The journey ended in what became known as Indian Territory, then

much larger than present-day Oklahoma. These immigrants joined other groups already there, including the Osage, Pawnee, and Comanche. Not surprisingly, when a Choctaw chief was asked to name the re-divided territory in 1866, he chose "okla" ("people") and "homa" ("red"). The state kept the name when it entered the Union in 1907. Today, members of 67 tribes live here, making up almost 8 percent of the total population.

One of the easiest state shapes to recognize, Oklahoma resembles a cooking pan, complete with handle. Landforms range from mountains to flatlands, and habitats from deep woods to sparse grasslands. The Ozark Plateau, shared with Missouri and Arkansas, covers the state's northeast corner. This rugged region is eroded by fast-flowing streams, many of which have been dammed for hydropower, flood control, and recreation. Other highlands include the forested Ouachita Mountains in the southeast

1830—42
The forced march of the Cherokee from their homes in the Southeast to Indian Territory became known as the Trail of Tears.

1889
When the government opened former Indian land to settlement, thousands rushed in to stake their claims. Each settler got 160 acres.

1930s
Drought and poor conservation practices stripped farms of topsoil, forcing thousands of farmers to abandon their land.

1995
In an act of domestic terrorism, antigovernment militants destroyed the Murrah Federal Building in Oklahoma City.

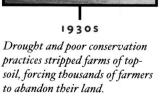

Oklahoma is right in the middle of Tornado Alley, a region of the Great Plains where more twisters strike than any place else on Earth. Critical research is carried out here by scientists who attempt to predict tornadoes and their destructive paths.

OKLAHOMA
Sooner State

OKLAHOMA

STATEHOOD	November 16, 1907; 46th state
CAPITAL	Oklahoma City
LARGEST CITY	Oklahoma City Population 519,034
TOTAL AREA	69,898 sq mi; 181,036 sq km
LAND AREA	68,667 sq mi; 177,847 sq km
POPULATION	3,751,351
POPULATION DENSITY	53 people per sq mi
MAJOR RACIAL/ETHNIC GROUPS	72.2% white; 8.6% Native American; 7.4% African American; 1.7% Asian. Hispanic (any race) 8.9%.
INDUSTRY	manufacturing, services, government, finance, insurance, real estate
AGRICULTURE	cattle, wheat, hogs, poultry, nursery stock

SCISSOR-TAILED FLYCATCHER

MISTLETOE

Did you know?

1. The country's first parking meters were installed in Oklahoma City in 1935.
2. In 1930 an oil gusher called Wild Mary Sudik sprayed so much oil and gas that people in Oklahoma City couldn't light matches for fear of causing explosions.
3. The famous ballerina Maria Tallchief was an Osage from Fairfax, Oklahoma. The ballerina mural in the rotunda of the state capitol honors this Native American's talent.
4. Oklahoma has had 14 official flags during its history.
5. The state capitol building in Oklahoma City has a working oil well on its grounds.
6. Tulsa is known as the Oil Capital of the World.
7. Oklahoma has more artificial lakes than any other state, with over one million surface acres of water.
8. Until statehood, Oklahoma was known as Indian Territory. Today 39 tribes have their headquarters in the state.

and the Wichita Mountains in the southwest. Much of the rest of the pan is filled with a mixture of hills and plains, rolling out to the Panhandle. There, the drier High Plains are topped by Black Mesa, Oklahoma's highest point, at 4,973 feet (1,516 m).

COLORADO
Black Mesa
4,973 ft
1,516 m
Cimar
Bois
City
Highest point
in Oklahoma
KIOWA AND
RITA BLANCA
NATIONAL
GRASSLAND

Oklahoma's resources lie both below and above ground. Oil is found all across the varied landscape, with "black gold" pumped even on the state capitol grounds in Oklahoma City. Oil refining is a major industry, as is manufacturing of aviation components, auto parts, and electronics. Data processing is a growing service business. Top agricultural activities include cattle ranching and wheat growing. Peanuts, cotton, and vegetables are grown in the Red River Valley bordering Texas.

In the 1930s Oklahoma farmers fell victim to drought and to farming practices that had stripped the soil of its natural protection. Wind eroded their plowed fields, sending thousands of "Okies" on the road, some as far as California. Better care of the fragile soil has allowed much of the farmland to recover, but the wind can still be a problem. Cold fronts clash with warm and humid air each spring, often producing destructive tornadoes. One twister struck near Oklahoma City in 1999, with winds of 318 miles per hour (512 kph)— the highest ever recorded for a tornado.

Oklahoma today has great promise, but problems as well. Average income is among the lowest in the nation, with many Native Americans living in poverty. Farms and ranches are struggling to survive. The state is still recovering from the terrible tragedy of the Oklahoma City bombing that killed 168 people in 1995. But with its diversity and a wealth of natural resources, Oklahoma is bound to prosper "sooner" rather than later.

KANSAS

MO.

HIGH
PLAINS

Beaver • Beaver

Guymon
OPTIMA
N.W.R.
Optima
Lake

TEXAS

Miami

Buffalo

Alva
SALT PLAINS
N.W.R.

Blackwell

Ponca
City

Salt Fork
Great
Salt Plains
Lake

Rock Cr.

Kaw
Lake

Osage
Nation
Reservation

Bartlesville

Pawhuska

Oologah
Lake

Vinita
Grove

Woodward

Fairview

Enid

Perry

Sooner
Lake

Skiatook
Lake

Owasso

Pryor

Lake O' The
Cherokees

Wolf Creek

North Canadian

Cimarron

Stillwater

Cushing

Sand Springs

CIMARRON TPK.

Keystone
Lake

Tulsa

Broken Arrow

Jenks

Sapulpa

Bixby

Wagoner

Lake
Hudson

OZARK PLATEAU

Tahlequah

Stilwell

BLACK KETTLE
NATIONAL
GRASSLAND

WASHITA
N.W.R.

Watonga

Kingfisher

Guthrie

Edmond

O K L A H O M A

Yukon

Deep Fork

Bristow

Muskogee

Ft.
Gibson L.

Tenkiller
Lake

WASHITA
BATTLEFIELD
N.H.S.

Weatherford

Clinton

El Reno

Bethany

Oklahoma City

DEEP FORK
N.W.R.

Okmulgee

Henryetta

Checotah

SEQUOYAH
N.W.R.

Sallisaw

Sayre

Elk
City

Moore

Shawnee

Tecumseh
Seminole

N. Canadian

Arkansas

Washita

North Fork Red

Hobart

Anadarko

Norman

Wewoka

Holdenville

Robert S.
Kerr Lake

Poteau

Mangum

Elm Fork Red

Lake Altus

Wichita Mts.

Chickasha

Purcell

Canadian

Little

Eufaula
Lake

McAlester

Wilburton

Heavener

Salt Fork Red

WICHITA MTS.
WILDLIFE
REFUGE

H.E. BAILEY TURNPIKE

Pauls
Valley

Ada

Sardis
Lake

OUACHITA
NATIONAL FOREST

Hollis

Altus

Lawton

Marlow

Washita

Kiamichi

Ouachita Mountains

Red

Frederick

Duncan

Sulphur

CHICKASAW
N.R.A.

McGee
Creek
Lake

Little

Mtn. Fork

Broken
Bow
Lake

Walters

Waurika
Lake

Arbuckle Mts.

Atoka

Muddy Boggy

Antlers

Hugo
Lake

LITTLE
RIVER
N.W.R.

Broken
Bow

Lone
Grove

Ardmore
Madill

Tishomingo

TISHOMINGO
N.W.R.

Coleman

Blue

Hugo

Red

Idabel

OUACHITA
NATIONAL
FOREST.

Durant

TEXAS

Lake
Texoma

INDIAN NATION TURNPIKE

TURNER TURNPIKE

WILL ROGERS TPK.

Claremore

Chikaskia

Arkansas

ARKANSAS

0   40   80 miles
0   40   80 kilometers
Albers Conic Equal-Area Projection

*Rigs for pumping oil, like the one shown
here, can be found all across Oklahoma.
While Bartlesville was the site of the
first commercial oil well in 1897, nearby
Tulsa soon became—and remains—the
state's oil center. The Sooner State
ranks sixth among U.S. states in oil
production and fourth in output of
natural gas, which has recently become
a more valuable resource for the state.*

TEXAS

★ *Lone Star State* ★

TEXAS IS BIGGER than most countries—and it once was one! In 1836, Texans fought Mexico for independence. The best-known battle took place in San Antonio at a mission called the Alamo. There, a band of volunteers fought for days against General Antonio López de Santa Anna's Mexican Army—and died. But six weeks later, on April 21, other Texans defeated Santa Anna near San Jacinto. Their famous battle cry? "Remember the Alamo!"

When it entered the Union in 1845 as the 28th state, Texas was considered so large that Congress gave it the chance to split into five separate states. It never did divide itself, so it's not surprising that sprawling Texas has an amazing mix of environments. Sun-baked deserts and cold peaks in the west contrast with warm, swampy bayous along the Louisiana border. Ranchers in the Texas Panhandle may endure bitter winter winds on the same day that grapefruit is picked in the Rio Grande Valley 800 miles (1,280 km) to the south.

The Spanish first arrived on Texas's Gulf shores in 1519, and the area became part of New Spain. For nearly two centuries France struggled with Spain for control of the region. Then New Spain won its independence in 1821 and became Mexico. Texas became an independent republic in 1836, and nine years later, it joined the United States.

Within a dozen years, cattle was king in Texas. Cowboys on horseback let their longhorns graze freely across the range. Huge herds were driven to market along the Chisholm Trail all the way to Kansas. Such cattle drives ended as the open range was fenced. Angus, Hereford, and other cattle breeds now join longhorns on Texas ranches large and small. Cattle ranching is still big business, and the rugged individualism of "cowboy culture" lives on in Texas.

1718

San Antonio de Valero, later known as the Alamo, was one of several missions built throughout Texas by the Spanish.

1836

Sam Houston defeated Santa Anna in the Battle of San Jacinto, winning Texas independence from Mexico.

1901

The discovery of oil at Spindletop near Beaumont led to the building of refineries that support the state's oil and gas industries.

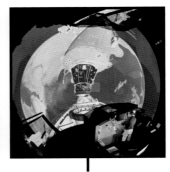

Present day

The Lyndon B. Johnson Space Center, site of this mission simulator, is the foundation of the space technology industry in Houston.

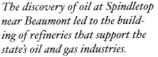

While most Texans today live in urban and suburban areas, real-life cowboys—some on horseback—still herd cattle on ranches in the Lone Star State.

TEXAS
Lone Star State

STATEHOOD	December 29, 1845; 28th state
CAPITAL	Austin
LARGEST CITY	Houston Population 2,009,834
TOTAL AREA	268,581 sq mi; 695,621 sq km
LAND AREA	261,797 sq mi; 678,051 sq km
POPULATION	25,145,561
POPULATION DENSITY	93 people per sq mi
MAJOR RACIAL/ ETHNIC GROUPS	70.4% white; 11.8% African American; 3.8% Asian; 0.7% Native American. Hispanic (any race) 37.6%.
INDUSTRY	chemicals, machinery, electronics and computers, food products, petroleum and natural gas, transportation equipment
AGRICULTURE	cattle, sheep, poultry, cotton, sorghum, wheat, rice, hay, peanuts, pecans

MOCKINGBIRD   BLUEBONNET

Did you know?

1. Texas is bigger than the combined area of all seven countries in Central America. It is also bigger than every country in Europe except Russia.
2. In 1900 a storm surge caused by a hurricane killed 6,000 people in Galveston.
3. Six national flags have flown over Texas during the course of its history: Spanish, French, Mexican, Texan, Confederate, and American.
4. Texas is noted for having towns with strange names, such as Goodnight, Cut and Shoot, Wink, Muleshoe, North Zulch, Birthright, Turkey, and Noodle. A city named Iraan is made up of the first names of Ira and Ann Yates who struck oil on their farm in 1926.
5. Both the silicon computer chip and the electronic calculator were invented by engineers at a company named Texas Instruments.

The Panhandle has some of the state's best farmlands, where wheat, sorghum, and soybeans are grown. Year-round warmth allows winter vegetables and citrus fruits to be produced in the far south. Irrigated cotton is grown on the dry plains. Scenic rivers run from the higher lands of west and central Texas southeast across the coastal plain to the Gulf of Mexico. Shrimp, crabs, and oysters are caught in Gulf waters.

The discovery of East Texas oil in 1901 brought wealth and propelled the state into the modern era. World War II fueled state manufacturing. San Antonio became a major military hub and biotechnology research center. In recent decades, Texas cities have become leaders in banking, electronics, and many high-tech industries.

Today Texas is second only to Alaska in area and second only to California in population (about 22 million). In 2001, another "second" was achieved when George W. Bush became the second Texas Bush to live in the White House. The state ranks first among states in number of counties (254), number of farms and amount of farmland, cattle and beef production, and oil and gas output. Texas surely ranks high in the influence of Hispanic, mostly Mexican, culture. One-third of its people are Hispanic. As early as 2026, Hispanic Texans could be in the majority.

Texans face problems, too. A long border and massive immigration sometimes brings trouble. The U.S. Border Patrol works to keep out illegal migrants and drugs. The Texas economy rides unsteady oil prices. Pollution comes from oil industries and millions of Texas cars and trucks. State population has increased by five million since 1990. But the promise of the Lone Star State shines for newcomers and old hands alike. The future for big, friendly Texas sure seems bright.

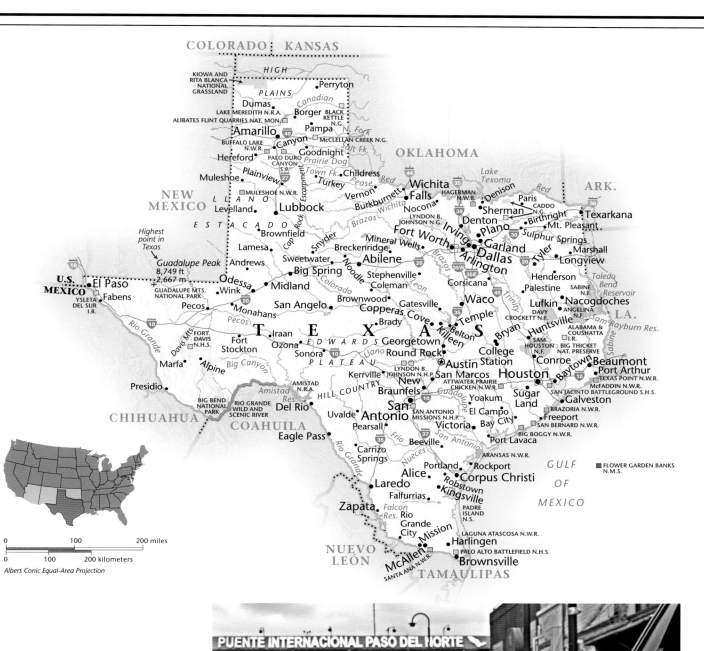

COLORADO KANSAS

HIGH

KIOWA AND
RITA BLANCA
NATIONAL
GRASSLAND

PLAINS

Canadian

Perryton

Dumas
LAKE MEREDITH N.R.A.   Borger   BLACK
ALIBATES FLINT QUARRIES NAT. MON.   KETTLE
                                              N.G.
Amarillo   Pampa
                McCLELLAN CREEK N.G.
BUFFALO LAKE   Canyon   OKLAHOMA
N.W.R.
Hereford   Goodnight   Prairie Dog
        PALO DURO   Town Fk.
        CANYON   Childress
Muleshoe   Plainview   S.P.   Turkey   Pease   Red
                                                    Lake
NEW   Levelland   MULESHOE N.W.R.   Vernon   Texoma   ARK.
MEXICO   LLANO   Wichita   HAGERMAN   Denison   Paris
                                Falls   N.W.R.
Highest   ESTACADO   Lubbock   Burkburnett   Sherman   CADDO   Texarkana
point in   Brazos   Nocona   N.G.
Texas   Brownfield   Wichita   Denton   Birthright   Mt. Pleasant   30
                                LYNDON B.   Plano
Guadalupe Peak   Lamesa   Cap Rock   JOHNSON N.G.   Fort Worth   Irving   Sulphur Springs
8,749 ft   Andrews   Snyder   Mineral Wells   Garland   Tyler
2,667 m   Sweetwater   Breckenridge   Dallas   Marshall
GUADALUPE MTS.   Big Spring   Abilene   Arlington   Longview
U.S.   NATIONAL PARK   Odessa   Colorado   20   35E   Corsicana   Toledo
MEXICO   El Paso   Wink   Midland   Stephenville   Leon   Henderson   Bend
    Fabens   Coleman   Palestine   SABINE   Reservoir
YSLETA   Pecos   Monahans   San Angelo   Brownwood   Waco   45   N.F.
DEL SUR   Copperas Cove   Gatesville   Lufkin   Nacogdoches
I.R.   Pecos   Iraan   Brady   Temple   Trinity   ANGELINA   DAVY
                        T E X A S   Belton   Bryan   CROCKETT N.F.   Huntsville   N.F.
Fort   EDWARDS   Georgetown   Killeen   SAM   ALABAMA &
Marfa   DAVIS   Ozona   Sonora   Llano   Round Rock   College   HOUSTON   COUSHATTA
    MTS.   PLATEAU   LYNDON B.   Austin   Station   N.F.   NAT. PRESERVE   I.R.
N.H.S.   Fort   JOHNSON N.H.P.   San Marcos   Conroe   Sam Rayburn Res.
Alpine   Stockton   HILL COUNTRY   Kerrville   ATTWATER PRAIRIE   Houston   Baytown   Beaumont
Big Canyon   New   CHICKEN N.W.R.   BIG THICKET   Port Arthur
Presidio   AMISTAD   Braunfels   Guadalupe   Sugar   SAN JACINTO BATTLEGROUND S.H.S.   TEXAS POINT N.W.R.
        N.R.A.   Yoakum   Land   McFADDIN N.W.R.
BIG BEND   Amistad   San   SAN ANTONIO   El Campo   BRAZORIA N.W.R.   Galveston
NATIONAL   Res.   Del Rio   Antonio   MISSIONS N.H.P.   Bay   Freeport
PARK   RIO GRANDE   Uvalde   Victoria   City   SAN BERNARD N.W.R.
CHIHUAHUA   WILD AND   Pearsall   BIG BOGGY N.W.R.
COAHUILA   SCENIC RIVER   Frio   37   San Antonio   Port Lavaca
        Eagle Pass   Beeville
                    Nueces   ARANSAS N.W.R.
        Carrizo   35   Portland   Rockport   GULF   FLOWER GARDEN BANKS
        Springs   Alice   Robstown   Corpus Christi   N.M.S.
                Rio Grande   Laredo   Falfurrias   Kingsville   OF
        Zapata   Falcon   Rio   PADRE   MEXICO
NUEVO   Res.   Grande   ISLAND
LEON   City   Mission   LAGUNA ATASCOSA N.W.R.   N.S.
                Harlingen
            McAllen   Brownsville   PALO ALTO BATTLEFIELD N.H.S.
TAMAULIPAS   SANTA ANA N.W.R.

0   100   200 miles
0   100   200 kilometers
Albers Conic Equal-Area Projection

PUENTE INTERNACIONAL PASO DEL NORTE

*Many Mexicans along the 1,250-mile-
(2,010-km-) long Texas-Mexico border
have developed a cross-border life.
Thousands, like this taxi driver, live
in their home country and commute
each day across the international
boundary to work in El Paso and
other Texas border cities. Others risk
their lives to enter the U.S. illegally
by crossing the Rio Grande.*

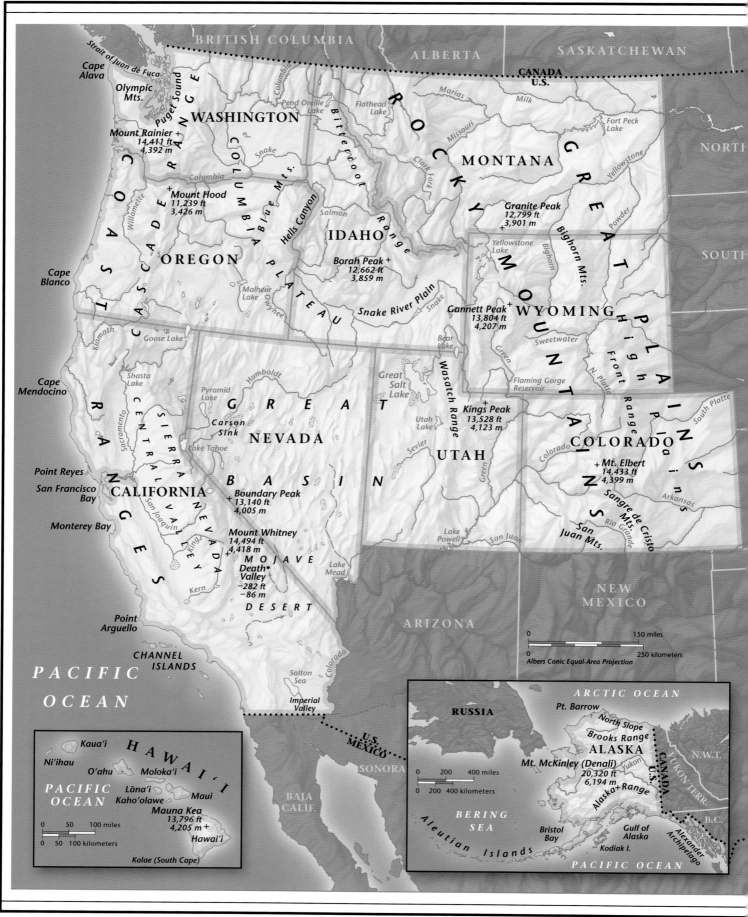

BRITISH COLUMBIA

ALBERTA

SASKATCHEWAN

Strait of Juan de Fuca

Cape Alava

Olympic Mts.

CANADA
U.S.

WASHINGTON

Mount Rainier +
14,411 ft
4,392 m

Columbia

Pend Oreille Lake

Flathead Lake

Marias

Milk

Missouri

Fort Peck Lake

NORTH

R O C K Y

MONTANA

Yellowstone

+Mount Hood
11,239 ft
3,426 m

Columbia

Blue Mts.

Snake

Salmon

Clark Fork

IDAHO

Granite Peak
12,799 ft
+3,901 m

Powder

SOUTH

OREGON

Willamette

Hells Canyon

Borah Peak +
12,662 ft
3,859 m

Range

Bighorn

Bighorn Mts.

Bitterroot

M O U N T A I N

G R E A T

Cape Blanco

Malheur Lake

Owyhee

Snake River Plain

Snake

Gannett Peak+
13,804 ft
4,207 m

WYOMING

Yellowstone Lake

Green

Sweetwater

Front

Bear Lake

Flaming Gorge Reservoir

Cape Mendocino

Klamath

Shasta Lake

Goose Lake

Great Salt Lake

Wasatch Range

Kings Peak +
13,528 ft
4,123 m

COLORADO

Range

P L A I N S

Plains

Humboldt

Pyramid Lake

G R E A T

Sacramento

Point Reyes

San Francisco Bay

Carson Sink

Lake Tahoe

NEVADA

Utah Lake

UTAH

+ Mt. Elbert
14,433 ft
4,399 m

South Platte

High

Colorado

Sierra

Central Valley

CALIFORNIA

B A S I N

Boundary Peak
+ 13,140 ft
4,005 m

Sevier

Green

Arkansas

Sangre de Cristo

Monterey Bay

San Joaquin

Kings

NEVADA

SIERRA

Mount Whitney
14,494 ft
+4,418 m

Lake Powell

San Juan

Rio Grande

Mts.

San Juan Mts.

Point Arguello

Kern

M O J A V E

Death Valley
–282 ft
–86 m

Lake Mead

NEW MEXICO

RANGES

D E S E R T

Colorado

CHANNEL ISLANDS

Salton Sea

Colorado

ARIZONA

0   150 miles

0   250 kilometers

Albers Conic Equal-Area Projection

P A C I F I C

O C E A N

Imperial Valley

U.S.
MEXICO

SONORA

ARCTIC OCEAN

RUSSIA

Pt. Barrow

North Slope

Brooks Range

ALASKA

CANADA
U.S.

N.W.T.

BAJA
CALIF.

0   200   400 miles

0   200   400 kilometers

Mt. McKinley (Denali)
20,320 ft
6,194 m

Yukon

YUKON TERR.

Kaua'i

Ni'ihau

H A W A I ' I

O'ahu

Moloka'i

B E R I N G
S E A

Alaska+Range

B.C.

PACIFIC OCEAN

Lāna'i

Maui

Aleutian Islands

Bristol Bay

Gulf of Alaska

Alexander Archipelago

Kaho'olawe

Mauna Kea
13,796 ft
4,205 m +

Kodiak I.

0   50   100 miles

0   50   100 kilometers

Hawai'i

PACIFIC OCEAN

Kalae (South Cape)

The West

THE WEST BEGINS where the Great Plains meet the Rocky Mountains. Between the Rockies and the Sierra Nevada is a vast, crumpled land called the Great Basin where rivers vanish beneath desert sand or drain into seasonal lakes. North of the Great Basin, rich volcanic soils from ancient lava flows cover the Columbia Plateau.

Along the western rim, coastal mountains wring moisture from Pacific storms. The rain and snow nourish forests of spruce, cedar, hemlock, and redwood. The great Central Valley in California and the Willamette Valley in Oregon are the largest of many fertile lowlands. The vast Alaskan peninsula stretches from its forested panhandle in the southeast, over towering peaks and treeless plains to the Arctic Ocean, then west almost to Asia. Tropical Hawaii, a chain of volcanic islands, is located in the Pacific Ocean more than 2,400 miles (3,900 km) from the U.S. mainland.

A Restless and Enduring Frontier

GEOGRAPHIC EXTREMES rule in the West. The nation's highest, lowest, wettest, and driest places are here, along with volcanoes, earthquakes, flash floods, mudslides, and wildfires. For thousands of years the Nez Perce thrived in the northwest by spearing salmon and collecting berries. Paiute irrigated fields of corn and squash in the Great Basin, and Blackfeet hunted game in the Rockies.

Europeans did not reach this region of the New World until 1542 when Juan Cabrillo sailed up the coast. Vitus Bering navigated the Alaska Panhandle during 1741, and in 1778 Captain James Cook reached Hawaii. The Spanish built a string of missions along the California coast beginning in 1769. But the rest of the region remained largely unsettled until the 1840s, when thousands of people followed the Oregon and California Trails across the West. Other groups, such as Brigham Young's Mormon pioneers, settled Utah's Salt Lake Valley. With the discovery of gold in California in 1848, the world literally rushed in.

By 1869 the Transcontinental Railroad, built with the help of Chinese and Irish labor, linked the eastern and western halves of the country. New arrivals from every corner of the globe fanned out across the West to take advantage of the untapped riches of America's newest frontier. In Oregon and Washington logging employed thousands of workers. The introduction of cattle and other domestic stock and crops, followed by the invention of barbed wire, altered natural grasslands forever. Mineral strikes created boom towns as far away as Alaska. In Hawaii lush tropical forests gave way to sugarcane and fruit fields. By the early 1900s—50 years after the California gold rush—Americans had largely displaced Mexicans in California, Native Hawaiians, and Indians throughout the West. At the same time the American conservation movement emerged when Congress created the world's first national park: Yellowstone (1872).

Today, mining, logging, ranching, and fishing remain important in rural areas. Every Western state depends upon farming, especially California where huge corporate operations employ migrant field workers from Mexico and other Latin American countries. However, providing water both to farms and growing cities in this mostly arid land is an enormous challenge that will require creative leadership to solve.

Since the 1920s, a variety of new industries has emerged to energize the economies and cultures of this vast region. Southern California and Las Vegas are famous for entertainment. A Seattle suburb is home to software giant Microsoft, and electricity harnessed from the Columbia River powers aerospace and aluminum industries. California's Silicon Valley, near San Francisco, is a global hub of high-tech industries. Hawaii tops the nation in macadamia nuts and some tropical fruits. Alaska's North Slope is

"Out where the hand clasp's a little stronger, Out where the smile dwells a little longer, That's where the West begins."

ARTHUR CHAPMAN,
"OUT WHERE THE WEST BEGINS"

a leading source of crude oil, but proposals to lessen the country's dependency on foreign oil by drilling in the Arctic National Wildlife Refuge stir controversy among oil companies, conservationists, government leaders, and ordinary citizens. For mountain states, ski resorts and vacation/retirement homes now make up an increasingly important part of their economies.

Although the West clings to its frontier image, most people live in rapidly growing and ethnically diverse cities such as Seattle, Los Angeles, and Denver. The continuing challenge will be to provide a decent standard of living for the millions of people who live here while preserving the scenic beauty and natural resources that attracted them to the region.

This brown bear gets ready to enjoy a meal of fresh salmon from a river in southeastern Alaska. Known as grizzlies in some areas, brown bears are smart and adapt readily to their environment, eating roots, insects, small mammals, and berries as well as fish.

ALASKA

★ *Last Frontier* ★

"SEWARD'S ICEBOX." That's what critics called the continent's vast, mostly unexplored northwestern peninsula when William Seward arranged for its purchase from Russia in 1867. But few complained when Joe Juneau discovered gold in 1880. By the end of the century, people were pouring through the Chilkoot Pass enroute to the Klondike goldfields—a scene now shown on some Alaska license plates.

The newcomers found more than gold. There were huge catches of salmon and impressive timber harvests. Today the state is still a leading source for salmon, crab, halibut, and herring. Although Alaska ranks first among the states in amount of forestland, only 10 percent of it is used for timber.

Alaska's strategic importance to the United States became critical when the Japanese invaded the Aleutian Islands during World War II. The 1,522-mile (2,450-km) Alaska-Canada (Alcan)

Highway was completed in just eight months. Originally built as a military supply road, it is still the only land route to Alaska. Population in the territory grew steadily after the war, and the Last Frontier became the 49th state in 1959.

More than twice as large as Texas, the state totals one-sixth of the country's entire area. Mountains abound, topped by massive Mount McKinley (Denali), North America's highest peak. Snow-fed rivers rush to the sea while tens of thousands of blue-ice glaciers inch their way across the land. Cold northern treeless plains called tundra contrast with the dense evergreen trees of the Tongass National Forest a thousand miles to the milder southeast. Alaska's position on the Arctic Circle brings long and sometimes warm "midnight sun" summer days, while winters can be brutally cold with long hours of darkness.

Powerful forces are at work far beneath the land. The 1912 eruption of Mount Katmai was

1867

The agreement to purchase Alaska from Russia was a bold and controversial move to expand U.S. territory.

1896–1900

Gold rushes, first in Canada's Klondike region and then in Alaska, focused U.S. attention on the territory's vast resources.

1942

The Japanese invasion of the Aleutians in World War II led to the building of a military supply route called the Alcan Highway.

1968–Present

The Trans Alaska Pipeline is capable of carrying 2.1 million barrels of oil each day from Prudhoe Bay to Valdez.

Massive Hubbard Glacier loses a chunk of its ice to Russell Fiord (opposite) through a process called calving. One of more than 600 named glaciers in the state, the Hubbard flows from the St. Elias Mountains to the sea near the north end of Alaska's southeast panhandle.

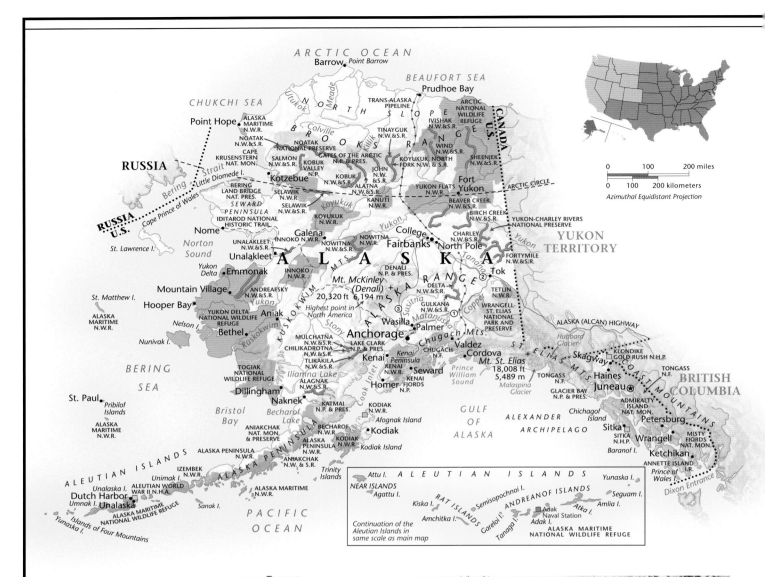

ARCTIC OCEAN

Barrow • Point Barrow

BEAUFORT SEA

CHUKCHI SEA

Prudhoe Bay

TRANS-ALASKA PIPELINE

Point Hope •

ALASKA MARITIME N.W.R.
NOATAK N.W.&S.R.
NOATAK NATIONAL PRESERVE
GATES OF THE ARCTIC N.P. & PRES.

IVISHAK N.W.&S.R.
ARCTIC NATIONAL WILDLIFE REFUGE

TINAYGUK N.W.&S.R.

WIND N.W.&S.R.

SHEENJEK N.W.&S.R.

CANADA
U.S.

RUSSIA

Bering Strait

Little Diomede I.

CAPE KRUSENSTERN NAT. MON.

SALMON N.W.&S.R.

KOBUK VALLEY N.P.

NORTH FORK N.W. & S.R.

JOHN N.W.&S.R.

KOYUKUK N.W. & S.R.

Kotzebue •

BROOKS RANGE

Killik

Colville

Meade

Utukok

NORTH SLOPE

Fort Yukon

RUSSIA U.S.

BERING LAND BRIDGE NAT. PRES.

SELAWIK N.W.R.
SELAWIK N.W.&S.R.

ALATNA N.W.&S.R.

KANUTI N.W.R.

YUKON FLATS N.W.R.

BEAVER CREEK N.W.&S.R.

ARCTIC CIRCLE

Cape Prince of Wales

SEWARD PENINSULA

IDITAROD NATIONAL HISTORIC TRAIL

Nome •

Koyukuk

KOYUKUK N.W.R.

BIRCH CREEK N.W.&S.R.

YUKON-CHARLEY RIVERS NATIONAL PRESERVE

YUKON TERRITORY

St. Lawrence I.

Norton Sound

UNALAKLEET N.W.&S.R.

Galena •

INNOKO N.W.R.

NOWITNA N.W.R.

College

Fairbanks

North Pole

Yukon

CHARLEY N.W.&S.R.

Unalakleet •

ALASKA

FORTYMILE N.W.&S.R.

St. Matthew I.

Emmonak •

INNOKO N.W.R.

Mts

NOWITNA N.W.R.

Tanana

Tok

Yukon Delta

Mountain Village •

ANDREAFSKY N.W.&S.R.

DENALI N.P. & PRES.

DELTA N.W.&S.R.

②

TETLIN N.W.R.

Yukon

Mt. McKinley (Denali) +

RANGE

Hooper Bay •

YUKON DELTA NATIONAL WILDLIFE REFUGE

20,320 ft 6,194 m

GULKANA N.W.&S.R.

ALASKA (ALCAN) HIGHWAY

Nelson I.

Aniak •

Highest point in North America

ALASKA

①

Copper

WRANGELL-ST. ELIAS NATIONAL PARK AND PRESERVE

Nunivak I.

Bethel •

Stony

Wasilla

Susitna

③

Hubbard Glacier

Kuskokwim

MULCHATNA N.W.&S.R.

Matanuska

Anchorage

Palmer

Valdez

ST. ELIAS MTS.

BERING SEA

CHILIKADROTNA N.W.&S.R.

LAKE CLARK N.P. & PRES.

Chugach Mts.

Cordova

Mt. St. Elias

Skagway

KLONDIKE GOLD RUSH N.H.P.

TLIKAKILA N.W.&S.R.

Kenai

CHUGACH N.F.

18,008 ft 5,489 m

TONGASS N.F.

COAST MOUNTAINS

TONGASS N.F.

BRITISH COLUMBIA

Iliamna Lake

ALAGNAK N.W.&S.R.

Kenai Peninsula

Seward

Malaspina Glacier

TOGIAK NATIONAL WILDLIFE REFUGE

Cook Inlet

KENAI N.W.R.

Prince William Sound

Haines

Juneau ⊛

St. Paul

Dillingham •

Naknek

Becharof Lake

Homer

KENAI FJORDS N.P.

GLACIER BAY N.P. & PRES.

ALEXANDER

Chichagof Island

ADMIRALTY ISLAND NAT. MON.

Petersburg

Pribilof Islands

Bristol Bay

KODIAK N.W.R.

GULF OF ALASKA

ARCHIPELAGO

Sitka

SITKA N.H.P.

Wrangell

ALASKA MARITIME N.W.R.

KATMAI N.P. & PRES.

Afognak Island

Baranof I.

MISTY FIORDS NAT. MON.

ANIAKCHAK NAT. MON. & PRESERVE

BECHAROF N.W.R.

Kodiak

Ketchikan

ALASKA PENINSULA N.W.R.

KODIAK N.W.R.

Kodiak Island

ANNETTE ISLAND I.R.

ALASKA PENINSULA

ANIAKCHAK N.W. & S.R.

Trinity Islands

Prince of Wales I.

Dixon Entrance

ALEUTIAN ISLANDS

IZEMBEK N.W.R.

Unimak I.

ALEUTIAN WORLD WAR II N.H.A.

Unalaska I.

Dutch Harbor

Umnak I. Unalaska

ALASKA MARITIME NATIONAL WILDLIFE REFUGE

Sanak I.

PACIFIC OCEAN

Yunaska I.

Islands of Four Mountains

NEAR ISLANDS

Attu I.

Agattu I.

ALEUTIAN ISLANDS

Yunaska I.

Kiska I.

RAT ISLANDS

Semisopochnoi I.

ANDREANOF ISLANDS

Seguam I.

Amchitka I.

Gareloi I.

Adak Naval Station

Atka I.

Amlia I.

Continuation of the Aleutian Islands in same scale as main map

Tanaga I.

Adak I.

ALASKA MARITIME NATIONAL WILDLIFE REFUGE

0   100   200 miles
0   100   200 kilometers
Azimuthal Equidistant Projection

A bull moose pays a surprise visit to a home in downtown Anchorage. Standing as tall as seven feet (2 m) and weighing as much as 1,200 pounds (540 kg), they are the world's largest deer. In Alaska, moose have traditionally been sources of food, hides, and bone for tools. Today, hunters kill 6,000 to 8,000 moose a year in Alaska, yielding some 3.5 million pounds (1.6 million kg) of meat. The animals are also a favorite with tourists, who love to photograph them.

the largest in North America in the last century, and the 1964 earthquake that rocked Anchorage was among the most powerful ever recorded.

The discovery of huge oil reserves on the North Slope in 1968 spurred the state's most recent growth. Workers by the thousands moved from other states to help build an 800-mile- (1,290-km-) long pipeline from Prudhoe Bay to the ice-free port of Valdez. On average almost a million barrels of crude oil a day move through the pipeline, making Alaska a top oil producer.

Thanks to wise legislation, every Alaskan shares in these oil earnings. But costs to the environment can be high. The biggest oil spill in the country's history blackened hundreds of miles of shoreline in 1989. Coastal ecosystems and fishing towns still feel the effects. A debate over plans to drill for oil in the Arctic National Wildlife Refuge pits those who want to preserve the wilderness against those who want to exploit its energy reserves. The issue is far from being resolved.

Alaskans today are still pioneers in many ways. Their state is a mix of wild and tamed that is unlike any other. Huge moose and brown bears sometimes stroll right into Alaskan cities. Legislators must travel to the state capital by water or air because no highway connects Juneau to the rest of the world. Where schools are few and far between, children attend school over the Internet, and doctors often travel by bush plane to see patients. Alaska's Native peoples make up a higher percentage of the population than in any other state, and many follow their traditional lifestyles. Alaskans face amazing opportunities and tough challenges—especially concerning the state's rich natural resources and fragile environments. But it's easy for them to see that Seward got a great bargain in buying this great land.

ALASKA

STATEHOOD	January 3, 1959; 49th state
CAPITAL	Juneau
LARGEST CITY	Anchorage Population 268,983
TOTAL AREA	663,267 sq mi; 1,717,854 sq km
LAND AREA	571,951 sq mi; 1,481,347 sq km
POPULATION	710,231
POPULATION DENSITY	1 person per sq mi
MAJOR RACIAL/ ETHNIC GROUPS	66.7% white; 14.8% Native American; 5.4% Asian; 3.3% African American; Hispanic (any race) 5.5%.
INDUSTRY	petroleum products, state, local, and federal government, services, trade
AGRICULTURE	shellfish, seafood, nursery stock, vegetables, dairy products, feed crops

WILLOW PTARMIGAN   FORGET-ME-NOT

Did you know?

1. Alaska has the northernmost and westernmost points in the United States and is the only state with land in the Eastern Hemisphere.
2. The distance from southeast Alaska to the tip of the Aleutian chain roughly equals the distance from Miami to Los Angeles.
3. The most powerful earthquake ever recorded in North America struck Anchorage in 1964. It was 80 times more powerful than the 1906 San Francisco quake and measured 9.2 on the Richter scale.
4. Little Diomede Island is only 2.5 miles (4 km) from Russian territory.
5. Barrow, the northernmost U.S. city, has 67 days of continuous darkness in winter and 84 days of continuous daylight in summer.
6. Alaska's first people came from Asia across a land bridge.

CALIFORNIA

★ *Golden State* ★

"JUST ADD WATER." Californians have followed this simple recipe for more than a century to grow their state. Snowmelt from Sierra Nevada slopes and Colorado River water make distant deserts produce and temperate croplands produce more. Water sharing also helped propel the state into the modern era by allowing industries to sprout and cities to bloom.

California's fields and factories make it the nation's leading producer of food and manufactured goods. So colossal is the state's economy that if California were an independent country it would be among the ten richest in the world. In terms of money earned, milk and grapes are the state's leading farm products. It also grows more than 99 percent of the nation's total of more than a dozen specialty crops, including artichokes, raisins, walnuts, and kiwifruit. California is an industrial powerhouse, too. The state's assembly lines turn out a multitude of products—everything from jets and missiles to high-tech hardware and software.

The Golden State has a stunning array of natural resources and environments. There are abundant minerals, vast forests of gigantic pines and redwoods, and unrivaled fisheries along its nearly one-thousand-mile coast. In the north stand the majestic peaks of the Cascade Range. Deep within Death Valley, the driest and hottest place on the continent, lies Badwater. At 282 feet (86 m) below sea level, it is North America's lowest point. Eighty-plus miles west—and nearly three miles higher—stands 14,494-foot (4,418-m) Mount Whitney in the Sierra Nevada. The Coast Ranges rise along the Pacific Ocean. In between lies the fertile Central Valley, source of most of California's agricultural wealth.

1769

Mission San Diego de Alcalá was the first of 21 missions built by the Spanish in an effort to convert native people to Christianity.

1848

The discovery of gold brought fortune seekers from around the world and sparked the westward movement across the country.

1906

The San Francisco earthquake led to the first government-sponsored study of the cause of earthquakes in the U.S.

2003

In a special recall election, California voted to remove its governor from office, the first state ever to take such action.

The Golden Gate Bridge (opposite) rises above the fog over San Francisco Bay. Each day thousands travel back and forth across the bridge from homes in northern suburbs to high-tech jobs in the Silicon Valley between Palo Alto and San Jose.

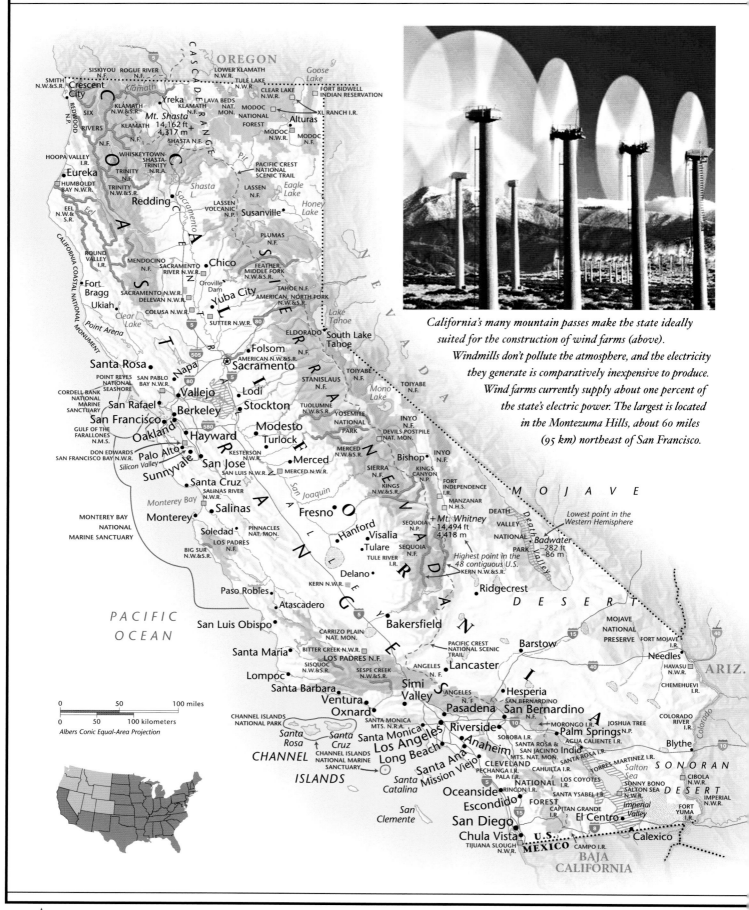

California's many mountain passes make the state ideally suited for the construction of wind farms (above). Windmills don't pollute the atmosphere, and the electricity they generate is comparatively inexpensive to produce. Wind farms currently supply about one percent of the state's electric power. The largest is located in the Montezuma Hills, about 60 miles (95 km) northeast of San Francisco.

OREGON

SISKIYOU N.F.
ROGUE RIVER N.F.
LOWER KLAMATH N.W.R.
TULE LAKE N.W.R.
Goose Lake

SMITH N.W.&S.R.
Crescent City
Klamath
Yreka
LAVA BEDS NAT. MON.
CLEAR LAKE N.W.R.
FORT BIDWELL INDIAN RESERVATION

KLAMATH N.W.R.
MODOC
XL RANCH I.R.
Alturas

REDWOOD N.P.
SIX RIVERS
KLAMATH N.F.
Mt. Shasta 14,162 ft +4,317 m
SHASTA N.F.
MODOC N.W.R.
MODOC NATIONAL FOREST
MODOC N.F.

N.F.
WHISKEYTOWN-SHASTA-TRINITY N.R.A.
TRINITY N.F.
Pit
PACIFIC CREST NATIONAL SCENIC TRAIL

HOOPA VALLEY I.R.
Eureka
HUMBOLDT BAY N.W.R.
TRINITY N.W.&S.R.
Shasta L.
LASSEN N.F.
Eagle Lake

EEL N.W.& S.R.
Fel
Redding
Sacramento
LASSEN VOLCANIC N.P.
Susanville
Honey Lake

ROUND VALLEY I.R.
MENDOCINO N.F.
Chico
PLUMAS N.F.

CALIFORNIA COASTAL NATIONAL MONUMENT
Fort Bragg
Ukiah
SACRAMENTO N.W.R.
Oroville Dam
FEATHER, MIDDLE FORK N.W.&S.R.

Clear Lake
SACRAMENTO N.W.R. DELEVAN N.W.R.
Yuba City
AMERICAN, NORTH FORK N.W.&S.R.
TAHOE N.F.

Point Arena
COLUSA N.W.R.
SUTTER N.W.R.
Lake Tahoe

ELDORADO N.F.
South Lake Tahoe

Santa Rosa
Napa
Folsom
AMERICAN N.W.&S.R.

POINT REYES NATIONAL SEASHORE
SAN PABLO BAY N.W.R.
Sacramento
TOIYABE N.F.
STANISLAUS N.F.
TOIYABE N.F.

CORDELL BANK NATIONAL MARINE SANCTUARY
San Rafael
Vallejo
Lodi
Mono Lake

GULF OF THE FARALLONES
Berkeley
Stockton
TUOLUMNE N.W.&S.R.
YOSEMITE NATIONAL PARK
INYO N.F.
DEVILS POSTPILE NAT. MON.

San Francisco
Oakland
Hayward
Modesto
Turlock
MERCED N.W.&S.R.
INYO N.F.

DON EDWARDS SAN FRANCISCO BAY N.W.R.
Palo Alto
KESTERSON N.W.R.
Bishop
KINGS CANYON N.P.

Silicon Valley
Sunnyvale
San Jose
Merced
MERCED N.W.R.
SIERRA N.F.
FORT INDEPENDENCE I.R.

Santa Cruz
SALINAS RIVER N.W.R.
SAN LUIS N.W.R.
KINGS N.W.&S.R.
MANZANAR N.H.S.

Monterey Bay
Salinas
San Joaquin
Fresno
DEATH VALLEY

MONTEREY BAY NATIONAL MARINE SANCTUARY
Monterey
Hanford
Visalia
SEQUOIA N.P.
Mt. Whitney 14,494 ft +4,418 m
NATIONAL PARK
Lowest point in the Western Hemisphere
Badwater -282 ft -86 m

Soledad
PINNACLES NAT. MON.
Tulare
SEQUOIA N.F.
Highest point in the 48 contiguous U.S.
KERN N.W.&S.R.

BIG SUR N.W.&S.R.
LOS PADRES N.F.
TULE RIVER I.R.
Delano

Paso Robles
Ridgecrest

Atascadero
KERN N.W.R.
DESERT

PACIFIC OCEAN
San Luis Obispo
Bakersfield
Barstow
MOJAVE NATIONAL PRESERVE
FORT MOJAVE I.R.

CARRIZO PLAIN NAT. MON.
PACIFIC CREST NATIONAL SCENIC TRAIL
Needles

Santa Maria
BITTER CREEK N.W.R.
LOS PADRES N.F.
ANGELES N.F.
Lancaster
HAVASU N.W.R.
ARIZ.

Lompoc
SISQUOC N.W.&S.R.
SESPE CREEK N.W.&S.R.
Hesperia
CHEMEHUEVI I.R.

Santa Barbara
Simi Valley
ANGELES N.F.
San Bernardino
COLORADO RIVER I.R.

Ventura
Oxnard
SANTA MONICA MTS. N.R.A.
Pasadena
San Bernardino
SAN BERNARDINO N.F.
MORONGO I.R.
JOSHUA TREE N.P.

CHANNEL ISLANDS NATIONAL PARK
Santa Monica
Riverside
SOBOBA I.R.
Palm Springs
AGUA CALIENTE I.R.

Santa Rosa
Santa Cruz
Los Angeles
Anaheim
Indio
SANTA ROSA & SAN JACINTO MTS. NAT. MON.
Blythe

CHANNEL ISLANDS NATIONAL MARINE SANCTUARY
Long Beach
Santa Ana
Mission Viejo
CLEVELAND
PECHANGA I.R.
PALA I.R.
CAHUILLA I.R.
TORRES-MARTINEZ I.R.
SONORAN DESERT

CHANNEL ISLANDS
Santa Catalina
Oceanside
NATIONAL
RINCON I.R.
LOS COYOTES I.R.
SANTA YSABEL I.R.
Salton Sea
SONNY BONO SALTON SEA N.W.R.
CIBOLA N.W.R.

San Clemente
Escondido
FOREST
CAPITAN GRANDE I.R.
El Centro
Imperial Valley
IMPERIAL N.W.R.

San Diego
Chula Vista
U.S.
CAMPO I.R.
Calexico
FORT YUMA I.R.

TIJUANA SLOUGH N.W.R.
MEXICO
BAJA CALIFORNIA

Colorado

SIERRA NEVADA

CASCADE RANGE

COAST RANGES

0 50 100 miles
0 50 100 kilometers
Albers Conic Equal-Area Projection

The seafaring explorer Juan Rodríguez Cabrillo claimed California for Spain in 1542. But it was not until 1769 that colonization began. Father Junípero Serra established the first of a string of missions. There, priests worked to convert the native people to Christianity. With the missions came presidios (forts) and pueblos (towns). Some of these, such as San Francisco, San Jose, and San Diego, now rank among the nation's largest urban areas. In 1821 control passed to Mexico and then in 1848 to the United States after the Mexican-American War. That same year gold was discovered on the American River. In 1849 thousands of "forty-niners" headed for California to strike it rich. By the time statehood was achieved in 1850, the population had grown to almost 100,000.

Today, nearly one out of eight Americans lives in California, making it by far the most populous state. More than 90 percent of the people live in urban areas. One in three Californians is Hispanic, and one in ten is of Asian descent.

Such a diverse land is not without problems. There are frequent earthquakes, forest fires, and other natural disasters. A downturn in the high-tech industry boosted unemployment figures, and recurring problems with water supply, freeway congestion, and air quality have been joined by massive power outages and budget shortages. In 2003 Californians expressed their frustration by recalling their governor. In a special election, actor-turned-politician Arnold Schwarzenegger replaced Gray Davis as chief executive. Whether he can solve California's problems remains to be seen, but one thing is certain. There are plenty of opportunities. People will continue to seek their fortunes in the Golden State.

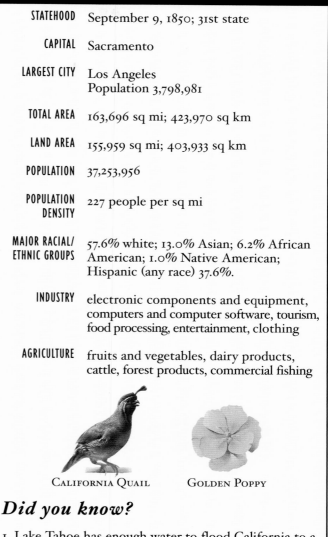

CALIFORNIA
Golden State

CALIFORNIA REPUBLIC

STATEHOOD	September 9, 1850; 31st state
CAPITAL	Sacramento
LARGEST CITY	Los Angeles Population 3,798,981
TOTAL AREA	163,696 sq mi; 423,970 sq km
LAND AREA	155,959 sq mi; 403,933 sq km
POPULATION	37,253,956
POPULATION DENSITY	227 people per sq mi
MAJOR RACIAL/ ETHNIC GROUPS	57.6% white; 13.0% Asian; 6.2% African American; 1.0% Native American; Hispanic (any race) 37.6%.
INDUSTRY	electronic components and equipment, computers and computer software, tourism, food processing, entertainment, clothing
AGRICULTURE	fruits and vegetables, dairy products, cattle, forest products, commercial fishing

CALIFORNIA QUAIL   GOLDEN POPPY

Did you know?

1. Lake Tahoe has enough water to flood California to a depth of 14 inches (36 cm).
2. California has the highest and lowest points in the lower 48 states: Mount Whitney at 14,494 feet (4,418 m) and Death Valley at 282 feet (86 m) below sea level.
3. California contains the tallest, biggest, and oldest trees in the world: a 369.4-foot- (112.6-m-) tall coast redwood, a giant sequoia measuring 275 feet (84 m) high by 103 feet (31 m) around, and a 4,789-year-old bristlecone pine.
4. California is the largest producer of solar energy in the United States.
5. California grows more than half the nation's fruits, nuts, and vegetables, and produces more milk than the state of Wisconsin.
6. More Native Americans live in California than in any other U.S. state.

COLORADO

★ *Centennial State* ★

REACH FOR THE SKY! Colorado is known around the world for its lofty mountains and its Mile-High City of Denver. The state has more than 50 peaks higher than 14,000 feet (4,200 m), and averages an elevation of 6,800 feet (2,070 m). No other state measures up to that.

Yet Colorado is more than snow-capped peaks. The flatter, drier High Plains cover its eastern third. Here cattle are ranched where buffalo once roamed. In a broad southern valley that was once the bed of an ancient sea lies Great Sand Dunes National Park, with dunes topping 700 feet (210 m). The state's western third is rugged plateau, cut by rivers into deep valleys and flat-topped mesas.

Colorado's snow-capped peaks provide water for wildlife, farms, and cities far from the state. Like spokes of a wheel, life-giving rivers flow from high peaks to drier lands around. The state takes its name from its most famous river.

Spanish explorers, who saw the rusty-colored waters cutting through red stone canyons far downstream from its source in what is now Rocky Mountain National Park, named it Colorado, meaning "colored red." The Rio Grande runs south and east all the way to the Gulf of Mexico. To the northeast flows the South Platte; to the southeast the Arkansas.

Along a creek flowing from the Front Range, prospectors found another Colorado treasure in 1858—gold. Thousands of fortune-seekers moved in, and the city of Denver was founded. The Cheyenne and Arapaho fought to hold onto their lands, but the settlers won out. By 1870, railroads linked the territory with the rest of the country, bringing more people. Some settlers ranched cattle on the High Plains, while others farmed crops in irrigated fields. Towns sprang up in mountain valleys across the territory with the discovery of silver, other minerals,

1833

Bent's Fort, a prominent land-mark and trading center on the Santa Fe Trail, was Colorado's first permanent settlement.

1858

With the discovery of gold in the Front Range north of Pikes Peak, thousands of fortune seekers headed to Colorado in covered wagons.

1954

President Eisenhower celebrated the growth of reclamation pro-jects that use dams and canals to carry river water to farmlands.

Present day

The North American Aerospace Defense Command (NORAD) keeps watch for air attacks directed at the U.S. or Canada.

Ancestral Puebloans built spectacular villages into the sandstone walls of canyons. Cliff Palace (opposite), preserved in Mesa Verde National Park, once housed from 100 to 125 people in its 140-plus rooms. It was mysteriously abandoned more than 700 years ago.

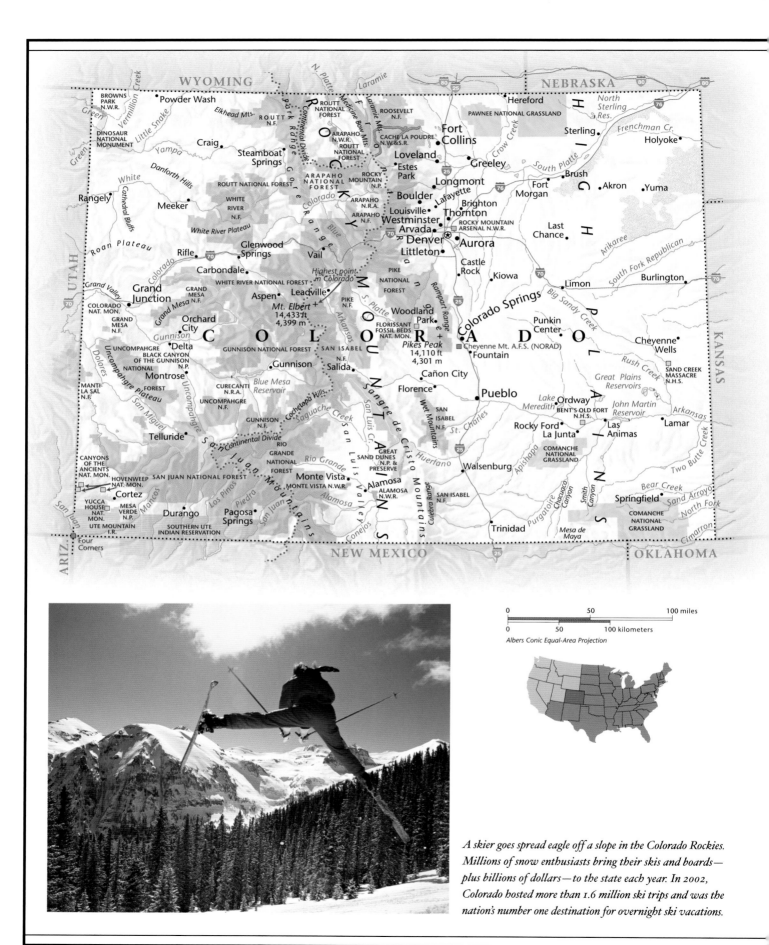

A skier goes spread eagle off a slope in the Colorado Rockies. Millions of snow enthusiasts bring their skis and boards—plus billions of dollars—to the state each year. In 2002, Colorado hosted more than 1.6 million ski trips and was the nation's number one destination for overnight ski vacations.

and more gold. In 1876, on the nation's 100th birthday, the Centennial State entered the Union.

Colorado grew rapidly through the 20th century. Oil and natural gas deposits were tapped in both the eastern plains and western plateaus. Coal and iron helped Pueblo become a steel center. Denver, located where the Plains meet the mountains, grew into the trade, transportation, and financial center for the entire Rocky Mountain region. Its many federal government offices and nearby military facilities have earned it the nickname Washington of the West. As the population grew so did the demand for water. Most of the runoff from rain and snow flows into rivers on the western side of the Rockies, but most of the people live and work on the eastern side. To solve this problem rivers have been dammed and tunnels built to carry water through the mountains for homes, industry, and irrigation.

Colorado's fresh, powdery snow attracts millions of skiers and snowboarders to its slopes each year. Reborn mining towns, such as Aspen and Telluride, boom each winter, and Vail is one of the country's largest ski resorts. Some people even move to Colorado just for the snow!

Colorado's treasures can be the source of problems, too. Sand laced with deicing chemicals is damaging mountain streams. Toxic minerals from abandoned mines pollute water supplies. Since 1990 the population has increased from 3.3 million to more than 4.5 million. The heavy volume of traffic and industry creates smog that hangs like a huge brown cloud over the Denver region. Although progress has been made in cleaning up the air, there is pressure to weaken some of the controls. These are a few of the issues the people of Colorado must try to solve to preserve the quality of life they prize so highly.

COLORADO
Centennial State

STATEHOOD	August 1, 1876; 38th state
CAPITAL	Denver
LARGEST CITY	Denver Population 560,415
TOTAL AREA	104,094 sq mi; 269,601 sq km
LAND AREA	103,718 sq mi; 268,627 sq km
POPULATION	5,029,196
POPULATION DENSITY	48 people per sq mi
MAJOR RACIAL/ ETHNIC GROUPS	81.3% white; 4.0% African American; 2.8% Asian; 1.1% Native American; Hispanic (any race) 20.7%.
INDUSTRY	real estate, state, local, and federal government, durable goods, communications, health and other services, nondurable goods, transportation
AGRICULTURE	cattle, corn, wheat, dairy products, hay

LARK BUNTING   COLUMBINE

Did you know?

1. As protection against earthquakes or nuclear explosions, the Cheyenne Mountain Operations Center of NORAD is mounted on 1,319 giant springs that allow it to sway up to 12 inches (30 cm) in any direction.
2. The 700-foot- (210-m-) high, wind-shaped sand dunes in Great Sand Dunes National Monument occupy an area that was covered by an ancient sea more than one million years ago.
3. The benefits of fluorides for healthy teeth were discovered when a study determined that fluoride in the drinking water of Colorado Springs caused residents to have fewer cavities.
4. The Unsinkable Molly (Margaret Tobin) Brown was a citizen of Leadville where her husband struck it rich when he found gold in 1893. She earned her nicname by helping women and children leave the *Titanic* before the luxury liner sank in 1912.

HAWAI'I

★ *Aloha State* ★

MARK TWAIN CALLED THEM "the loveliest fleet of islands that lies anchored in any ocean." Though they look like green jewels in an ocean-blue setting, these islands were formed by a red-glowing force of nature. As the Pacific plate grinds slowly to the northwest, molten rock pushes up through a "hot spot" to form the islands one by one. The oldest, worn down by millions of years of weather and waves, lie near Russia's Kamchatka Peninsula, far to the northwest of today's main islands. The newest is the "Big Island" of Hawai'i where eruptions from Kīlauea and gigantic Mauna Loa continue to build new land. Thousands of years from now there will be a new island. Molten material is slowing pushing a seamount called Lo'ihi toward the surface.

The first settlers were Polynesians who paddled double-hulled canoes from islands farther west, perhaps 1,500 years ago. They established thriving communities on each of the eight major islands. Captain James Cook claimed the islands for the British Empire in 1778, naming them the Sandwich Islands for the Earl of Sandwich. But the name didn't last long. By 1810 a native chieftan, King Kamehameha I, had succeeded in unifying the islands, and the entire island group became known as Hawai'i.

Change came rapidly. Hawai'i became a center of the Pacific whaling industry. Imported Christianity took root among many native Hawaiians, while imported diseases took the lives of many more. A special trade agreement allowed American businesses to export sugar tax-free. This led to a boom in sugarcane production. Workers were brought in mostly from Asia to work the plantations. Eventually, this resulted in greater ethnic diversity and fewer pure Hawaiians. In 1893, the powerful sugar barons helped overthrow Queen Lili'uokalani,

1782–1810
King Kamehameha gained control of the islands from local chiefs and became the first king of a unified Hawai'i.

1898
Profits from sugarcane, shown being harvested, led U.S. businessmen to pressure the government to make Hawai'i part of the U.S.

1941
Japan's attack on the naval base at Pearl Harbor on December 7 caused the United States to officially enter World War II.

Present day
Resort areas like Waikīkī (above), in the shadow of Diamond Head, have made tourism Hawai'i's most important industry.

Kīlauea (opposite), the world's most active volcano, has been spilling lava down its slopes in one eruption after another since 1983. Where it flows into the sea, lava extends the coast. More than 380 acres (154 ha) have been added to the Big Island's edge.

HAWAI‘I
Aloha State

STATEHOOD	August 21, 1959; 50th state
CAPITAL	Honolulu
LARGEST CITY	Honolulu Population 378,155
TOTAL AREA	10,931 sq mi; 28,311 sq km
LAND AREA	6,423 sq mi; 16,635 sq km
POPULATION	1,360,301
POPULATION DENSITY	124 people per sq mi
MAJOR RACIAL/ ETHNIC GROUPS	38.6% Asian; 24.7% white; 10.0% Hawaiian/Pacific Islander; 1.6% African American; Hispanic (any race) 10.5%.
INDUSTRY	tourism, trade, finance, food processing, petroleum refining, stone, clay, and glass products
AGRICULTURE	sugarcane, pineapples, nursery stock, tropical fruit, livestock, macadamia nuts

HAWAIIAN GOOSE (NENE)

HIBISCUS

Did you know?

1. There are no racial or ethnic majorities in Hawai‘i because everyone is part of a minority.
2. More animals and plants native to Hawai‘i are on the endangered species list than in any other state. Even its state bird is endangered.
3. You can ski two different ways on the same day in Hawai‘i: on water at the beach and on snow on the slopes of Mauna Kea, a 13,796-foot- (4,205-m-) high volcano on the Big Island.
4. Mount Wai‘ale‘ale, on the island of Kaua‘i, is the wettest place in the United States, with 460 inches (1,168 cm) of rainfall per year.
5. Hawai‘i's state fish is the humuhumunukunukuapua‘a, a type of trigger fish.
6. There are only 12 letters in the Hawai‘ian alphabet: *A, E, I, O, U, H, K, L, M, N, P,* and *W.*

Hawaiian surfer Megan Abubo performs at a competition on Maui in 2003. Surfers from around the world visit the Aloha State to experience what many think is the world's best surfing. The biggest waves, as high as 12 feet (4 m) or more, usually crash against O‘ahu's North Shore beaches during winter, generated by North Pacific storms. Smaller waves for beginning surfers are found on other beaches.

the last monarch. Hawai‘i became a U.S. territory in 1900. By the following year the naval station at Pearl Harbor was under construction.

The Japanese attack on Pearl Harbor brought the United States into World War II and brought Hawai‘i into the modern era. Thousands of people from the U.S. mainland moved in to work for the war effort, and many stayed on after peace was restored. More people immigrated in the post-war years. In 1959 Hawai‘i entered the Union as the 50th state.

The introduction of jet airline passenger service to Hawai‘i opened the doors to tourism. By 1970 this industry had replaced agriculture as the state's chief economic activity. These days the

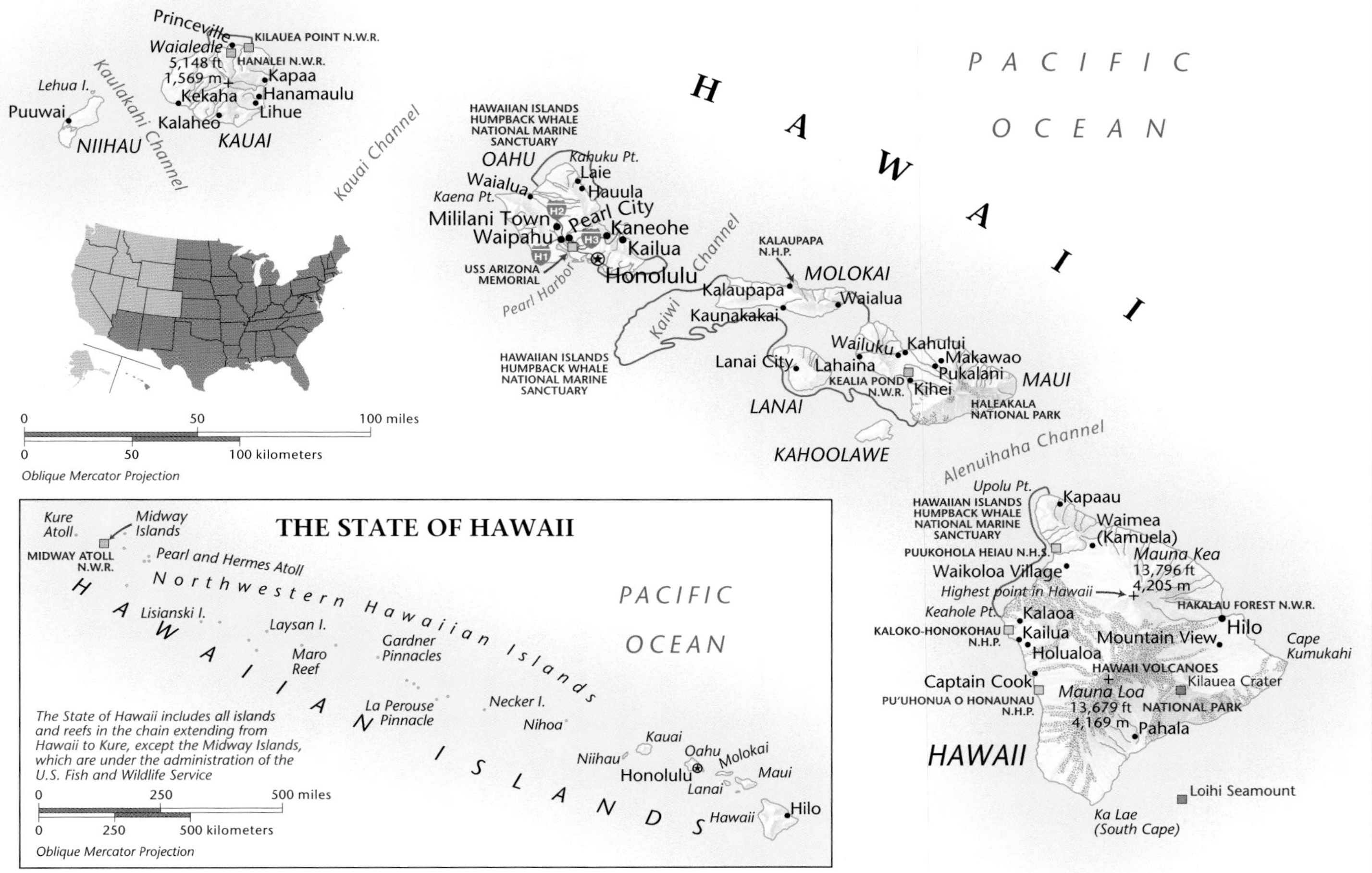

PACIFIC OCEAN
HAWAII
Princeville
KILAUEA POINT N.W.R.
Waialeale
5,148 ft
1,569 m
HANALEI N.W.R.
Kapaa
Hanamaulu
Lihue
Kekaha
Kalaheo
KAUAI
Lehua I.
Puuwai
NIIHAU
Kaulakahi Channel
Kauai Channel
HAWAIIAN ISLANDS HUMPBACK WHALE NATIONAL MARINE SANCTUARY
OAHU
Kahuku Pt.
Laie
Hauula
Waialua
Kaena Pt.
Mililani Town
Pearl City
Waipahu
Kaneohe
Kailua
Honolulu
USS ARIZONA MEMORIAL
Pearl Harbor
Kaiwi Channel
KALAUPAPA N.H.P.
MOLOKAI
Kalaupapa
Kaunakakai
Waialua
Wailuku
Kahului
Makawao
Pukalani
Lanai City
Lahaina
KEALIA POND N.W.R.
Kihei
MAUI
LANAI
HALEAKALA NATIONAL PARK
KAHOOLAWE
Alenuihaha Channel
Upolu Pt.
Kapaau
Waimea (Kamuela)
PUUKOHOLA HEIAU N.H.S.
Waikoloa Village
Mauna Kea
13,796 ft
4,205 m
Highest point in Hawaii
Keahole Pt.
Kalaoa
HAKALAU FOREST N.W.R.
Hilo
KALOKO-HONOKOHAU N.H.P.
Kailua
Holualoa
Mountain View
Cape Kumukahi
HAWAII VOLCANOES NATIONAL PARK
Captain Cook
Mauna Loa
13,679 ft
4,169 m
Kilauea Crater
PU'UHONUA O HONAUNAU N.H.P.
Pahala
HAWAII
Loihi Seamount
Ka Lae (South Cape)
0 50 100 miles
0 50 100 kilometers
Oblique Mercator Projection
THE STATE OF HAWAII
Kure Atoll
Midway Islands
MIDWAY ATOLL N.W.R.
Pearl and Hermes Atoll
Northwestern Hawaiian Islands
HAWAIIAN ISLANDS
Lisianski I.
Laysan I.
Maro Reef
Gardner Pinnacles
La Perouse Pinnacle
Necker I.
Nihoa
PACIFIC OCEAN
Kauai
Niihau
Oahu
Molokai
Honolulu
Lanai
Maui
Hawaii
Hilo
The State of Hawaii includes all islands and reefs in the chain extending from Hawaii to Kure, except the Midway Islands, which are under the administration of the U.S. Fish and Wildlife Service
0 250 500 miles
0 250 500 kilometers
Oblique Mercator Projection

islands are a peaceful getaway for vacationers especially from Japan and the U.S. mainland. Millions each year enjoy the state's scenic delights and tropical climate. Tourists hike in lush Kaua'i rain forests, view volcanoes on the Big Island and whales off Maui, or shop in the famous Waikīkī district of O'ahu. Many enjoy surfing or sunning on beautiful beaches—some of volcanic black sand—all over the islands.

Hawai'i has the greatest ethnic diversity of any U.S. state. Fewer than one in four residents are white, and roughly four in ten are of primarily Asian descent. Though few "pure" Hawaiians remain, it is believed that many of the people born here are part Hawaiian. There is a movement among native Hawaiians for some form of self-government that ranges from leaving the Union to reclaiming land taken from them when the monarchy was overthrown. Other issues affect daily lives. A heavy dependence on tourism means that a drop in the number of visitors can cause difficulty for residents who live in a state where the high cost of importing goods makes everyday items expensive. The loss of habitat, which places more and more native plants and animals on the endangered species list, is also linked to this industry. The state has its problems. But it also has what Hawaiians call a "spirit of aloha" that places value on working together for the betterment of their island home.

IDAHO

★ *Gem State* ★

GEM OF THE MOUNTAINS, another nickname for Idaho, fits the state in several ways. Among the rich variety of minerals found here, the deep purple Idaho star garnet is treasured by gem collectors. The state's snow-topped peaks sparkle jewel-like in the sun. And cold, clear streams, like the Clearwater and Salmon Rivers, are strung like sparkling necklaces through the state's mountain valleys. The state's official name comes from the *Idaho,* a Columbia River steamship. With the discovery of gold in 1860 along the Clearwater River, the diggings came to be called the Idaho mines. When a state name was needed, Idaho won the prize.

Prospectors traveled up the Columbia and Snake Rivers, staking claims to gold, silver, and other minerals in the mountain valleys north of present-day Boise. Ranchers and others followed the miners, and by 1890 the population reached 90,000. That year, with "leftover" lands from neighboring Wyoming and Montana, Idaho was admitted as the 43rd state with Boise as its capital.

Today, most residents live south and east of Boise on the Snake River Plain. This broad valley, though poor in rainfall, is rich with both hydro-electricity and water for fields thanks to a series of dams built across the river. Fertile volcanic soils combine with mild temperatures to support the state's famous potato crop.

Forested mountains cover most of sparsely populated central Idaho and the northern panhandle. Lewis and Clark crossed the Bitterroot Range in 1805, opening the region to trappers who supplied beaver pelts for markets in the East. Until the 1830s, these mountain men would gather to trade furs, supplies, and tall tales. One popular spot for these rendezvous was near Bear Lake on the Idaho-Utah border.

The natural resources that first brought

1805

With the help of Indian guides, Lewis and Clark crossed the Bitterroot Range on their quest to find the Pacific Ocean.

1877

The Army's arrest of a Nez Perce chief (above) led to a war that ended with the Indians being forced to move to reservations.

1976

The Teton Dam collapse increased inspections of existing dams, cancelled some projects, and promoted the use of concrete in future dams.

Present day

Idaho's mountains, lakes, rivers, and wildlife have made tourism, including snow sports, an important year-round industry.

Posing serious hazards for trappers and other early travelers, Idaho's whitewater rivers provide thrills and chills for today's tourists. This group of rafters (opposite) flashes through rapids on the Selway River in central Idaho.

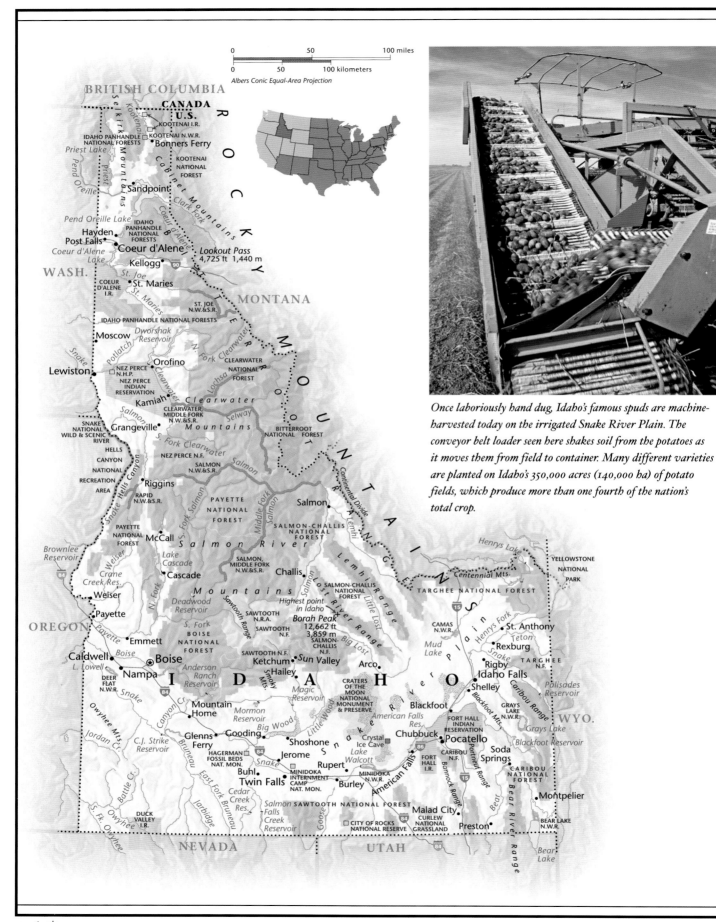

0   50   100 miles
0   50   100 kilometers
Albers Conic Equal-Area Projection

BRITISH COLUMBIA

CANADA
U.S.
KOOTENAI I.R.
IDAHO PANHANDLE
NATIONAL FORESTS
KOOTENAI N.W.R.
Bonners Ferry

KOOTENAI
NATIONAL
FOREST

Priest Lake

Sandpoint

Pend Oreille Lake
IDAHO
PANHANDLE
NATIONAL
FORESTS

Hayden
Post Falls
Coeur d'Alene
Coeur d'Alene Lake
Kellogg
Lookout Pass
4,725 ft 1,440 m

WASH.
COEUR
D'ALENE
I.R.
St. Maries
St. Joe
MONTANA
St. Maries
ST. JOE
N.W.&S.R.
IDAHO PANHANDLE NATIONAL FORESTS

Moscow
Dworshak Reservoir
Orofino
CLEARWATER
NATIONAL
FOREST

Lewiston
NEZ PERCE
N.H.P.
NEZ PERCE
INDIAN
RESERVATION
Kamiah
CLEARWATER,
MIDDLE FORK
N.W.&S.R.
Clearwater
Selway
BITTERROOT
NATIONAL FOREST

SNAKE
NATIONAL
WILD & SCENIC
RIVER
Grangeville
S Fork Clearwater
NEZ PERCE N.F.
Mountains

HELLS
CANYON
NATIONAL
RECREATION
AREA
Riggins
RAPID
N.W.&S.R.
PAYETTE
NATIONAL
FOREST
SALMON
N.W.&S.R.
Salmon

Brownlee Reservoir
PAYETTE
NATIONAL
FOREST
McCall
Lake Cascade
S Fork Salmon
Middle Fork Salmon
SALMON-CHALLIS
NATIONAL
FOREST
Lemhi
Henrys Lake
YELLOWSTONE
NATIONAL
PARK

Crane Creek Res.
84
Weiser
Weiser
N. Fork
Deadwood Reservoir
SALMON,
MIDDLE FORK
N.W.&S.R.
Salmon River
Challis
SALMON-CHALLIS
NATIONAL
FOREST
Centennial Mts.
TARGHEE NATIONAL FOREST

OREGON
Payette
Payette
S. Fork
BOISE
NATIONAL
FOREST
Mountains
SAWTOOTH
N.R.A.
SAWTOOTH
N.F.
Highest point in Idaho
Borah Peak
12,662 ft
3,859 m
SALMON-
CHALLIS
N.F.
Lost River Range
Little Lost
Big Lost
CAMAS
N.W.R.
Mud Lake
15
St. Anthony
Rexburg
Teton
TARGHEE
N.F.

Emmett
Boise
Caldwell
L. Lowell
Nampa
DEER
FLAT
N.W.R.
Anderson Ranch Reservoir
SAWTOOTH RANGE
SAWTOOTH N.F.
Ketchum
Sun Valley
Hailey
Smoky Mts.
Arco
CRATERS
OF THE
MOON
NATIONAL
MONUMENT
& PRESERVE
Rigby
Idaho Falls
Shelley
Palisades Reservoir
WYO.

I   D   A   H   O

84
Mountain
Home
Snake
Mormon Reservoir
Magic Reservoir
Big Wood
Little Wood
Blackfoot
American Falls
FORT HALL
INDIAN
RESERVATION
GRAYS
LAKE
N.W.R.
Blackfoot Mts.
Grays Lake
Caribou Range
Blackfoot Reservoir

Owyhee Mts.
Jordan Cr.
C.J. STRIKE
Reservoir
Bruneau
Glenns
Ferry
Gooding
HAGERMAN
FOSSIL BEDS
NAT. MON.
Snake
Shoshone
Jerome
Rupert
Crystal Ice Cave
Lake Walcott
Chubbuck
FORT
HALL
I.R.
86
Pocatello
CARIBOU
N.F.
Soda
Springs
Portneuf Range
CARIBOU
NATIONAL
FOREST
Bear River Range

Battle Cr.
East Fork Bruneau
Cedar Creek Res.
Buhl
MINIDOKA
INTERNMENT
CAMP
NAT. MON.
Twin Falls
MINIDOKA
N.W.R.
Burley
American Falls
FORT HALL I.R.
15
Bannock Range
Montpelier
BEAR LAKE
N.W.R.
Bear Lake

S. FK. Owyhee
DUCK
VALLEY
I.R.
Salmon Falls Creek Reservoir
SAWTOOTH NATIONAL FOREST
84
CITY OF ROCKS
NATIONAL RESERVE
CURLEW
NATIONAL
GRASSLAND
Malad City
Preston
Goose

NEVADA   UTAH
84

R   O   C   K   Y

Selkirk Mountains
Kootenai
Priest
Cabinet Mountains
Clark Fork
Coeur d'Alene
90
BITTERROOT
MOUNTAINS
Pend Oreille
Snake
Potlatch
Clearwater
N. Fork Clearwater
Lochsa

M   O   U   N   T   A   I   N   S

Continental Divide
Lemhi Range
Henrys Fork
Snake

L   O   S   T   ... R   A   N   G   E

Boise ⊛

Once laboriously hand dug, Idaho's famous spuds are machine-harvested today on the irrigated Snake River Plain. The conveyor belt loader seen here shakes soil from the potatoes as it moves them from field to container. Many different varieties are planted on Idaho's 350,000 acres (140,000 ha) of potato fields, which produce more than one fourth of the nation's total crop.

people to the state still provide Idahoans with work. Precious metals are declining in importance, but mining remains a key industry. Idaho supplies the nation with a broad array of industrial minerals, including lead, zinc, and copper. Phosphate, used as fertilizer and even in soft drinks, is mined in the arid far southeast. Processing of the huge potato crop into various frozen styles also provides work for residents. Many are employed in the harvesting and processing of spruce, fir, and pine trees from the state's vast forests. Indeed, national forests cover more than a third of the state, an area exceeded only by Alaska.

Among the most rugged and remote in the United States, Idaho's wild lands attract tourists who want to "get away from it all." Thrill-seekers come to raft roaring rivers, hike rocky trails, and fish icy streams in the Salmon River, Sawtooth, and Bitterroot ranges. Winter sports are popular, too, such as skiing at one of the country's biggest resorts—Sun Valley.

Wild and scenic Idaho faces challenges, too. Its population of nearly 1.4 million places it just 40th among states—but it is the fifth fastest-growing state. Forests are being cut down as demands for housing increase. As mining and logging operations downsize, computer and other high-technology businesses provide new employment opportunities. The rise of dairy farms has led to complaints about waste management. Adventure tourism provides an ever-growing economic boost to the state, but increasing visitor numbers may threaten the wilderness experience they seek. It is crystal clear that Idaho's people must seek a balance between the use and the protection of plentiful natural resources for their state to continue as a gem of the mountains.

IDAHO
Gem State

STATEHOOD	July 3, 1890; 43rd state
CAPITAL	Boise
LARGEST CITY	Boise Population 189,847
TOTAL AREA	83,570 sq mi; 216,446 sq km
LAND AREA	82,747 sq mi; 214,314 sq km
POPULATION	1,567,582
POPULATION DENSITY	18 people per sq mi
MAJOR RACIAL/ ETHNIC GROUPS	89.1% white; 1.4% Native American; 1.2% Asian; 0.6% African American; Hispanic (any race) 11.2%.
INDUSTRY	electronics and computer equipment, tourism, food processing, forest products, mining, chemicals
AGRICULTURE	potatoes, dairy products, cattle, wheat, alfalfa hay, sugar beets, barley, trout

MOUNTAIN BLUEBIRD   SYRINGA (MOCK ORANGE)

Did you know?

1. To prepare for missions to the Moon, NASA's Apollo astronauts spent time learning about volcanic rocks at Craters of the Moon National Monument.
2. The Big Wood River, sometimes known as the Upside Down River, has the curious feature of changing from 100 feet (30 m) wide by 4 feet (1.2 m) deep to 4 feet wide by 100 feet deep a short distance away.
3. Idaho's first sizable potato crop was planted by Mormon colonists from Salt Lake City. They found a ready market with the gold miners of 1860.
4. Crystal Ice Cave's features include a frozen river and waterfall. Even when the outside temperature is 95°F (35°C), the cave stays at freezing: 32°F (0°C). It is located near Craters of the Moon National Monument.
5. Arco was the first city in the world to be lighted with electricity generated by nuclear power.

MONTANA

★ *Treasure State* ★

RECIPE FOR MONTANA: Take three parts shortgrass prairie and two parts mountain. Lace with small streams and large rivers. Sprinkle with gold, silver, copper, lots of animals, and a few people. Freeze in winter and warm in summer under a Big Sky.

Fourth largest state, sprawling Montana—a Spanish word meaning "mountainous"—has dozens of ranges in its west and flat to gently rolling prairies in its east. The Continental Divide winds along Rocky Mountain ridges that form its border with Idaho, splitting waterways along the way. To the west rivers flow to the Pacific; to the east the mighty Missouri River runs through grassy plains to the Mississippi then south to the Gulf of Mexico. Montana's climate divides there as well. The west is comparatively wet and mild year-round. Extremes are typical in the east, with very cold winters and hot, dry summers.

In a pattern typical of western settlement, mineral riches brought fortune seekers to Montana. Many cities trace their beginnings to mining in the 1860s. Prospectors found gold in Last Chance Gulch along what is now state-capital Helena's main street. A massive copper deposit called "the richest hill on earth" put Butte on the map. Virginia City, once rich with gold, is now a ghost town. Mineral wealth propelled Montana to territorial status in 1864 and statehood in 1889.

Livestock grazing on open range in eastern Montana was followed by fenced cattle and sheep ranches and wheat farms. Miners were joined by loggers and sawmill workers, who turned spruce, fir, pine, and cedar trees into lumber and other wood products for the rest of the country. Gold, silver, and even sapphires are still mined in Montana's mountain west. But these days minerals even more vital for the

1860s

The arrival of steamboats at Fort Benton, a key trading post on the Missouri River, made it the world's most remote inland port.

1876

The Plains Indian victory at the Battle of the Little Bighorn was short-lived. Within a year they were forced onto reservations.

1886–1887

The bitter winter of 1886–87, coupled with too many cattle grazing on too little land, almost destroyed the cattle industry.

Present day

Efforts to treat unsafe water seeping into Berkeley Pit copper mine, closed since 1982, have turned it into an environmental laboratory.

Unlike its human-built namesake, this "Chinese Wall" (opposite) is a natural feature running along the Continental Divide in western Montana. It was created by mountain-building forces that lifted the limestone reef of an ancient seabed a thousand feet.

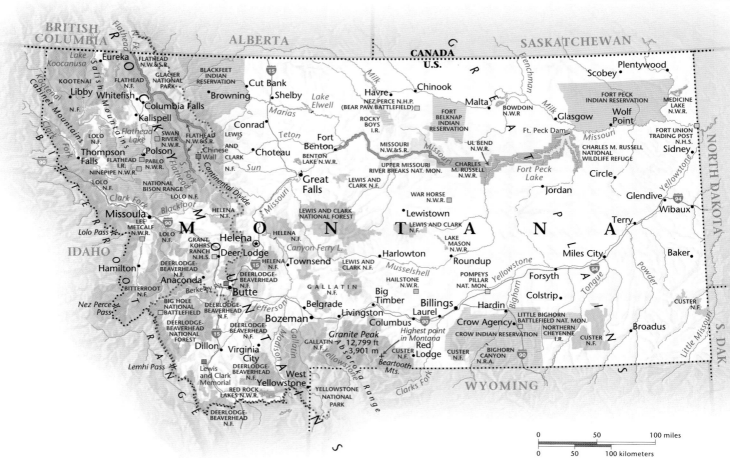

A boy connects the Old West to the New at a guest ranch in the Blackfoot River Valley in western Montana. These days visitors can help work cattle on real ranches, or relax at modern resorts. Horseback riding, river float trips, fly fishing, and hiking are all offered in summer, while winters bring out snowmobiles, skis, and snowshoes. For those who prefer a true Big Sky Country getaway, Montana maintains 14 wilderness areas.

nation—oil and coal—come from the state's Great Plains. More recently, there has been an increase in jobs in the tourist industry. People come to fish and canoe the state's plentiful rivers, and to hike and hunt the state's vast wild lands. Glacier National Park features snow-capped peaks, deep glacier-carved valleys, and spectacular lakes. The scenic Beartooth Highway passes through two of Montana's many national forests on its way to Yellowstone National Park.

There's lots of history to see in Montana, too. Lewis and Clark traveled more miles in Montana than in any other present-day state. They met mostly friendly and helpful native people as they followed the Missouri. On June 25, 1876, near another Montana river—the Little Big Horn—a meeting between whites and Indians was anything but friendly. Crazy Horse led 2,000 Lakota and Cheyenne warriors against George Armstrong Custer and about 215 U.S. Army troops. It was the last major victory by Native Americans in the Indian Wars. Blackfeet, Crow, Flathead, Cheyenne, Lakota, and other native peoples still live in Montana, making up more than 6 percent of the state's population. Most live on one of seven reservations across the state.

In recent years, a number of celebrities have bought homes and ranches in Montana. Some residents do not welcome the increased land prices and other changes this trend has brought. There is also a struggle over logging and mining decisions that impact the natural environment. Although Montana's population has increased by more than 100,000 since 1990, great expanses of the state remain largely untouched by people. While some of Montana's ingredients may change a little in the future, the state's basic recipe will continue to be treasured under its Big Sky.

MONTANA
Treasure State

STATEHOOD	November 8, 1889; 41st state
CAPITAL	Helena
LARGEST CITY	Billings Population 92,008
TOTAL AREA	147,042 sq mi; 380,838 sq km
LAND AREA	145,552 sq mi; 376,979 sq km
POPULATION	989,415
POPULATION DENSITY	6 people per sq mi
MAJOR RACIAL/ ETHNIC GROUPS	89.4% white; 6.3% Native American; 0.6% Asian; 0.4% African American; Hispanic (any race) 2.9%.
INDUSTRY	forest products, food processing, mining, construction, tourism
AGRICULTURE	wheat, cattle, barley, hay, sugar beets, dairy products

WESTERN MEADOWLARK   BITTERROOT

Did you know?

1. Montana is the only state with river systems that empty into the Gulf of Mexico, Hudson Bay, and the Pacific Ocean.
2. Montana holds the records for rapid temperature changes. In Great Falls on January 11, 1980, the temperature rose from -32°F (-36°C) to 15°F (-9°C) in seven minutes, and at Browning on January 23–24, 1916, the temperature fell from 44°F (7°C) to -56°F (-49°C) in 24 hours.
3. Montana has a tribally-controlled college on each of its Indian reservations. Tribes include the Crow, Northern Cheyenne, and Blackfeet.
4. Many dinosaur fossils have been found in Montana, including nests with eggs and juveniles. The nests led paleontologist Jack Horner, consultant to the movie *Jurassic Park,* to conclude that dinosaurs exhibited family behavior.
5. One of the world's highest sports centers is located in Butte, which has an elevation of 5,549 feet (1,691 m).

NEVADA
★ *Silver State* ★

LIKE A BIG SLICE OF PIE, Nevada angles between California, Utah, and Arizona. The Sierra Nevada, the mountains that give the state its name, rise along the long border with California and block rain and snow moving in from the Pacific Ocean. This helps make Nevada, which averages only about nine inches (23 cm) of precipitation each year, the driest of the 50 states.

Nevada's dry landscape looks like wrinkled paper. Parallel rows of more than 150 north-south mountain ranges rise between at least 90 broad valleys in this Great Basin region. Most rivers flowing into these basins dry up in the summer heat. The Paiute, Shoshone, and Washoe peoples and their ancestors roamed this basin-and-range landscape for thousands of years before Europeans and their descendants came to this remote region. In the 1770s the Spanish blazed a trail across the southeast corner to connect their settlements in New Mexico with their missions in California. After the Mexican-American War in 1848, Nevada and much of the Southwest came under U.S. control. Mormons from Utah followed the Spanish Trail in the 1850s to settle in a mountain-ringed valley named Las Vegas ("the meadows"). Here and in other settlements they irrigated crops and raised livestock. Then came mining riches.

Prospectors struck silver and gold in Virginia City, northeast of Lake Tahoe, in 1859. The so-called Comstock Lode turned out to be one of the richest silver deposits ever found. This mineral wealth helped Nevada become a U.S. territory in 1861 and the 36th state in 1864, as hordes of hopeful settlers arrived. Carson City, a nearby mining camp, was made the capital. Though great wealth came from many mines over the next half century, mining created a "boom or bust" economy. Prosperity would be

1843–1845

Lieutenant John C. Frémont, during his exploration of the Great Basin, named Pyramid Lake for this rock formation.

1859

The 1859 discovery of silver and gold led to a rush in settlement, the opening of many mines, and statehood in 1864.

1931

After lawmakers legalized gambling, casinos began to attract tourists, laying the foundation for Nevada's largest industry.

Present day

The U.S. government's plan to make Yucca Mountain a storage site for radioactive waste, is vigorously opposed by many residents.

An Egyptian sphinx, the Eiffel Tower, and the Statue of Liberty can all be seen in replica in Las Vegas (opposite). Gambling, superstar-studded stage shows, and a year-round tourist season have fueled the area's rapid urban growth.

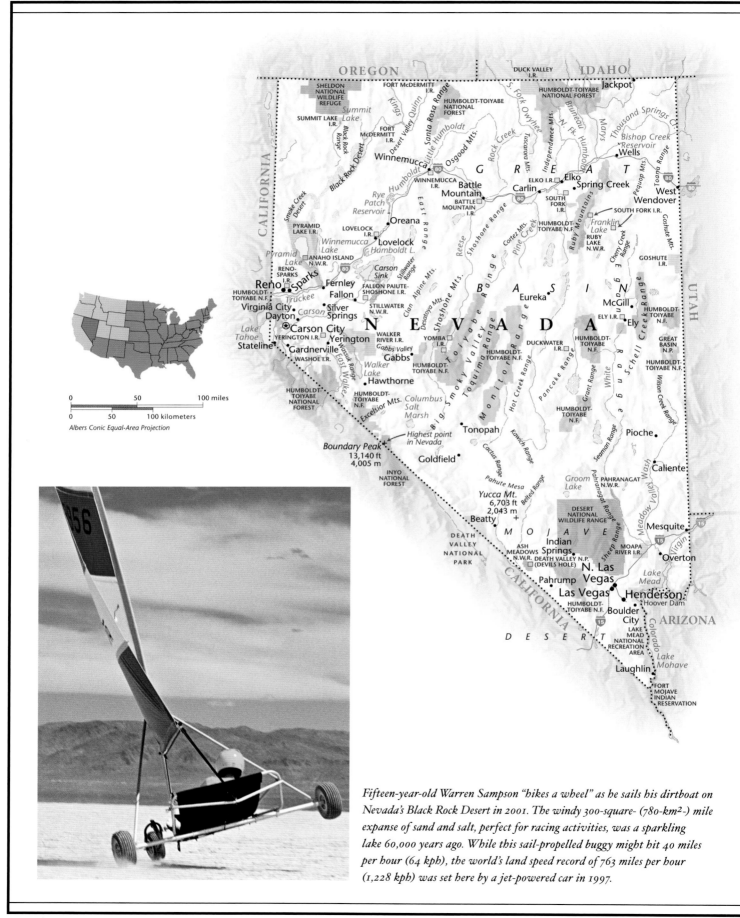

Fifteen-year-old Warren Sampson "hikes a wheel" as he sails his dirtboat on Nevada's Black Rock Desert in 2001. The windy 300-square- (780-km²-) mile expanse of sand and salt, perfect for racing activities, was a sparkling lake 60,000 years ago. While this sail-propelled buggy might hit 40 miles per hour (64 kph), the world's land speed record of 763 miles per hour (1,228 kph) was set here by a jet-powered car in 1997.

replaced by hard times after each mineral deposit was "played out." Nevada was hit hard by the Great Depression in the 1930s. The state needed to find a more stable base for its economy. Making gambling legal was one answer to the up-and-down mining activity. Water was needed to irrigate desert valleys and provide light to homes, hotels, and gaming tables. Federal money and thousands of imported workers built spectacular 726-foot- (221-m-) high Hoover Dam. The project, which spans the Colorado River, supplies water and power to cities and farms across several states and, by forming Lake Mead, provides water recreation in the middle of a desert, too.

Like a desert flower after a rain, Nevada has blossomed. Las Vegas, Reno, and Lake Tahoe attract millions of tourists each year. People come to live, too. Beyond the cities are cattle and sheep ranches, farms, and mines. The state still produces more gold and silver than any other state.

While Nevada now bets on its gaming wealth, future good luck is not a sure thing. Tourists visit less often when the nation's economy is weak or when the cost of transportation is high, creating a big problem in a state where many wages depend on these visitors. Nevada's population has grown, too, from 1.2 million in 1990 to more than 2.2 million. In 2003, the U.S. Census Bureau announced that Nevada has been the fastest-growing state for 17 years straight. This growth puts stress on already limited water supplies. Nevada must share Colorado River water with neighbor states as well as with Mexico. There is concern, too, about the long-term effects of past nuclear testing on federal land and the plan to bury nuclear wastes from around the country in Yucca Mountain. Whatever awaits Nevada, a good bet is that its people will work hard to keep on winning.

NEVADA
Silver State

STATEHOOD	October 31, 1864; 36th state
CAPITAL	Carson City
LARGEST CITY	Las Vegas Population 508,604
TOTAL AREA	110,561 sq mi; 286,351 sq km
LAND AREA	109,826 sq mi; 284,448 sq km
POPULATION	2,700,551
POPULATION DENSITY	24 people per sq mi
MAJOR RACIAL/ ETHNIC GROUPS	66.2% white; 8.1% African American; 7.2% Asian; 1.2% Native American; Hispanic (any race) 26.5%.
INDUSTRY	tourism and gaming, mining, printing and publishing, food processing, electrical equipment
AGRICULTURE	cattle, hay, dairy products

MOUNTAIN BLUEBIRD   SAGEBRUSH

Did you know?

1. In the early days, mail was delivered to Carson Valley by a Norwegian mailman on homemade skis.
2. Samuel Clemens (now better known as Mark Twain) started his career writing for the Virginia City *Territorial Enterprise* newspaper in the spring of 1862 for $25 per week. He later described his salary as "bloated luxury" in his book *Roughing It.*
3. The top-secret U.S. Air Force base known as Area 51, whose existence was denied for years and where believers in UFOs claim alien spacecraft are hidden underground, is located about 100 miles (160 km) northwest of Las Vegas on Groom Lake.
4. Between 1975 and 2000 the population of Clark County, home of Las Vegas, grew by almost 250 percent. It is still one of the fastest-growing counties in the nation.
5. More than a thousand atomic bomb tests have been conducted in Nevada by the U.S. Army.

OREGON
★ *Beaver State* ★

"IF YOU POKE A BROOMSTICK in the ground, it will grow!" To an 1840s farm family looking for a new life in the American West, such words about the rich soils of Oregon's Willamette Valley pulled like a magnet. Tens of thousands of hopeful settlers came by wagon train across the Oregon Trail, generating enough population for Oregon to become a state in 1859. Most Oregonians still call this broad and beautiful valley home.

East of the Willamette loom the giant, snow-crowned volcanoes of the Cascade Range—Hood, Jefferson, and the Three Sisters. To the west, the Coast Ranges stand shrouded in fog and covered in mossy forest. A string of picturesque fishing towns, jewel-like state parks, and lonely lighthouses stretch along the rocky coast. Howling winds blast the shore in winter, whipping up huge waves that crash against it, chipping away the land. Rocky sea stacks stand as remnants of a long-ago shoreline.

The mountains split the state into two main climate regions. They force Pacific moisture out on the western slopes but block most precipitation from reaching the Columbia Plateau and Great Basin lands to the east. Here, semi-arid lands favor cattle ranching and farming of wheat, hay, sugar beets, and other specialty crops with water from the Snake and other rivers. Oregon's diverse agriculture yields more than 200 different farm products. The state ranks first in production of Christmas trees, hazelnuts, peppermint, raspberries, blackberries, loganberries, and grass seed. That's right, the green grass on a lawn near you may have had its beginnings on an Oregon seed farm.

Trees—big trees!—also love Oregon's climate. They cover nearly half the state. Forests of towering Douglas fir and western hemlock carpet the slopes of the Coast and Cascade Ranges,

Early 1800s

John McLoughlin and his fur trading company helped newcomers settle in the region. He is known as the "Father of Oregon."

1850s

Development boomed with the Donation Land Law of 1850, which gave 320 acres to settlers who farmed land for four years.

Late 1800s

Logging of vast stands of trees began in the late 1800s and provided the basis for the state's forest-products industry.

1990–Present

Since 1990 logging and any other type of disturbance is illegal near a known nesting site of the endangered northern spotted owl.

Crater Lake (opposite), at 1,932 feet (589 m) is the deepest in the United States. It fills a depression created when an eruption caused the top of a volcano to collapse. Wizard Island, in the 6-mile- (10-km-) wide lake, was created by a later eruption.

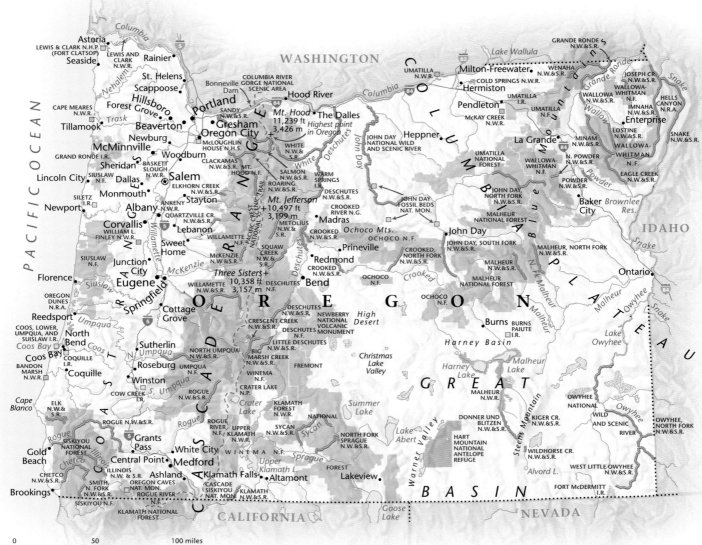

WASHINGTON

Astoria
LEWIS & CLARK N.H.P. (FORT CLATSOP)
Seaside
LEWIS AND CLARK N.W.R.
Rainier
St. Helens
Scappoose
CAPE MEARES N.W.R.
Hillsboro
Forest Grove
Tillamook
Beaverton
Newburg
Portland
Gresham
Oregon City
McMinnville
Woodburn
GRAND RONDE I.R.
Sheridan
BASKETT SLOUGH N.W.R.
Dallas
Lincoln City
SIUSLAW I.R.
Monmouth
Salem
Stayton
Newport
Albany
SILETZ I.R.
Corvallis
WILLIAM L. FINLEY N.W.R.
Lebanon
Sweet Home
SIUSLAW N.F.
Junction City
Florence
Eugene
Springfield
OREGON DUNES N.R.A.
Cottage Grove
Reedsport
COOS, LOWER, UMPQUA, AND SIUSLAW I.R.
Coos Bay
North Bend
Sutherlin
BANDON MARSH N.W.R.
Coquille
COQUILLE I.R.
Roseburg
Winston
Cape Blanco
ELK N.W. & S.R.
COW CREEK I.R.
Gold Beach
Grants Pass
White City
CHETCO N.W.&S.R.
Central Point
Medford
Ashland
Klamath Falls
Altamont
Brookings
SMITH, N. FORK N.W.&S.R.
OREGON CAVES NAT. MON.
ROGUE RIVER N.F.
CASCADE SISKIYOU NAT. MON.
SISKIYOU N.F.
KLAMATH NATIONAL FOREST

CALIFORNIA

Columbia
Bonneville Dam
COLUMBIA RIVER GORGE NATIONAL SCENIC AREA
Hood River
Mt. Hood 11,239 ft 3,426 m
The Dalles
Highest point in Oregon
SANDY N.W.&S.R.
McLOUGHLIN HOUSE N.H.S.
CLACKAMAS
MT. HOOD N.F.
WHITE N.W.&S.R.
ELKHORN CREEK
White
SALMON N.W.&S.R.
ROARING RIVER N.W.&S.R.
ANKENY N.W.R.
QUARTZVILLE CR. N.W.&S.R.
Mt. Jefferson +10,497 ft 3,199 m
WARM SPRINGS I.R.
METOLIUS N.W. S.R.
McKENZIE N.W.&S.R.
SQUAW CREEK N.W.&S.R.
Three Sisters + 10,358 ft 3,157 m
WILLAMETTE N.W.&S.R.
CRESCENT CREEK N.W.&S.R.
DESCHUTES N.W.&S.R.
BIG MARSH CREEK N.W.&S.R.
NORTH UMPQUA N.W.&S.R.
UMPQUA N.F.
WINEMA N.F.
CRATER LAKE N.P.
Crater Lake
ROGUE N.W.&S.R.
ROGUE RIVER N.F.
UPPER KLAMATH N.W.R.
KLAMATH FOREST N.W.R.
NATIONAL
SYCAN N.W.&S.R.
Sycan
Upper Klamath L.
WINEMA N.F.
KLAMATH N.W.&S.R.

DESCHUTES N.W.&S.R.
Deschutes
Madras
CROOKED RIVER N.G.
CROOKED N.W.&S.R.
Prineville
Redmond
CROOKED N.W.&S.R.
Bend
DESCHUTES N.W.&S.R.
NEWBERRY NATIONAL VOLCANIC MONUMENT
DESCHUTES N.W.&S.R.
LITTLE DESCHUTES N.W.&S.R.
FREMONT
High Desert
Christmas Lake Valley
Summer Lake
NORTH FORK SPRAGUE N.W.&S.R.
Sprague
FOREST
Lakeview
Goose Lake

Lake Wallula
UMATILLA N.W.R.
Milton-Freewater
COLD SPRINGS N.W.R.
Hermiston
Pendleton
UMATILLA I.R.
McKAY CREEK N.W.R.
Heppner
JOHN DAY NATIONAL WILD AND SCENIC RIVER
GRANDE RONDE N.W.&S.R.
WENAHA N.W.&S.R.
La Grande
UMATILLA NATIONAL FOREST
WALLOWA-WHITMAN N.F.
Enterprise
JOSEPH CR. N.W.&S.R.
WALLOWA-WHITMAN N.F.
IMNAHA N.W.&S.R.
HELLS CANYON N.R.A.
LOSTINE N.W.&S.R.
MINAM N.W.&S.R.
SNAKE N.W.&S.R.
WALLOWA-WHITMAN N.F.
EAGLE CREEK N.W.&S.R.
POWDER N.W.&S.R.
Baker City
Brownlee Res.
IDAHO

JOHN DAY, NORTH FORK N.W.&S.R.
JOHN DAY FOSSIL BEDS NAT. MON.
MALHEUR NATIONAL FOREST
John Day
JOHN DAY, SOUTH FORK N.W.&S.R.
OCHOCO Mts.
OCHOCO N.F.
CROOKED, NORTH FORK N.W.&S.R.
OCHOCO N.F.
MALHEUR, NORTH FORK N.W.&S.R.
MALHEUR N.W.&S.R.
MALHEUR NATIONAL FOREST
Ontario
Snake

Burns
BURNS PAIUTE I.R.
Harney Basin
Harney Lake
Malheur Lake
MALHEUR N.W.R.
Lake Owyhee
Malheur
OWYHEE NATIONAL
Owyhee
DONNER UND BLITZEN N.W.&S.R.
KIGER CR. N.W.&S.R.
WILD AND SCENIC RIVER
Lake Abert
Warner Valley
HART MOUNTAIN NATIONAL ANTELOPE REFUGE
Steens Mountain
WILDHORSE CR. N.W.&S.R.
WEST LITTLE OWYHEE N.W.&S.R.
OWYHEE, NORTH FORK N.W.&S.R.
Alvord L.
FORT McDERMITT I.R.

GREAT BASIN

NEVADA

COLUMBIA
BLUE MOUNTAINS
PLATEAU
COAST RANGE
CASCADE RANGE
OREGON
PACIFIC OCEAN

0   50   100 miles
0   50   100 kilometers

Albers Conic Equal-Area Projection

A member of the Warm Springs tribe fishes in the Deschutes River of north-central Oregon. Net fishing for salmon, lamprey eels, and other species has been a way of life here for generations. Today, sediments from logging, farming, industrial pollution, and dams on Oregon's rivers have caused the fish populations to decline, threatening Native American traditions.

while ponderosa pines thrive in the eastern highlands. Logging has been one of Oregon's leading economic activities for decades. Although forest protection agreements have reduced the state's tree harvest in recent years, Oregon still leads the country in timber output.

Oregon is more than forests and fields. Where the Willamette River flows into the Columbia, a trading center bloomed into Portland, the City of Roses. Its docks import cars from Asia, and its factories process wood products and computer components. Portland is recognized as a model city for its success in keeping its downtown healthy and active.

Oregon faces challenges in managing its rich natural resources and sources of scenic beauty in a way that will maintain the quality of life that its people long have enjoyed. The Columbia River provides water to run massive hydroelectric plants that generate most of Oregon's electricity and power metal-processing plants. While a boon to industry, the dams have disrupted river flow and contributed to the decline of the state's once-rich salmon fishery. Opportunities in computer and other high-tech jobs have encouraged people to emigrate from California and other states. There has also been an increase in the number of Hispanic and Asian residents. With the population increasing at a rate of more than 50,000 people each year, there is major concern over the loss of agricultural land and the competition for water. Renewed logging of old-growth forests that have been standing for centuries—long before there ever *was* an Oregon—stirs controversy. While the struggle to balance economic growth and preserve the environment will be ongoing, a fine Pacific Coast position and plentiful natural assets hold great promise for Oregon's future.

OREGON
Beaver State

STATE OF OREGON 1859

STATEHOOD	February 14, 1859; 33rd state
CAPITAL	Salem
LARGEST CITY	Portland Population 539,438
TOTAL AREA	98,381 sq mi; 254,805 sq km
LAND AREA	95,997 sq mi; 248,631 sq km
POPULATION	3,831,074
POPULATION DENSITY	38 people per sq mi
MAJOR RACIAL/ ETHNIC GROUPS	83.6% white; 3.7% Asian; 1.8% African American; 1.4% Native American; Hispanic (any race) 11.7%.
INDUSTRY	real estate, retail and wholesale trade, electronic equipment, health services, construction, forest products, business services
AGRICULTURE	nursery stock, hay, cattle, grass seed, wheat, dairy products, potatoes

WESTERN MEADOWLARK   OREGON GRAPE

Did you know?

1. During World War II, Japan tried unsuccessfully to start huge fires along the Oregon coast by launching fire bombs.
2. Beneath the streets of Pendleton, Oregon, you can tour a labyrinth of tunnels built between 1870 and 1930 by Chinese laborers who were forced to live and work underground to escape discrimination. A Chinese laundry, ice house, and butcher shop are among the businesses restored in 1989.
3. The U.S. Department of Energy's Bonneville Power Administration, headquartered in Portland, provides about 45 percent of the electricity used in the Pacific Northwest. Most of this power comes from 31 hydroelectric plants along the Columbia River.
4. Oregon takes its nickname from the abundant beaver that gave rise to a thriving fur trade in the early 1800s.

UTAH
★ *Beehive State* ★

"THIS IS THE RIGHT PLACE." So said Brigham Young, as he looked out over the Great Salt Lake Valley from the Wasatch Mountains on July 24, 1847. Young had just led a hardy group of Mormon pioneers to find freedom in the west to practice their religion. From the 1847 group of some 1,500 immigrants, Mormon communities grew quickly to 40,000 by 1860. Irrigation helped communities thrive on the thin strip of fertile soil along the Wasatch Front. Today, seven of ten Utah residents are Mormons, and the region between Brigham City and Provo is still the most populated.

Utah brims with scenic landforms. The north-south running Wasatch join the Uinta Mountains, which reach east along the Wyoming border. Topped by Kings Peak at 13,528 feet (4,123 m), the Uintas are the only major range in the Rockies that run east-west. The dry valleys and rugged ranges of the Great Basin stretch west and southwest of the Wasatch. Here, rivers may flow into low areas during spring, but none flow out. Salts carried from the surrounding mountains are left behind as the water evaporates. When mountain man Jim Bridger first tasted the water of the Great Salt Lake in 1824, he thought he had reached the Pacific Ocean! In Utah's southern section stands the Colorado Plateau, a huge raised tableland shared with Colorado, New Mexico, and Arizona. Here the Colorado and other rivers slice down through layers of colored rocks, forming scenic canyon lands.

For thousands of years the Ute, Paiute, and Shoshone peoples lived in small groups in this remote region. But it was the Mormons who settled in great numbers. They dug ditches to channel water from streams to their fields. With hard work and cooperation they turned the desert into productive farmland. Arrival of

1847
Brigham Young, with an advance group of 148 followers, arrived in Salt Lake Valley and established Utah's first Mormon settlement.

1869
The completion of the first Transcontinental Railroad brought settlers and opened new markets for Utah's farm and mining products.

1952
Uranium deposits near Moab provided a basis for weapons development industries that now raise environmental concerns.

Present day
Desert expanses make excellent testing grounds and have helped make Utah a leader in defense systems and aerospace technology.

Millions of years of wind and weather have chiseled away at domes of red sandstone to create the more than 2,000 landforms, including Delicate Arch (opposite), preserved in Arches National Park. The largest arch stretches 306 feet (93 m) end to end.

This exquisitely preserved backbone is on display at Dinosaur National Monument's Quarry Visitor Center. Fifteen hundred fossils are preserved here, including parts of Stegosaurus, Apatosaurus, Camptosaurus, Ceratosaurus, turtle species, crocodiles, and mammals. The bodies of these creatures were covered in sand by a river about 150 million years ago. Dissolved minerals fossilized the bone structures; mountain building tilted the riverbed up onto the side of a steep hill; then erosion exposed the mass of fossils.

Map of Utah

0   50   100 miles
0   50   100 kilometers
Albers Conic Equal-Area Projection

IDAHO

SAWTOOTH N.F. Raft River Mts.

Spring Bay

Newfoundland Evaporation Basin

GOLDEN SPIKE N.H.S. (PROMONTORY)

Promontory

BEAR RIVER MIGRATORY BIRD REFUGE

Great Salt Lake Desert

Great Salt Lake

Smithfield
Logan
Providence
Tremonton
Wellsville
WASATCH-CACHE NATIONAL FOREST
Brigham City
North Ogden
Ogden
Clearfield
Layton
Farmington
Centerville
Bountiful

Bear Lake

WYOMING

Flaming Gorge Reservoir

WASATCH-CACHE NATIONAL FOREST

Highest point in Utah
Kings Peak
13,528 ft
4,123 m
Uinta Mountains

FLAMING GORGE N.R.A.

ASHLEY NATIONAL FOREST

Wendover

Salt Lake City
W. Jordan
Murray
Grantsville
Riverton
Sandy
Tooele
WASATCH-CACHE N.F.
SKULL VALLEY I.R.
TIMPANOGOS CAVE NAT. MON.
Lehi
Pleasant Grove
Orem
Provo
Spanish Fork
Springville
Payson

Heber City

UINTA NATIONAL FOREST

Strawberry Reservoir

Roosevelt

Vernal

DINOSAUR NATIONAL MONUMENT

OURAY N.W.R.

Green

UINTAH AND OURAY INDIAN RESERVATION

COLORADO

GREAT

GOSHUTE INDIAN RESERVATION

FISH SPRINGS N.W.R.

Sevier Desert

WASATCH-CACHE N.F.

Utah Lake

ASHLEY N.F.

Nine Mile Creek

Willow Creek
Bitter Creek
White

Confusion Range

Nephi

UINTA N.F.

Helper
Price

Desolation Canyon
Currant Hill Cr.

Roan

East Tavaputs Plateau

BASIN

Sevier Lake

Delta
FISHLAKE
Manti

Moroni
Mount Pleasant
Ephraim

MANTI-LA SAL NATIONAL FOREST

Castle Dale

San Rafael

Price

Cliffs

NEVADA

U   T   A   H

Fillmore

Richfield

Green River

Green

ARCHES NATIONAL PARK

I-70

FISHLAKE N.F.

San Rafael Swell

Milford

Beaver

FOREST

Piute Res.

Otter Creek Reservoir

CAPITOL REEF NATIONAL PARK

Fremont

Dirty Devil

Moab

MANTI-LA SAL N.F.

CANYONLANDS NATIONAL PARK

Little Salt Lake

Sevier

Panguitch

DIXIE NATIONAL FOREST

Escalante

C   O   L   O   R   A   D   O

Henry Mts.

Halls Creek

Bullfrog Creek

Colorado

MANTI-LA SAL N.F.

Blanding

Cedar City

CEDAR BREAKS NAT. MON.

BRYCE CANYON NATIONAL PARK

GRAND STAIRCASE-ESCALANTE NATIONAL MONUMENT

GLEN CANYON N.R.A.

Lake Powell

NATURAL BRIDGES NAT. MON.

HOVENWEEP NAT. MON.

DIXIE N.F.

ZION NATIONAL PARK

Virgin

Kanab Creek

Paria

RAINBOW BRIDGE NAT. MON.

San Juan

PAIUTE I.R.
Hurricane
Santa Clara
St. George
Kanab

Monument Valley

Four Corners

N. MEX.

ARIZONA

P   L   A   T   E   A   U

NAVAJO NATION RESERVATION

the railroad brought non-Mormons and other immigrants. In 1869 the Golden Spike that completed the first transcontinental railroad was driven into the ground near Promontory, north of Great Salt Lake. Mining of copper and other minerals brought more people and wealth to Utah in the 20th century.

Mormons wanted Utah to enter the Union with the name Deseret, meaning "honeybee," in recognition of all their hard work. Congress thought that sounded too much like "desert," so the state was named Utah after the native Ute people. But its nickname, Beehive State, honors its Mormon settlers.

Nearly two-thirds of the state is owned by the federal government. Government building of weapons parts and rockets has been important to the economy since World War II. The vast western flatlands make perfect testing grounds for fast cars and missiles. But the government has also helped make tourism a huge industry for the state. Some of the best opportunities for skiing, rock climbing, mountain biking, hiking, and boating are on government land. Manufacturing, especially of computer and other high-tech equipment, is another key industry.

Utah does face challenges. Mormons sometimes argue with non-Mormons over land use, civil versus religious rights, and other issues. Decades of mining and military weapons testing have damaged some land areas. Struggles continue over further mining and building on Utah's fragile natural areas. Drought and water shortages are always a concern, and danger could come from a hidden source. Movement along a fault near Salt Lake City could trigger an earthquake. But with careful planning, Utah should continue to be the "right place" for residents and visitors alike.

UTAH
Beehive State

STATEHOOD	January 4, 1896; 45th state
CAPITAL	Salt Lake City
LARGEST CITY	Salt Lake City Population 181,266
TOTAL AREA	84,899 sq mi; 219,887 sq km
LAND AREA	82,144 sq mi; 212,751 sq km
POPULATION	2,763,885
POPULATION DENSITY	32 people per sq mi
MAJOR RACIAL/ ETHNIC GROUPS	86.1% white; 2.0% Asian; 1.2% Native American; 1.1% African American; Hispanic (any race) 13.0%.
INDUSTRY	government, manufacturing, real estate, construction, health services, business services, banking
AGRICULTURE	cattle, dairy products, hay, poultry and eggs, wheat

CALIFORNIA GULL

SEGO LILY

Did you know?

1. Rainbow Bridge, in the national monument of the same name, is the world's largest natural stone bridge. It is 290 feet (88 m) high and 275 feet (84 m) across.
2. Members of The Church of Jesus Christ of Latter Day Saints are also known as Mormons. This name comes from the Book of Mormon, which is the church's holy text, or bible. There are more than eleven million Mormons worldwide.
3. The Great Salt Lake is three to five times saltier than the ocean and the largest lake west of the Mississippi River. It is the remnant of a much larger ancient inland sea called Lake Bonneville.
4. Utah's spectacular scenery is preserved in five national parks, seven national monuments, two national recreation areas, and six national forests.
5. The names Utah, Uinta, and Wasatch all derive from the Ute people.

WASHINGTON

★ *Evergreen State* ★

WET AND MILD, hip and wild. Washington State is all of these and more. While the weather, especially in the western third, is known to be foggy and rainy with mild temperatures, it does not dampen the spirit and creativity of the people who live there. The forces of nature that created its spectacular landscapes are still at work. Washington State residents enjoy the beauty and deal with the wildness.

Washington forms the northwest corner of the Lower 48 states. The Coast Ranges are topped by the towering Olympic Mountains. These slopes are drenched with moisture—an average of 12 to 14 *feet* (3–4 *m*) a year. Temperate rain forests of spruce, hemlock, fir, and cedar thrive there. Just east is glacially-carved Puget Sound along which most of the state's residents live. On clear days, they can see majestic, snow-clad Mount Rainier, an active volcano in the nearby Cascade Range. In 1980 Mount St. Helens,

in the southern part of the range, literally blew its top—a dramatic reminder that powerful forces are still at work here. These western mountains block most precipitation from moving to the eastern part of the state, where it is dry enough for sagebrush and short grasses to grow.

Zigzagging from northeast to southwest across the state is the massive Columbia. The largest-volume river in the western U.S., the Columbia is perhaps the hardest working, too. A huge system of dams, topped by the Grand Coulee, spin turbines to create electricity and form reservoirs to provide water for agriculture.

Sea journeys brought early explorers to the area, and sea otters brought fur traders. But it was Lewis and Clark's overland route to the Pacific and the opening of the Oregon Trail that spurred settlement in the mid 1800s. Native Americans, including the Nez Perce, Yakima, and Spokane, fought to keep their lands but

1775–1792

Spanish explorers were followed by British and American fur traders and merchants. At various times, each claimed the region.

1880s

Riots in Seattle between Chinese workers and white newcomers seeking jobs led to the establishment of labor unions.

1940s

Boeing Company began building military aircraft during World War II. Today it is the world's largest aircraft manufacturer.

1970s–Present

Microsoft, founded by computer gurus Bill Gates and Paul Allen, has greatly enhanced the state's economy, especially in the 1990s.

The observation deck of Seattle's 605-foot- (184-m-) high Space Needle (opposite) provides great views of the entire Puget Sound region as well as stately Mount Rainier, which at 14,411 feet (4,392 m) is Washington's highest peak.

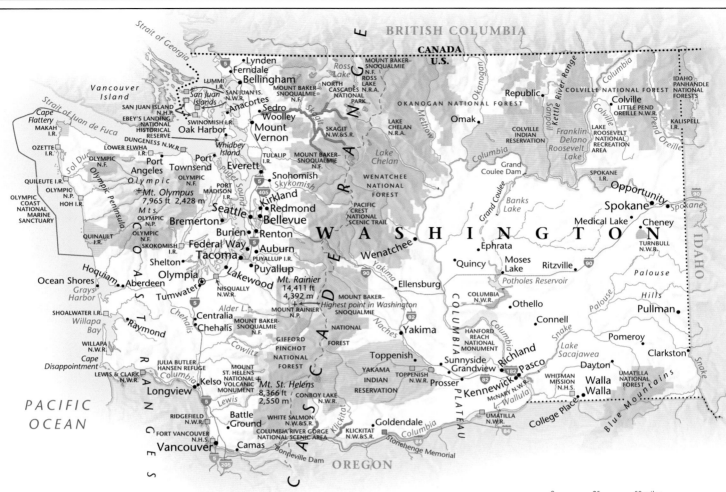

Ten to twelve billion apples are hand-picked each year from Washington's orchards. (There are no apple-picking machines.) In 2003 the state accounted for more than half of the nation's total harvest of this fruit. Varied soils and climate coupled with irrigation from the Columbia and its tributary rivers, allow growers to also produce bountiful crops of grapes, cherries, and pears.

lost. The first railroad reached the territory in the 1880s, and by the end of the decade Washington gained statehood. When gold was discovered in Canada's Yukon Territory in the 1890s, Washington became the shipping gateway to the goldfields. The Evergreen State boomed, growing from 75,000 people in 1889 to 1.25 million by 1920.

Its nickname suits the state, with more than half the land cloaked in forests. Early development centered on logging, along with fishing from coastal waters, cattle and wheat farming in the east, and orchards—especially apple—scattered throughout. Manufacturing "took off" when aircraft builders, aluminum companies, and defense industries set up shop in the Puget Sound area during the two world wars. The success of a coffee company and a computer software giant caused Seattle's population to explode in the 1990s.

Over the years, residents have learned lessons about economic growth and state resources. The state's once-thriving salmon catch has been greatly reduced, in part through over-harvest and dam construction. Concerns about forest preservation have led to less logging, though the forest industry is still huge. Washington's successful aircraft and computer industries face intense global competition. Seattle, regarded as one of the country's most beautiful cities, is jammed with traffic. The discovery in December 2003 that one of the state's dairy cows had mad cow disease raised concerns about the safety of U.S. beef.

Bright spots in the economic forecast for the state include growth in biotechnology research, a likely increase in shipping from Puget Sound ports, and a renewed emphasis on preserving resources through wise management to ensure that future generations of Washingtonians will benefit from the state's natural riches.

WASHINGTON
Evergreen State

STATEHOOD	November 11, 1889; 42nd state
CAPITAL	Olympia
LARGEST CITY	Seattle Population 570,426
TOTAL AREA	71,300 sq mi; 184,665 sq km
LAND AREA	66,544 sq mi; 172,348 sq km
POPULATION	6,724,540
POPULATION DENSITY	94 people per sq mi
MAJOR RACIAL/ ETHNIC GROUPS	77.3% white; 7.2% Asian; 3.6% African American; 1.5% Native American; Hispanic (any race) 11.2%.
INDUSTRY	aerospace, tourism, food processing, forest products, paper products, industrial machinery, printing and publishing, metals
AGRICULTURE	seafood, apples, dairy products, wheat, cattle, potatoes, hay

AMERICAN GOLDFINCH   COAST RHODODENDRON

Did you know?

1. Washington is the only state named for a President. As a territory it was almost called "Columbia" in honor of the Columbia River.
2. Sam Hill built a concrete replica of England's Stonehenge on a bluff overlooking the Columbia River as a memorial to the soldiers from Klickitat County who fought and died in World War I.
3. The Olympic Peninsula, where rainfall averages 12–14 feet (3–4 m) a year, is home to the only temperate rain forest in the lower 48 states. The forest is dominated by Sitka spruce and western hemlock, some of which are 300 feet (90 m) high and 23 feet (7 m) around.
4. Washington has more glaciers than all of the other 47 contiguous U.S. states combined.
5. The northwesternmost point in the contiguous United States is Cape Flattery on the Olympic Peninsula.
6. The first Father's Day was observed in Spokane in 1910.

WYOMING

★ *Equality State* ★

HIGH, WIDE, AND WINDY—all describe Wyoming. The state is second only to Colorado in elevation, averaging 6,700 feet (2,040 m). It stretches 360 miles (580 km) east to west and 280 miles (450 km) north to south. Winds blow hard across rugged mountains and dry basins, making Wyoming the windiest state. In winter, winds can pick up dry snow, creating "ground blizzards" even on clear days. Wyoming could be described as lonely, too. Though ninth largest in area, the state has the lowest population. More people live in the city of Denver, Colorado, than in all of Wyoming!

Wyoming may be short on people, but it is tall on scenery. Mysterious Devils Tower, which perhaps is more famous for its role in the movie *Close Encounters of the Third Kind* than it is for being the nation's first national monument, is a reminder of an ancient volcanic past. Three hundred miles to the west, heat from Earth's

core still reaches the surface. Yellowstone National Park contains more geysers than any other place in the world. These and other geothermal features share the park with canyons, waterfalls, forests, and wildlife. In fact, Wyoming's huge variety of wildlife—elk, moose, pronghorn, bison, bear (both black and grizzly), deer, coyote, mountain lions and eagles—makes the entire state seem like a big game park.

Just south of Yellowstone stand the jagged, glacier-carved peaks of the Tetons, youngest range in the Rockies. Like a teenager, the Tetons are still growing—about a foot every four centuries. Near the end of the Wind River Range, ruts from Oregon Trail wagons can still be seen along South Pass. This natural gateway through the Rockies opened the West to settlement beginning in the 1830s.

Oil was discovered in the Wind River Basin

1825

The Green River Rendezvous was the annual meeting place for trappers who came to trade furs for food and other supplies.

1869

Wyoming's territorial legislature was the first in the U.S. to allow women to vote and to hold office on an equal basis with men.

1880s

By 1887 overgrazing and a series of terrible winters had caused many ranches to fail, crippling Wyoming's cattle industry.

1910—Present

The development of Salt Creek (above) and other oil fields around Casper made the city the center of Wyoming's oil industry.

The majestic peaks of the Tetons, youngest range in the Rocky Mountains, rise above the Snake River (opposite). Nearby Jackson Hole provides year-round recreational opportunities and is the winter home of the nation's largest elk herd.

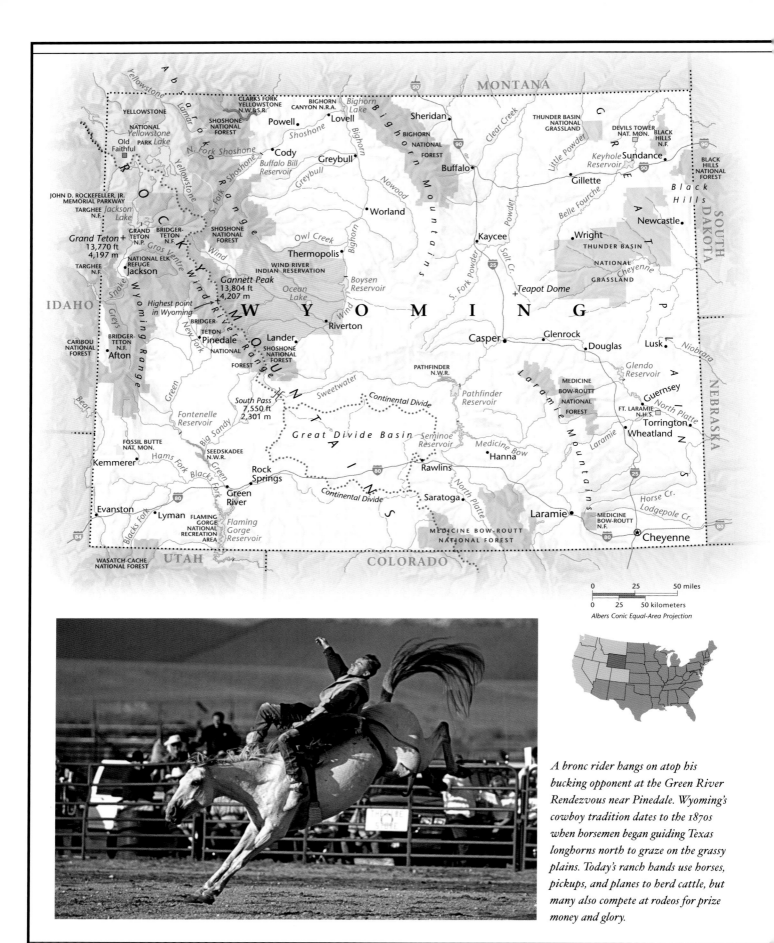

MONTANA

YELLOWSTONE

CLARKS FORK
YELLOWSTONE
N.W.&S.R.

BIGHORN
CANYON N.R.A.

Bighorn
Lake

THUNDER BASIN
NATIONAL
GRASSLAND

DEVILS TOWER
NAT. MON.

BLACK
HILLS
N.F.

NATIONAL

Powell

Lovell

Sheridan

Clear Creek

Little Powder

Sundance

BLACK
HILLS
NATIONAL
FOREST

Yellowstone
PARK *Lake*

Old
Faithful

SHOSHONE
NATIONAL
FOREST

BIGHORN
NATIONAL
FOREST

Buffalo

Keyhole
Reservoir

N. Fork Shoshone

Cody

Greybull

Shoshone

S. Fork Shoshone

Buffalo Bill
Reservoir

Greybull

Gillette

JOHN D. ROCKEFELLER, JR.
MEMORIAL PARKWAY

TARGHEE
N.F.

Jackson
Lake

Nowood

Worland

Kaycee

Wright

THUNDER BASIN

Belle Fourche

Newcastle

Black
Hills

SOUTH
DAKOTA

Grand Teton +
13,770 ft
4,197 m

GRAND
TETON
N.P.

BRIDGER-
TETON
N.F.

SHOSHONE
NATIONAL
FOREST

Owl Creek

Thermopolis

NATIONAL

TARGHEE
N.F.

NATIONAL ELK
REFUGE

Jackson

Gros Ventre

Wind

Gannett Peak
13,804 ft
4,207 m

WIND RIVER
INDIAN
RESERVATION

Boysen
Reservoir

Bighorn

S. Fork Powder

Teapot Dome +

Casper

GRASSLAND

Cheyenne

Glenrock

IDAHO

Snake

Greys

Highest point
in Wyoming

BRIDGER-
TETON
N.F.

Pinedale

Ocean
Lake

W Y O M I N G

Douglas

Lusk

Niobrara

Afton

New Fork

BRIDGER-
TETON
NATIONAL
FOREST

Lander

SHOSHONE
NATIONAL
FOREST

Riverton

Wind

PATHFINDER
N.W.R.

Pathfinder
Reservoir

MEDICINE
BOW-ROUTT
NATIONAL
FOREST

Glendo
Reservoir

Guernsey

CARIBOU
NATIONAL
FOREST

Green

South Pass
7,550 ft
2,301 m

Sweetwater

Continental Divide

Laramie

FT. LARAMIE
N.H.S.

North Platte

Torrington

Fontenelle
Reservoir

Big Sandy

Great Divide Basin

Seminoe
Reservoir

Medicine Bow

Wheatland

FOSSIL BUTTE
NAT. MON.

Bear

SEEDSKADEE
N.W.R.

Rock
Springs

Hanna

Rawlins

Laramie

Horse Cr.

Lodgepole Cr.

Kemmerer

Hams Fork

Green

Continental Divide

North Platte

Saratoga

MEDICINE
BOW-ROUTT
N.F.

Evanston

Lyman

FLAMING
GORGE
NATIONAL
RECREATION
AREA

Flaming
Gorge
Reservoir

MEDICINE BOW-ROUTT
NATIONAL FOREST

Cheyenne

WASATCH-CACHE
NATIONAL FOREST

UTAH

COLORADO

0   25   50 miles
0   25   50 kilometers
Albers Conic Equal-Area Projection

*A bronc rider hangs on atop his
bucking opponent at the Green River
Rendezvous near Pinedale. Wyoming's
cowboy tradition dates to the 1870s
when horsemen began guiding Texas
longhorns north to graze on the grassy
plains. Today's ranch hands use horses,
pickups, and planes to herd cattle, but
many also compete at rodeos for prize
money and glory.*

in 1833. A year later Fort Laramie, the first real settlement in Wyoming, was founded as a trading post on land where Cheyenne, Arapahoe, and other native peoples had long lived. As a military post, it played a key role both in protecting settlers and in the wars and treaties that eventually gave them control of the land.

The Union Pacific Railroad, which reached Wyoming in 1867, brought a boom in settlement and spurred economic activities that are still important to the state. Ranching became a big business. Cattle, at first longhorns from Texas, were fattened on the open range and then shipped by train to the East. Other homesteaders came to ranch sheep and farm crops. Coal deposits were mined along the early rail route. Now, massive machinery strips vast seams of coal, making Wyoming the nation's largest producer of this resource. Most is exported by rail to eastern power plants.

People came in search of other minerals, too. In 1888 oil was struck near Casper. Today, the refining of oil and natural gas is the state's most important industry. Uranium was found in the 1950s. Wyoming is now the nation's top producer.

The opening of Yellowstone National Park in 1872 brought tourists to Wyoming, and this industry is key to Wyoming's future. Visitors come to re-live the Wild West, staying at dude ranches and cheering at rodeos in towns across the state. The U.S. government owns about half the state. Much of this land is used for recreation and tourism, but logging, grazing, and mining are permitted in selected areas. Some people are concerned that these activities could hurt the land and the state's future. Careful management can ensure that Wyoming's wild, wide-open spaces will be around for all to enjoy for many years to come.

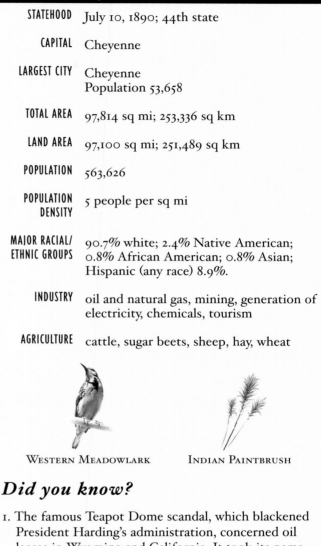

WYOMING
Equality State

STATEHOOD	July 10, 1890; 44th state
CAPITAL	Cheyenne
LARGEST CITY	Cheyenne Population 53,658
TOTAL AREA	97,814 sq mi; 253,336 sq km
LAND AREA	97,100 sq mi; 251,489 sq km
POPULATION	563,626
POPULATION DENSITY	5 people per sq mi
MAJOR RACIAL/ ETHNIC GROUPS	90.7% white; 2.4% Native American; 0.8% African American; 0.8% Asian; Hispanic (any race) 8.9%.
INDUSTRY	oil and natural gas, mining, generation of electricity, chemicals, tourism
AGRICULTURE	cattle, sugar beets, sheep, hay, wheat

WESTERN MEADOWLARK   INDIAN PAINTBRUSH

Did you know?

1. The famous Teapot Dome scandal, which blackened President Harding's administration, concerned oil leases in Wyoming and California. It took its name from the shape of a rock formation above the oil reserves in Wyoming.
2. Butch Cassidy's Wild Bunch gang lived in and around Kaycee, Wyoming, on the Powder River.
3. Wyoming is called the Equality State because it was the first state to give women the right to vote, granted in 1869 when it was still a territory.
4. The horse on Wyoming's license plate is named Old Steamboat in honor of a legendary bucking bronco that no one could ride.
5. Devils Tower was named the country's first national monument by President Teddy Roosevelt in 1906. It is a sacred site of worship to many Plains Indians, who know it as Bears Lodge.
6. Cody, Wyoming, is named for "Buffalo Bill" Cody.

U.S. TERRITORIES

FAR-FLUNG TROPICAL ISLANDS. The United States claims 13 island territories scattered across ten time zones. Of these, only the five largest—Puerto Rico and the U.S. Virgin Islands in the Caribbean Sea and the Northern Marianas, Guam, and American Samoa in the Pacific Ocean—have their own governments, cultures, and economies. Each of these was acquired from another country as the result of a war or international agreement, and each is a valued part of the United States.

Residents of all but American Samoa are U.S. citizens, and all except the Northern Marianas have a non-voting delegate in the U.S. House of Representatives. Many island people, seeking new opportunities, have moved to the United States. The country's population now includes 2.7 million Puerto Ricans, and tens of thousands of American Samoans live in Hawaii and other Pacific states. Meanwhile, each year millions of mainlanders are lured by the promise of sun and sand to these distant shores.

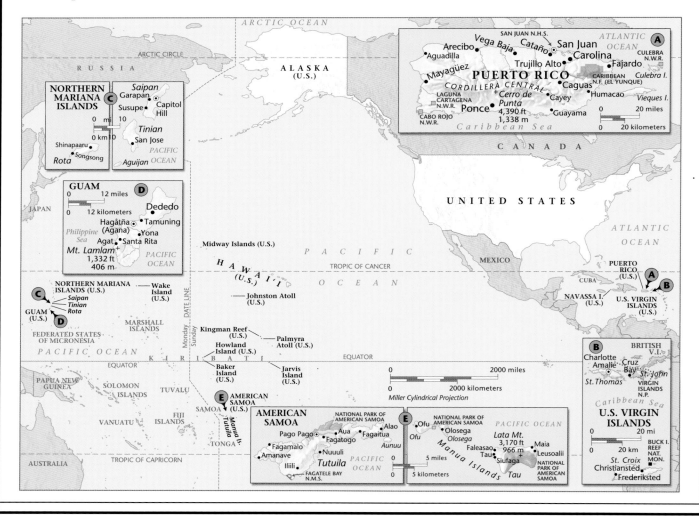

AMERICAN SAMOA (Pop.: 62,000)

Populated mainly by descendants of Polynesian seafarers who arrived here some 4,000 years ago, American Samoa processes huge tuna catches for U.S. markets. Fagatele Bay National Marine Sanctuary (left) serves as a symbol of the concern Samoan people have for the environment.

GUAM (Pop.: 164,000)

Much of Guam belongs to the U.S. military. More than half of its 164,000 people were born elsewhere. Tourism, especially in the form of tropic-seeking Japanese visitors, is the island's most important economic activity. At right, a native Taotao dancer performs at a Pacific Arts Festival.

NORTHERN MARIANA ISLANDS (Pop.: 78,000)

Most people here live on Saipan, the center for commercial and government activities. Chamorros, people whose ancestors came from Southeast Asia, make up the native population. Many islanders farm, work in the garment industry, or hold government jobs. Tourism is growing thanks to fabulous beaches (left).

PUERTO RICO (Pop.: 3,879,000)

Spanish-speaking Puerto Rico has more people than 25 U.S. states. Manufacturing, especially of medicines and electronics, has surpassed an agricultural economy based on sugar, coffee, and tobacco. El Yunque rain forest (right) is among the attractions that fuel a thriving tourist industry.

VIRGIN ISLANDS (Pop.: 110,000)

The islands of St. Thomas, St. Croix, and St. John—purchased from Denmark in 1917—make up most of the U.S. Virgin Islands. Sugar-mill ruins (left) are evidence of a past dominated by plantation farming. Today, profits come mainly from tourism and the refining of imported oil.

★ Facts & Figures ★

All 50 States

Capital City
Washington, D.C.

Largest City
New York City
Population 8,084,316

Total Area
3,794,083 sq mi;
9,826,630 sq km

Land Area
3,537,439 sq mi;
9,161,923 sq km

Population 290,809,777

Population Density
82 people per sq mi

Major Racial/Ethnic Groups
75.1% white; 12.3% African American; 3.6% Asian;.9% Native American. Hispanic (any race) 12.5%

Top States

Top Ten in Farm Products (by net farm income)
1. Texas
2. California
3. North Carolina
4. Georgia
5. Florida
6. Iowa
7. Nebraska
8. Alabama
9. Illinois
10. Arkansas

Top Five in Fisheries
1. Alaska
2. Louisiana
3. Maine
4. Florida
5. Texas

Top Ten in Minerals
1. Texas
2. Louisiana
3. Alaska
4. California
5. Oklahoma
6. Wyoming
7. New Mexico
8. West Virginia
9. Kentucky
10. Colorado

Extremes

World's Strongest Surface Wind
231 mph (372 kph),
Mount Washington, NH,
April 12, 1934

World's Oldest Living Tree
Methuselah bristlecone
pine, California; 4,789
years old

World's Tallest Living Tree
The "Stratosphere Giant,"
a coast redwood in
Humboldt Redwoods State
Park in California,
369.4 ft (112.6 m) high

World's Largest Gorge
Grand Canyon, Arizona:
275 mi (443 km) long along
the river; 590 ft to 18 mi
(180 m to 29 km) wide;
about 1 mile (1.6 km) deep

Highest U.S. Temperature
134°F (56.6°C),
Death Valley, California,
July 10, 1913

Lowest U.S. Temperature
Minus 80°F (-62.2°C)
at Prospect Creek, Alaska,
January 23, 1971

Highest U.S. Point
Mount McKinley
(Denali), Alaska;
20,320 feet (6,194 m)

Lowest U.S. Point
Death Valley, California;
282 feet (86 m) below
sea level

Longest U.S. River System
Mississippi-Missouri;
3,710 mi (5,971 km) long

Rainiest U.S. Spot
Wai'ale'ale (mountain),
Hawai'i: average annual
rainfall 460 in (1,168 cm)

U.S. Metropolitan Areas with More Than Five Million People
(A metropolitan area is a city and its surrounding suburban areas.)
1. New York,
   pop. 21,199,900
2. Los Angeles,
   pop. 16,373,600
3. Chicago,
   pop. 9,157,500
4. Washington, D.C.,
   pop. 7,608,100
5. San Francisco,
   pop. 7,039,400
6. Philadelphia,
   pop. 6,188,500
7. Boston,
   pop. 5,819,100
8. Detroit,
   pop. 5,456,400
9. Dallas-Fort Worth,
   pop. 5,221,800

Map Key

- ⊛ State capital
- + Elevation
- ▪ Point of interest
- —— River
- – – Intermittent river
- ⊥⊥⊥⊥ Canal
- ——— Interstate or selected other highway
- - - - Trail
- ••••• National boundary
- •••••• State boundary
- •••••• Continental divide
- ⊨ Lake and dam
- ⟳ Intermittent lake
- ⟳ Dry lake
- ⟳ Swamp
- ⊞⊞ Glacier
- ⟳ Below sea level
- ▨ Sand
- ▨ Lava

City and Town Population:
- ● **New York** *1,000,000 and over*
- ● San Jose *100,000 to 999,999*
- ● Frankfort *25,000 to 99,999*
- ● Aspen *under 25,000*

- ▫ National Battlefield, **N.B.**
  National Battlefield Park, **N.B.P.**
  National Battlefield Site, **N.B.S.**
  National Historic Site, **N.H.S.**
  National Historical Area
  National Historical Park, **N.H.P.**
  National Lakeshore
  National Military Park, **N.M.P.**
  National Memorial, **NAT. MEM.**
  National Monument, **NAT. MON.**
  National Park, **N.P.**
  National Parkway
  National Preserve
  National Recreation Area, **N.R.A.**
  National River
  National Riverway
  National Scenic Area
  National Seashore
  National Volcanic Monument

- ▨ □ National Forest, **N.F.**
- ▨ □ National Grassland, **N.G.**
- ➤ National Wild & Scenic River, **N.W.& S.R.**
- ▨ □ National Wildlife Refuge, **N.W.R.**
- ▨ □ State Park, **S.P.**
  State Historical Park, **S.H.P.**
  State Historic Site, **S.H.S.**
- ▨ □ Indian Reservation, **I.R.**
- ⟳ ▪ National Marine Sanctuary, **N.M.S.**

★ Resources ★

Bibliography

—————. *Atlas of North America.* National Geographic Society. Washington, DC: 1985.

—————. *Discover America: A Comprehensive Travel Guide to Our Country's Greatest Destinations.* Reader's Digest. Pleasantville, NY: 2004.

—————. *Historical Atlas of the United States.* National Geographic Society. Washington, DC: 1988.

—————. *National Geographic United States Atlas For Young Explorers,* Updated Edition. National Geographic Society. Washington, DC: 2004

—————. *Webster's New Geographical Dictionary,* 3rd edition. G. & C. Merriam Co. Springfield, MA: 1997.

—————. *The World Almanac and Book of Facts 2004.* World Almanac Books. New York: 2004

Barber, Nathan. *Get Wise! Mastering U.S. History.* Peterson's. Lawrenceville, NJ: 2004.

Ciovacco, Justine, et al. *State-by-State Atlas.* DK Publishing. New York: 2003.

Garrington, Sally. *United States.* Facts on File. New York: 2003.

Hakim, Joy. *A History of Us,* 11 vols., 2nd rev. ed. Oxford University Press Children's Books. New York: 1999.

Hintz, Martin. *United States of America,* 2nd series. Scholastic, Inc. New York: 2004.

Johnston, Robert D. *The Making of America.* National Geographic Society. Washington, DC: 2002.

Lyon, James and Andrew Dean Nystrom. *Lonely Planet USA,* 2nd edition. Lonely Planet Publications. Oakland, CA: 2002.

Pogany, Don. *Our Flag Was Still There: 50 States in 100 Days.* Barnes and Noble. New York: 2002.

Rogers, Mary M., ed. *United States—in Pictures.* Lerner Publications. Minneapolis, MN: 1995.

Sedeen, Margaret, ed. *National Geographic Picture Atlas of Our Fifty States.* National Geographic Society. Washington, DC: 1991.

Stewart, George R. *Names on the Land: A Historical Account of Place-Naming in the United States,* 3rd edition. Houghton Mifflin. Boston: 1967.

More advanced texts include:

Boyer, Paul S., et al. *The Oxford Companion to United States History.* Oxford University Press. New York: 2001.

Conzen, Michael P., ed. *The Making of the American Landscape.* Unwin Hyman. Boston: 1990.

Davis, Kenneth C. *Don't Know Much About History: Everything You Need to Know About American History but Never Learned.* Harper Collins. New York: 2003.

Faragher, John Mack, et al. *Out of Many: A History of the American People,* 4th ed. Prentice Hall. Upper Saddle River, NJ: 2002.

Halberstam, David. *Defining a Nation: Our America and the Sources of Its Strength.* National Geographic Society, Washington, DC: 2003.

Hine, Robert V. and John Mack Faragher. *The American West: A New Interpretive History.* Yale University Press. New Haven, CT: 2000.

Hudson, John C. *Across This Land: A Regional Geography of the United States and Canada.* Johns Hopkins University Press. Baltimore, MD: 2002.

Useful Web sites:

State facts: http://www.50states.com
http://www. infoplease.com/states
http://www.ipl.org/youth/stateknow/skhome.html

State Web sites: http://www.state. [state postal abbreviation].us (for example, Alabama's web site is http://www.state.al.us)

State of the State addresses: http://www.nga.org

National Park Service: http://www.nps.gov

U.S. Census Bureau: http://www.census.gov

The United States Mint—50 State Quarters Program: http://www.usmint.gov

Agricultural information, including state rankings from the US Department of Agriculture, National Agriculture Statistics Service: http://www.usda.gov/nass/aggraphs/graphics.htm
http://www.usda.gov/nass/pubs/agstats.htm
http://www.usda.gov/nass/sso-rpts.htm (for links to state offices)

USDA crop data is housed in the Mann Library at Cornell University. For listings of Crop Production Annual Summaries, go to: http://usda.mannlib.cornell.edu/

For mineral resource information, go to the US Geological Survey Web site:
http://minerals.usgs.gov/minerals/pubs/state/

★ Index ★

Boldface indicates illustrations.

★ A ★

Abenaki people (tribe) 37
Adirondack Mtns., NY 15, **15**, 45
Aerospace industry 129, 131, 221, **221**, 223, 225, **225**, 227
Alabama **64–67**, 89
  maps 60, 66
Alamo (mission), TX 181, **181**
Alaska 187, **187**, **188–191**, 227
  maps 184, 190
Alcan Highway, AK-Can. 189
Algonquin (language group) 25, 33, 45, **57**, 69, 93, 121, 141
Alibamu (tribe) 65
Allen, Ethan 57
American Samoa 232, **233**
Anchorage, AK 190, **190**, 191
Annapolis, MD 29
Apache (tribe) 169, **169**, 171
Apple farming 226, **226**
Arapaho (tribe) 197
Arches N.P., NV **220**, 221
Arizona **168–171**, 221
  maps 164, 170
Arkansas **68–71**
  maps 60, 70
Atlanta, GA **76**, 77, 79
Atlantic City, NJ **40**, 41
Atomic testing and research 117, 173, **173**, 175, 215
Augusta, GA 77
Auto racing 121, **121**, 123
Automobile industry 101, **101**, 123, **132**, 133, **133**, 134, 154, **154**, 155

★ B ★

Badlands, SD **156**, 157
Baltimore, MD 29, **29**, 29–30
Barley farming 150, **150**
Baseball bats 81, **81**
Battle Creek, MI 133, **133**
Beaches 21, **21**, 43, **201**, 203, **233**
Birmingham, AK 67
Black Hawk War 125, 161
Black Hills, SD 157, 158, **158**, 159
Black Rock Desert, NV 214, **214**
Blackfeet (tribe) 211
Blueberry farming 26, **26**, 43, 135
Boeing Corp. 225, **225**
Boll weevils 67, 78, 97, **97**, 99
Boone, Daniel 81, **81**
Boston, MA 32, **32**, **33**, 34, 35
Branson, MO 141, **141**, 143
Bridger, Jim 221
Brown, John 109, **109**, 130
Bryan, William Jennings 145, **145**
Bush, George W. 183

★ C ★

Cabot, John 25, **25**
Cabrillo, Juan Rodríguez 195
California 171, **192–195**, 213
  maps 184, 194
Calvert, George 29
Cape Canaveral, FL **73**
Cape Hatteras, NC **92**, 93
Carson City, NV 213
Carter, Jimmy 7, 79
Casinos **212**, 213, 215
Caves 106, **106**
Champlain, Samuel de 45, 57
Charleston, SC **96**, 97, 99
Charleston, WV 109
Chattanooga, TN 101
Chemical industry 21, **21**, 23, 31, 41, **41**, 111, 143
Cherokee (tribe) 69, 77, 81, 93, 101, 177, **177**
Cherry growing 134, **134**, 135
Chesapeake & Ohio Canal, DC-MD, 21, 30, **30**
Chesapeake Bay, DE-MD-VA **28**, 29, 31, 105
Cheyenne (tribe) 129, 147, 197, 211, 231
Chicago, IL **116**, 117, 119
Chickasaw (tribe) 89, 102, 177
Chimney Rock, NE **144**, 145
Choctaw (tribe) 69, 89, 177
Cincinnati, OH 153
Civil War, U.S. 89
  Midwest 127, 141
  Northeast 23, 29, **29**, 31, 35, 39, 41, 47, 49, **49**, 51, 55
  Southeast 65–66, **69**, 77, 78, 81–82, 85, **85**, 90, 97, **97**, 99, 101, **101**, 102, 105, **105**, 107
Cleveland, OH 153, **153**
Clovis points 173
Coal mining
  Midwest 151, 155
  Northeast 51, 109, **109**, 111
  Southeast **81**, 82, 83
  West 111, 199, 211, 231
Colonial Williamsburg, VA **104**, 105
Colorado **196–198**, 221, 229
  maps 184, 198
Colt, Samuel 19
Columbia, SC 97
Columbus, OH 153
Comanche (tribe) 177
Connecticut **16–19**
  maps 12, 18
Continental Divide **208**, 209
Cook, James 201
Copper mining 133, 169, 171, 209, **211**, 223
Corn farming 119, 146, **146**
Coronado, Francisco Vásquez 129
Cotton gin 17, 77, **77**, 99
Cotton industry
  Midwest 143
  Northeast 53
  Southeast 65, 67, 77, 79, 89, **89**, 90, 91, **91**, 93, 97, 99, 102
  Southwest 171
Cranberry farming 35, **35**, 43, 161
Crater Lake, OR **216**, 217
Crazy Horse (chief) 157, **157**, 159, 211
Creeks (tribe) **65**, 77, 93, 177
Crow (tribe) 211

Custer, George Armstrong 157, 211
Cuyahoga River, OH 153, **153**

★ D ★

Dairy farming 59, 139, 161, **161**, 162, **162**, 207, 227
Dakota (tribe) 137, **137**
de León, Juan Ponce **73**
de Soto, Hernando 69, 89
de Tonty, Henri 69
Deere, John 117
Delaware **20–23**
  maps 12, 22
Delaware (tribe) 49
Denver, CO 197, 199, 229
Detroit, MI 123, 135
District of Columbia **10**, 11, 29, 30, 107
du Pont, E. I. 21, 23
Dust storms 131, 157, **157**, 177, **177**, 178

★ E ★

Earthquakes 191, 193, **193**, 195
Edison, Thomas 41, **41**
Eisenhower, Dwight D. 197
Ellis Island, NY 45
Empire State Building **44**, 45
Ericson, Leif 25
Erie Canal, NY 45, **45**, 153
Everglades, FL 73, 74
Evers, Medgar 89

★ F ★

Fish-farming 90, 219
Fishing industry 31, 54, **54**, 189, 227
  see also Seafood industry
Flagler, Henry M. 73, **73**
Flathead (tribe) 211
Floods 125, **125**
Florida **72–75**
  maps 60, 75
Food processing and packaging 42, **42**, 127, 131, 146, 153, 155, 159, 163
Ford, Henry 133
Forest fires 173, **173**, 195
Fort Benton, MT 209, **209**
Fort Laramie, WY 231
Fort Sumter, SC 97, **97**, 99
Fossils 223, **223**
Fox (tribe) 125
Frémont, John C. 213
Furniture making 94, **94**, 95

★ G ★

Gambling 213, 215
Gates, Bill 225
Gateway Arch, St. Louis, MO **140**, 141, 143
Gauley River, WV **109**
Georgia **76–79**
  maps 60, 79
Geronimo (Apache chief) **169**
Gettysburg, PA 49, **49**
Glaciers **188**, 189
Glass-making 110, **110**, 111
Gold mining

Alaska 189, **189,** 227
California 193, **193,** 195
Colorado 197, 199
Idaho 205
Montana 209
Nevada 213, 215
South Dakota 157, **157**
Goodyear, Charles 19
Grand Canyon, AZ **168,** 169
Grant, Ulysses S. 107
Great Salt Lake, UT 221
Great Smoky Mtns., NC-TN 95, **100,**   101,
    102
Green Mtns., VT 57
Green River Rendezvous, WY 229, **229**
Groton, CT 17, **17**
Guam 232, **233**

★ H ★

Hamlin, Hannibal 25, **25**
Harley Davidson Motor Co. 161
Hawai'i **200–203,** 232
    maps 184, 203
Hennepin, Louis 137, **137**
Henry, John 109
Higley, Brewster 129
Hohokam (tribe) 169
Homestake Mine, SD 157, **157,** 159
Hooker, Thomas 17, **17**
Hooper Strait Lighthouse, MD **28,** 29
Hopewell (tribe) 153
Hopi (tribe) 169, 173
Houston, Sam 181, **181**
Hudson, Henry 21, 45, 47
Hurricanes 74, 97

★ I ★

Idaho **204–207**
    maps 184, 206
Illini (tribe) 117, 141
Illinois **116–119**
    maps 112, 118
Indiana **120–123**
    maps 112, 122
Iowa **124–127**
    maps 112, 126
Iron and steel industry
    Midwest 119, 121, **121,** 123, 133, 137,
    137, 155
    Northeast 19, 49, **49,** 51
    Southeast **65**
    West 199
Ironclad ships 105, **105**
Iroquois (tribe) 45, 153

★ J ★

Jackson, Andrew 65, 89, 101, **101,** 102
Jackson, MS 89, 90
Jamestown, VA 105
Jefferson, Thomas 105
Joliet, Louis 117, 125, 161
Juneau, Joe 189

★ K ★

Kamehameha I, King (Hawai'i) 201, **201**
Kansa (tribe) 129
Kansas **128–131**
    maps 112, 131
Kansas City, MO 143
Kennedy Space Center, FL 74
Kentucky **80–83,** 121
    maps 60, 82–83
Kīlauea (volcano), HI 201
King Philip's War 33, 53

Kiowa (tribe) 129
Kitt Peak National Observatory, Tuscon, AZ
169
Ku Klux Klan 102

★ L ★

La Follette, "Fighting Bob" 161, **161**
La Salle 85
Lakota (tribe) 157, 159, 211
Lead production 143, 161, **161**
Lenni-Lenape (tribe) 21, 41, **41**
Lewis and Clark expeditions 141, 149, **149,**
    157, 205, **205,** 211, 225
Liberty Bell **48,** 49
Lighthouses **24,** 25, **28,** 29
Lili'uokalani, Queen (Hawaii) 201, 202
Lincoln, Abraham 117, **117**
Little Bighorn, MT 209, **209,** 211
Little Rock, AR **69**
Log cabins 21, **21**
Logging and timber industry
    Midwest 133, 137, 139, 163
    Northeast 25, 27, 59
    Southeast 109, 111
    West 207, 209, 211, 217, **217,** 219, 227
Long, Huey **85**
Long, Stephen 145
Los Alamos, NM 175
Louisiana 63, **84–87**
    maps 60, 86
Louisiana Purchase (1803) 69, 85, 129, 141
Louisville, KY 82
Luray Caverns, VA 106, **106**

★ M ★

Madison, WI 163
Maine **24–27**
    maps 12–13, 26
Mandan (tribe) 149
Maple syrup industry 39, 47, 58, **58**
Marietta, OH 153
Marlow, NH **36,** 37
Marquette, Jacques 117, 125, 133, 161
Maryland 11, **28–31**
    maps 12, 30–31
Massachusetts 25, **32–35,** 37
    maps 12, 34–35
McCauly, Mary Ludwig Hays **41**
McLoughlin, John 217, **217**
Memphis, TN 102
Menominee (tribe) 161
Mesa Verde N.P., CO **196,** 197
Mexican-American War 169, 175, 195, 213
Michigan 125, **132–135**
    maps 112, 134
Midwest (region) **112–115**
    see also states by name
Military installations
    Midwest 131, 145, **145,** 231
    Northeast 17, **17,** 18, **18,** 19, 39, 55
    Southeast 74, 90, 93, **93,** 99, 102, 107
    Southwest 171, 201, **201,** 202
    West 197, **197,** 199, 221, **221,** 223, 225, **225**
Mineral mining 207, 211, 223
Minneapolis, MN 137, 139
Minnesota **136–139**
    maps 112, 138
Minqua (tribe) 21
Minuit, Peter 45, **45**
Mississippi **88–91**
    maps 60, 91
Missouri 25, 129, **140–143**
    maps 112, 142
Mitten Buttes, UT-AZ 167, **167**

Mobile, AL 65, 67
Montana 157, 205, **208–211**
    maps 184, 210
Montgomery, AL 65
Montpelier, VT 59
Mormons 213, 221, **221,** 223
Motorcycles 161, **161**
Mystic Seaport, CT **16,** 17

★ N ★

Nanticoke (tribe) 21
Narragansett (tribe) 53
Nashville, TN 101, 102
Natchez (tribe) 89
Nation, Carrie A. 129, **129,** 131
Navajo (tribe) 169, 173, **173**
Nebraska **144–147**
    maps 112, 146
Nevada 171, **212–215**
    maps 184, 214
New Hampshire **36–39,** 57
    maps 12, 38
New Jersey **40–43**
    maps 12, 42
New London, Conn. 19
New Mexico **172–175,** 213, 221
    maps 164, 174
New Orleans, LA **84,** 85, **85,** 87
New York 37, 41, 43, **44–47,** 57
    maps 12, 46
Newark, NJ 41
Newport, RI 53, **53,** 55
Nez Perce (tribe) 205, **205,** 225
Niagara Falls, NY-Ont. 47, **47**
Nicolet, Jean 161, **161**
NORAD 197, **197**
North Carolina **92–95**
    maps 60–61, 94–95
North Dakota **148–151**
    maps 112, 150
Northeast (region), U.S. **12–15**
    see also states by name
Northern Marianas 232, **233**
Nuclear industry 49, **49,** 175, 213
    see also Atomic testing and research

★ O ★

Oglethorpe, James **77**
Ohio **152–155**
    maps 112–113, 154
Oil and natural gas industry
    Midwest 131, 149, 151, 155
    Northeast 23
    Southeast 85, **85,** 90, 109
    Southwest 175, 179, 180, **180,** 181, **181,** 183
    territories 233
    West 189, 191, 199, 211, 229, **229,** 231
Ojibwa (tribe) 133, 137, 161
Oklahoma **176–179**
    maps 164–165, 178–179
Oklahoma City, OK 177, **177,** 178
Omaha, NE 145
Oregon **216–219**
    maps 184, 218
Osage (tribe) 129, 141, 177
Ottawa (tribe) 133, **133**
Outer Banks, NC **92,** 93, 95
Owls, northern spotted **217**

★ P ★

Paiute (tribe) 213, 221
Paper and pulp industry 27, 59, 79, 99,   137,
    163
Parks, Rosa **65**

Peanut farming 78, **78–79**
Pearl Harbor, HI 201, **201,** 202
Penn, William 49, **49**
Pennsylvania 23, **48–51**
  maps 12, 50
Pequot (tribe) 17
Philadelphia, PA 41, 43, 49, 51
Phoenix, AZ 171
Pierre, SD 157
Pine Barrens, NJ 43
Pitcher, Molly **41**
Pittsburgh, PA 49, 51
Plains Indians 209, **209**
Platte River, NE 145
Pocahontas **105**
Pontiac (chief) **133**
Pony Express 141, **141**
Portland Head (lighthouse), ME **24,** 25
Portland, OR 219
Portsmouth, NH 37, 39
Portsmouth, RI 53
Potato farming 27, 205, 206, **206,** 207
Potawatomi (tribe) 133
Poultry industry 21, 31, **70,** 71, 79, 90, 95
Powhatan 105
Powwows **172,** 173
Providence, RI 53, **53**
Pueblo, CO 199
Puebloans (tribe) 169, 197
Puerto Rico 232, **233**
Punxsutawney Phil 51, **51**
Pyramid Lake, NV 213, **213**

★ Q ★

Quakers 49
Quarries 59, 98, 122, **122**

★ R ★

Railroads
  Midwest 125, **125,** 127, 129, **129,** 133, 147, 149,
    153
  Southeast 30, 73, **73,** 78, 99, 109, **109**
  West 197, 221, **221,** 222, 227, 231
Rainier, Mt., WA **224,** 225
Raleigh, Sir Walter 93
Rhode Island **52–55**
  maps 12, 54
Rice farming 71, 97, **97,** 143
Richmond, VA 107
Roanoke Island, NC 93, **93**
Rodeos 230, **230**
Roosevelt, Theodore 169
Rubber and plastics industry 153, **153,** 155
Rushmore, Mt., NM, SD 158, **158,** 159

★ S ★

Sakakawea, Lake, ND 149, **149**
San Antonio, TX 183
San Diego de Alcalá (mission), CA 193, **193**
San Francisco, CA **192,** 193, **193,** 195
San Xavier del Bac (mission), near Tuscon,
  AZ **169**
Santa Anna, Antonio Lopez de 181
Santa Fe, NM 173, **173,** 175
Sauk (tribe) 125, **125**
Sault Saint Marie, MI 133
Savannah, GA 78
Seafood industry 25, 29, 31, 87, 89, **89,**   90,
  189
  see also Fishing industry
Seattle, WA **224,** 225, **225,** 227
Seminole (tribe) 73, 177
Serpent Mound, OH **152,** 153

Serra, Junípero 195
Seward, William 189
Sheep farming 57, **57,** 59
Shipbuilding 17, 19, 25, **25,** 27, 35, 107
Shipping industry 34, 143, 155, 227
Shopping malls **137**
Shoshone (tribe) 149, 213, 221
Silver mining 213, 215
Sioux (tribe) 147, 157
Slater, Samuel 53
Slavery **81**
  Midwest 25, 117, 121, 129, 130, 141, 155
  Northeast 17, 23, 25, 35, 39, 59
  Southeast 29, 30, 53, 55, 65, 69, 77, 81, 90,
    93, 97, **97,** 99, 105, 107, 109
Smith, John 29, **105**
Soo Canal, MI 133, **133**
South Carolina 93, **96–99**
  maps 60, 98
South Dakota **156–159**
  maps 112, 158
Southeast (region), U.S. 60–63
  see also states by name
Southwest (region), U.S. 164–167
  see also states by name
Soybean production 118, **118,** 119
Space Camp, Huntsville, AL **65,** 67
Space industry 73, 175, 181, **181**
  see also Aerospace industry
Spanish-American War 73, 233
Spokane (tribe) 225
Springfield, IL 117
St. Augustine, FL 73
St. Helens, Mt., WA 225
St. Louis, MO **140,** 141, **141,** 143
St. Paul, MN 139
Stark, John 37
Statue of Liberty **2–3,** 240
Ste. Genevieve, MO 141, **141**
Steamboats
  Midwest 69, 125, 133, **140,** 141, 153, 157
  Southeast 85, **88,** 89, 111
  West 205, 209
Steel industry see Iron and steel industry
Strategic Air Command, Omaha, NE   145,
  145
Submarines 17, **17,** 19
Sugarcane production 201, **201,** 233
Sunflowers **148,** 149, 151, 159
Surfing 202, **202,** 203
Swedes 21, 23

★ T ★

Tallahassee, FL 73
Tennessee **100–103**
  maps 60, 102–103
Tennessee Valley Authority 67, 102
Terrorist attacks
  N.Y. 45, **45**
  Okla. 177, **177,** 178
Tetons (range), WY **228,** 229
Tewa (tribe) 173
Texas 173, **180–183**
  maps 164–165, 183
Textile industry
  Northeast 33, **33,** 37, **37,** 39, 53, 55, 57, 59
  Southeast 93, **93,** 95, 99, 107
Theme parks 74, 75, **75**
Theodore Roosevelt Dam, AZ **169**
Tobacco industry 29, 81, 93, 95, 97, 99, 107
Tornadoes 129, **176,** 177, 178
Trail of Tears 77, 89, 177, **177**
Trans-Alaska Pipeline 189, **189,** 191
Trenton, NJ 41

Tucson, AZ **169,** 17
Tunbridge, VT **56,** 57

★ U ★

U.S. Virgin Islands 232, **233**
UFO festival, NM 174
Underground Railroad 121, **121,** 155
United Nations 47
United States political map 8–9
Uranium mining 221, **221**
Utah 184, **220–223,** 222

Ute (tribe) 221, 223

★ V ★

Vermont 47, **56–59**
  maps 12, 58
Vikings 25
Vincennes, IN 121, **121**
Virginia 11, 93, **104–107,** 109
  maps 60–61, 106–107
Volcanoes 189, 191, **200,** 201, **216,** 217, **224,**
  225, 233

★ W ★

Wal-Mart **69**
Walt Disney World, Orlando, FL 75, **75**
Wampanoag (tribe) 33
War of 1812 29, **29,** 65
Warm Springs (tribe) 218
Washington **224–227**
  maps 184, 226
Washington, D.C. see District of Columbia
Washington, George 11, 105, **105**
Washoe (tribe) 213
Wayne, "Mad" Anthony 153
West (region) 184–187
  see also states by name
West Virginia **108–111**
  maps 60, 110
Whaling 19, 35, 201
Wheat farming **128,** 129, 131, 149, 151,
  209, 217
White Mtns., NH 37
Whitney, Eli 17, 19, 77, **77**
Wichita (tribe) 129
Williams, Roger 53, **53**
Wind farms 194, **194**
Winnebago (tribe) 161
Winnibigoshish, Lake, MN **136,** 137
Wisconsin 125, **160–163**
  maps 112, 162
World War II 55, 189, **189,** 201, **201,** 202
World War II Memorial, Washington, D.C.
  79, 98
World's Fairs **141,** 143
Wounded Knee, SD 159
Wyoming 205, **228–231**
  maps 184, 230

★ Y ★

Yakima (tribe) 225
Yellowstone N.P., ID-MT-WY 229, 231
Yorktown, VA 105, **105**
Young, Brigham 221, **221**
Yucca Mtn., NV 213, **213,** 215

★ Z ★

Zuni (tribe) 173

★ Illustration Credits ★

Cover (wheat), Darrell Gulin/CORBIS; (mountains), Jeff Vanuga/CORBIS; (sky), L. Clarke/CORBIS; (eagle), Ron Sanford/CORBIS.

Front Matter
2–3, Mitchell Funk/Getty Images; 4 (up), John Henley/CORBIS; 4 (ctr), Siegfried Layda/Getty Images; 4 (lo), Philip Gould/CORBIS; 5 (up), Layne Kennedy/CORBIS; 5 (ctr), Bruce Dale; 5 (lo), Michael Melford/Getty Images; 6, John Henley/CORBIS; 9, Layne Kennedy/CORBIS; 10, Charles O'Rear/CORBIS.

The Northeast
15, James L. Amos/CORBIS; 16, Michael Melford/Getty Images; 17 (le), North Wind Picture Archives; 17 (ctr, le), Bettmann/CORBIS; 17 (ctr, rt), Talladega College; 17 (rt), AP Photos; 18, James Marshall/CORBIS; 20, Courtesy, Winterthur Museum; 21 (le), courtesy Library of Congress; 21 (ctr, le), Hagley Museum and Library; 21 (ctr, le), ©Hulton-Deutsch Collection/CORBIS; 21 (rt), Kevin Fleming/CORBIS; 22, Pat Crowe; 24, Owaki-Kulla/CORBIS; 25 (le), CORBIS; 25 (ctr, le), CORBIS; 25 (ctr, rt), courtesy Maine Historical Society; 25 (rt), Owaki-Kulla/CORBIS; 26, David H. Wells/CORBIS; 28, Medford Taylor; 29 (le), St. Mary's County Museum Division; 29 (ctr, le), Bettmann/CORBIS; 29 (ctr, rt), CORBIS; 29 (rt), David Ball/CORBIS; 30, Pat & Chuck Blackley; 32, Dave Bartruff/CORBIS; 33 (le), Bettmann/CORBIS; 33 (ctr, le), courtesy National Army Museum, Chelsea; 33 (ctr, rt), CORBIS; 33 (rt), Andy Ryan; 35, Robert Holmes/CORBIS; 36, Siegfried Layda/Getty Images; 37 (le), North Wind Picture Archives; 37 (ctr, le), CORBIS; 37 (ctr, rt), Bettmann/CORBIS; 37 (rt), Kevin Lamarque/Reuters/CORBIS; 38, AP Photos; 40, PictureNet/CORBIS; 41 (le), North Wind Picture Archives; 41 (ctr, le), Bettmann/CORBIS; 41 (ctr, rt), Bettmann/CORBIS; 41 (rt), Brownie Harris/CORBIS; 42, Mark Peterson/CORBIS; 44, Alan Schein Photography/CORBIS; 45 (le), North Wind Picture Archives; 45 (ctr, le), Bettmann/CORBIS; 45 (ctr, rt), Bettmann/CORBIS; 45 (rt), Sean Adair/CORBIS; 46, Cosmo Condina/Getty Images; 48, Francesco Ruggeri/Getty Images; 49 (le), Bettmann/CORBIS; 49 (ctr, le), Bettmann/CORBIS; 49 (ctr, rt), CORBIS; 49 (rt), Wally McNamee/CORBIS; 50, AP Photos; 52, Onne van der Wal/CORBIS; 53 (le), Bettmann/CORBIS; 53 (ctr, le), Bettmann/CORBIS; 53 (ctr, rt), Bob Krist/CORBIS; 53 (rt), Mark E. Gibson/CORBIS; 54, Onne van der Wal/CORBIS; 56, Randy Olson; 57 (le), North Wind Picture Archives; 57 (ctr, le), North Wind Picture Archives; 57 (ctr, rt), Vermont Historical Society; 57 (rt), Steven E. Frishling/CORBIS; 58, Kevin Fleming/CORBIS.

The Southeast
63, Bob Clemenz; 64, David Muench; 65 (le), Alabama Department of Archives and History; 65 (ctr, le), COR-BIS; 65 (ctr, rt), Bettmann/CORBIS; 65 (rt), courtesy NASA; 66, Richard Howard; 68, Bernie Jungkind; 69 (le), North Wind Picture Archives; 69 (ctr, le), North Wind Picture Archives; 69 (ctr, rt), Bettmann/CORBIS; 69 (rt), ©Reuters/CORBIS; 70, AP Photo; 72, Getty Images; 73 (le), Bettmann/CORBIS; 73 (ctr, le), North Wind Picture Archives; 73 (ctr, rt), Flagler Museum Archives; 73 (rt), AP Photo; 75, Richard T. Nowitz/COR-BIS; 76, Gary Randall/Getty Images; 77 (le), North Wind Picture Archives; 77 (ctr, le), Bettmann/CORBIS; 77 (ctr, rt), CORBIS; 77 (rt), ©THIERRY ORBA/CORBIS SYGMA; 78, Inga Spence/Index Stock Imagery; 80, Kevin R. Morris/Getty Images; 81 (le), George Caleb Bingham, "Daniel Boone Escorting Settlers through the Cumberland Gap, 1851–52." Oil on canvas, 36 1/2 x 50 1/4". Washington University Gallery of Art, St. Louis. Gift of Nathaniel Phillips, 1890.; 81 (ctr, le), North Wind

Picture Archives; 81 (ctr, rt), Underwood & Underwood/CORBIS; 81 (rt), Randy Duchaine/COR-BIS; 83, Kevin R. Morris/CORBIS; 84, Philip Gould/CORBIS; 85 (le), Louisiana Historical Society; 85 (ctr, le), North Wind Picture Archives; 85 (ctr, rt), Bettmann/CORBIS; 85 (rt), CORBIS; 86, Philip Gould/CORBIS; 88, Dave Bartruff/Index Stock Imagery; 89 (le), North Wind Picture Archives; 89 (ctr, le), CORBIS; 89 (ctr, rt), Flip Schulke/CORBIS; 89 (rt), Philip Gould/CORBIS; 91, Richard Hamilton Smith/CORBIS; 92, Randy Wells/Getty Images; 93 (le), North Wind Picture Archives; 93 (ctr, le), Bettmann/CORBIS; 93 (ctr, rt), Bettmann/CORBIS; 93 (rt), courtesy US Army; 94, Brownie Harris/CORBIS; 96, Benn & Esther Mitchell/Getty Images; 97 (le), North Wind Picture Archives; 97 (ctr, le), CORBIS; 97 (ctr, rt), George D. Lepp/CORBIS; 97 (rt), Tom Salyer/CORBIS; 98, Tim Dominick; 100, David Muench/CORBIS; 101 (le), courtesy Library of Congress; 101 (ctr, le), The Philadelphia Print Shop; 101 (ctr, rt), Bettmann/COR-BIS; 101 (rt), John Madere/CORBIS; 103, Hiroyuki Matsumoto/Getty Images; 104, Colonial Williamsburg Foundation; 105 (le), North Wind Picture Archives; 105 (ctr, le), North Wind Picture Archives; 105 (ctr, rt), Francis G. Mayer/CORBIS; 105 (rt), Virginia Polytechnic Institute and State University; 106, Ann Purcell/CORBIS; 108, Anna Susan Post; 109 (le), Kansas State Historical Society; 109 (ctr, le), The Museum of African American Art, Los Angeles, California, Palmer C. Hayden Collection, gift of Miriam A. Hayden; 109 (ctr, rt), Bettmann/CORBIS; 109 (rt), Kit Kittle/COR-BIS; 110, James L. Amos/CORBIS.

The Midwest
115, Layne Kennedy/CORBIS; 116, Adrian Lyon/Getty Images; 117 (le), North Wind Picture Archives; 117 (ctr, le), Bettmann/CORBIS; 117 (ctr, rt), Bettmann/COR-BIS; 117 (rt), FermiLab; 118, Richard Hamilton Smith/CORBIS; 120, Ron Goltry/Index Stock Imagery; 121 (le), North Wind Picture Archives; 121 (ctr, le), Bettmann/CORBIS; 121 (ctr, rt), Calumet Regional Archives, Indiana University Northwest; 121 (rt), Reuters/CORBIS; 122, AP Photos/Darron Cummings; 124, Craig Aurness/CORBIS; 125 (le), North Wind Picture Archives; 125 (ctr, le), Stock Montage; 125 (ctr, rt), State Historical Society of Iowa; 125 (rt), Les Stone/CORBIS; 126, Julie Habel/CORBIS; 128, Joel Sartore/www.joelsartore.com; 129 (le), Bettmann/COR-BIS; 129 (ctr, le), Bettmann/CORBIS; 129 (ctr, rt), Bettmann/CORBIS; 129 (rt), courtesy Raytheon Aircraft; 130, AP Photo/Dodge City (Kan.) *Daily Globe,* Michael Schweitzer; 132, Andy Sacks/Getty Images; 133 (le), North Wind Picture Archives; 133 (ctr, le), courtesy Library of Congress; 133 (ctr, rt), CORBIS; 133 (rt), courtesy Kellogg's Cereal City USA; 134, AP Photo/*Traverse City Record Eagle*/John L. Russell; 136, Paul Harris/Getty Images; 137 (le), North Wind Picture Archives; 137 (ctr, le), Minnesota Historical Society; 137 (ctr, rt), Keystone View Company/CORBIS; 137 (rt), Bob Cole; 138, Layne Kennedy/CORBIS; 140, Sam Abell, National Geographic Photographer; 141 (le), Missouri State Historical Society; 141 (ctr, le), Charles Hargens, Pony Express Museum, St. Joseph, Missouri; 141 (ctr, rt), Schenectady Museum; Hall of Electrical History Foundation/CORBIS; 141 (rt), Ralph Krubner/Index Stock Imagery; 142, Randy Olson; 144, Jeff Gnass; 145 (le), North Wind Picture Archives; 145 (ctr, le), Nebraska State Historical Society; 145 (ctr, rt), Bettmann/COR-BIS; 145 (rt), Jim Sugar/CORBIS; 146, Richard Hamilton Smith/CORBIS; 148, Annie Griffiths Belt; 149 (le), Michael Haynes; 149 (ctr, le), Minnesota Historical Society/CORBIS; 149 (ctr, rt), Bettmann/CORBIS; 149 (rt), Annie Griffiths Belt/CORBIS; 150, Andy Sacks/Getty Images; 152, Richard A. Cooke/CORBIS; 153 (le), North Wind Picture Archives; 153 (ctr, le), Bettmann/CORBIS; 153 (ctr, rt), Cleveland State University Library; 153 (rt), Wes Thompson/CORBIS;

154, Andy Sacks/Getty Images; 156, Sarah Leen/NG Image Collection; 157 (le), Joslyn Art Museum, Omaha, Nebraska; 157 (ctr, le), CORBIS; 157 (ctr, rt), photo courtesy of the South Dakota State Historical Society-State Archives; 157 (rt), AP Photo/Charles Bennett; 158, Charles Thatcher/Getty Images; 160, Jim Richardson; 161 (le), Wisconsin Historical Society; 161 (ctr, le), Wisconsin Historical Society; 161 (ctr, rt), CORBIS; 161 (rt), Peter Turnley/CORBIS; 162, Layne Kennedy/CORBIS.

The Southwest
167, Lester Lefkowitz/CORBIS; 168, Bruce Dale; 169 (le), Buddy Mays/CORBIS; 169 (ctr, le), CORBIS; 169 (ctr, rt), Bettmann/CORBIS; 169 (rt), Roger Ressmeyer/CORBIS; 170, David Hiser/Getty Images; 172, R.W. Jones/CORBIS; 173 (le), Museum of New Mexico; 173 (ctr, le), Museum of New Mexico; 173 (ctr, rt), CORBIS; 173 (rt), SANTA FE NEW MEXICO/CORBIS SYGMA; 174, AP Photo/Eric Draper; 176, CORBIS; 177 (le), Victor R. Boswell, Woolaroc Museum, Bartlesville Oklahoma; 177 (ctr, le), Bettmann/CORBIS; 177 (ctr, rt), Bettmann/CORBIS; 177 (rt), Anthony Suau/BLACK STAR; 179, Richard Hamilton Smith/CORBIS; 180, Joseph McNally/Getty Images; 181 (le), CORBIS; 181 (ctr, le), Bettmann/CORBIS; 181 (ctr, rt), CORBIS; 181 (rt), courtesy/NASA; 183, AP Photo.

The West
187, Kennan Ward/CORBIS; 188, Michael Melford/Getty Images; 189 (le), Bettmann/CORBIS; 189 (ctr, le), Alexander Alland/CORBIS; 189 (ctr, rt), Horace Bristol/CORBIS; 189 (rt), Nevada Wier/CORBIS; 190, Paul A. Souders/CORBIS; 192, Morton Beebe/CORBIS; 193 (le), CORBIS; 193 (ctr, le), North Wind Picture Archives; 193 (ctr, rt), Bettmann/CORBIS; 193 (rt), Kenneth James/CORBIS; 194, Lester Lefkowitz/COR-BIS; 196, David Muench; 197 (le), Richard Frajola; 197 (ctr, le), Bettmann/CORBIS; 197 (ctr, rt), Bettmann/CORBIS; 197 (rt), courtesy NORAD; 198, Paul Chesley/NG Image Collection; 200, Jim Sugar/COR-BIS; 201 (le), Richard Cummins/CORBIS; 201 (ctr, le), Bettmann/CORBIS; 201 (ctr, rt), Bettmann/CORBIS; 201 (rt), David Sailors/CORBIS; 202, Reuters/CORBIS; 204, Michael Melford; 205 (le), Doris S. Clymer; 205 (ctr, le), Jo Proferes, graphic from Nez Perce Bicentennial Exhibit; 205 (ctr, rt), courtesy Bureau of Reclamation; 205 (rt), David Stoecklein/CORBIS; 206, Mark Gibson/Index Stock Imagery; 208, Dewitt Jones; 209 (le), North Wind Picture Archives; 209 (ctr, le), North Wind Picture Archives; 209 (ctr, rt), Buffalo Bill Historical Center, Cody, Wyoming; gift of Charles Ulrick and Josephine Bay Foundation, Inc.; 88.60; 209 (rt), Tony DiFronzo; 210, Jan Burchofsky-Houser/CORBIS; 212, Bob Krist/CORBIS; 213 (le), North Wind Picture Archives; 213 (ctr, le), CORBIS; 213 (ctr, rt), Bettmann/CORBIS; 213 (rt), Dan Lamont/CORBIS; 214, Scott S. Warren; 216, AP Photo/*Herald and News,* Ron Winn; 217 (le), Bettmann/CORBIS; 217 (ctr, le), North Wind Picture Archives; 217 (ctr, rt), F. Burns/CORBIS; 217 (rt), Galen Rowell/CORBIS; 218, AP Photo/Don Ryan; 220, George H. H. Huey/CORBIS; 221 (le), Bettmann/CORBIS; 221 (ctr, le), Bettmann/CORBIS; 221 (ctr, rt), Utah State Historical Society; 221 (rt), courtesy NASA; 222, Tom Bean; 224, Joel W. Rogers/CORBIS; 225 (le), Don Crook; 225 (ctr, le), courtesy Museum of History and Industry; 225 (ctr, rt), Bettmann/CORBIS; 225 (rt), James Leynse/CORBIS; 226, CORBIS; 228, Lester Lefkowitz/CORBIS; 229 (le), Alfred Jacob Miller, The Walters Art Gallery, Baltimore; 229 (ctr, le), Bettmann/CORBIS; 229 (ctr, rt), Buffalo Bill Historical Center, Cody, Wyoming; 7.69; 229 (rt), Jonathan Blair/CORBIS; 230, Kevin R. Morris/CORBIS; 233 (up, le), Kip Evans, National Marine Sanctuaries; 233 (up, rt), James Davis; Eye Ubiquitous/CORBIS; 233 (rt), Michael S. Yamashita/CORBIS; 233 (lo, rt), Wolfgang Kaehler/CORBIS; 233 (lo, le), CORBIS.

Published by the National Geographic Society

JOHN M. FAHEY, JR.
President and Chief Executive Officer

GILBERT M. GROSVENOR
Chairman of the Board

NINA D. HOFFMAN
Executive Vice President. President of Books and Education Publishing Group

ERICKA MARKMAN
Senior Vice President, President of Children's Books and Education Publishing Group

Staff for this book

Nancy Laties Feresten
Vice President, Editor-in-Chief of Children's Books

Suzanne Patrick Fonda
Project Editor

Bea Jackson
Art Director

Carl Mehler
Director of Maps

Kay Kobor Hankins
Illustrations Editor

Janet A. Dustin
Illustrations Coordinator

Jennifer Emmett
Virginia Ann Koeth
Editors

Susan Kehnemui Donnelly
Editorial Assistant

Matt Chwastyk
Gregory Ugiansky
XNR Productions
Map Research and Production

Jocelyn G. Lindsay
Text Research

David Lindsay
Research Assistant

Daniel L. Sherman
David M. Seager
Production Design

Mark A. Wentling
Indexing

Heidi Vincent
Director of Direct Response Sales and Marketing

Jeff Reynolds
Marketing Director, Children's Books

Rebecca E. Hinds
Managing Editor

R. Gary Colbert
Production Director

Lewis R. Bassford
Production Manager

Alan V. Kerr
Vincent P. Ryan
Manufacturing Managers

Consultants

NORTHEAST
Sari Bennett
Director, Center for Geography Education University of Maryland Baltimore County

Cathleen McAnneny
Associate Professor of Geography University of Maine at Farmington

Chester E. Smolski
Professor Emeritus of Geography Rhode Island College

SOUTHEAST
Kurt Butefish
Tennessee Geographic Alliance University of Tennessee

Truman Hartshorn
Professor of Geography Georgia State University

Joseph T. Manzo
Geography Department Concord University West Virginia

Robert Morrill
Professor Emeritus Virginia Tech University

Keith Mountain
Kentucky Geographic Alliance Department of Geography and Geosciences University of Louisville

Steve Pierce
North Carolina Geographic Alliance

Bobbie Richardson
Mississippi Geographic Alliance Blue Mountain College

William R. Strong
Alabama Geographic Alliance University of Alabama

MIDWEST
Carol Craig
Missouri Geographic Alliance

Darrell P. Kruger
Illinois Geographic Alliance Illinois State University

John Heinrichs
Kansas Geographic Alliance Fort Hays State University

Kathy Lamb Kozenski
Geography Educators Network of Indiana

David A. Lanegran
John S. Holl Professor of Geography Macalester College Minnesota

Michael Libbee
Michigan Geographic Alliance Central Michigan University

Kay E. Weller
Geographic Alliance of Iowa University of Northern Iowa

SOUTHWEST
Sarah Bednarz
Associate Professor of Geography Texas A&M University

Richard Boehm
Texas Alliance for Geographic Education Texas State University

Ronald Dorn
Arizona Geographic Alliance Arizona State University

Gale Ekiss
Arizona Geographic Alliance

WEST
Jody Smothers Marcello
Alaska Geographic Alliance

Mark Montgomery
Colorado Geographic Alliance University of Denver

Virgil M. Young
Professor Emeritus College of Education Boise State University

To my father, Blaine V. "Buck" Bockenhauer (1926–1995),
who taught me to love life and to learn through travel. Thanks, Dad!—MHB

In memory of Meg Cunha, who introduced me to reading—SFC

Acknowledgments

I've learned much on this fifty states writing adventure. I've marveled at the dizzying diversity across this vast country while appreciating the connections that bind its people and regions together into a single great nation.

I've also learned how rewarding it is to work with the dedicated team of people at the Children's Books Division of National Geographic. I appreciated working with Steve Cunha, who brought energy and creativity to the regional essays. Thanks much to the coordinators of state geographic alliances and other geographers who provided feedback on my state essays. And to former President Jimmy Carter, a special thanks for penning a beautiful Foreword.

I could not have completed this book without the constant support of my family. My freshman son Sam took time from his studies at the University of Wisconsin to compile resources and offer incisive commentary about many state essays. Sixteen-year-old Karen and fourteen-year-old Thomas read drafts, found useful Web sites, and organized resources. Now and then one of them would read a passage and say, "A middle-school kid won't understand *that,* Dad!" I needed that. I also valued weekly phone calls of support from my mother, Dolores. Most of all, my wife, Nancy, not only provided daily encouragement but agreed—when impossible deadlines loomed—to draft many of the timeline legends for the book. Without her I wouldn't be writing these lines.

Published by the National Geographic Society
1145 17th Street, NW
Washington, D.C. 20036-4688

Library of Congress Cataloging-in-Publication Data

Bockenhauer, Mark H.
  National Geographic our fifty states / written by Mark H. Bockenhauer and Stephen F. Cunha.
    p. cm.
  Includes bibliographical references and index.
  ISBN 0-7922-6402-9 (trade edition)
  ISBN 0-7922-6992-6 (library edition)
  1. U.S. states. 2. United States—Geography. 3. United States—History, Local.
I. Title: Our fifty states. II. Cunha, Stephen F. III. Title.
  E180.B635 2004
  917.3—dc22

                        2004001190

One of the world's largest nonprofit scientific and educational organizations, the National Geographic Society was founded in 1888 "for the increase and diffusion of geographic knowledge." Fulfilling this mission, the Society educates and inspires millions every day through its magazines, books, television programs, videos, maps and atlases, research grants, the National Geographic Bee, teacher workshops, and innovative classroom materials. The Society is supported through membership dues, charitable gifts, and income from the sale of its educational products. This support is vital to National Geographic's mission to increase global understanding and promote conservation of our planet through exploration, research, and education.

For more information, please call 1-800-NGS LINE (647-5463) or write to the following address:

NATIONAL GEOGRAPHIC SOCIETY
1145 17th Street N.W.
Washington, D.C. 20036-4688 U.S.A.
Visit the Society's Web site at www.nationalgeographic.com

ISBN: 978-0-7922-9764-2 (regular)   ISBN: 978-0-7922-8268-6 (deluxe)

PRINTED IN CHINA
12/RRDS/9

Today there are many state-flag displays (above), but in the past they were rare. One of the first was assembled after World War I and included 48 flags. For many years these flags could be seen in the Old Post Office Building in Washington, D.C.

Flags of OUR FIFTY STATES

a special supplement to Our Fifty States *that includes the flags of the District of Columbia, the U.S. Territories, and the national flag of the United States*

BY WHITNEY SMITH, PH.D.
Director, Flag Research Center
Winchester, Massachusetts

NATIONAL GEOGRAPHIC
WASHINGTON, D.C.

for Austin

★ TABLE OF CONTENTS ★

★ INTRODUCTION ★ 247

★ ALPHABETICAL LISTING OF STATE FLAGS ★ 248

★ DISTRICT OF COLUMBIA AND THE U.S. TERRITORIES ★ 298

★ U.S. NATIONAL FLAG ★ 301

★ ★ ★

★ PARTS OF A FLAG ★ 302

★ GLOSSARY ★ 302

★ RESOURCES ★ 303

★ CREDITS & MISSION STATEMENT ★ 304

INTRODUCTION

★ *The Flags of Our Fifty States* ★

FLAGS HAVE BEEN USED for thousands of years. Their presence has long inspired soldiers in war and helped show the course of battle, the position of leaders, and the eventual winners and losers. For centuries they have been used in official ceremonies when a ruler or leader appeared.

Many of the earliest flaglike objects consisted of a wooden or metal pole with an emblem at the top made of metal, leather, or even feathers. At least two thousand years ago cloth flags were introduced. The Romans, for example, hung a red flag on a crossbar attached to a staff and used it as a signal, a reward, and as a standard for a military unit. That *vexillum* was the basis for the word "vexillology," which means "the study of flags."

The first modern national flag—one created by a people to symbolize their country and its ideals—was the Continental Colors of the United States *(see page 300)*. It combined the red and white stripes of the Sons of Liberty (a radical group that fought for American independence) and the British Union Jack. Over the years the design of this flag has changed to become the familiar Stars and Stripes that is today's U.S. national flag. As colonies and territories became U.S. states, they designed their own flags as symbols of their unique identity within the Union.

Although the fascinating story of U.S. state flags has never been told in full, this book offers the reader some idea of their unusual designs and the stories behind them. It includes a number of older flags unknown even to most citizens in the states that once flew them. It also gives resources for readers who want to learn more about this colorful and significant area of study.

WHITNEY SMITH, PH.D.
Director, Flag Research Center

John van Arsdale robbed British troops of the satisfaction of seeing their flag flying over America as they sailed for home in 1783. Climbing a flag pole, greased by departing soldiers (opposite), he tore down the Union Jack and raised the Stars and Stripes.

ALABAMA
★ *Heart of Dixie* ★

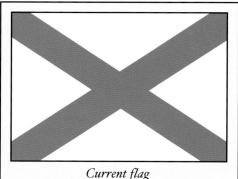

Current flag

OFFICIAL STATE NAME: State of Alabama

STATE ABBREVIATION: AL

DATE OF STATEHOOD: December 14, 1819

ORDER OF STATEHOOD: 22

FLAG DESIGNER: Unknown

STATE MOTTO: We Dare Maintain Our Rights

STATE BIRD: Northern Flicker

STATE TREE: Longleaf Pine

STATE FLOWER: Camellia

FLAG FACT: The 1861 Alabama flag is one of a few flags to feature a flag in its design.

*1861 Alabama independence flag
(obverse above, reverse below)*

THE SALTIRE (diagonal cross) in the current state flag was chosen to remind people of the Confederate Battle Flag carried by Alabama troops during the Civil War. Because the design only hints at the Battle Flag, Alabama's flag has not been criticized by people who dislike Confederate symbols. Adopted 30 years after the Civil War, the flag has often been shown as a square, like the Battle Flag. Since state law doesn't say anything about the flag's proportions, the Alabama Supreme Court decided that the flag is official whether it is square or oblong.

Alabama's first flag (below, left) was very complex. The obverse had a woman holding both a sword and an unofficial flag favoring secession that was popular just before Alabama joined the Confederacy in 1861. The word "Alabama" was over a yellow star. The woman defends it beneath the slogan "Independent Now And Forever." The reverse of the 1861 flag showed a cotton plant above a Latin motto meaning "None Dare Touch Me." At the foot of the cotton plant was a coiled snake. The message to the North was clear: Leave the cotton-planting people of Alabama alone.

The 1861 flag was hoisted over Alabama's capitol in January of that year. It celebrated the state's decision to secede from the United States. However, strong winds tore it, and it was taken down. In 1865 after the Civil War was over, a Union soldier took the flag home with him. In 1939 the flag was returned to the state of Alabama.

ALASKA

★ *Last Frontier* ★

Current flag

OFFICIAL STATE NAME: State of Alaska

STATE ABBREVIATION: AK

DATE OF STATEHOOD: January 3, 1959

ORDER OF STATEHOOD: 49

FLAG DESIGNER: Benny Benson

STATE MOTTO: North to the Future

STATE BIRD: Willow ptarmigan

STATE TREE: Sitka spruce

STATE FLOWER: Forget-me-not

FLAG FACT: Only Alaska has a state flag
with stars arranged as a constellation.

Russian-American Company flag

IN 1926 BENNY BENSON was an orphan living at the Mission Territorial School near Seward, Alaska. He heard about a contest, sponsored by the American Legion, to design a flag for the territory. Like many other school children, Benny made a picture of his idea for an Alaska flag. The judges liked his idea, and the territorial legislature adopted it in May 1927.

That design (above, left), in use today by the State of Alaska, is very simple. The background of blue symbolizes the forget-me-not (the state flower), mountain lakes, and the evening sky. Benny picked the golden color of the stars as a reminder of the gold that had sparked a gold rush to Alaska in the 1890s.

Seven of the stars form the Great Bear, or Big Dipper, constellation. The single star at the upper fly end represents the North Star and a promise that the territory would someday become a state in the Union. It was also chosen because Alaska is the northernmost part of the United States. The different symbols of the flag are referred to in the song "Alaska's Flag," for which Marie Drake wrote the words and Elinor Dusenbury the music.

When the Russians ruled Alaska from the late 1700s until 1867, they used a variety of flags. A special one, used exclusively for display in Alaska, showed the imperial Russian double-headed eagle on a flag of white, blue, and red horizontal stripes (below, left). A scroll in the eagle's claws proclaimed the "Russian-American Company."

ARIZONA
★ *Grand Canyon State* ★

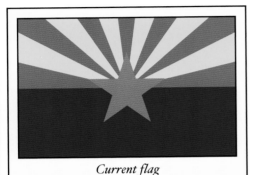

Current flag

OFFICIAL STATE NAME: State of Arizona

STATE ABBREVIATION: AZ

DATE OF STATEHOOD: February 14, 1912

ORDER OF STATEHOOD: 48

FLAG DESIGNER: Colonel Charles W. Harris

STATE MOTTO: *Ditat Deus* (God Enriches)

STATE BIRD: Cactus Wren

STATE TREE: Paloverde

STATE FLOWER: Saguaro

FLAG FACT: When Arizona was deciding on its flag design, one of the proposals included a picture of the Gila monster lizard.

18th-century Spanish flag

THE CURRENT STATE FLAG IS A STYLIZED picture of the Arizona desert in the evening with the last rays of the sun over the dark blue of the land. The large, central, copper-colored star speaks proudly of copper deposits and the other mineral wealth of the state.

Blue and yellow are the official state colors, and the star is a symbol of statehood. Red and yellow were colors long used in Spain (below, left), where they were found in the coat of arms of Spanish regions such as Castile, Aragon, and Navarre. Spanish explorers were the first Europeans to visit Arizona.

The original flag design was created in 1911, a year before Arizona became a state. Rifle teams from different state National Guard units were having a competition in Ohio. The captain of the Arizona team, Colonel Charles W. Harris, wanted Arizona represented by a distinctive flag. He made a design, which was sewn by Nan Hayden, wife of his friend Carl. Although everyone liked the design, nothing was done about it until six years later.

In 1917 different flag proposals were submitted to the new state legislature. They included designs resembling other state flags—ones showing the state seal, the name of the state, local wildlife, etc. Someone even proposed adopting the Stars and Stripes as the state flag. Finally Harris's design won approval. An Arizona flag was on the battleship U.S.S. *Arizona* in 1941 when it was sunk at Pearl Harbor, Hawaii, during World War II.

ARKANSAS
★ *Natural State* ★

Current flag

OFFICIAL STATE NAME: State of Arkansas

STATE ABBREVIATION: AR

DATE OF STATEHOOD: June 15, 1836

ORDER OF STATEHOOD: 25

FLAG DESIGNER: Ms. Willie Hawker

STATE MOTTO: *Regnat Populus*
(The People Rule)

STATE BIRD: Mockingbird

STATE TREE: Pine

STATE FLOWER: Apple blossom

FLAG FACT: The flags of Arkansas and Brazil, a country in South America, are among the very few flags bearing a diamond shape.

1913 Arkansas state flag

IN 1912 THE DAUGHTERS of the American Revolution (D.A.R.) wanted a state flag to present to the battleship U.S.S. *Arkansas,* but the state legislature had never adopted a flag. In the D.A.R. design competition, the winner was Ms. Willie Hawker of the Pine Bluff Chapter. The state legislature approved her design in February 1913.

That design had white stars on a blue frame, set against a red background (below, left). Those symbols resembled ones found in the Battle Flag of the Confederate States of America, of which Arkansas had been part. The central emblem was a lozenge, or diamond shape, chosen because Arkansas is the only state that produces diamonds. The colors of the flag are the same as the colors of the United States flag.

Twenty-five white stars proclaim Arkansas as the 25th state of the Union. The three stars in the center of the 1913 flag represented the three countries—France, Spain, and the United States—that had ruled the territory that became Arkansas. They also represented the year of the Louisiana Purchase (1803) and Arkansas as the third state carved from the Louisiana Territory.

In 1923 the legislature agreed to add a fourth star to stand for Arkansas as part of the Confederacy. The final design change was made a year later when the four central stars were arranged in the pattern still official today (above, left). Students recite the pledge, "I salute the Arkansas Flag with its diamond and stars. We pledge our loyalty to thee."

CALIFORNIA

★ *Golden State* ★

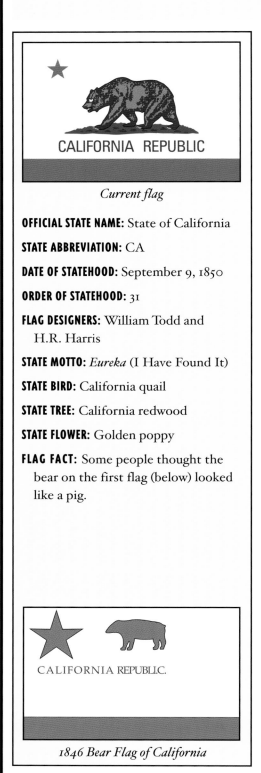

Current flag

OFFICIAL STATE NAME: State of California

STATE ABBREVIATION: CA

DATE OF STATEHOOD: September 9, 1850

ORDER OF STATEHOOD: 31

FLAG DESIGNERS: William Todd and H.R. Harris

STATE MOTTO: *Eureka* (I Have Found It)

STATE BIRD: California quail

STATE TREE: California redwood

STATE FLOWER: Golden poppy

FLAG FACT: Some people thought the bear on the first flag (below) looked like a pig.

1846 Bear Flag of California

BEFORE THE GOLD RUSH OF 1849 few people lived in the northwestern part of Mexico that later became California. Some were Indians (who had no flags) and some were Mexicans—settlers, missionaries, and government officials. The Americans who increasingly came to settle there were unhappy. They wanted opportunities not available under Mexican rule.

In June 1846 a group of Americans living in Sonoma, in what is now the State of California, designed and hoisted a new flag (below, left). Like the Stars and Stripes, it included the colors red and white, but it had a single star and a single stripe. The most important symbol was the large grizzly bear that appeared over the words "California Republic."

This Bear Flag, as it was called, proclaimed a new country independent of Mexico. That new "nation" did not survive long. Just at that time the United States declared war on Mexico. U.S. Commodore John Sloate landed near Monterey in July 1846 and proclaimed California an American territory under the Stars and Stripes.

The Bear Flag was not forgotten (although most of the real bears soon died off). The flag became more popular over the years. In 1911 the state finally recognized the old Bear Flag as the official state banner, and it came to be flown throughout California. Because many flags were made and sold each year, the artwork for the bear was standardized in 1953 so that all flags would look the same (above, left).

COLORADO

★ *Centennial State* ★

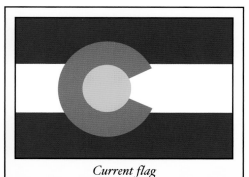

Current flag

OFFICIAL STATE NAME: State of Colorado

STATE ABBREVIATION: CO

DATE OF STATEHOOD: August 1, 1876

ORDER OF STATEHOOD: 38

FLAG DESIGNER: Andrew Carlisle Carson

STATE MOTTO: *Nil Sine Numine* (Nothing Without the Deity)

STATE BIRD: Lark bunting

STATE TREE: Colorado blue spruce

STATE FLOWER: Columbine

FLAG FACT: Colorado, North Carolina, and Ohio are the only states with flags that display the first letter or letters of the state's name.

1907 Colorado state flag

COLORADO'S CURRENT FLAG has a very simple design. This makes it easy to recognize, even at a distance. The symbolism, on the other hand, contains many elements. The big red C stands for Colorado and the Columbine State. Colorado is also known as the Centennial State because it joined the Union in 1876 when the country was celebrating the hundredth anniversary of the Declaration of Independence.

The state flag colors—blue, yellow, and white—reflect the colors of the state flower, the columbine. Gold and silver mining was one of the important occupations among early Colorado settlers, and in flags gold and silver can be represented by yellow and white. The U.S. national colors (red, white, and blue) also appear in the Colorado flag. The red and yellow hint at the old territorial claims of Spain in the area and the fact that Spain's flag was red and yellow. The Spanish word for red, *colorado,* gave the state its name.

The first Colorado flag showed the state coat of arms (below, left). It had crossed mining tools on a shield below snow-capped mountains. Above appeared the ancient Roman *fasces* (a bundle of rods tied together) bound with ribbons proclaiming "Union" and "Constitution." The "eye of God" at the top was referred to in the Latin motto on a scroll at the bottom, meaning "Nothing Without the Deity." This complex design hints at why Colorado decided to develop an entirely new, simpler flag, which became official in June 1911 (above, left).

CONNECTICUT

★ *Constitution State* ★

Current flag

OFFICIAL STATE NAME: State of Connecticut

STATE ABBREVIATION: CT

DATE OF STATEHOOD: January 9, 1788

ORDER OF STATEHOOD: 5

FLAG DESIGNER: Unknown

STATE MOTTO: *Qui Transtulit Sustinet* (He Who Brought Us Over Will Sustain Us)

STATE BIRD: Robin

STATE TREE: White oak

STATE FLOWER: Mountain laurel

FLAG FACT: In the first state seal, the hand of God appeared above the grape vines.

1775 Connecticut military flag

SINCE GRAPES ARE NOT a major local resource, it may not be clear why both Connecticut's first official flag (below, left) and its current one (above, left) have three grape vines as their central design. Those vines, which also appear on the state coat of arms and seal, are part of a message expressed partly by words and partly by symbols.

The 17th century English settlers of Connecticut created three towns—Hartford, Wethersfield, and Windsor—and, later, three colonies—New Haven, Seabrook, and Connecticut. The grape vines are a reference to those towns and, possibly, to the colonies.

The Latin motto on the flag is based on the 80th Psalm in the Bible. Translated, it means "He Who Brought Us Over Will Sustain Us." The people who chose the motto insisted that, just as those who plant grape vines take care of them, so God would look after the English settlers who had been "planted" in the colony of Connecticut.

In 1775 military leaders created the first official Connecticut flags. Each regiment used the state coat of arms in the center of its flag, but the field, or background, color of each flag varied. For example, the Second Regiment, which served at the Battle of Bunker (Breed's) Hill, had a red field (below, left). Its flag is the only regimental flag that has survived. In June 1897 a standard blue background was chosen for the official non-military state flag. The current version of that flag (above, left) dates from August 1972.

DELAWARE

★ *First State* ★

Current flag

OFFICIAL STATE NAME: State of Delaware

STATE ABBREVIATION: DE

DATE OF STATEHOOD: December 7, 1787

ORDER OF STATEHOOD: 1

FLAG DESIGNER: Flag commission

STATE MOTTO: Liberty and Independence

STATE BIRD: Blue hen chicken

STATE TREE: American holly

STATE FLOWER: Peach blossom

FLAG FACT: Delaware, the "First State," did not separate from Pennsylvania until 1776.

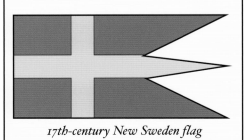

17th-century New Sweden flag

THE LAST OF THE 13 ORIGINAL STATES to adopt a flag, Delaware finally approved the design it still uses in July 1913 (above, left). A special committee of three chose the symbols of this flag. In 1953 the flag law was omitted from the *Delaware Code* by mistake, and the flag had to be adopted again. A special law in 1955 regulated the exact shades of blue and buff for the flag's background and its diamond emblem.

During the Revolutionary War, a Delaware militia group used a green flag with 13 red and white stripes in its canton. At the 1876 Centennial Exposition the state was represented by a white pennant bearing "Delaware" in blue. A flag with the state coat of arms appeared at the 1907 Jamestown Exposition and, three years later, on the battleship U.S.S. *Delaware*.

In the colonial era, Delaware was part of the New Sweden settlement. The blue Swedish flag had a yellow cross (below, left). Those colors may have influenced the design of the state flag, although blue and buff were favored for uniforms during the Revolutionary War. The coat of arms on the flag, adopted in 1777, features symbols of life in the 18th century. A ship stands for commerce, a farmer with a hoe plus the sheaf of wheat and ear of corn symbolize agriculture, while an ox representing cattle-raising completes the design. The date December 7, 1787 refers to the day Delaware ratified the U.S. Constitution. Delaware is proud that it was the first state to approve that document.

FLORIDA

★ *Sunshine State* ★

Current flag

OFFICIAL STATE NAME: State of Florida

STATE ABBREVIATION: FL

DATE OF STATEHOOD: March 3, 1845

ORDER OF STATEHOOD: 27

FLAG DESIGNER: Francis P. Fleming

STATE MOTTO: In God We Trust

STATE BIRD: Mockingbird

STATE TREE: Sabal palmetto palm

STATE FLOWER: Orange blossom

FLAG FACT: For a long time, the state seal showed the wrong type of palm tree.

1845 Florida state flag

THE FIRST FLORIDA STATE FLAG (below, left) included the Stars and Stripes in the canton to show Florida's pride in being part of the United States. At the same time, the flag expressed the opposition of the new state to federal government interference in its affairs. The five stripes of blue, orange, red, white, and green are unique among state flags. Unfortunately, no one bothered to write down what was intended by the number of stripes and their coloring.

Although part of the Confederacy during the Civil War, Florida had several flags based on the Stars and Stripes. With the Confederate defeat, a neutral flag design was adopted in August 1868. It showed the state seal on a plain white flag. The red diagonal bars were added in November 1900 to form the current flag (above, left) because the 1868 design looked too much like a flag of surrender. Florida probably chose the saltire (diagonal cross) because it recalled the Confederate Battle Flag.

After the Civil War, Florida also got rid of its old state seal, which showed a map and an American eagle. The new design, which appears in the center of the saltire, featured a steamship and a setting sun with an Indian woman in the foreground dropping flowers into the water. In 1985 all the details of the seal were carefully examined. Artists made a new official version which corrected previous errors. For example, the tree is now the sabal palmetto palm, which grows throughout the state.

GEORGIA

★ *Empire State of the South* ★

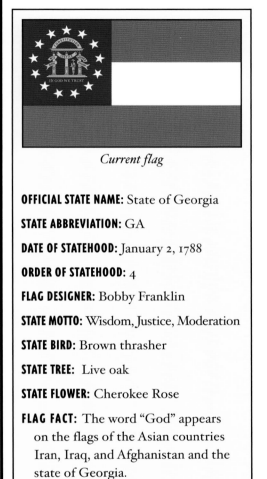

Current flag

OFFICIAL STATE NAME: State of Georgia

STATE ABBREVIATION: GA

DATE OF STATEHOOD: January 2, 1788

ORDER OF STATEHOOD: 4

FLAG DESIGNER: Bobby Franklin

STATE MOTTO: Wisdom, Justice, Moderation

STATE BIRD: Brown thrasher

STATE TREE: Live oak

STATE FLOWER: Cherokee Rose

FLAG FACT: The word "God" appears on the flags of the Asian countries Iran, Iraq, and Afghanistan and the state of Georgia.

1956 Georgia state flag

GEORGIA HAS HAD MORE FLAGS than any other state. In the 19th century, flags with the state coat of arms or seal on either red or blue backgrounds were in use. When Georgia seceded from the Union, a white flag with a red or blue star was hoisted. During the years 2001 to 2003, three different designs flew over buildings and homes.

In 1879 Confederate soldiers convinced the legislature to adopt a state flag similar to the Confederate Stars and Bars. It had horizontal stripes of red, white, and red with a blue bar along the hoist. The state coat of arms was added, and later the date 1799 in the arms was changed to 1776.

The U.S. Supreme Court ordered school desegregation in the 1950s, ending separate schools for blacks and whites. In protest, Georgia made the Confederate Battle Flag part of its flag (below, left). Its 13 stars stood for the Confederate states. Many Georgians, especially African Americans, opposed that flag and its symbolism. In 2001 a complicated new flag included the state seal, the motto "In God We Trust," and five small flags on a ribbon marked "Georgia's History."

Compromises in May 2003 resulted in the present flag based on the Stars and Bars (above, left). It has 13 stars for the original 13 U.S. states (including Georgia). It also has the state coat of arms and the motto "In God We Trust." Students salute it, saying "I pledge allegiance to the Georgia Flag and to the principles for which it stands, Wisdom, Justice, and Moderation."

HAWAI‘I
★ *Aloha State* ★

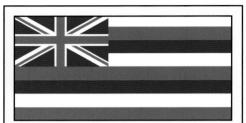

Current flag

OFFICIAL STATE NAME: State of Hawai‘i

STATE ABBREVIATION: HI

DATE OF STATEHOOD: August 21, 1959

ORDER OF STATEHOOD: 50

FLAG DESIGNER: King Kamehameha I

STATE MOTTO: *Ua Mau Ke Ea O Ka Aina I Ka Pono* (The Life of the Land is Perpetuated in Righteousness)

STATE BIRD: Hawaiian goose (Nene)

STATE TREE: Kukui (Candlenut)

STATE FLOWER: Hibiscus

FLAG FACT: Hawai‘i is the only state that once used a throne, a crown, and a royal flag.

19th-century Hawaiian royal flag

WHEN KING KAMEHAMEHA I united the Hawaiian islands in 1795, flags were not part of traditional Polynesian culture. Vessels from the United States, Britain, Russia, and other countries introduced the concept of national and naval flags. When Hawaiians gradually came to feel that their islands should have a flag, the first (unofficial) Hawaiian flag was the British Union Jack.

A variation of that flag was created in 1816 when the *Kaahumanu,* the first Hawaiian ship to travel abroad, sailed for China. It had the new (1801) Union Jack in the canton and horizontal stripes of red, white, and blue. As with many early flags, there was no uniform design. The kings and queens of Hawai‘i displayed a royal standard (below, left). It showed the shield and crown from the royal coat of arms in the center of a striped field.

In 1843, in their attempt to seize control of the islands, the British destroyed all Hawaiian flags. When Hawaiian independence was again proclaimed, the new flag resembled the old one but with eight stripes instead of nine (above, left). Those stripes stood for the main islands—Hawai‘i, O‘ahu, Moloka‘i, Maui, Lāna‘i, Ni‘ihau, Kaua‘i, and Kaho‘olawe.

That flag has continued in use ever since, despite changes in Hawai‘i’s status. In 1893 American settlers overthrew the royal government and in 1898, at the time of the Spanish-American War, Hawai‘i became an American territory. Finally, in 1959, Hawai‘i became the 50th U.S. state.

IDAHO
★ *Gem State* ★

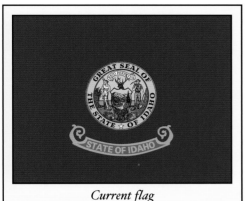

Current flag

OFFICIAL STATE NAME: State of Idaho

STATE ABBREVIATION: ID

DATE OF STATEHOOD: July 3, 1890

ORDER OF STATEHOOD: 43

FLAG DESIGNER: General C. A. Elmer

STATE MOTTO: *Esto Perpetua*
(May It Last Forever)

STATE BIRD: Mountain bluebird

STATE TREE: White pine

STATE FLOWER: Syringa (Mock orange)

FLAG FACT: Idaho has the only state
seal designed by a woman. Her name
was Emma Edwards.

1907 Idaho state flag

ADJUTANT GENERAL C. A. ELMER, head of the state's militia, gave Idaho its complicated flag design. The legislature authorized a flag in March 1907 (below, left). It was blue, the favorite color for state flags, based on extensive Civil War usage. The state name was supposed to appear in the center, "in such colors and of such size and dimensions as shall be prescribed by the adjutant general."

Elmer put "State of Idaho" on a scroll, but he added a picture of the state seal. Despite the conflict between the flag described by the legislature and the one Elmer designed, no further action was taken until March 1927. The legislature, changing its mind, formally accepted the flag in actual use (above, left), although the seal made it very costly to manufacture.

Below a blue sky, local products spill from cornucopias—apples, pears, grapes, corn, potatoes, tomatoes, plus other fruits and vegetables and a sheaf of wheat. A miner in khaki clothes and red bandanna holds a pick and shovel. To his left, rocks seem to threaten to roll down on him.

Facing away from the miner on the seal is a woman with symbols of justice (scales) and liberty (a liberty cap of the type used in ancient Rome by freed slaves). On a central shield is a mill, a farmer with a horse-drawn plow, a huge fir tree, and a sun rising over snow-covered mountains that stand above the Snake River. An elk head peers over the shield, and the state motto is written above on a scroll.

ILLINOIS

★ *Land of Lincoln* ★

Current flag

OFFICIAL STATE NAME: State of Illinois

STATE ABBREVIATION: IL

DATE OF STATEHOOD: December 3, 1818

ORDER OF STATEHOOD: 21

FLAG DESIGNER: Rockford Chapter, Daughters of the American Revolution

STATE MOTTO: State Sovereignty, National Union

STATE BIRD: Cardinal

STATE TREE: White oak

STATE FLOWER: Violet

FLAG FACT: The dates on the boulder that appears on the current flag indicate when state seals were made.

1918 Illinois 100-year anniversary flag

BEFORE THE CIVIL WAR many Americans favored states' rights as a way of protecting the institution of slavery. Even in the free states of the North, many supported more power for states and less for the federal government. The state seal adopted in 1820 hints at the dispute over state versus national power.

The motto added at that time read "State Sovereignty, National Union." Even after the Civil War, the legislature refused to reverse the order of the words. However, the man who made the seal for use on official state documents drew the ribbon bearing the motto so that "National Union" appeared prominently at the top.

The state flag was designed by the Rockford Chapter of the Daughters of the American Revolution. When it was adopted in 1915, the design of the seal—without its surrounding inscription—was supposed to appear on a white field. The seal could be shown in full color or in black and white, but the latter was usually preferred. In July 1970 the state decided that the name "Illinois" should be added at the bottom (above, left).

An entirely different flag, designed by Wallace Rice, celebrated Illinois's centennial as a state in 1918 (below, left). The flag's three horizontal bars had a large star for Illinois and 10 stars for the free states plus 10 for the slave states that preceded Illinois in statehood. In 1968, on its 150th "birthday," a special sesquicentennial flag was created.

INDIANA

★ *Hoosier State* ★

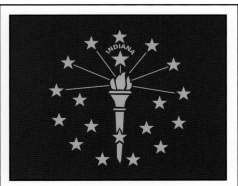

Current state banner

OFFICIAL STATE NAME: State of Indiana

STATE ABBREVIATION: IN

DATE OF STATEHOOD: December 11, 1816

ORDER OF STATEHOOD: 19

FLAG DESIGNER: Paul Hadley

STATE MOTTO: The Crossroads of America

STATE BIRD: Cardinal

STATE TREE: Tulip poplar

STATE FLOWER: Peony

FLAG FACT: Although Indiana became a state in 1816, its star was not added to the Stars and Stripes until 1818.

1901 Indiana state flag

THE INDIANA STATE BANNER (as the current flag is officially known) could be mistaken for the flag of the European Union. Both have a dark blue background with a ring of gold stars—13 on Indiana's and 12 on the European Union's. In addition, Indiana has seven rays extending outward from the flames of a golden torch. Five more stars appear in an inner arc at the bottom and a large star above the torch has the word "Indiana" written over it. The torch is for knowledge and liberty, with the rays suggesting their spread across the country.

The flag's designer, Paul Hadley, won a competition sponsored by the Daughters of the American Revolution in 1916, when Indiana completed its first century of statehood. Hadley recommended stars of either gold or buff, a color that had been used in military uniforms during the American Revolution. While the flag law of May 1917 allowed for either option, golden yellow has always been preferred by flag manufacturers. It is almost impossible to find flags that use metallic gold.

Union veterans of the Civil War generally opposed state flags. They wanted people to fly only the national flag. As a result, the first state flag of Indiana, adopted in March 1901, was simply the national Stars and Stripes. The one shown here (below, left) was the 45-star version in use until 1908. Since the flag law is still in force, Indiana today recognizes the 50-star U.S. flag as its state flag.

IOWA

★ *Hawkeye State* ★

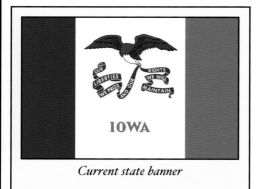

Current state banner

OFFICIAL STATE NAME: State of Iowa

STATE ABBREVIATION: IA

DATE OF STATEHOOD: December 28, 1846

ORDER OF STATEHOOD: 29

FLAG DESIGNER: Dixie C. Gebhardt

STATE MOTTO: Our Liberties We Prize and Our Rights We Will Maintain

STATE BIRD: American goldfinch

STATE TREE: Oak

STATE FLOWER: Wild rose

FLAG FACT: The governor's flag has the state seal in color on a blue field.

1917 Iowa state flag

THE DAUGHTERS OF THE American Revolution asked Iowa's General Assembly for a state flag. It approved a special commission in 1913 that was supposed to recommend a design. The commission found itself in the midst of a dispute. Civil War veterans opposed recognizing any flag except the Stars and Stripes, while the D.A.R. strongly favored the creation of a state flag.

When the United States entered World War I in 1917, the D.A.R. took the opportunity to promote their concept again. A white flag bearing the bald eagle of the state seal was chosen. Above the state name, that flying eagle was shown holding a ribbon on which the state motto was written. Flags of this design were sent to Iowa troops abroad (below, left).

Finally, in March 1921 the state legislature officially approved the design of that World War I flag with modifications (above, left). To please the Civil War veterans, the new design was officially labeled a banner rather than a flag. At the recommendation of D.A.R. member Dixie C. Gebhardt, the plain white background was replaced by vertical bars. Stripes of blue at the hoist and red in the fly were added to the white, as in the French Tricolor. Another French connection was that Iowa had been part of the Louisiana Purchase, which transferred a vast territory from France to the United States in 1803. France was on the minds of many Iowans in 1921 because it had been a major U.S. ally in the "Great War" (World War I).

KANSAS

★ *Sunflower State* ★

KANSAS

Current flag

OFFICIAL STATE NAME: State of Kansas

STATE ABBREVIATION: KS

DATE OF STATEHOOD: January 29, 1861

ORDER OF STATEHOOD: 34

FLAG DESIGNER: Unknown

STATE MOTTO: *Ad Astra Per Aspera*
(To the Stars Through Difficulties)

STATE BIRD: Western meadowlark

STATE TREE: Cottonwood

STATE FLOWER: Sunflower

FLAG FACT: The name "Kansas" refers to an Indian tribe and a nearby river.

1953 Kansas state banner

IN THE MID-19TH CENTURY very few states had flags of their own. Even state capitols rarely displayed a flag. There was little need for an official flag because state governments were much smaller than today. That flag situation changed during the Civil War.

Although red, white, and blue were considered the national colors, a darker blue was always preferred by the Army. Therefore, most state militias from the North carried a blue color (military flag) bearing the state seal or coat of arms. After the Civil War when states began adopting flags, many Northern legislatures simply selected their familiar militia color as the basic design. Today, almost half of all U.S. state flags, including that of Kansas, are blue with the state seal or coat of arms.

The blue state *flag* adopted by Kansas in March 1927 included the state seal and a small sunflower. That flag was expensive to manufacture, and it was not easy to identify quickly. Then in June 1953 Kansas approved a simple state *banner.* A large sunflower, which most Americans recognized as the Kansas state flower, was centered on a blue field (below, left).

Although the 1953 banner was simple, easy to make and to recognize, and had clear symbolism, it was almost never used. In June 1963 the legislature modified the 1927 flag. The sunflower and seal were reduced in size and "Kansas" was written below them. Then in December 1985 some seal details were changed, resulting in the current flag (above, left).

KENTUCKY

★ *Bluegrass State* ★

Current flag

OFFICIAL STATE NAME: Commonwealth of Kentucky

STATE ABBREVIATION: KY

DATE OF STATEHOOD: June 1, 1792

ORDER OF STATEHOOD: 15

FLAG DESIGNER: Mrs. Joseph Burgess

STATE MOTTO: United We Stand, Divided We Fall

STATE BIRD: Cardinal

STATE TREE: Tulip poplar

STATE FLOWER: Goldenrod

FLAG FACT: Massachusetts, Pennsylvania, and Virginia are also commonwealths.

1861 Kentucky military flag

THE KENTUCKY STATE SEAL, adopted in 1793, combines words and pictures to tell a story. The emblem consists of two men shaking hands: One is wearing formal clothing and the other, frontier garb. They represent city dwellers of the east and pioneers of the west. When Kentucky became a state in 1792, it was considered to be on the western edge of the country!

The motto "United We Stand, Divided We Fall" expressed the idea that the two parts of the state needed each other. The motto was not exclusive to Kentucky. In 1768 a patriotic song by John Dickinson had included the words "Then join hand in hand, brave Americans all. By uniting we stand, by dividing we fall." The same concept had appeared in one of Æsop's fables written in the 5th century B.C.

During the Civil War, Kentucky, which was a slave state, had both a Union and a Confederate government. Kentucky men favoring the North used a blue color (military flag) featuring the state seal. Some troops fighting for the South carried an 1861 flag based on the Stars and Bars of the Confederacy with the state name added (below, left).

In March 1918 the basic design of the current flag was approved. Based on Kentucky's Union military colors, it had the state seal in the center of a blue field. The seal was surrounded by the goldenrod—the state flower—and the official name of the state. Artistic changes were made to the design in June 1962 to create today's state flag (above, left).

LOUISIANA

★ *Pelican State* ★

Current flag

OFFICIAL STATE NAME: State of Louisiana

STATE ABBREVIATION: LA

DATE OF STATEHOOD: April 30, 1812

ORDER OF STATEHOOD: 18

FLAG DESIGNER: Unknown

STATE MOTTO: Union, Justice, Confidence

STATE BIRD: Brown pelican

STATE TREE: Cypress

STATE FLOWER: Magnolia

FLAG FACT: Within four weeks in 1803, Louisiana flew French, Spanish, and U.S. flags.

1861 Louisiana state flag

CENTURIES AGO PEOPLE saw pelicans feeding their young by passing fish to them, beak to beak. It looked as though the parent were scraping its breast and the young were consuming drops of blood. Christians saw the pelican as a symbol of parents sacrificing for their children. The bird was highly regarded for its concern for its young.

French settlers and merchants who developed a colony at the mouth of the Mississippi River in the 17th and 18th centuries saw the many pelicans in the area as a favorable sign for success. The bird thus became the unofficial Louisiana emblem.

Even after Louisiana passed to Spain and then to the United States in 1803, the pelican was associated with the territory. It appeared on the seal of the first U.S. territorial governor. When Louisiana left the Union in 1861, it hoisted the Pelican Flag. In July 1912 the legislature created a state flag with pelicans and the state motto (above, left). Since then there have been artistic variations in that flag.

Louisiana had an entirely different flag during the Civil War. Adopted in February 1861, it featured the horizontal stripes and canton design of the Stars and Stripes (below, left). The single yellow star represented statehood. The stripes included the blue, white, and red colors of the flags of the United States, the Confederate States, and France. The red and yellow of the Spanish flag were also part of the design. This simple design expresses the state's historic traditions.

MAINE

★ *Pine Tree State* ★

Current flag

OFFICIAL STATE NAME: State of Maine

STATE ABBREVIATION: ME

DATE OF STATEHOOD: March 15, 1820

ORDER OF STATEHOOD: 23

FLAG DESIGNER: Unknown

STATE MOTTO: *Dirigo* (I Guide)

STATE BIRD: Chickadee

STATE TREE: Eastern white pine

STATE FLOWER: White pine cone and tassel

FLAG FACT: The single star on the flag below symbolizes statehood, as on the flag of Massachusetts.

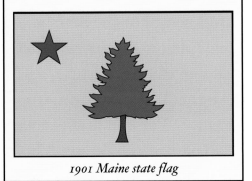

1901 Maine state flag

THE PINE TREE, which has provided revenue for Maine since English settlers arrived in the 17th century, has appeared in the state's seal, coat of arms, naval flag, and state flag. Maine militia colors (military flags) were traditionally white with the state coat of arms, but the state flag adopted in March 1901 (below, left) had a background of buff, a color associated with Revolutionary War military uniforms. The pine tree appeared in natural colors, and in the upper hoist was a blue star—the North Star, which for centuries guided sailors.

The North Star also was featured in the state seal and coat of arms with a Latin motto meaning "I Guide." Maine was proud to be the northernmost U.S. state (from 1820 to 1858). In February 1909 a new flag was chosen by the state. Based on Civil War military flags, it is supposed to have the state seal in the center, although in practice the coat of arms appears instead. That flag is still official (above, left).

In July 1939, recalling its strong connections with the Atlantic Ocean, Maine adopted a "merchant and marine flag." To the white background and green tree, dating to the Revolutionary War, the state motto and state name were added. The blue anchor below the tree makes the usage of the flag clear. Although infrequently seen, the Maine maritime flag is still official. Today, Massachusetts is the only other state with a special maritime flag. Maine was part of Massachusetts until 1820.

MARYLAND
★ *Old Line State* ★

Current flag

OFFICIAL STATE NAME: State of Maryland

STATE ABBREVIATION: MD

DATE OF STATEHOOD: April 28, 1788

ORDER OF STATEHOOD: 7

FLAG DESIGNER: Unknown

STATE MOTTO: *Fatti Maschi Parole Femine* (Deeds Are Manly, Words Feminine)

STATE BIRD: Northern (Baltimore) oriole

STATE TREE: White oak

STATE FLOWER: Black-eyed Susan

FLAG FACT: Avalon, a settlement on the island of Newfoundland in eastern Canada, had the same flag as colonial Maryland because they were both owned by the Lords Baltimore.

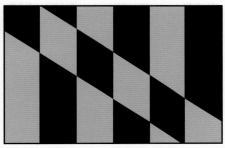

17th-century Maryland flag

IN ENGLAND women generally were not allowed to have coats of arms of their own. However, some women were heiresses who, as heads of families, were permitted to have their own personal coats of arms and banners. Alicia Crossland was an heiress and her family, the Crosslands of Yorkshire, displayed a quartered shield of white and red bearing a cross "counterchanged." That means the cross and the field used the same colors but in different places.

When Leonard Calvert married Alicia, he was permitted to combine her arms with his—black and gold vertical stripes with a diagonal stripe counterchanged. According to the law of heraldry, Calvert was authorized to use an armorial banner—a flag featuring his coat of arms design (below, left). As the lord proprietor of Maryland, Calvert displayed the family banner, although he did not include the Crossland arms. Documents from as early as 1638 indicate that the black and gold banner was carried as a military color. Just before the American Revolution, the British Union Jack was added as a canton to that banner. When the Calvert flag was revived in the mid-19th century, it included the Crossland arms. Some design elements were featured in the state's Civil War flags. In 1901 the whole design was recognized as the official flag of the governor of Maryland. In March 1904, it was adopted as the state flag (above, left). Today, Maryland is proud of its heraldic banner, one of the few among the 50 states.

MASSACHUSETTS

★ *Bay State* ★

Current flag

OFFICIAL STATE NAME: Commonwealth of Massachusetts

STATE ABBREVIATION: MA

DATE OF STATEHOOD: February 6, 1788

ORDER OF STATEHOOD: 6

FLAG DESIGNER: Unknown

STATE MOTTO: *Ense Petit Placidam Sub Libertate Quietem* (By the Sword We Search for Peace and Quiet Only Under Liberty)

STATE BIRD: Chickadee

STATE TREE: American elm

STATE FLOWER: Mayflower

FLAG FACT: In 1971 the star was changed from silver to white to reduce costs.

APPEAL TO HEAVEN

18th-century Massachusetts flag

THE MASSACHUSETTS LEGISLATURE created the first state flag in 1908. It combined the flag carried by the state militia (front) and the state's naval flag (reverse), which dates to the Revolutionary War. That flag was white with a green pine tree and the motto "Appeal to Heaven" (below, left). The militia flag was also white but bore the state coat of arms in the center.

In October 1971 the legislature simplified the state flag. Since then the same design—the coat of arms of the commonwealth—has been on both the front and the back (above, left). The old ensign (naval flag), with its motto omitted, was revived as a separate flag. Maine, the only other state with its own maritime flag, has a similar design.

When Massachusetts put a single star on its coat of arms in 1790, it became the first state to use that symbol to show that it was part of the United States. The Indian in the center of the arms has been a Massachusetts symbol since 1629. In a seal created that year for the Massachusetts-Bay Company, there is an Indian standing between two pine trees saying "Come Over and Help Us."

The Massachusetts motto is expressed partly by the Latin words appearing on the scroll around the shield and partly by the arm holding a sword shown in the crest. Combined and translated, these elements provide the entire motto: "This Hand Opposed To Tyrants Searches with a Sword for Peaceful Conditions Under Liberty."

MICHIGAN

★ *Great Lake State* ★

Current flag

OFFICIAL STATE NAME: State of Michigan

STATE ABBREVIATION: MI

DATE OF STATEHOOD: January 26, 1837

ORDER OF STATEHOOD: 26

FLAG DESIGNER: Unknown

STATE MOTTO: *Si Quæris Peninsulam Amœnam Circumspice* (If You Seek a Pleasant Peninsula, Look Around You)

STATE BIRD: Robin

STATE TREE: White pine

STATE FLOWER: Apple blossom

FLAG FACT: One of three state flag mottos is *Tuebor*—"I Will Defend."

Michigan governor's flag

A VISITOR TO THE CATHEDRAL OF ST. PAUL in London complained that no credit was given architect Sir Christopher Wren for his work. The response was, "If you seek his monument, look around you." A modified version of that saying appears in the coat of arms of Michigan. Translated from Latin it reads, "If You Seek a Pleasant Peninsula, Look Around You."

Another motto in the Michigan coat of arms appears on a shield with a setting sun and a man standing next to a lake. He bears a rifle but holds up his hand as a peaceful greeting. The Latin motto *Tuebor* means "I Will Defend." It refers to the determination of Americans to protect their homes against the British in neighboring Canada. The Michigan-Canada border has been peaceful since 1815.

Another motto appears on a ribbon above the American eagle, which is shown with olive branches and arrows but no U.S. shield. *E Pluribus Unum,* the national motto, means "One Out of Many." Although it was adopted in 1782 as part of the U.S. Great Seal, its use on the Michigan seal and coat of arms dates only from 1835. The elk and moose shield supporters may have been taken from the arms of the Hudson's Bay Company.

Like Pennsylvania, Michigan uses a special version of its state flag—the background is white instead of blue—as the governor's personal flag (below, left). It is displayed in the governor's office, car, and boat, and when the Michigan National Guard is being reviewed.

MINNESOTA

★ *Gopher State* ★

Current flag

OFFICIAL STATE NAME: State of Minnesota

STATE ABBREVIATION: MN

DATE OF STATEHOOD: May 11, 1858

ORDER OF STATEHOOD: 32

FLAG DESIGNER: Unknown

STATE MOTTO: *L'Etoile du Nord*
(The Star of the North)

STATE BIRD: Common loon

STATE TREE: Red pine

STATE FLOWER: Showy lady's slipper

FLAG FACT: One flag maker mistakenly showed the Minnesota motto as "The Canvas of the North."

1893 Minnesota state flag

SOME MINNESOTA WOMEN decided to present a state flag to display at the World's Columbian Exposition held in Chicago in 1893. They based the design on a Minnesota color (military flag), but omitted the name of the troop appearing on the reverse side of the original. As a result, their pattern—officially recognized by the state legislature as the Minnesota flag in April of that year—had a plain blue reverse side.

The front of the flag had 19 stars to show that Minnesota was the 19th state after the original 13 (below, left). It also had the state name, the state flower (the showy lady's slipper), and the state seal. That seal showed the Falls of St. Anthony, near present-day Minneapolis, which were first seen by a European in 1680. There was also an Indian retreating into the setting sun and a farmer plowing his field. The seal's French motto means "The Star of the North," a reference to the fact that Minnesota was the northernmost U.S. state from 1858 until 1959.

So that the flag would be less expensive to make, the central design was simplified in March 1957 and placed on a blue background. In August 1983 the Indian was changed. Instead of fleeing the farmer, he was facing him (above, left). This symbolized that both Native Americans and Europeans have contributed to the development of the state. The basic design of the current flag resembles those of many neighboring states, as well as the militia colors carried by Minnesota troops during the Civil War.

MISSISSIPPI

★ *Magnolia State* ★

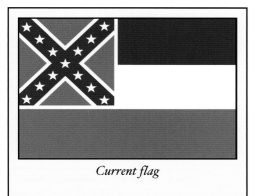

Current flag

OFFICIAL STATE NAME: State of Mississippi

STATE ABBREVIATION: MS

DATE OF STATEHOOD: December 10, 1817

ORDER OF STATEHOOD: 20

FLAG DESIGNER: Unknown

STATE MOTTO: *Virtute et Armis*
(By Valor and Arms)

STATE BIRD: Mockingbird

STATE TREE: Magnolia

STATE FLOWER: Magnolia

FLAG FACT: In a referendum held in 2001, voters rejected a proposal to remove the Confederate Battle Flag from the state flag.

1861 Mississippi state flag

TODAY THE STAR IS POPULAR as a symbol around the world. More than one-third of all national flags show one or more stars. When the Stars and Stripes was created in 1777, however, no other national flag displayed a star. The stars in the Mississippi flag were inspired by the 13 stars on the Battle Flag of the Confederate States of America, created in 1861.

The current state flag (above, left) was adopted in February 1894. The canton corresponds to that used in the second and third Confederate national flags. The stripes, unlike those of the Confederate Stars and Bars, are blue, white, and red. The flagstaff is decorated with a combined battle-ax and spear finial. The whole design is intended to emphasize the commitment of Mississippi to the states' rights principles of the South.

The star was a Mississippi symbol even before the Civil War. When the United States bought the Louisiana Territory (including the area that would become the state of Mississippi) from France, the Spanish insisted that West Florida, the coastal area east of the Mississippi River, was legally theirs, not France's. Local American settlers then proclaimed the Republic of West Florida under a blue flag with a white star.

At the beginning of the Civil War a design of a star on a blue field, known as the Bonnie Blue Flag, was widely flown in all Southern states. When Mississippi adopted its first state flag in January 1861 (below, left) the canton was the Bonnie Blue Flag. The central flag emblem, within a red border, was a magnolia tree.

MISSOURI

★ *Show Me State* ★

Current flag

OFFICIAL STATE NAME: State of Missouri

STATE ABBREVIATION: MO

DATE OF STATEHOOD: August 10, 1821

ORDER OF STATEHOOD: 24

FLAG DESIGNER: Mrs. Robert B. Oliver

STATE MOTTO: United We Stand, Divided We Fall; *Salus Populi Suprema Lex Esto* (The Welfare of the People Is the Highest Law)

STATE BIRD: Eastern bluebird

STATE TREE: Dogwood

STATE FLOWER: Hawthorn

FLAG FACT: The U.S. coat of arms appears on the state seal—and on the one-dollar bill.

1909 proposed Missouri flag

MISSOURI HAD NO STATE FLAG IN 1909. Dr. G. H. Holcomb submitted a flag design to the Missouri legislature (below, left). It had the 13 red and white stripes and the blue canton of the national flag, but there was a circle of 24 stars to indicate the order of Missouri's admission to the Union. The state abbreviation (MO.) appeared within the circle. That flag and other designs based on the Confederate Battle Flag, which had been carried by some Missouri regiments in the Civil War, were rejected.

In March 1913 a different design, created by Mrs. Robert B. Oliver of the Daughters of the American Revolution, was approved as the first official state flag (above, left). Stripes of the red, white, and blue national colors were overlaid by a white disk. It featured the state coat of arms set within a blue border bearing 24 white stars. The coat of arms was part of the state's great seal, which had been adopted in 1821.

The 24 stars are also represented against a background of sky blue in the crest of the arms. Two grizzly bears support the central shield, which is divided vertically. Another bear appears on a red background below a blue area with a white crescent, which symbolizes Missouri as the second state carved from the Louisiana Purchase. The other half of the shield presents the coat of arms of the United States. Missouri is unusual in having two mottoes as part of its coat of arms and flag. One is printed in English, the other in Latin.

MONTANA

★ *Treasure State* ★

Current flag

OFFICIAL STATE NAME: State of Montana

STATE ABBREVIATION: MT

DATE OF STATEHOOD: November 8, 1889

ORDER OF STATEHOOD: 41

FLAG DESIGNER: Unknown

STATE MOTTO: *Oro y Plata* (Gold and Silver)

STATE BIRD: Western meadowlark

STATE TREE: Ponderosa pine

STATE FLOWER: Bitterroot

FLAG FACT: Of the many state mottoes that appear on state flags, only Montana's is in Spanish.

1973 proposed Montana flag

THE MILITARY FLAG of the First Montana Infantry, U.S. Volunteers, lost the fringe at its outer end while in service during the 1898 Spanish-American War. When the Montana legislature adopted it as the state flag in February 1905, its unusual "fringe on top and bottom edges only" became official. The state seal on that flag showed a scene from nature—the Great Falls on the Missouri River, surrounded by mountains and symbols of mining and agriculture. The state motto "Gold and Silver" appeared in Spanish.

The flag with its central emblem and dark blue field resembled those of many other states. Therefore, as collections of state flags became common, the Montana flag was hard to tell from all the others. In 1981 the legislature ordered that the name of the state be added to the design (above, left).

An alternative flag had been endorsed in 1973 by the state's House of Representatives (below, left). It showed stripes of blue, white, and green with white mountains in the canton. (The Spanish word *montana* means "mountainous.") The blue stripe was for the "Big Sky State" while the white peaks recalled another state nickname, "Land of Shining Mountains." Green symbolized fields and forests, and the white was for the pure waters of Montana's rivers and lakes. Flag designer James Croft chose a copper arrowhead as a flagpole finial. It was intended to represent the Indian inhabitants of the state. The Montana Senate narrowly rejected this distinctive flag.

NEBRASKA

★ *Cornhusker State* ★

Current flag

OFFICIAL STATE NAME: State of Nebraska

STATE ABBREVIATION: NE

DATE OF STATEHOOD: March 1, 1867

ORDER OF STATEHOOD: 37

FLAG DESIGNER: Unknown

STATE MOTTO: Equality Before the Law

STATE BIRD: Western meadowlark

STATE TREE: Cottonwood

STATE FLOWER: Goldenrod

FLAG FACT: The seal shows the Rocky Mountains, which are located 125 miles (200 km) west of Nebraska.

1917 Nebraska National Guard flag

THE FIRST PRINTED PRESENTATION of state flags appeared in the October 1917 NATIONAL GEOGRAPHIC magazine. The Nebraska flag published there—the state seal on a yellow background (below, left)—was not an official state flag. During World War I, the men of the Nebraska National Guard trained in state camps before going to Europe to fight. Families decided to show their support for those men by creating flags. Women designed and made flags with the Nebraska seal on backgrounds of different colors. The yellow versions ended up being used as headquarters flags for the Nebraska National Guard, although they were not official.

In 1920 the first proposal for a state banner called for changes in the state seal. The Nebraska chapter of the Daughters of the American Revolution developed a new design that included the state flower, but their idea was rejected by the legislature. The current flag (above, left), promoted by Mrs. B. G. Miller, was adopted in April 1925. It is still in use, although since 1963 it has been called a flag instead of a banner.

The state seal is represented in blue, gold, and silver on a field of dark blue. Metallic gold and silver are occasionally used in flags, but they are normally—as in the Nebraska flag—replaced by golden yellow and silver gray. The Nebraska seal shows a blacksmith in front of a scene showing wheat and corn, a settler's cabin, a railroad train, and a scroll with the state motto, "Equality Before the Law."

NEVADA

★ *Silver State* ★

Current flag

OFFICIAL STATE NAME: State of Nevada

STATE ABBREVIATION: NV

DATE OF STATEHOOD: October 31, 1864

ORDER OF STATEHOOD: 36

FLAG DESIGNER: Louis Shellback III

STATE MOTTO: All For Our Country

STATE BIRD: Mountain bluebird

STATE TREE: Single-leaf piñon and bristlecone pine

STATE FLOWER: Sagebrush

FLAG FACT: The slogan "Battle Born" refers to the fact that Nevada became a state during the Civil War.

1905 Nevada state flag

SETTLERS WERE DRAWN to Nevada by mineral resources, especially gold and silver. They are featured in the various state symbols. The first Nevada state flag adopted in February 1905, had the words "Silver" and "Gold" emblazoned on a dark blue background (below, left). It also bore the state name and 18 stars in each of the two colors. Those were actually represented in gray and golden yellow, since it would have been difficult and expensive to use metallic silver and gold.

In March 1915 a more traditional state flag was substituted. The 36 gold and silver stars plus the state name were retained, but the motto "All For Our Country" and the shield from the state seal were added in the center of the blue field. The state seal showed a mill, smelter, and horse-drawn cart, all under a sun rising over mountains. A railroad on a trestle and agricultural symbols (a sheaf of wheat, a sickle, and a plow) completed the design. Such a complex design meant that few flags were made.

The legislature changed its mind again in 1929 and simplified the state flag. Within a wreath of sagebrush—the state flower—appeared a single white star and the state name, all below a scroll with the slogan "Battle Born." The final change occurred when the current state flag (above, left) was adopted in October 1991. Aside from artistic improvements, the only modification was having the state name appear below the star rather than between its points.

NEW HAMPSHIRE

★ *Granite State* ★

Current flag

OFFICIAL STATE NAME: State of New Hampshire

STATE ABBREVIATION: NH

DATE OF STATEHOOD: June 21, 1788

ORDER OF STATEHOOD: 9

FLAG DESIGNER: Unknown

STATE MOTTO: Live Free or Die

STATE BIRD: Purple finch

STATE TREE: White birch

STATE FLOWER: Purple lilac

FLAG FACT: The nine stars on the flag identify New Hampshire as the ninth state to enter the Union.

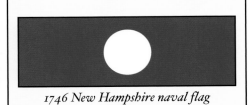

1746 New Hampshire naval flag

THE SHIP IN NEW HAMPSHIRE'S state seal and flag is supposedly the *Raleigh,* which served in the Revolutionary War. That vessel was built in 1776. However, the ship's flag is shown as the Stars and Stripes, which was not adopted by Congress until 1777. What flags the *Raleigh* actually displayed in the shipyard (shown on the seal) or at sea is unknown.

The *Raleigh's* shipyard was located on an island in the Piscataqua River, which was claimed by both New Hampshire and Maine. The Supreme Court of the United States eventually decided the island belonged to Maine. Therefore New Hampshire has the unusual distinction of featuring a scene from another state on its state flag and seal (above, left).

New Hampshire's first flag was adopted in 1792 as a color to be carried by the state militia. While similar to the modern state flag, it was never displayed on public buildings. In 1909 a regular state flag was authorized. It had the state seal framed by nine stars and a wreath of laurel leaves. The seal was slightly altered in January 1932.

New Hampshire once had a "vane"—a small, narrow flag flown on a ship for identification. It was used on transport ships in 1746 when troops from New Hampshire, Rhode Island, and Connecticut went to Nova Scotia. There, combined British and American forces successfully attacked France's Fort Louisburg. Although not used for other purposes, that vane is the earliest known New Hampshire flag (below, left).

NEW JERSEY

★ *Garden State* ★

Current flag

OFFICIAL STATE NAME: State of New Jersey

STATE ABBREVIATION: NJ

DATE OF STATEHOOD: December 18, 1787

ORDER OF STATEHOOD: 3

FLAG DESIGNER: Unknown

STATE MOTTO: Liberty and Prosperity

STATE BIRD: American goldfinch

STATE TREE: Red oak

STATE FLOWER: Violet

FLAG FACT: Congressman Francis Hopkinson designed the state seal—and Old Glory, the U.S. national flag.

Chartered West India Company flag

NEW JERSEY IS ONE of the most urban and industrial states of the Union. However, its state flag, seal, and coat of arms (above, left) commemorate its agricultural wealth. New Jersey was rural when its seal was adopted in 1777, and the legislature has never changed it. The head of a horse serves as the crest for a shield that displays three plows. One of the shield supporters is Ceres, the Roman goddess of agriculture, who holds a cornucopia of fruits. The other supporter, Liberty, holds her traditional staff with a red liberty cap. The ancient Phrygians were the first to give a red cap to anyone who was freed from slavery. When the Romans followed the custom, that cap became the classical symbol of liberty.

During the revolutions in America and France and for many decades afterward, the liberty cap was a popular symbol in both countries. In its motto "Liberty and Prosperity," New Jersey honors both liberty and agriculture.

The blue and buff flag colors may indirectly derive from old flags of the Netherlands. In the early 17th century parts of New York and New Jersey, as colonies of the Netherlands, flew its orange, white, and blue tricolor. The same flag with the initials GWC represented the Dutch Chartered West India Company (below, left). Those orange and blue flags may have inspired the buff and blue colors of Revolutionary War uniforms that were the basis for the state flag colors adopted in March 1896.

NEW MEXICO

★ *Land of Enchantment* ★

Current flag

OFFICIAL STATE NAME: State of New Mexico

STATE ABBREVIATION: NM

DATE OF STATEHOOD: January 6, 1912

ORDER OF STATEHOOD: 47

FLAG DESIGNER: Dr. Harry Mera

STATE MOTTO: *Crescit Eundo* (It Grows As It Goes)

STATE BIRD: Roadrunner

STATE TREE: Piñon

STATE FLOWER: Yucca

FLAG FACT: A 2001 Internet vote hailed New Mexico's flag as having the best state flag design.

1915 New Mexico state flag

VEXILLOGRAPHY, the art of creating flags, requires simple design and complex meaning. Many who create flags fail to understand this. By showing only everyday objects, they reduce the possibility for subtle and multiple meanings. Also, such flags are often difficult and expensive to manufacture and impossible to identify at a distance.

The first New Mexico state flag, approved in 1915 (below, left), included the state's order of admission to the Union (47), its name (separately and in the complex state seal), and the 48-star United States flag. Few of these flags were ever made.

The Daughters of the American Revolution held a competition for a more appropriate flag. Dr. Harry Mera, an archaeologist and physician, created the winning design. Although most revised state flags do not improve the flags they replace, Mera's strikingly simple design was an exception. The state legislature accepted it in March 1925 (above, left). The yellow and red colors suggest the banners of Spain, flown in New Mexico when the first Europeans explored it. The central design is an ancient sun symbol used by the Zia, a Pueblo people native to New Mexico.

The flag is honored by this pledge: "I salute the flag of the state of New Mexico, the Zia symbol of perfect friendship among united cultures." The Zia people have unsuccessfully tried to obtain payment from the state government for its widespread use of their traditional symbol.

NEW YORK
★ *Empire State* ★

Current flag

OFFICIAL STATE NAME: State of New York

STATE ABBREVIATION: NY

DATE OF STATEHOOD: July 26, 1788

ORDER OF STATEHOOD: 11

FLAG DESIGNER: Unknown

STATE MOTTO: *Excelsior* (Loftier)

STATE BIRD: Eastern bluebird

STATE TREE: Sugar maple

STATE FLOWER: Rose

FLAG FACT: A rising sun was the heraldic badge of the English dukes of York.

18th-century New York flag

IN THE 17TH CENTURY beaver pelts were so valuable they served as a unit of payment. A beaver appeared in the coats of arms of the Dutch colonies of New Amsterdam and New Netherland. Today it is the state animal of New York, and beavers appear in the New York City seal and flag.

During the Revolution, a beaver flag flew in New York, but little record of its design or how it was used survives. A silk beaver flag, more likely displayed by the military than hoisted on a ship, still exists (below, left). Today the beaver no longer appears on the New York State flag. It has been replaced by two women holding a shield showing the Hudson River, mountains, and a rising sun. On the coat of arms, an American eagle over a globe suggests the Empire State has helped the United States become a world power.

That coat of arms was adopted in 1777. Except for artistic variations, it has continued in use ever since. A blue military flag with that coat of arms, used by the Third New York Regiment during the Revolution, has survived. The first regulation for a state flag dates from 1858. It was simply the state arms on a white field of an unusual size—10 feet by 12 feet (3 x 3.7 m).

In 1896 the background of that flag was changed from white to buff. (The uniforms of New York troops during the Revolution had been dark blue with buff collar, cuffs, and trim.) Finally in 1901 the background of the state flag was altered to blue, a design which has continued in use to this day (above, left).

NORTH CAROLINA

★ *Tar Heel State* ★

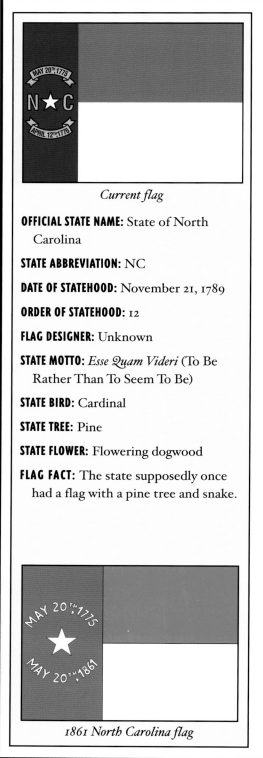

Current flag

OFFICIAL STATE NAME: State of North Carolina

STATE ABBREVIATION: NC

DATE OF STATEHOOD: November 21, 1789

ORDER OF STATEHOOD: 12

FLAG DESIGNER: Unknown

STATE MOTTO: *Esse Quam Videri* (To Be Rather Than To Seem To Be)

STATE BIRD: Cardinal

STATE TREE: Pine

STATE FLOWER: Flowering dogwood

FLAG FACT: The state supposedly once had a flag with a pine tree and snake.

1861 North Carolina flag

MANY BELIEVE THAT NORTH CAROLINA had a Revolutionary War flag showing a hornet's nest, but the existence of that flag has not been proven. It is known, however, that a British general complained that Americans in Charlotte, North Carolina, fought so fiercely that he felt as though he were in a hornet's nest there.

North Carolina adopted its first official flag in 1861 during the Civil War (below, left). Its design honored two historic documents. It bore the date of the state's secession from the Union (May 20, 1861) and the date of the Mecklenburg Declaration of Independence (May 20, 1775), which supposedly was the first American proclamation of independence. Unfortunately, historians have serious doubts that this document ever existed. The flag had horizontal stripes of blue over white and a red stripe at the hoist. The two dates frame a white star. This flag was used by both the state government and the state militia.

After the Civil War, the 1861 flag was no longer flown. In 1885 the state legislature created a new design that was similar to the 1861 design. The positions of the red and blue stripes were reversed, and the state initials (NC) were added. The date of the Mechlenburg Declaration of Independence stayed, but the date of secession was dropped. Instead, the Halifax Resolves were recognized by the addition of the date April 12, 1776. This flag is still in use as the state flag (above, left).

NORTH DAKOTA
★ *Flickertail State* ★

Current flag

OFFICIAL STATE NAME: State of North Dakota

STATE ABBREVIATION: ND

DATE OF STATEHOOD: November 2, 1889

ORDER OF STATEHOOD: 39

FLAG DESIGNER: Colonel John H. Fraine

STATE MOTTO: Liberty and Union Now and Forever One and Inseparable

STATE BIRD: Western meadowlark

STATE TREE: American elm

STATE FLOWER: Wild prairie rose

FLAG FACT: The Indian arrowhead shape of the state coat of arms (shown below) is unique.

North Dakota "government" flag

THE EAGLE HAS BEEN A FAVORITE symbol for at least 2,000 years. Kings and emperors in Germany, Spain, Austria, Russia, Poland, and elsewhere have featured it in their banners and coats of arms. The coat of arms of the United States shows the bald eagle, a species native to North America.

That eagle was popular on early American military flags. It usually carried an olive branch symbolizing peace and a bundle of arrows standing for war, although sometimes these were omitted. Over its head, 13 stars and sun rays often appeared, while the national motto—*E Pluribus Unum* (One Out of Many)—was written on a ribbon held in the eagle's beak. The U.S. shield rested on its breast.

That design was placed on the flag of North Dakota adopted in March 1911 (above, left). The design was the standard U.S. Army military flag in the late 19th century when the First North Dakota Infantry served during the Spanish-American War. The scroll below the eagle originally bore the words "First North Dakota Infantry."

In 1957 a "government" flag was created (below, left), although it is used only by the North Dakota National Guard. The flag colors are green for agriculture and yellow for livestock. The stars on the flag came from the personal coats of arms of two early French explorers, while the fleur-de-lis had been used by another. The stars also suggest the three branches of government: executive, legislative, and judicial.

OHIO

★ *Buckeye State* ★

Current flag

OFFICIAL STATE NAME: State of Ohio

STATE ABBREVIATION: OH

DATE OF STATEHOOD: March 1, 1803

ORDER OF STATEHOOD: 17

FLAG DESIGNER: John Eisenmann

STATE MOTTO: With God All Thing Are Possible

STATE BIRD: Cardinal

STATE TREE: Buckeye

STATE FLOWER: Scarlet carnation

FLAG FACT: This flag and that of Nepal, a country in Asia, have similar shapes.

Ohio governor's flag

JOHN EISENMANN DESIGNED and patented a flag that was recognized in May 1902 as the Ohio state flag (above, left). Its shape makes it unusual. Most modern flags, including all other current U.S. state flags, are rectangular. The Ohio flag stands out in a display, but it is also expensive to manufacture.

Eisenmann was inspired by the shape of the U.S. Cavalry flag. During the Civil War a cavalry troop typically used a Stars and Stripes with a triangular area cut from the fly. Its canton had metallic gold stars, and the unit number of the troop flying the flag often appeared in the flag's center. Eisenmann reduced the number of stars and stripes and added a white-bordered red disk to stand for the official Ohio tree, the buckeye.

The 17 stars indicate that Ohio was the 17th state to join the Union. The flag shape suggests the hills and valleys of Ohio, and the stripes suggest its roads and waterways. Many of those elements are part of the state seal. The seal also has a sun with 13 rays that does not appear in the flag.

The Ohio governor has a flag with the state's coat of arms within a ring of 17 stars (below, left). Four corner stars indicate the governor's rank as commander-in-chief of the Ohio National Guard. Red, a traditional Army color, serves as the background. This flag, the design of which dates to 1905, did not become legal until 1945. It is used in the governor's office and when reviewing the National Guard.

OKLAHOMA

★ *Sooner State* ★

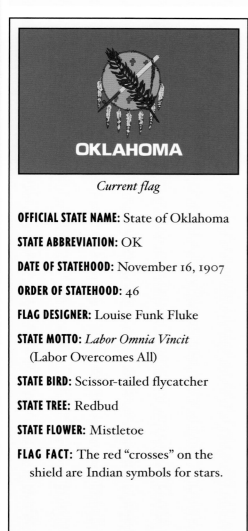

Current flag

OFFICIAL STATE NAME: State of Oklahoma

STATE ABBREVIATION: OK

DATE OF STATEHOOD: November 16, 1907

ORDER OF STATEHOOD: 46

FLAG DESIGNER: Louise Funk Fluke

STATE MOTTO: *Labor Omnia Vincit*
(Labor Overcomes All)

STATE BIRD: Scissor-tailed flycatcher

STATE TREE: Redbud

STATE FLOWER: Mistletoe

FLAG FACT: The red "crosses" on the shield are Indian symbols for stars.

1911 Oklahoma state flag

PROUD OF THEIR NEW STATEHOOD, Oklahoma legislators adopted a state flag in March 1911 (below, left). The red background was probably intended to symbolize the "Red Men" (Native Americans) who were an important part of the population. The large star in the center was marked "46" to indicate that Oklahoma was the 46th state to join the Union. The design incorporated the three national colors found in the Stars and Stripes.

By 1918, however, Americans had come to associate a red flag bearing a large star with the Communists and Soviet Russia, who were considered America's enemies at that time. The Oklahoma flag seemed to give the wrong message, so in April 1925 it was replaced by a new design created by Louise Funk Fluke.

Her flag had been the winner in a competition sponsored by the state chapter of the Daughters of the American Revolution. Its blue background was based on a Choctaw flag and was intended to symbolize loyalty and devotion. The central shield was a distinctive Osage bison-hide shield. Across the shield were two traditional symbols of peace—the Indian peace-pipe and the European olive branch.

That flag served Oklahoma until the eve of World War II, when the name "Oklahoma" was added (above, left). Then in 1988 the central emblem was carefully reviewed for accuracy. The state decided to modify some design details and color shades and to issue specifications as a guide to flag makers.

OREGON

★ *Beaver State* ★

Current flag (front)

OFFICIAL STATE NAME: State of Oregon

STATE ABBREVIATION: OR

DATE OF STATEHOOD: February 14, 1859

ORDER OF STATEHOOD: 33

FLAG DESIGNER: Unknown

STATE MOTTO: *Alis Volat Propriis*
(It Flies with Its Own Wings)

STATE BIRD: Western meadowlark

STATE TREE: Douglas fir

STATE FLOWER: Oregon grape

FLAG FACT: This state flag is the only current state flag that has different designs on each side.

Current flag (back)

THE OREGON SEAL, shown on the current state flag, was adopted in 1859. It pictures important details connected with the recognition of American rule in the Pacific Northwest. Russian and Spanish claims to the area had disappeared by 1826, but Canada (then ruled by Britain) and the United States still competed for control over the coast and the Columbia River.

Both powers wanted the promised wealth suggested in Oregon's seal—rich agricultural lands (the sheaf and plow) and mineral resources (the pickax). Settlers from both countries, represented by the covered wagon, were filling the area. The campaign slogan of U.S. presidential candidate James K. Polk in 1844 was "Fifty-Four Forty or Fight." That meant that the United States felt it should own all the land up to latitude 54 degrees, 40 minutes. Since neither side wanted war, the border was finally set at the 49th parallel of north latitude. As the seal shows, British men-of-war left the Oregon coast, and American steamers arrived.

Oregon became the 33rd state in 1859 when the chief political issue was a possible civil war. Since Oregon was proud of its support for national unity, it chose as its slogan "The Union." The stars and eagle complete the American symbolism of the design.

The beaver appeared on the reverse of the flag (below, left). It is shown in gold on a blue field, the two official state colors. The flag, adopted in February 1925, was displayed in Lexington, Massachusetts, at the 150th anniversary of the Revolution's first battle.

PENNSYLVANIA

★ *Keystone State* ★

Current flag

OFFICIAL STATE NAME: Commonwealth of Pennsylvania

STATE ABBREVIATION: PA

DATE OF STATEHOOD: December 12, 1787

ORDER OF STATEHOOD: 2

FLAG DESIGNER: Unknown

STATE MOTTO: Virtue, Liberty, and Independence

STATE BIRD: Ruffled grouse

STATE TREE: Hemlock

STATE FLOWER: Mountain laurel

FLAG FACT: Cords and tassels of blue and white decorate the staff of the state flag.

Pennsylvania governor's flag

THE TALE OF BETSY ROSS, one of the best known woman in American history, was first told before the country's hundredth anniversary. With the Civil War over, Americans celebrated economic growth, westward expansion, and the transcontinental railway. The story of George Washington asking a widow seamstress to make the first American flag was very appealing.

Vexillologists generally agree the story is fiction. Ross did make colors (military flags) for the Pennsylvania Navy in 1776, when the Stars and Stripes was still a year in the future. It is possible that these were Pennsylvania flags, which had been used as early as 1738. The design may have been the family banner of William Penn, founder of Pennsylvania.

Pennsylvania's seal changed after the state separated from Britain. The new design, a coat of arms created in 1777, is basically the same as what appears on the governor's flag today (below, left). The shield has a ship to symbolize commerce and a plow and wheat sheaves standing for agriculture. There is an American eagle in the crest, and work horses support the shield. For its motto, the new commonwealth chose "Virtue, Liberty, and Independence."

In April 1799 Pennsylvania militia regiments were ordered to carry flags in which the shield of Pennsylvania appeared on the breast of an eagle. Similar Pennsylvania military flags were carried during the Civil War. The first official state flag for general use, dating from June 1907, is still the state flag (above, left).

RHODE ISLAND

★ *Ocean State* ★

Current flag

OFFICIAL STATE NAME: State of Rhode Island and Providence Plantations

STATE ABBREVIATION: RI

DATE OF STATEHOOD: May 29, 1790

ORDER OF STATEHOOD: 13

FLAG DESIGNER: Unknown

STATE MOTTO: Hope

STATE BIRD: Rhode Island red

STATE TREE: Red maple

STATE FLOWER: Violet

FLAG FACT: The governor's flag of the smallest state has the longest official state name.

1877 Rhode Island state flag

EARLY CHRISTIANS put themselves in danger if they displayed a cross openly, so that symbol was sometimes made to look like an anchor. Thus the anchor became a Christian symbol of hope. Early Rhode Island settlers chose the anchor and the word "hope" as official state symbols.

The first Rhode Island flags were blue with a white disk (1746) and white with a blue anchor and ring (1822). White, the official Rhode Island color since 1779, was based on the white trim of its infantry uniforms. Rhode Island troops carried white colors (military flags) during the Revolution, some of which still exist.

The first official Rhode Island state flag was adopted in March 1877 (below, left). It had a white background with a blue anchor and a ring of 38 blue stars for the 38 states in the Union. In February 1882 the flag was modified. An anchor of yellow was placed within a ring of 13 yellow stars on a blue background. That number symbolized that Rhode Island was the 13th of the original 13 states to ratify the U.S. Constitution.

Finally, in 1897 the present flag was adopted (above, left). Although the golden stars and anchor remained from the previous design, the white background made it look very different. The blue background had made the symbols on the flag stand out. They were harder to see on white. However, white had been the traditional Rhode Island flag color since the Revolutionary War, and Rhode Island legislators preferred it.

SOUTH CAROLINA

★ *Palmetto State* ★

Current flag

OFFICIAL STATE NAME: State of South Carolina

STATE ABBREVIATION: SC

DATE OF STATEHOOD: May 23, 1788

ORDER OF STATEHOOD: 8

FLAG DESIGNER: Unknown

STATE MOTTO: *Dum Spiro Spero* (While I Breath I Live); *Animis Opibusque Parati* (Ready In Spirit and Resources)

STATE BIRD: Carolina wren

STATE TREE: Palmetto

STATE FLOWER: Yellow jessamine

FLAG FACT: Proposals made in 1899 to change the flag to purple failed.

1861 South Carolina flag

IN 1775 SOUTH CAROLINA troops wore blue uniforms when they fought for American freedom. The badge on the caps of the Second Infantry Regiment was a crescent with the slogan "Liberty or Death." (In English heraldry the crescent was a symbol for the second son in a family, so it made sense to use it for the Second Infantry Regiment.) In June 1776, when Americans successfully defended a nameless fort in Charleston harbor, the fort's flag was blue with a white crescent in the upper corner. The word "Liberty" may have been written on the crescent.

British cannonballs are said to have bounced off the palmetto logs used to build the American fort, saving the lives of its defenders. As a result, that tree became another South Carolina symbol. Militia colors in the early 19th century combined a palmetto tree and a crescent on a dark blue field. This tree was often seen as a rival of the pine popular in the North.

After Lincoln was elected president in 1860, South Carolina became the first state to secede from the Union. At first, South Carolinians flew unofficial flags, many of which showed a palmetto tree. When the new republic finally chose an official flag, it was blue with a white crescent and a white oval (below, left). The palmetto appearing on that oval was golden yellow. Almost immediately, however, the legislature changed its mind and adopted the design still in use today, a crescent and palmetto of white on a blue flag (above, left).

SOUTH DAKOTA

★ *Mount Rushmore State* ★

Current flag

OFFICIAL STATE NAME: State of South Dakota

STATE ABBREVIATION: SD

DATE OF STATEHOOD: November 2, 1889

ORDER OF STATEHOOD: 40

FLAG DESIGNER: Will G. Robinson

STATE MOTTO: Under God the People Rule

STATE BIRD: Ring-necked pheasant

STATE TREE: Black Hills spruce

STATE FLOWER: Pasqueflower

FLAG FACT: South Dakota, like Idaho, includes its name twice on its flag.

1909 South Dakota state flag

MOST PEOPLE KNEW FLORIDA as the "Sunshine State." This created problems for South Dakota's claim to the nickname, which was written on its state flag. In July 1992 state legislators changed the slogan. Proud of the huge carvings of Presidents Washington, Lincoln, Jefferson, and Theodore Roosevelt, they proclaimed South Dakota the "Mount Rushmore State."

That slogan accompanies the state seal and name on the current flag (above, left). The 19th-century seal shows a man with a horse-drawn plow near a river with mountains in the background. A smelter, cattle, several houses and Indian teepees, and a paddlewheel steamer appear below a scroll proclaiming "Under God the People Rule."

In 1908 Spanish-American war veteran Captain Seth Bullock and State Historical Society secretary Doane Robinson created the first state flag (below, left). It was simply a blazing yellow sun framed by the words "South Dakota" and "The Sunshine State" on a field of light blue. When the legislature approved the design in July 1909, however, it added the state seal in dark blue outline on the flag's back side.

That double-sided flag was costly to make and too heavy to fly freely. In March 1963 legislators decided to combine the designs so that the seal and the sun and slogan showed on both sides of the flag. Although the new design is less costly to make and more like the majority of state flags, its sun now is reduced to a zigzag frame around the seal.

TENNESSEE

★ *Volunteer State* ★

Current flag

OFFICIAL STATE NAME: State of Tennessee

STATE ABBREVIATION: TN

DATE OF STATEHOOD: June 1, 1796

ORDER OF STATEHOOD: 16

FLAG DESIGNER: Captain LeRoy Reeves

STATE MOTTO: Commerce and Agriculture

STATE BIRD: Mockingbird

STATE TREE: Tulip poplar

STATE FLOWER: Iris

FLAG FACT: The stars on the state flag come as close to each other as possible without touching.

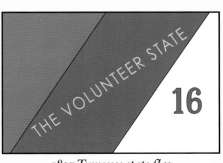

1897 Tennessee state flag

IN 2001 IT WAS PROPOSED to add "In God We Trust" to the state flag, written on the blue stripe at the fly end. The proposed change was rejected by the legislature. In general, inscriptions on flags are not a good idea. They appear backward on the flag reverse and even on the front are usually difficult to read when a flag is flying.

The current state flag (above, left) was designed by Captain LeRoy Reeves of the Tennessee National Guard. Approved in April 1905, it replaced an earlier design. Reeves found many meanings in the simple design he drafted. The three stripes, for example, suggest the three geographical regions of the state. The fact that Tennessee was the third state after the original 13 to join the Union is represented by the three stars. Three American presidents lived in Tennessee—Andrew Jackson, James Polk, and Andrew Johnson.

The first Tennessee flag was a standard militia flag of blue with the state seal. In April 1897 a distinctive banner was chosen as the first state flag (below, left). Approved at the time of the Tennessee Centennial Exposition, it had the nickname "The Volunteer State" crossing the field at an angle. That slogan recalled Tennessee's reputation for providing great numbers of volunteers whenever the nation was threatened. The figure 16 was a reference to its order of statehood. The 1897 design, like the current flag, featured the national colors red, white, and blue.

TEXAS
★ *Lone Star State* ★

Current flag

OFFICIAL STATE NAME: State of Texas

STATE ABBREVIATION: TX

DATE OF STATEHOOD: December 29, 1845

ORDER OF STATEHOOD: 28

FLAG DESIGNER: Unknown

STATE MOTTO: Friendship

STATE BIRD: Mockingbird

STATE TREE: Pecan

STATE FLOWER: Bluebonnet

FLAG FACT: In 1879 the flag description was omitted from the state laws by mistake. In 1933 lawmakers officially reestablished the flag.

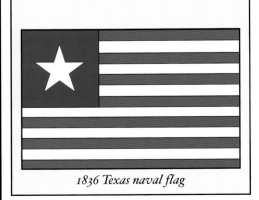

1836 Texas naval flag

THE STORY OF TEXAS FLAGS is so rich that two major books have been published on the subject. That history is also reflected in the fact that six flags have flown over Texas—those of Spain, France, Mexico, the Texas Republic, the Confederacy, and the United States.

Texas was an independent country from 1835 until it joined the Union in 1845. It had distinctive flags for its navy, fortresses, and merchant vessels. It even had its own signal code flags. Military units used a variety of flags during the Texas War of Independence. Many included the single star, the national symbol of Texas.

Americans who settled in the northern part of Mexico became unhappy with the policies of the Mexican government. In 1835 they revolted against the Mexican authorities and successfully established a new country: the Republic of Texas. Their first flag was Mexico's green, white, and red tricolor with the date of the old Mexican constitution (1824). The first national flag of Texas was adopted in December 1836. It featured a central golden yellow star on a blue field.

The Texas navy had an ensign that resembled that of the United States. The field bore 13 red and white horizontal stripes, but there was only a single white star in the blue canton (below, left). A new national flag became official in January 1839, and Texas adopted the current state flag (above, left) when it joined the Union. Today that flag with its three stripes of blue (with a white star), white, and red is one of the most widely used and most familiar of all the state flags.

UTAH
★ *Beehive State* ★

Current flag

OFFICIAL STATE NAME: State of Utah

STATE ABBREVIATION: UT

DATE OF STATEHOOD: January 4, 1896

ORDER OF STATEHOOD: 45

FLAG DESIGNER: Unknown

STATE MOTTO: Industry

STATE BIRD: California gull

STATE TREE: Blue spruce

STATE FLOWER: Sego lily

FLAG FACT: The Stars and Stripes shown in the coat of arms have too few stars.

1911 Utah state flag

IN 1849 THE MORMONS who had settled the Great Salt Lake region hoped to obtain recognition for their "State of Deseret," but the U.S. Congress refused to grant it. Finally, almost a half century later, statehood was granted for Utah, a name that came from the local Ute Indians. The new Utah seal had a bald eagle and two American flags to stress the patriotism of the people.

The flag emblem contains the dates 1847 (when Mormon settlement began) and 1896, when statehood was achieved. The shield, designed by Harry Edwards, presents a beehive and the motto "Industry," meaning "hard work." ("Deseret" is a Mormon word meaning "honeybee.") The beehive is surrounded by the sego lily, the state flower. That lily was sometimes eaten by Mormon settlers in the early years when food was scarce.

A local chapter of the Daughters of the American Revolution created the first Utah flag (below, left). A copy of the design, showing the Utah coat of arms in white, was given to Governor Heber M. Wells in 1903. It was officially adopted in March 1911.

The Sons and Daughters of Utah Pioneers ordered a flag to present to the battleship U.S.S. *Utah* in 1912. It came from the flag maker with its emblem in full color instead of white. Pleased with its appearance, the state legislature modified the law to make the full-color version the official state flag in March 1913 (above, left).

VERMONT

★ *Green Mountain State* ★

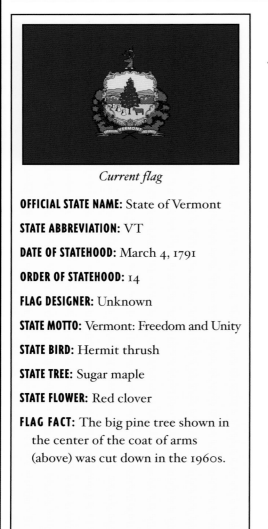

Current flag

OFFICIAL STATE NAME: State of Vermont

STATE ABBREVIATION: VT

DATE OF STATEHOOD: March 4, 1791

ORDER OF STATEHOOD: 14

FLAG DESIGNER: Unknown

STATE MOTTO: Vermont: Freedom and Unity

STATE BIRD: Hermit thrush

STATE TREE: Sugar maple

STATE FLOWER: Red clover

FLAG FACT: The big pine tree shown in the center of the coat of arms (above) was cut down in the 1960s.

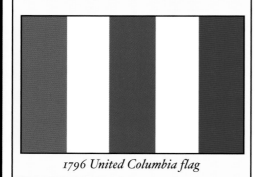

1796 United Columbia flag

VERMONT PROCLAIMED INDEPENDENCE in January 1777 and briefly used the name New Connecticut. It did not join the Union until March 1791. During its 14 years as an independent country, it never had an official national flag.

In 1796 Vermont leader Ethan Allen created a multi-colored flag when Vermont considered joining Quebec to become a large independent republic called United Columbia (below, left). The green stripe in the center referred to the state name, which means "green mountains." Red, white, and blue were the colors of France (from which Allen hoped to obtain aid) and of the United States.

After it was recognized as a U.S. state, Vermont showed its loyalty by adopting a state flag in May 1804. That banner was a 17-star version of the American flag (there were 17 states at the time) with 17 stripes and the word "Vermont." (Many incorrectly assumed that each state would automatically be given its own star and stripe in the national flag.)

In October 1837 a new Vermont state flag was approved. It had 13 red and white stripes and a blue canton with the state seal framed by an 8-point star. In 1919 the star was replaced by the more usual 5-point star. Just four years later—in June 1923—the current state flag was adopted (above, left). Its blue field shows the state coat of arms with pine branches, mountains, a cow, and the head of a deer. The ribbon bears the state motto, "Vermont: Freedom and Unity."

VIRGINIA
★ *Old Dominion State* ★

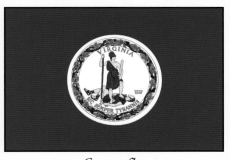

Current flag

OFFICIAL STATE NAME: Commonwealth of Virginia

STATE ABBREVIATION: VA

DATE OF STATEHOOD: June 25, 1788

ORDER OF STATEHOOD: 10

FLAG DESIGNER: Governor John Floyd

STATE MOTTO: *Sic Semper Tyrannis* (Thus Ever to Tyrants)

STATE BIRD: Cardinal

STATE TREE: Dogwood

STATE FLOWER: Flowering dogwood

FLAG FACT: Only the front of the two-sided state seal appears on the flag.

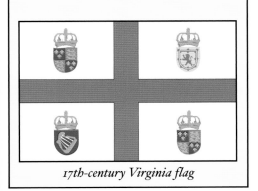

17th-century Virginia flag

IN 1619 A COAT OF ARMS was granted to the English royal colony of Virginia. The white shield bore the red cross of St. George, patron saint of England. In the corners were crowned shields over the coats of arms of the four kingdoms claimed by King James VI—England, France, Scotland, and Ireland. The Latin motto in the Virginia coat of arms means "Behold, Virginia Gives the Fifth [kingdom]." No example of the banner of the "Kingdom of Virginia" survives, but its design would have looked like the flag shown below, left.

The state seal adopted by Virginia in 1776 presents a classical Roman scene. "Virtue," a woman representing the Commonwealth, stands over the body of a man, symbolizing tyranny. His crown lies to one side, and his whip and chain are useless. The Latin motto proclaims "Thus Ever To Tyrants." The design is a not very subtle reference to the goal of the American Revolution.

In 1830 a blue flag with the state seal in the center was chosen by Governor John Floyd at a time when Virginia was asserting its rights against the federal government. In 1861 when Virginia seceded from the Union, that flag was officially adopted. It was re-adopted in 1871 after the Civil War. The wreath of ivy was added in 1931, and details of the coloring for the design were approved in 1949 (above, left). The Virginia flag is decorated with white fringe (not shown) that appears only along the fly end of the flag.

WASHINGTON
★ *Evergreen State* ★

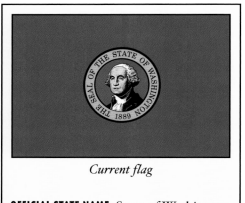

Current flag

OFFICIAL STATE NAME: State of Washington

STATE ABBREVIATION: WA

DATE OF STATEHOOD: November 11, 1889

ORDER OF STATEHOOD: 42

FLAG DESIGNER: Unknown

STATE MOTTO: *Al-Ki* (Bye and Bye)

STATE BIRD: American goldfinch

STATE TREE: Western hemlock

STATE FLOWER: Coast rhododendron

FLAG FACT: The seal on the flag is supposed to read correctly from both the front and the back sides of the flag.

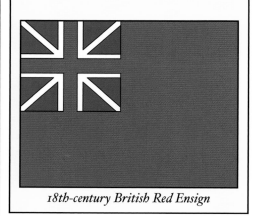

18th-century British Red Ensign

IT IS REMARKABLE that of the approximately 150 current and former U.S. state flags, the only ones with a green background are those of Washington and the little-used green-background government flag of North Dakota.

During World War I, Washington militia carried blue flags bearing the state seal. Since it is known as the Evergreen State, Washington also had special flags with a green field. One was created for the State Nautical School and another for display at the headquarters of the Daughters of the American Revolution in Washington, D.C. Finally in June 1923 official recognition was given to a state flag with the state seal centered on a green background (above, left).

The seal, adopted at the time of statehood in 1889, was designed by Charles Talcott, owner of a jewelry store in Olympia, the capital city. When asked to make the new state seal, he placed a postage stamp picturing George Washington within a double ring inscribed "The Seal of the State of Washington 1889."

The first flag that appeared in the area was the British Red Ensign (below, left). In the late 18th century, British explorers Captains James Cook and George Vancouver explored along the coast. That flag had been used on the East Coast a quarter century before as the symbol of British rule. The Revolutionary War established American independence, but only in the 1840s was the boundary drawn between British and American control in the Pacific Northwest.

WEST VIRGINIA

★ *Mountain State* ★

Current flag

OFFICIAL STATE NAME: State of West Virginia

STATE ABBREVIATION: WV

DATE OF STATEHOOD: June 20, 1863

ORDER OF STATEHOOD: 35

FLAG DESIGNER: Unknown

STATE MOTTO: *Montani Semper Liberi* (Mountaineers Are Always Free)

STATE BIRD: Cardinal

STATE TREE: Sugar maple

STATE FLOWER: Rhododendron

FLAG FACT: To celebrate 50 years of statehood, West Virginia gave each of its schools a state flag.

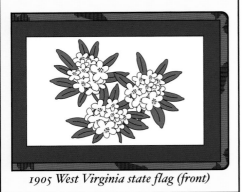

1905 West Virginia state flag (front)

LIKE MANY STATES, West Virginia has a complex seal. The reverse shows factories, homes, livestock, mountains, and even "the viaduct of the Baltimore and Ohio Railroad." West Virginia has a different design on the front of its seal. It was adapted for use in color on the current state flag, official since March 1929 (above, left).

Below a scroll with the name of the state is a fancy shield framed by rhododendrons, the state flower. In the center of the shield is the date of statehood (June 20, 1863) carved on a boulder guarded by a miner and a frontiersman. Those occupations were common in West Virginia at the time it separated from Virginia and entered the Union as a free state.

The Latin motto *Montani Semper Liberi* proudly proclaims "Mountaineers Are Always Free." An anvil and hammer, a cornstalk, a sheaf of wheat, two crossed rifles, and a liberty cap fill out the shield. The liberty cap was a popular symbol during the American Revolution and for decades afterward. Often such a cap was placed at the top of a "liberty pole" raised in the center of a town.

The first West Virginia state flag was adopted in February 1905 (below, left). It had the coat of arms on the back side and the "big laurel," or rhododendron, on the front. That flag was first used unofficially at the 1904 St. Louis world's fair. In February 1907 the same design with front and back sides reversed was officially recognized.

WISCONSIN

★ *Badger State* ★

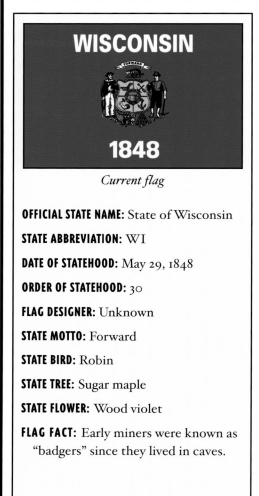

Current flag

OFFICIAL STATE NAME: State of Wisconsin

STATE ABBREVIATION: WI

DATE OF STATEHOOD: May 29, 1848

ORDER OF STATEHOOD: 30

FLAG DESIGNER: Unknown

STATE MOTTO: Forward

STATE BIRD: Robin

STATE TREE: Sugar maple

STATE FLOWER: Wood violet

FLAG FACT: Early miners were known as "badgers" since they lived in caves.

1863 Wisconsin state flag (back)

IN 1887 WHEN THE LEGISLATURE was standardizing state laws, the legal description of the state flag was mistakenly omitted. State flags were not often used in that era, so it was not until April 1913 that the state flag was readopted. Like many other states, Wisconsin placed its coat of arms—which appears on the state seal—on a blue background. In collections of state flags it was difficult to recognize, so in May 1981 the legislature added the state name above the coat of arms and the date of statehood below (above, left).

The state seal has a badger as a crest. A sailor and a miner support the shield. At their feet are lead ingots (symbolizing mining) and cornucopias with fruits and vegetables spilling out (symbolizing agriculture). The shield is quartered and bears the national coat of arms in the center. Other symbols include a plow, crossed pick and shovel, an anchor, and an arm holding a hammer. A ribbon with the state motto appears at the top.

The first Wisconsin state flag was adopted in March 1863 when the state was fighting to preserve the Union. Militia regiments displayed the standard flag of that era, a dark blue field with a painted or embroidered version of the state coat of arms in full color. Wisconsin's law also required that the reverse of the flag bear a different design, one that featured the coat of arms of the United States, with its bald eagle, 13 stars, olive branches, and arrows, and the national shield and motto (below, left).

WYOMING

★ *Equality State* ★

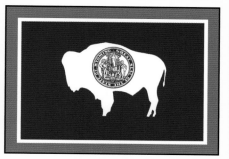

Current flag

OFFICIAL STATE NAME: State of Wyoming

STATE ABBREVIATION: WY

DATE OF STATEHOOD: July 10, 1890

ORDER OF STATEHOOD: 44

FLAG DESIGNER: Verna Keays Keyes

STATE MOTTO: Equal Rights

STATE BIRD: Western meadowlark

STATE TREE: Plains cottonwood

STATE FLOWER: Indian paintbrush

FLAG FACT: The designer of the "buffalo" flag (above) was from the town Buffalo, Wyoming.

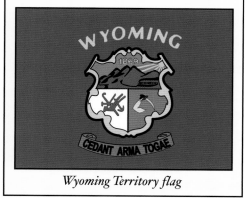

Wyoming Territory flag

WYOMING'S FLAG FEATURES, as part of the state seal, a woman holding a banner inscribed "Equal Rights" (above, left). Wyoming is proud to have been the first major government in the world to grant unrestricted voting rights to women. The figure was based on the famous Winged Victory of Samothrace statue in the Louvre Museum in Paris, France.

The two men on the seal represent a cowboy and a miner, important occupations in Wyoming when it became a territory in 1869. State resources (livestock, mines, grain, and oil) and the dates of territorial government (1869) and statehood (1890) are also shown. The United States shield with a star and the number 44, indicating Wyoming's order of statehood, is topped by an American eagle.

The most important symbol, the bison, appears as a reminder of the past. The colors are those of the United States, but they have other symbolism as well. Red is for the Indians and the blood of early pioneers, while white stands for purity and integrity. Blue suggests the sky, justice, and faithfulness.

The current state flag was the only official one until February 1991, when the state legislature created a flag for Wyoming Territory (below, left). Such a flag had never existed when Wyoming was a territory, although the coat of arms and motto were used. Wyoming is the only state or nation to have adopted, after the fact, a flag representing a past era, although countries sometimes use authentic historical flags.

DISTRICT OF COLUMBIA AND THE U.S. TERRITORIES

Current flag

DISTRICT OF COLUMBIA

This flag corresponds to the family coat of arms of George Washington. Some mistakenly think the Stars and Stripes is based on these arms. In England the "stars" were originally spur rowels, symbol of a horseman. The District of Columbia became the United States capital on December 1, 1800. This flag was the first to represent the District, which has only limited self-government. It was adopted in October 1938.

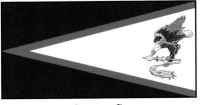
Current flag

AMERICAN SAMOA

Sixty years after the hoisting of the first U.S. flag here, American Samoa raised its own flag on April 27, 1960. The design includes American symbols—the colors red, white, and blue and the bald eagle. Red and white were also flag colors of the old Samoan kingdom. In the eagle's claws are traditional emblems. The *fue* (in the lower claw) represents the wisdom of the council of chiefs, while the *uatogi* (pronounced WAH-tong-ghee) is a war club and refers to state power.

Current flag

GUAM

On July 4, 1917, the flag of Guam, designed by Mrs. Carrol Paul, became official two decades after the United States acquired the island from Spain. The red border, added in February 1948, symbolizes the sacrifices made by Guamanians under Japanese occupation during World War II. The central emblem is shaped like the traditional slingshot stone used by ancestors of the local Chamorro people. The scene shows the Hagåtña River, a flying proa canoe, and a cliff called Two Lovers' Leap, which recalls a favorite island legend.

Current flag

NORTHERN MARIANA ISLANDS

This flag, with a white star and blue field representing this group of islands in the Pacific Ocean, was designed in March 1972. It was first flown on July 4, 1976. Behind the star is a latte stone (an ancient house foundation), which honors the legendary hero Taga. A wreath of flowers was added as a symbol of the islands' Chamorro and Carolinian people. The new flag was approved in 1988, two years after the Northern Marianas became a U.S. commonwealth. Other slight changes were made in 1990.

Current flag

PUERTO RICO

The Puerto Rican and Cuban flags were similar when both sought freedom from Spain in the 1890s. Puerto Rico's 1895 flag was for decades promoted by island nationalists opposed to American rule, which began in 1898. When Puerto Rico became a U.S. commonwealth in 1952, its first official action legalized the 1895 flag. Earlier Puerto Rican flags had been based on its 1511 coat of arms, the flag of the Dominican Republic, and the naval signal flag of San Juan, the island's capital.

Current flag

VIRGIN ISLANDS

Many flags, including those of Spain, England, France, and the Duchy of Brandenburg have flown over the Virgin Islands. In March 1917 the islands became a U.S. territory after they were purchased from Denmark. In May 1921 the governor authorized a local flag, still in use today. It includes the letters *VI* (for Virgin Islands) and a simplified version of the coat of arms of the United States. Many consider that the three arrows are symbols for the islands of St. Croix, St. John, and St. Thomas.

OUR CHANGING NATIONAL FLAG

★ *1776 to the Present* ★

Continental Colors: 1 January 1776 - 14 June 1777

15 June 1777 - 30 April 1795

1 May 1795 - 3 July 1818

4 July 1818 - 3 July 1819

4 July 1819 - 3 July 1820

4 July 1820 - 3 July 1822

4 July 1822 - 3 July 1836

4 July 1836 - 3 July 1837

4 July 1837 - 3 July 1845

4 July 1845 - 3 July 1846

4 July 1846 - 3 July 1847

4 July 1847 - 3 July 1848

4 July 1848 - 3 July 1851

4 July 1851 - 3 July 1858

4 July 1858 - 3 July 1859

4 July 1859 - 3 July 1861

4 July 1861 - 3 July 1863

4 July 1863 - 3 July 1865

4 July 1865 - 3 July 1867

4 July 1867 - 3 July 1877

4 July 1877 - 3 July 1890

4 July 1890 - 3 July 1891

4 July 1891 - 3 July 1896

4 July 1896 - 3 July 1908

4 July 1908 - 3 July 1912

4 July 1912 - 3 July 1959

4 July 1959 - 3 July 1960

Future (51 stars)

4 July 1960 - Present

★ U.S. NATIONAL FLAG ★

EVERYONE IS FAMILIAR with the national flag of the United States. Its design is probably the best known symbol in the world. Americans fly a huge number of flags, but there are more "Stars and Stripes" sold and used than all the other flags put together.

This was not always true. People didn't fly flags on homes, churches, schools, or even public buildings in the early days of the country. The national flag identified American ships and forts. It was used by the Armed Forces, but not all troops carried the Stars and Stripes until the late 1840s.

The big surge in flag usage came in 1861 when the attack by Confederate forces on the American flag flying on Fort Sumter in South Carolina began the Civil War. In the North that event was considered an attack on the country and everything it stood for. The Union states immediately made the flag the central focus of their patriotism and of their struggle for survival. Similarly, Americans everywhere proudly displayed the flag after the September 11, 2001, terrorist attacks.

Over the years the flag has also represented the country in its acquisition of western territories, its scientific and commercial ventures, in exploration around the world (and in outer space), and in armed conflict abroad. For more than two centuries it has represented the highest ideals of the nation.

In recent decades the U.S. flag has become part of the nation's popular culture. Clothing, advertising and packaging, household goods, and toys and games are just a few examples of how the flag or its image is being used. The American flag belongs to and is used by everyone, from the President to the most recent immigrant. The flag lapel pin and inexpensive flags for lawns and homes make the same statement of respect and love of country as the ceremonial banners of a military color guard.

The real meaning of the flag, however, is not in the cloth, the thread, the dyes with which it is made, or in its design. Its message is found in the hearts and minds of people all across the land. To maintain and advance the highest ideals of our nation's flag is the responsibility and privilege of each and every American.

No country has changed its flag as often as the United States. An 1817 law limited the number of stripes to 13 and provided for a star for each state but did not specify the arrangement of the stars.

★ THE PARTS OF A FLAG ★
★ GLOSSARY ★

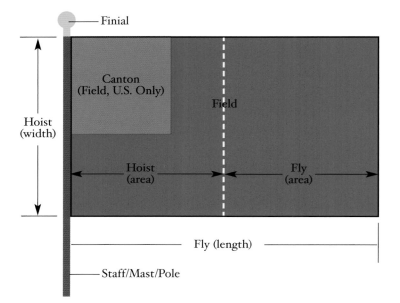

Arms: a symbolic design made according to heraldic rules

Banner: a flag, especially one hung vertically or with a design on one side only

Canton: the rectangular area in the flag's upper hoist area

Coat of arms: *see* "Arms"

Color: a military flag

Crest: the symbol at the very top of a coat of arms

Ensign: a national flag used on a ship

Field: the background of a flag; in the U.S. flag, the blue area bearing the stars

Finial: a symbolic figure attached to the top of a flagstaff

Fly: the length of a flag or the area farthest from the staff

Fringe: decorative threads, usually yellow, attached to the edges of a flag

Heraldry: a formal system for presenting symbols in coats of arms and on flags

Hoist: the width of a flag or the area nearest the staff; also, to raise a flag

Militia: a band of local soldiers

Obverse: the side of a flag seen when its staff is to the left; front of the flag

Pledge: to make a formal promise to a person, flag, etc.

Proportions: the ratio between the width and length of a flag (e.g. 2:3)

Reverse: the side of a flag seen when its staff is to the right; the back of a flag

Royal standard: the personal flag of a king or queen

Saltire: a diagonal cross

Scroll: a ribbon, usually bearing a motto, found in coats of arms and on flags

Seal: a stamp for impressing a design on paper or wax; the design made by a seal that often appears on a flag

Secede: to separate from a country or other area

Standard: a flag, especially one used by an army or an important person

Stars and Bars: the first national flag of the Confederate States of America

Tricolor: a flag of three stripes, each of a different color

Vexilloid: an object used like a flag, usually consisting of a pole with a symbol at the top

Vexillology: the study of flags

Vexillum: a Roman standard

★ RESOURCES ★

Contact the Flag Research Center, Box 580, Winchester, MA, 01890 (which has the largest collection of information on state flags) for information about its bimonthly journal, *The Flag Bulletin,* and for answers to specific questions.

Visit the Flag Research Center Web site at www.FlagSmith.com
Other useful Web sites include Flags of the World at www.flagspot.net/flags/
or: www.crwflags.com/fotw/flags/.

★

The best books on the subject of state flags and symbols are:

Howe, Randy. *Flags of the Fifty States and their Incredible Histories.* Globe Pequot. Guilford, CT: 2002.

Schnapper, M. B. *American Symbols: The Seals and Flags of the Fifty States.* Public Affairs. Washington, D.C.: 1974.

Shearer, Benjamin F. and Barbara S. Shearer. *State Names, Seals, Flags and Symbols: A Historical Guide.* Greenwood. Westport, CT: 1994.

Smith, Whitney. *The Flag Book of the United States.* William Morrow. New York: 1975.

_____. *The Flags of the Fifty States.* Fleetwood. Cheyenne, WY: 1976.

_____. *Flags Through the Ages and Across the World.* McGraw-Hill. New York: 1975.

★ CREDITS ★
★ MISSION STATEMENT ★

★ ★ ★

One of the world's largest nonprofit scientific and educational organizations, the National Geographic
Society was founded in 1888 "for the increase and diffusion of geographic knowledge."
Fulfilling this mission, the Society educates and inspires millions every day through its magazines,
books, television programs, videos, maps and atlases, research grants, the National Geographic Bee,
teacher workshops, and innovative classroom materials. The Society is supported
through membership dues, charitable gifts, and income from the sale of its educational products.
This support is vital to National Geographic's mission to increase global understanding
and promote conservation of our planet through exploration, research, and education.

For more information, please call 1-800-NGS LINE (647-5463) or write to the following address:

NATIONAL GEOGRAPHIC SOCIETY
1145 17th Street N.W.
Washington, D.C. 20036-4688 U.S.A.
Visit the Society's Web site at www.nationalgeographic.com.

PRINTED IN CHINA
12/RRDS/9